TEACHING ETHNIC
DIVERSITY WITH FILM

TEACHING ETHNIC DIVERSITY WITH FILM

Essays and Resources for Educators in History, Social Studies, Literature, and Film Studies

Edited by Carole Gerster
with Laura W. Zlogar

McFarland & Company, Inc., Publishers
Jefferson, North Carolina, and London

LIBRARY OF CONGRESS CATALOGUING-IN-PUBLICATION DATA

Teaching ethnic diversity with film : essays and resources for
educators in history, social studies, literature and film studies /
edited by Carole Gerster with Laura W. Zlogar.
   p.   cm.
Includes bibliographical references and index.

ISBN 0-7864-2195-9 (softcover : 50# alkaline paper)

1. Multicultural education — Study and teaching —
United States. 2. Motion pictures in education — United States.
I. Gerster, Carole, 1943– II. Zlogar, Laura W., 1951–
LC1099.3.T432 2006
370.117 — dc22   2005011457

British Library cataloguing data are available

On the cover: Denzel Washington in the title role of *Malcolm X* (1992)

Manufactured in the United States of America

McFarland & Company, Inc., Publishers
 Box 611, Jefferson, North Carolina 28640
  www.mcfarlandpub.com

Acknowledgments

This book derives from teaching and researching films by and about American's ethnic minorities at the University of Wisconsin–River Falls and the University of California–Santa Cruz, but primarily from our work in planning and directing three National Endowment for the Humanities Summer Institutes for secondary teachers. Carole Gerster directed and Laura Zlogar assisted for each of these institutes, all on the topic "Picturing America: Cinematic Representations of America's Ethnic Diversity." We thank the Endowment for granting us the funds to direct these institutes (in 1996, 2000, and 2001) as well as the high school teachers who participated. For five weeks each of these three summers, 20 to 25 high school teachers from across the nation spent six to eight hours a day, five days a week, screening, analyzing, interpreting, and discussing the historical, cultural, social, literary, and film history significance of films about and by America's ethnic minorities. These teachers, committed to including ethnically diverse representations and perspectives in their history, social studies, literature, and film studies classes, each devised a curriculum unit teaching ethnic films as primary texts and then incorporated the units in their curricula during the academic year. A number of teachers were inspired to rewrite their units, based on the experience of teaching them, for consideration in this book. Because of space limitations, we include only a few representative essays but wish to thank everyone for their contributions to the success of the institutes at large, for the assistance they offered fellow teachers, for supporting this endeavor, and for their own continuing work in focusing on multicultural and visual literacy as an effective means to teach ethnic studies across the curriculum. Phil Fitzgerald and Harold Tiffany each returned the year following their institutes to assist as Master Teachers, and Barbara Markham and Robert Gabrick returned to report on how to manage a joint ethnic film curriculum project in classrooms across the country (hers in New Jersey and his in Minnesota). We are grateful for their help. We would also like to thank the guest lecturers who came to the various institutes to share their insights about ethnic representations and ethnic issues on film. American film and American ethnicity scholars, filmmakers, and diversity activists provided backgrounds, enriched our collective ethnic understandings, and led us to spirited conversations. They include Thomas Cripps, Iverson White, Ed Guerrero, and Vincent Rocchio for African Americans on film; David Mura, Renee Tajima-Pena, and Gina Marchetti for Asian Americans on film; Diane Glancy, Jay Rosenstein and Charlene Teters, Michael Hilger, Rayna Green, and Jacquelyn Kilpatrick for American Indians on film; and Carlos Cortes and Joaquin Alvarado for Latino/as on film. We read their books and articles, watched their films, and absorbed and reflected their knowledge in our teaching and in our essays in this book. Four of these scholars have contributed essays to this book — on the film history of African Americans, Asian Americans, American Indians, and Latino/as.

The University of Wisconsin–River Falls deserves our thanks for hosting each of these three institutes, as well as supporting Carole's role in helping to design and in directing the Film Studies Minor, encouraging us to design and teach ethnic film and literature courses, providing grants to purchase hundreds of ethnic videos and scholarly books, and supporting our research to write this book. We are indebted to the endorsement and support of Chancellors Gary Thibodeau and Ann Lydecker, Deans Neal Prochow, Gorden Hedahl, and Nicholas Karolies, and English Department Chairs Richard Beckham and Marshall Toman; to the library and video collection assistance of Valerie Malzacher, John Laird, and Clio McLagan; to the video assistance of Leslie Bleskachek; and to the administrative and strategic psychological support of Sheri Fowler.

The University of California–Santa Cruz merits our thanks for supplying grant monies to purchase the film stills that we include to enrich the visual literacy component of this book, and the Educational Technology Center at the University of Wisconsin deserves our thanks for assisting Laura in obtaining a number film stills from videos and DVDs.

We dedicate this book to our husbands and children, Patrick Gerster, Rick Zlogar, Mark Gerster, Jennifer Studer, and Jason Gerster, and to the participants in our NEH institutes with our thanks for sharing the values of diversity and understanding. We hope that this book encourages others to teach ethnic films as a means to help their students better understand America's ethnic diversity and that it inspires high school and undergraduate college teachers, education majors, and especially today's media-mentored students to join with us in a multicultural conversation about the ways film representations both reflect and affect that understanding.

C.G. and L.W.Z.

Contents

vii

Preface

by Carole Gerster and Laura W. Zlogar

This book is designed as a textbook and reference tool for education majors, secondary school and undergraduate college teachers, and media specialists. We offer rationales, historical backgrounds, suggestions for specific ways to teach films (in VHS and DVD formats) about and by America's ethnic minorities, and supplemental resources. Although the focus is on incorporating ethnic films into high school and college undergraduate American history, social studies, literature, and film studies courses, this book should also prove useful for others who want to incorporate an ethnic studies component into their courses. The primary goal of this book is to provide teachers with the means to enable their students to attain both visual and multicultural literacy: to help their students understand how changing film representations of African Americans, Asian Americans, American Indians, and Latino/as both reflect and affect changing attitudes.

In the Introduction, Carole Gerster defines and examines the need for visual and multicultural literacy in our increasingly visual and multiethnic society, and Laura Zlogar outlines how including films about and by America's ethnic minorities in American history, social studies, literature, and film studies meets current high school standards.

Part I. Film Histories is organized by ethnic group. It offers four individual essays by experts on the film history background of African Americans, Asian Americans, American Indians, and Latino/as. Vincent Rocchio, author of *Reel Racism: Confronting Hollywood's Construction of Afro-American Culture* (Boulder: Westview, 2000), writes about the need to teach films about and by African Americans as mediated representations in his essay "Historical Overview of African Americans on Film: Challenges to Racial Ideology." Gina Marchetti, author of *Romance and the Yellow Peril: Race, Sex, and Discursive Strategies in Hollywood Fiction* (Berkeley: University of California Press, 1999), provides a film history of

1

Asian American Independent films and considers specific topics and films in her essay "Using Film and Video to Teach About Asians and Asian Americans Across the Curriculum." Jacqueline Kilpatrick, author of *Celluloid Indians: Native Americans and Film* (Lincoln: University of Nebraska Press, 1999), chronicles the film history of American Indian stereotypes and challenges to those stereotypes in her essay "American Indians and Film in the Classroom." And Joaquin Alvarado, coauthor of *Contemporary Chicana and Chicano Art*, volumes I and II (Tempe, Arizona: Bilingual Review Press, 2002), and writer, producer, and director of the film *The Silent Cross*, about immigration and violence along the U.S. /Mexican Border (2003), profiles the history of Latino/a representations in American cinema and discusses specific films and topics in his essay "Changing Faces: Exploring Latino/a History, Culture, and Identity through U.S. Cinema."

Part II. Methods, by Carole Gerster, is organized by the disciplines of American history, social studies, literature, and film studies. The chapters explore specific ways to teach visual and multicultural literacy with films about and by African Americans, Asian Americans, American Indians, and Latino/as in each of these disciplines. Each chapter includes suggested topics, methods, and corresponding films.

Part III. Classroom-Tested Curriculum Units offers four discipline-specific curriculum units that have been taught in various high school environments for a variety of students: in rural, suburban, and urban schools, in private and parochial schools, in schools with few and in schools with a majority of ethnic minority students, and in classes with disadvantaged, at-risk students as well as AP classes with advanced students. The curriculum unit for American history is Jennifer Pokorney's "Teaching American History: The American Dream and the History of Latinos and Latinas in America," which focuses on Latinos/as as one group throughout American history attempting to attain the American Dream. The social studies curriculum unit is Mel Didier's "Teaching Social Studies: The U.S. (Unfinished Sojourn) on Freedom Road," which teaches students about America's Civil Rights Movement and its continuing relevance. The unit for teaching American literature is Nancy Shay's "Teaching American Literature: Representations of Japanese American Internment," which compares internment representations in a novel and several film documentaries. For the film studies classroom, Billie Smith offers her "Teaching Film Studies: Images of Ethnicity and Justice in America," which looks at ways to read representations of ethnicity and justice in two Hollywood films. The teachers who offer these lesson plans invite other teachers to adapt them for their own classrooms.

Other sections provide teachers with the resources necessary to create their own curriculum units. In this Preface, Carole Gerster explores meanings and uses of the terms "race" and "ethnicity" to open inquiry into the topics of innate differences versus social constructions and imposed versus chosen categories of identity. The Appendix lists video distributors for ethnic films and videos as well as important web sites on independently produced media about ethnicity. The Glossary, Carole Gerster's "The Language of Film: Film Terms," is an essential resource for teaching visual literacy. It defines standard film techniques and describes how they guide viewer response. Teachers may want to use key definitions and concepts in teaching visual literacy to their students. The "Selected Filmography," organized by ethnic group, lists significant films in the history of ethnic representations most appropriate for high school and undergraduate college classrooms. The "Selected Bibliography" lists, also by ethnic group, background readings to complement those films.

A Note on Terminology: Race and Ethnicity

We prefer the term "ethnicity" to the term "race," but understand that this is an unresolved issue and that imprecision in terminology is often inevitable because the vocabulary to discuss the subject is still evolving. Although the terms "race" and "ethnicity" are often used interchangeably, there is disagreement about their meanings and their usefulness, in part because the definition of race has changed. In the past, racial groups were categorized in the United States according to ancestry and external features (including skin color, hair texture, and eye, nose, and lip shape), which supposedly indicated differing, fixed, and essential qualities of human beings of different races. Racial categories were not neutral: racial differences were thought to be biological (or, using current terminology, genetic) differences in mental, physical, and even moral capabilities that were passed on from parents to children. Today, however, racial categories are increasingly recognized as social constructions that were invented primarily to promote the idea of white (Euro-American) superiority in order to justify enslaving Africans, taking lands inhabited by American Indians and Latino/as under policies of Manifest Destiny, and ensuring the low wages of Asian immigrant workers and then all ethnic minorities in a country that also proclaimed freedom and equality. If some races were inferior, the arguments ran, they could benefit from the ruling guidance of the superior white race. Hollywood films provide a record of how race and racism have permeated American society.[1] Two recent independent films— Michael Moore's (2002) documentary *Bowling for Columbine* and

Paul Haggis's (2005) feature *Crash*—show how ideas about racial differences have been institutionalized and internalized. *Bowling* also contends and *Crash* dramatizes that we need to envision ourselves differently, and both suggest that understanding our interconnectedness can serve as an alternative to the destructive divisions in racial idealogy.

The fictive nature of racial categories has been proven by genetic studies showing that neither ancestral origins nor differences in external features (skin color, and so on) are indices of differences in mental, physical, or moral capabilities.[2] That racial categories are also fictive because they are subject to change is illustrated in studies chronicling how various groups (Irish Americans and Italian Americans) have successfully labored and lobbied to make their racial status white.[3] Ironically, racial categorizing itself also challenges the validity of racial categories. In America, a person considered biracial whose parents are, for example, Euro American and African American is considered African American, and a person born of an Asian American and a Euro American is considered Asian American. These categories reflect social rather than biological constructions.[4] Many now use the term "race" to refer to socially constructed categories and prefer to keep the term active until it is understood as such.

Films depicting recent scholarship on race as unrelated to genetics and on the influence that ideas about race have had on American society are an excellent means to help students understand the need to rethink racial categories. The three-part (2003) documentary film series, *Race: The Power of an Illusion* begins with Christine Herbes-Sommers' *Episode 1: The Difference Between Us*, which surveys recent scientific studies, including genetics, that disprove the biological basis of race. Tracy Heather Strain's *Episode 2: The Story We Tell* chronicles how, when, and why ideas about race took hold in the United States, tracing the idea of race from the European conquest of the Americas through its crystallization into an ideology of racial difference and white supremacy to justify American slavery and imperialism. And Llewellyn M. Smith's *Episode 3: The House We Live In* highlights the ways American society has retained the idea of racial superiority and institutionalized white privilege to the detriment of ethnic minorities.[5]

Advocates of the term "ethnicity" instead of "race" (and of ethnic and bi-ethnic identity rather than racial and bi-racial identity) insist that we are all members of the human race and that race is indeed a social construction rather than a scientific actuality, but also note that the term "race" will continue to be discriminatory because, by most people's definition, it attributes fixed characteristics to all members of a group. Ethnicity is also a social construction, but with the important distinction that it makes no pretence of being anything else. Ethnicity is a more neutral term than race in that when it defines groups of people in the United States by ancestral origin, it refers to ancestral cultural traits such as language, foods, and other cultural customs and traditions, not inherent human traits passed on, and it does not contend that all members of one ethnic group have any inherent superior or inferior mental, physical, or moral characteristics. Ethnicity recognizes, but de-emphasizes the importance of, common physical characteristics since the appearance of individuals within each group often varies widely. Ethnic distinctions also emphasize that Euro Americans are just another ethnic group, not the standard or norm by which all other ethnic groups should be measured. Using ancestral origin as a means of identity is the reason for the labels African American, Asian American, Native American, Latino/a, and Euro American, and the further distinctions preferred by some of Liberian American, Vietnamese American, Navajo, Mexican American, German American, and so on to ensure the recognition of multiple identities within the larger categories.

Categories of ethnic identity also recognize that persons of some ancestral origins and cultures live as minorities within a country dominated by persons of another ancestral origin and culture; since Euro Americans are the dominant group in the United States, all others are considered ethnic minorities. Although many do not care for the label "minority," ethnic minorities often choose their ethnicity as a means of identity to avoid neglect, invisibility, and cultural annihilation. Teachers wanting to explore this topic have many films to choose from in which filmmakers chronicle debates about and the efforts of ethnic minorities to define and retain their ethnic identity in America rather than to adopt Euro-American culture wholeheartedly and assimilate into an undifferentiated melting pot defined by Euro Americans. Tim Carrier's (1990) documentary *Family Across the Sea* and Julie Dash's feature film (1991) *Daughters of the Dust* both celebrate cultural connections between the Gullah people of South Carolina's sea islands and the people of Sierra Leone, West Africa. John Wehman's (1994) documentary *Filipino Americans: Discovering Their Past for the Future* profiles Filipino American history to highlight the importance of Filipino Americans maintaining their ethnic identity, while Renee Tajima-Pena's (1998) *My America ... or honk if you love Buddha* traces ethnic diversity among Asian Americans, and Lisa Hsia's (1986) *Made in China: A Search for Roots* chronicles the filmmaker's search for her ethnic roots and her decisions about which ethnic traits are viable for her as a young Chinese American. Jack Leustig's (1994) eight-part documentary, *500 Nations: Attack on Culture,* chronicles the continuing struggles of American Indians, from first European contact through the reservation system, to keep their culture alive, while Deb Wallwork's (1986) documentary *Keep Your Heart Strong: The Powwow* demonstrates how the contemporary powwow is one means to do so, and Jay Rosenstein's (1996) documentary *In Whose Honor?* profiles the ongoing efforts of Charlene Teters and others to stop the appropriation of Native American culture to provide names, mascots, and logos to promote professional, college, and high school sports teams. Marilyn Mulford's (1988) documentary *Chicano Park* explores how the creation of giant murals revitalized the cultural identity of a Mexican-American community in California, Radames Soto's seven-part (1998) documentary *Hispanic Americans* explores the diverse cultures maintained within the Latino/a community, and Sharon Weil's (1990) feature film *Sweet 15* spotlights the traditional Latina fifteenth birthday celebration (the *quinceanera*) that ushers a girl into adulthood as she examines the struggle of undocumented Mexican-American workers to be Mexican Americans.

Students encouraged to grapple with the terms "race" and "ethnicity" can become part of the effort to understand how the ideology of racial difference has served to create social inequities as if they were natural and to understand that cultural differences among Americans provide all of us a rich ethnic diversity we are only beginning to appreciate.

Introduction:
Why Teach Visual
and Multicultural Literacy?

by Carole Gerster and Laura W. Zlogar

"To be is to be perceived."
— Bishop Berkeley, *A Treatise Concerning the
Principles of Human Knowledge* (1710)

"How we are seen determines in part how we are
treated; how we treat others is based on how we see
them. Such seeing comes from representation."
— Richard Dyer, *The Matter of Images:
Essays on Representation* (1993)

We live in a visual culture with an increasing ethnic minority population. From the beginning of the twentieth century, film representations have both recorded and shaped beliefs about and behavior toward African Americans, Asian Americans, American Indians, and Latinos/as. Today, in large numbers, ethnic minority filmmakers are re-presenting their histories, cultures, and literature from the perspectives of their own experience. Films about and by ethnic minorities are historical, cultural, and literary texts that have mirrored prevailing attitudes as well as provided new images and promoted social change. Teaching Hollywood and independently produced feature films, narrative shorts, and documentaries provides an excellent means for students to gain multicultural and visual literacy: to understand changing images of and ideas about America's cultural diversity and to read the film images that continue to inform and persuade us. This book explores ways to teach films by and about America's ethnic minorities as visual texts in order to help students understand both the ever-changing dynamics of America's cultural diversity and the role of film in recording as well as shaping those dynamics.

Our Visual Culture

We live in an image-saturated culture where enticing advertisements dominate magazine pages, compete for our attention every few minutes on television, appear as spam on our computer screens, and greet us everywhere from building and roadway signs to movie screens and restaurant bathroom walls. In our visual culture, televisions find a place in several rooms of the house as well as the family van and in public establishments from airports and sports bars to shopping malls. Videos bring us movies from the 1890s to the present, sooth us in church sanctuaries, show us proper brushing techniques in dentists' offices, tell us stories of our past in museums, and allow us to win imaginary competitions and defeat imaginary enemies in video game galleries. In this visual culture, movie theatre and home video viewing are a major weekend pastime and new blockbuster films are the favorite topic of conversation from family rooms to boardrooms and classrooms. The documentary *Media Literacy: The New Basic* (Rutgers University, 1996) investigates the need for teaching media literacy in a culture where visual media surround us, noting that the information/technology age is a visual media age. Living in a visual culture means our source of knowledge is shifting from the written word to the visual image.[1] Much of what we know, and even more of what today's media-mentored students know — regarding attitudes, values, and especially how we define ourselves and others as Americans—comes from visual images. Living in a visual culture where individualism and experiential knowledge are primary values, Americans have been conditioned to believe what they see and to declare this belief in such popular clichés as "I saw it with my own eyes," "seeing is believing," and "the camera never lies." If not visually literate, viewers often unconsciously treat the moving image, even in Hollywood feature films (where the suspension of disbelief is essential to success), as evidence of reality.

We are in the midst of change regarding our sources of knowledge as well as what constitutes knowledge. The visual image has become central to how we represent and understand the world. The impact of movies on how we experience events became evident as images of the two airplanes crashing into the twin towers of the World Trade Center on September 11, 2001, replayed on television news broadcasts and the most frequent comment was that they looked just like a movie.[2] Images are also important to what some call a celebrity culture,[3] where today's young Americans learn the values of popular culture (wishing to look, feel, and live like media-famous and movie-star role models) from popular culture images, particularly the visual imagery of film. Americans of all ages now learn more about the world we live in from visual media than from written texts.[4] Historians note that most Americans now learn history through films,[5] cultural critics point to the efficacy of film to explain cultural and social issues, and narrative scholars categorize feature films as the literature of our age. For millions of Americans, feature films and documentaries not only record but also create American history and culture, and feature films are their literature. The power of the image to inform is neither a new nor a passing phenomenon, but cultural critics agree that visual imagery will serve as a primary source of information and knowledge for Americans in the twenty-first century.[6]

The challenge posed by this proliferation of visual images is that today's students are image consumers, but they do not know how to read the visual language of film or to read films as products of the times in which they were made and the filmmakers who made them. Students have few critical tools to examine the relation between film images and lived reality. In their vast variety, films can be the cause of both misunderstandings and better understandings. According to *Hollywood's America: United States History Through Its Films*, Hollywood is our "nation's dream factory, manufacturing fantasies and cultural myths," for "Hollywood has given Americans their most intensive — if highly distorted — picture of their country's past ... in shaping our deepest presuppositions about race, ethnicity, class, gender, and sexual conduct." The news from *Hollywood's America* is not all cautionary: as editors Steven Mintz and Randy Roberts also point out, our "movie culture has helped Americans adapt to an ever-changing society."[7] Film is a complex medium providing both misinformation and useful information and, just as students need to be able to read written texts with care, they need to read — to analytically and critically scrutinize — the film images that entertain and inform them on a daily basis.

Film is a powerful means of instruction both outside and inside the classroom and is an especially valuable tool for teaching topics in the humanities, social sciences, and the arts. Teachers, however, often know little about the medium and inadvertently encourage students to be passive recipients rather than careful readers of film texts. Too often, high school and college teachers use films as a break from the regular routine, a reward for students from what they regard as the real work of the class. Or they use films as visual aids, giving filmmakers ultimate authority by allowing films to teach themselves and encouraging students to passively accept what they see by testing only for remembered content — including the content in history by Hollywood. Teaching the form and content of films — by analyzing how the form directs viewers to read and react to the content — and teaching films as reflections of the times in which they were made and in relation to other (visual and written) texts can meet the challenge of teaching students to become visually literate.

Our Multi-Ethnic Culture

We also live in a multi-ethnic nation, where growing numbers of African Americans, Asian Americans, American Indians, and Latinos/as increasingly define American culture. While America was formed as a nation of ethnic cultures within a dominant Euro-American culture (with the motto *E Pluribus Unum*), cultural critics note that ethnic minorities will constitute America's demographic majority sometime before the year 2050 and are redefining the face of America.[8] This means the sources of American identity are rapidly shifting. Increasingly, what we define as American — our history and heritage, our music, our foods, and our languages and literature — derives from ethnic-minority Americans.

The challenge is that racial and ethnic tensions are high in American society at large and in high schools and undergraduate colleges in particular. Stereotypes prevail and hate crimes proliferate. Students unfamiliar with ethnic groups other than their own often deride rather than attempt to learn about that which they do not understand. Films can provide understanding: from films, students can learn about their own and others' ethnic histories and literatures as well as about contemporary ethnic cultures in addition to their own. Some films, however, encourage students to think of others in terms of popular stereotypes and as objects of derision. Learning to recognize recurring stereotypes — and to understand them as representations that reflect the times in which the films were made — helps students become critical readers of compelling images and persuasive film techniques rather than passive recipients. Teachers need to design curricula for an increasingly diverse student body that accurately reflects the diverse history, literature, and multi-sided social issues that define American culture.[9] And students need to examine recurrent issues in representations of American diversity to help them conceptualize and realize a democratically harmonious, multi-ethnic America in which to live.

Films about and by four American ethnic groups— African Americans, Asian Americans, American Indians, and Latinos/as— represent the way in which America defines itself as a multicultural nation, scholars define America's ethnic diversity, and American ethnic minority groups define themselves. These are four major classifications used by the U.S. Census Bureau in identifying its citizenry,[10] by the academic community in determining underrepresented groups to be included in disciplines across the curriculum, by textbook publishers and film distributors, and by ethnic minority groups in identifying and representing themselves in film. Examining film representations of these ethnic groups also offers comparative methods and issues to study other ethnic representations (of, for example, Arab Americans,[11] Jewish Americans, Italian Americans, Irish Americans) and provides a full and diverse account of American history and America's cultural and literary heritage.

Multicultural and Visual Literacy

Films about America's ethnic minorities demonstrate the reasons why students need to be critical viewers rather than passive recipients of what they see. African-American filmmaker Spike Lee points to a danger inherent in passive learning when he contends that ever since D.W. Griffith's (1915) *The Birth of a Nation*, it is from stereotyped misrepresentations "in movies that a lot of white Americans get their opinions of blacks."[12] From another perspective on the same issue, African-American Pulitzer- and Nobel-prize winning novelist Toni Morrison apprises readers in her first (1970) novel, *The Bluest Eye*, that movies are where many African Americans have derived false opinions of themselves as less worthy than whites.[13] Echoing Morrison, in Chinese American Nelly Wong's (1980) autobiographical poem "When I Was Growing Up," Wong confesses that watching movies as a child made her feel "un–American" to the point where she "longed to be white."[14] Conversely, in his (1994) memoir *Colored People*, Henry Louis Gates, Jr., recalls how black characters in particular films affected him positively and helped shape his identity as a black child.[15] For generations of Americans, films have been a powerful purveyor of cultural information about American ethnicity, and even films of the past continue to inform and influence the present. Rather than safely relegated to its place in film history, D.W. Griffith's (1915) *The Birth of a Nation* is still shown today by white supremacy groups, and this and other early films (some blatantly racist) are recycled and relabeled by television cable channels (e.g., Turner Classic Movies, American Movie Classics, the Westerns channel) as classics and are viewed alongside old and new films on other movie channels and in movie theatres— largely without the benefit of historical placement, cultural context, or critical analysis. David O. Selznick and Victor Fleming's (1939) film *Gone with the Wind*, which remains the most popular American historical film ever made,[16] continues to subject new generations to then popular racial stereotypes of dutiful and dim-witted African-American slaves with no attempt to depict the racial struggles of the antebellum, Civil War, and Reconstruction eras it portrays. For students whose knowledge about American ethnicity is limited, repeated stereotypes live in the perceptual present of film images and sustain their influence.

From the inception of the movie industry in the 1890s, film representations have included ethnic minority characters, most often as servants, foils, or antagonists to white protagonists, as comic relief, or as exotic peoples living outside the boundaries of accepted Euro-American values and norms. Today, ethnic minority filmmakers are recording and re-presenting their history and heritage for themselves and are re-informing others about the actualities of becoming and being an ethnic minority in American. For example, Arthur Dong's (1982) documentary *Sewing Woman* depicts the immigration experiences of his own Chinese American mother, as representative of all Chinese American immigrant women, to share his understanding of his ethnic heritage while recording a small part of the ethnically diverse history that has made America a multicultural society today. A number of filmmakers outside the ethnicity of the people whose stories they are filming are also researching their subjects and contributing historically accurate film records. Korean American Sonya Rhee's 2003 documentary *Soldados: Chicanos in Viet Nam* tells the story of Mexican-American soldiers' experiences before, during, and after the Vietnam war, based on her reading of Charley Trujillo's (1991) book of the same name, her consultations with Trujillo, and her desire to add images of their courage to the public record.[17] And Euro American David Riker's (1998) *La Ciudad* (*The City*) focuses on the immigrant experiences of Latinos/as from Mexico, Central America, South America, and the Caribbean. Riker learned Spanish, worked with community activists, interviewed and used immigrants from the community as actors, and recreated events he attended (such as a *quinceanera* party) in order to accurately reflect the current Latino/a immigrant experience in New York, portray Latinos/as as individuals, and denounce xenophobia.[18] Teachers can effectively include and distinguish between films that caricature ethnic minority Americans, by exploring the historical context and rationale behind such caricatures, and films that reflect the experiences and perspectives of ethnic minority communities themselves, by analyzing those perspectives to understand how these filmmakers have chosen to represent America's ethnic history, culture, and literature and their reasons for doing so.

Ethnic Film and Standards for Secondary Schools

High school teachers need to meet educational standards set for their students, and these standards can help college teachers know what their students have been required to learn. National, state, and discipline standards for secondary schools provide an important rationale for teaching multicultural and visual literacy. Schools, state departments of public instruction, and the professional organizations of a variety of disciplines— the National History Standards Project, the National Council for the Social Studies (NCSS), the National Council of Teachers of English (NCTE), the International Reading Association, and the Consortium of National Arts Education Association have all now recommended that teachers include in their curricula not only the events, experiences, and creative expressions of America's diverse cultures but also what has been more generally termed media literacy skills. Additionally, because the standards emphasize the interdisciplinary nature of learning, integrating ethnic film into course curricula becomes even more appropriate.

Teachers have been encouraged and even required to make significant changes in their course content to reflect the increasing diversity of America and the historical, cultural, social, and literary contributions of America's ethnic minorities. The history standards state that curricula should "reflect the nation's diversity" in terms of major events, policy issues, facets of human culture, and the history and cultures of diverse peoples.[19] NCSS recommends that social studies students understand "significant historical periods and patterns of change within and across cultures," that they be able to "investigate, interpret, and analyze multiple historical and contemporary viewpoints within and across cultures related to important events," that they understand cultural influences on the development of the self, and that they "compare and evaluate the impact of stereotyping" and other behaviors on individuals and groups.[20] The NCTE standards state that English Language Arts students should read a wide range of print and non-print texts of the various cultures of the U.S., and literature teachers should "help students become familiar with diverse peoples and cultures."[21] The Visual Arts standards recommended by the Consortium of National Arts Education Association state that students should be able to "describe the function and explore the meaning of specific art objects within varied cultures, times, and places" as well as understand the relationship of works of art to one another regarding "history, aesthetics, and culture."[22] Clearly, a film curriculum that includes ethnic film will meet these standards.

Media literacy — and particularly visual literacy — has been given somewhat less attention in high school curricula than multicultural literacy. While Australia, Poland, Hungary, Canada, and many others countries have had media literacy requirements for their students for many years, the country in which most media is produced — America — has been slower in incorporating analytical and critical media literacy skills into academics. In the most comprehensive survey of state media education standards, Robert Kubey and Frank W. Baker report that in November of 1998, only twelve states had curricular guidelines for media education, but by October of 1999, 48 states showed such frameworks,[23] and by 2001, the academic standards of all fifty states provided for media education as a part of its overall curriculum. But what exactly counts as "media education" and where it is taught — in English Language Arts or some other class— varies widely from state to state. Media education can mean reading a photograph, an advertisement, a newspaper editorial, a television newscast, a sitcom, or a film. And most books on teaching media are that wide-ranging and inclusive. Visual literacy, as we have used the term, with its emphasis upon teaching films as historical documents, as cultural documents, and as creative expressions of their makers using formal features specific to film, is perhaps the most important skill within the larger category of media literacy skills that teachers can help their students learn.

The standards of the various disciplines for teachers as well as for students emphasize the ability to critically read and interpret visual texts. Across disciplines, teachers are expected to use visual texts in their instruction, and students are expected to be able to read, interpret, and use these texts as they would print texts. The history standards state that students should be able to draw upon visual material, to formulate historical questions based upon historical documents— including visual ones— and to obtain data from such documents. Social studies students are expected to be "critical and copious readers of the best media, print, audio, and video content" and to be able to evaluate print and non-print sources of information. For English Language Arts, the NCTE standards recommend that students read a wide range of non-print texts and be able to "gather, evaluate, synthesize data" from them, to conduct research using them, and to use spoken, written, and visual language "for learning, enjoyment, persuasion, and exchange of information." NCTE's standards also encourage teachers to help "students to respond critically to different media," to use non-print as well as print media to help students understand human behavior, and — directly related to our focus on visual literacy — to help students "recognize that visual discourse (film, video, photographs) vary from culture to culture" and "understand how people are influenced by print and non-print media." Integrating ethnic minority film into course content allows teachers to meet both the visual literacy standards and diversity standards. The Visual Arts standards expect students to be able to "describe the origins of specific images and ideas and explain why they are of value in their artwork and in the work of others." Ethnic minority film study will allow students to study, for instance, the beginnings of ethnic stereotypes in film as well as recurring instances of and challenges to those stereotypes, analyzing the particular use of film types and film techniques to understand how viewers are invited to look at the stereotypes, in order to fulfill this standard.

Ethnic minority film study also provides teachers an opportunity to examine interdisciplinary relations between fields of study and to open their classrooms to such connections. The history standards note that in addition to consulting and understanding conventional historical documents, students should make use of visual, literary, and musical sources to understand historical narrative and that they should consult all types of historical records, including documentaries. The social studies standards claim that social studies teaching and learning "are powerful when they are integrative." Students are encouraged to read, consult, and evaluate a variety of sources, including photographs, films, and videos in formulating their understandings. Such interdisciplinary connections can be made by using fiction (historical novels and historical feature films) to teach history and visual literacy. Since many students will learn their history from these fictionalized accounts outside the classroom, teachers can use such sources effectively by having students compare them with current non-fiction accounts (history textbooks and documentaries) to explore differences, including point of view and the kinds of evidence and persuasive techniques each medium uses. Reminding students that the first historians were storytellers, teachers can also help students discover how such nonfiction texts as history textbooks and documentaries are not objective reports but reflect then-current ideas, have a point of view, and use the storytelling methods currently acceptable to the discipline to make history exciting and memorable. Social studies teachers can make interdisciplinary connections by including the historical and cultural contexts for films about social issues. Literature teachers can investigate the historical and cultural background of literary (both written and film narratives) texts. Comparative analysis of films and written texts—comparing film adaptations with the literary works from which they derive and comparing documentary and feature films with written accounts of historical and social issues— promotes critical reading of both visual and written texts. Comparing themes, point of view, evidence, and the persuasive techniques of different kinds of texts helps students to discover how investigating not just a variety of sources but a variety of kinds of sources can provide multiple perspectives. The Visual Arts standards encourage curricula to make connections between disciplines. Students are asked to compare media with other arts and with "ideas, issues, or themes in the humanities or sciences." Their achievement can be assessed on their ability to synthesize "the creative and analytical principles and techniques of the visual arts and other arts disciplines, the humanities, or the sciences." For Film Studies, having students create videos (about themselves, their families, and their communities, as well as about issues important to them) involves them in research and analysis of historical and cultural issues and allows them to apply their visual literacy skills in creative ways. Integrating ethnic film into the high school classroom can teach multicultural and visual literacy; promote critical reading, viewing, and thinking; and reveal the variety of ways history, culture, literature, and ethnic identity can be represented.

Appropriate Films

This book focuses on how and why to teach significant and representative films that are appropriate for high school and undergraduate college audiences—although individual teachers need to make individual decisions about what is or isn't appropriate for their students, their classrooms, their topics of study, and their schools only after previewing possible films. A few of the films we discuss contain scenes of violence, sexuality, and profane language, and only individual teachers can decide what is inappropriate or excessive.

We have limited our analysis of American cinema to Hollywood films, independently produced films and videos, and films made for television, and have generally excluded television programs. Feature films particularly appropriate for high school and undergraduate college audiences are often shown on television or were made for television, and many relevant documentaries have been shown on public television and advertised as available on video format for classroom study, some accompanied with study guides. We include a great number of these films but do not attempt to study television programming and the influence of television,[24] which is a large topic, but has a shorter history than film, especially of ethnic minority representations. Most of the films we have chosen are particularly relevant to high school and undergraduate college curricula in history, social studies, literature, and film studies classes, although journalism, music, and art teachers will find their disciplines mentioned, and history teachers, for example, may well find films recommended for a literature class most suitable to a history lesson, and vice versa. The purpose of this book is not to recommend particular films but to provide enough information for education majors, practicing teachers, and media specialists to make informed choices of their own.

PART I

FILM HISTORIES OF
AFRICAN AMERICAN,
ASIAN AMERICAN, AMERICAN
INDIAN AND LATINO/A
REPRESENTATIONS

1

Historical Overview of African Americans on Film: Challenges to Racial Ideology

by Vincent Rocchio

The history of African Americans on film is a long struggle over the meanings assigned to on-screen images of African Americans and the role those meanings exercise in society. That struggle — the conflicts that emerge over the circulation of denigrating and stereotypical images— provides evidence that more is at stake in the relationship between an image, its meaning, and the operations of society than first meets the eye. If, for example, meaning itself was inherent, fixed, and stable (and hence self-evident), then there would be no struggle: denigrating and stereotypical images would be seen and understood by all who viewed them as untruths, and they would have no social currency. It is, however, precisely because the meaning of race (or the perhaps more accurate term, ethnicity) is neither predetermined nor inherent that the meanings assigned to film images of African Americans are such a significant social battleground. For high school and undergraduate college students, learning to read these contested meanings is an essential step in learning visual and multicultural literacy. The constituencies in this struggle over meaning are many, but this essay will limit itself to only two such groups, loosely structured as they are: the Euro-American dominated Hollywood industry and African-American independent filmmakers.

The watershed moment in this conflict over meaning is certainly D.W. Griffith's 1915 film, *The Birth of a Nation.* For too long, Griffith and his film were the darlings of film history, which all too readily concluded that while the film's racism was deplorable, the film was, nonetheless, great art and a defining moment of American film history, if not film history itself.

If *The Birth of a Nation* is a defining moment in film history, however, it is due to the effect of the film's racism and the demonstrable attention that was paid to the film, not to its innovative or artistic merit. Indeed, there is little innovative about the film that can itself be considered the cause of its commercial success and status as great art.[1] Rather, the film seamlessly enmeshes its narrative drama in a racist ideology of racial difference. Griffith's highly skewed history of the Civil War and Reconstruction eras provided white spectators with seemingly realistic images of African Americans as uncivilized, violent, unintelligent, and overly libidinous. Moreover, the film provided these images at a specific historical juncture: in the transition from a rural-agricultural to an urban-industrial society. The traditional social order of America was in the process of being disrupted and displaced, threatened by the demands and pace of industrialization. *The Birth of a Nation* thus provided a rationale for this emerging mass society to maintain a white racial hierarchy in a developing social order. African Americans, the film so pointedly attempts to dramatize, were not capable of participating in the civilized world. Griffith thereby made the marginalization of African Americans seem not only justifiable but necessary.

The Birth of a Nation is thus a significant event in film history not because it is great art but because it demonstrates how meanings assigned to images of race could be effectively used to naturalize and justify the disenfranchisement of racial groups. Far from being a success despite its racism, *The Birth of a Nation* became a box office triumph because of its racism. Hollywood learned its lesson about box office success: for decades thereafter, Euro-American audiences consumed a steady stream of images whose function was to marginalize African Americans, Asian Americans, Latinos/as, and American Indians. Because film production is so capital intensive, Hollywood could do so with near — but not total — impunity. Several challenges, some from within the industry but most by independent African-American filmmakers, contested the dominant meanings Hollywood assigned to the image of African Americans.

One of the earliest challenges to Hollywood's portrayal of African Americans is the work of Oscar Micheaux, who is one of the first African-American independent filmmakers. Much of early American filmmaking (and film distribution for that matter) is lost to history, but the significance of Micheaux's films lies well beyond chronology, lost films, or even great artistic achievement. Micheaux was a pioneer, and his ability to produce and distribute commercially viable films featuring African Americans as early as 1919 warrants significant historical investigation. In addition, however, Micheaux's work is of significance for African-American independent film because it established what would become three fundamental parameters: using film as a means of uplifting the race, boldly challenging Hollywood's representations of African Americans, and experimenting with the structure of film style itself as an important part of contesting Hollywood.

Micheaux's skill as a filmmaker was focused on making films for African-American audiences that could compete with the content and the production values of Hollywood while countering its caricatures of African Americans. The predominately African-American casts of Micheaux's films offered more than positive African-American role models; they provided a variety of characters who confronted complex social issues, such as interracial romance and color hierarchy within the African-American community. Micheaux's films allowed African-American audiences to see representations of the social issues confronting them unencumbered by the denigrating and exaggerated stereotypes Hollywood insisted on for African-American characters.

In addition to opting for more complex images of African Americans, Micheaux directly confronted the images Hollywood produced. His 1920 film *Within Our Gates* is recognizable for its direct reversal of a rape scene from *The Birth of a Nation*. Griffith's film, focused on overly libidinous black men pursuing white women, includes no less than two attempted rapes. *Within Our Gates* replicates one of those scenes but reverses the racial roles: in Micheaux's film, a white man attempts to rape a black woman. Micheaux's skill at staging a visible replication is outweighed only by the social complexity that the scene brings to the fore. The black-on-white rape in *The Birth of a Nation* is narrative motivation for white vigilante violence — as white men in the film gather under the cloak of the Ku Klux Klan to enact their own ideas of racial hierarchy and racial justice — and an occasion for validating the social acceptability of lynching African Americans. The white-on-black rape scene of *Within Our Gates*, while also working within a structure of narrative causality, references a long history of unprosecuted crimes against African-American women. Micheaux's film not only confronts the racist iconography and ideology of Hollywood film, but also the racism within broader society that allowed such devastating injustices against African Americans.

Micheaux's work is noteworthy also in its challenge to the narrative and stylistic structure of Hollywood. Micheaux's films were always shot on tight budgets and tight schedules, the mark of most independent films. Such financial constraints, however, do not directly determine the film style of Micheaux's films, which subvert and create alternatives to such classical Hollywood conventions as strict narrative linearity and singular point of view. As *Within Our Gates* demonstrates with its overt challenge to *The Birth of a Nation*, Micheaux recognized that the stylistic structures of Hollywood film were not ideologically neutral but actively assigned meanings to African Americans (such as "threat," "dangerous," and "wicked") in order to marginalize them. Micheaux's significance rests in part on his combination of Hollywood production values with the subversion of its stylistic structures, techniques that have become a continuing legacy discernable in the work of such filmmakers as Spike Lee, Julie Dash, Robert Townsend, and John Singleton.

Like Griffith's work, Micheaux's films are perhaps too dated in terms of performance style and story lines to be accessible for serious study by high school and undergraduate college students. His impact and continuing legacy, however, are indispensable to understanding the history of African-American representation in film. Several books and articles provide detailed insight into his work for teachers of visual and multicultural literacy.[2] More accessible for students unschooled in film studies is *Midnight Ramble: The Story of the Black Film Industry*, a (1994) *American Experience* documentary that visualizes the issues at stake in Micheaux's work. Micheaux's career came to an end with the 1948 film *The Betrayal*. He survived both the Great Depression and the cinema's transition to sound, but the disruption of everyday life caused by America's entry into World War II prevented Micheaux from making another film until three years after the war's end. By the time he resumed, black audiences had abandoned him, judging his films to be outdated repetitions of the same themes. Forty years would pass before a vibrant African-American independent film industry would be revived and capture the attention of both audiences and the Hollywood establishment. In the interim, there would be very little to contest the dominant meanings assigned to African Americans by Hollywood film.[3]

Visual and Multicultural Literacy: Literature and Film Studies

To Kill a Mockingbird (Robert Mulligan, 1962) is an important film for understanding the limits of Hollywood films to challenge industry norms and practices. Mulligan's film and Harper Lee's Pulitzer-Prize winning 1960 novel (on which the film was based) provide film and literature students a means to compare the two media — not to determine how well the film does or does not reproduce the novel but to determine how the two media compare in challenging or reproducing the ideology of racial hierarchy. Both the novel and the film adaptation of *To Kill a Mockingbird* are about racism in the segregated South. As the narratives progress, there can be no doubt that both are anti-racist and hence progressive in their intentions. Atticus Finch, the white lawyer who defends Tom Robinson, a black man accused of raping a white woman, not only heroically stands up to a white lynch mob but also teaches his children to eschew racial bigotry. The plot in both allows Atticus to explicitly identify the prevailing racial prejudices of the community's racism and to fairly condemn them. The novel and the film alike render Tom's conviction as a travesty of justice and depict Tom's death in an attempted escape as an unnecessary tragedy.

Comparing characterizations reveals the limits of Hollywood filmmaking in terms of rendering complex African-American characters. The African Americans in *To Kill a Mockingbird* are dignified and respectable but also one-dimensional. Both the novel and the film pointedly counter the prevailing stereotype, so prominent in Griffith's film, of African-American men lusting after white women, as Atticus Finch proves to novel readers, films viewers, and his own children within the story that Tom is clearly innocent of the rape charge. In both novel and film, Tom Robinson is a virtuous victim. He has many times helped Mayella Ewell, a poverty-stricken white woman with an alcoholic father and no mother, doing whatever chores she asked him because he felt sorry for her having to take care of her many siblings with little or no help from her father. Tom Robinson is akin to another prominent stereotype, also depicted in Griffith's *The Birth of a Nation*, the Uncle Tom who is more than happy to serve white folks at the expense of his own personal interests. But Tom Robinson is an Uncle Tom with a difference: he does not serve out of loyalty to white people, and he is not applauded for faithful service. Instead, he feels sorry for Mayella, and his unpaid work for her is rewarded with her false accusation of rape and with the jury falsely convicting him. The novel and film depictions of Tom Robinson suggest that racism is so prominent in this small Southern town that his life and liberty are constantly in jeopardy. To make Tom a clear antithesis to the image of the stereotyped Black Brute threat to white women, in both the novel and the film, Tom is depicted as an innocent and naïve victim.

The novel and film differ somewhat in their depictions of Atticus Finch's maid, Calpurnia, but her only role in both is to serve the white family. Lee's novel gives Calpurnia a slimly depicted home life and has her take Atticus's daughter and son, Scout and Jem, to her own church one Sunday when Atticus cannot be home. While the African Americans there show the children great respect, one woman upbraids Calpurnia for bringing white children into what she perceives to be a safe space for African Americans only. Although Atticus does not allow his children to use the word, Calpurnia responds by calling the woman "a nigger," and she later tells Atticus that she hopes that the town's African-American community is not taking too many liberties in coming to his house with gifts in appreciation for his court defense of Tom Robinson. She has no opinions about the court case itself and seems only to care about the well-being of Scout, Jem, and Atticus. Mulligan's film goes one step further in marginalizing Calpurnia: it completely ignores her personal life. Viewers only learn that she has a life of her own when on one occasion Atticus asks her if she would mind staying overnight with the children. In both media, she is an updated reproduction of the old Mammy stereotype, also represented in Griffith's *The Birth of a Nation*, an African-American woman who is as happy to serve white folks as the faithful Uncle Tom. The novel and the film are important examples of how updating supposedly positive stereotypes does not prevent them from participating in the process of marginalizing African Americans.

For all of their progressive intent, the plot structure in both the novel and the film adaptation of *To Kill a Mockingbird* likewise assigns African Americans to the margins of society. Several elements of plot structure reproduce the structures of white privilege that racial ideology — and not just segregation — works to maintain. Chief among these is the narrative point of view. Atticus' daughter tells the story of one summer in her life as her childhood memory, and the story in both the novel and the film focuses on how racism affects the developing consciences of the white children. Even then, the racism is displaced. What impacts the children is not so much racism per se, but how their father stands up to it: they learn that their father is a hero. The fact that African Americans suffer under racism is subordinated to the figure of the white father. Nowhere is this made clearer than in the close of the trial scene. After witnessing an outrageous miscarriage of justice, the African-American community remains in the balcony of the courtroom, distant observers waiting for Atticus Finch to leave. As he does, they all stand silently as a sign of their respect and admiration for his noble fight, his willingness to speak and name his community's racism. The plot reinforces this gesture by having one of the leaders of the African-American community, a minister, tell Atticus' daughter Scout to stand with them. Only the novel has Jem later voice his anger at the verdict and vow to work to ensure better justice in the court system when he grows up. But, like the novel, the film leaves no space, no room for anger or outrage from African Americans, no doubt because of Hol-

To Kill a Mockingbird (Robert Mulligan, 1962). African Americans in the courtroom's segregated balcony rise to honor Atticus Finch, the Euro-American defense lawyer for Tom Robinson.

lywood's fear of legitimizing African-American outrage. Rather, African-American outrage and anger are subsumed by respect and admiration for a white man who is willing to battle for the African-American community. The African Americans are relegated to the role of testifying how great a white man is. African Americans, and for that matter racism, become subordinated to the role of character building for a white character.

In both novel and film, Atticus Finch and his children are given a preferential place within the plot. They are, in effect, more important — or privileged over — the African Americans who actually suffer the effects of racism. This narrative privileging replicates the social structure of white privilege — a social structure that works to secure preferential status — based on the "invisibility" of race for members of white society.[4] Several elements of the plot function together to make this privileging seem invisible and thus natural. The plot opens with the main characters, not the arrest or the alleged crime itself. In the film, the voice over of Atticus' daughter, Scout, within the opening replicates the novel and establishes the story from the children's point of view. The cause and effect structure of the narrative then links events to and through the children. This logical and fairly seamless organization of elements renders the privileging of white characters and the subordination of African Americans as an unnoticeable reflection of society (at least, unnoticeable and invisible to white audiences). This kind of invisible reproducing of the structure of privilege through the structure of plot became a staple for a Hollywood that eventually, because of the social effects of the Civil Rights Movement, had to retreat from the more obviously denigrating stereotypes of African Americans. Literature and film studies students can trace changing images of African Americans within this unchanging racial ideology from Griffith's (1915) *The Birth of a Nation* to Mulligan's (1962) *To Kill a Mockingbird* and beyond. Films such as *Guess Who's Coming to Dinner* (Stanley Kramer, 1967), *Cry Freedom* (Richard Attenborough, 1987), and the Academy Award winning (for best picture) *Driving Miss Daisy* (Bruce Beresford, 1989) continue to subordinate the issue of racism to the effect it has on main white characters.

Independent Challenges and Commercialization

The apparent ease with which Hollywood could contribute to the marginalization of African Americans through one-dimensional characterizations and the style and structure of its films was more than a little troubling to a group of African-American students at UCLA's film school in the 1970s. They resolved to make films that would confront Hollywood's representation of African Americans. Though their films were not immediate commercial successes, these students— Julie Dash, Haile Gerima, Charles Burnett, and others— helped build a foundation for black independent film upon which the next generation, led by Spike Lee, would ultimately be able to capitalize, creating a viable African-American independent cinema that would not only confront Hollywood but would also engage it commercially.

This commercial engagement, which saw Hollywood studios financing or distributing the work of black independents, such as Spike Lee's *School Daze* (1988) and *Do the Right Thing* (1989) and John Singleton's *Boyz 'N the Hood* (1991), reflected the complicated currents within the entertainment industry with respect to race. On one hand, as Ed Guerrero observes, the early to mid–1980s was, by and large, a return to repressing images of African-American culture from the screen.[5] On the other hand, Eddie Murphy was the biggest box office draw of the era, with interracial buddy films such as *48 Hours* (Walter Hill, 1982), *Another 48 Hours* (Walter Hill, 1990) and with *Beverly Hills Cop* (Martin Brest, 1984), *Beverly Hills Cop II* (Tony Scott, 1987), and *Beverly Hills Cop III* (John Landis, 1994) becoming huge commercial successes. Likewise, *The Cosby Show*, featuring actor-comedian Bill Cosby, was the top-rated television show. With these commercially viable examples of "black entertainment" and Spike Lee's crossover success, Hollywood became ready, as Sharon Willis notes, to change from repressing the image of African-American culture to marketing it as a commodity.[6] As Spike Lee's 2000 film *Bamboozled*—a parody of film and television caricatures and the marketing strategies behind them — would demonstrate, this commodification of African-American culture became yet another round in the struggle over the meanings assigned to the representation of African Americans.

Deconstructing the Ideology of Race

Teaching films about and by African Americans highlights several significant issues, but none is more central to the films specifically — and to African-American culture in general — than the meanings assigned to representations of African Americans. It is not just that many films repeat and thus perpetuate racist images but that, just as significantly, many films insist that there is a specific reality to race. They encourage audiences to accept the idea that race is a legitimate way to categorize human beings according to essential differences in mental and physical abilities. In this sense, films about African Americans (or any other perceived "non-white" social group), and the discourses they circulate about race, help to define what race is and thus what it means to be an African American. Contemporary studies of race, however, consistently point to the need to understand race not as a biological reality but rather as a social construction. Social definitions rather than biological realities define race. Skin color, for example, does not define race; a society defines skin color as a marker for so-called racial differences. The insistence on race as a biological reality that somehow determines the natural composition of social groups is the ideology of race. To attain visual and multicultural literacy, therefore, students must do more than identify the repeated imagery imposed on specific racial groups; they also need to learn how films perpetuate the ideology of racial difference by insisting that there is an inherent, natural, and unchanging way to be African American. Teaching students how to read images of African Americans on film forces a pedagogical decision. We can ignore ideology — and specifically the ideology of race — by limiting film analysis to content comparisons with the aim of determining how faithful a film is to a written version and by limiting analysis of film form to aesthetics or some other mode of film appreciation, or we can include the study of ideology as central to our task. The former approach, while relatively safe and neutral, runs the risk of maintaining the ideology of race by allowing it to remain concealed, for what we do not know to look for, we most often cannot see. The latter pedagogical option of focusing on racial ideology teaches students to read *how* a film perpetuates or dismantles racist ideas in the specific ways that it represents African Americans. Making the ideology of race central to our study of films about and by African Americans empowers students to confront not only the role and effects of racial hierarchy but also the ways films can maintain or dismiss such hierarchies.

Visual and Multicultural Literacy: History

Hollywood cinema has found a place within the history classroom precisely because its production values and adherence to codes of realism can effectively bring the past to life in a manner that engages students far beyond their textbooks. In this respect, most teachers' pedagogical approach becomes critical comparison: the film text engages the students' interest, and the teacher points out the differences between historical fact and fictional fantasy. Students come away with an appreciation for and knowledge of the past, and the field of history benefits accordingly. There is an added benefit, however, in also teaching students how to read racial ideology in film. The following analysis of Steven Spielberg's (1997) *Amistad*, Michael Mann's (2001) *Ali*, and two documentaries about the Civil Rights Movement demonstrates how students can read film representations of African Americans not as definitive or defective history but as representations with distinct ideological agendas.

Even before D. W. Griffith's 1915 *The Birth of a Nation*, black men have been depicted according to their place in a racial hierarchy. Thus, long before the film industry moved to Hollywood, white skin signified reason and civilization and black skin an inferiority and savagery that had to be controlled (the 1905 film *White Caps*, a precursor to *The Birth of a Nation*, is one such example). Griffith's skewed rendering of history from a white southern point of view in *The Birth of a Nation* is long and cumbersome, the acting is a melodramatic style no longer taken seriously, and the narrative transitions are exceedingly out of pace with contemporary film spectatorship. The film deserves serious study, but more important, and certainly more accessible for high school and undergraduate college students, is an examination of Griffith's legacy continuing in more recent films, such as Steven Spielberg's (1997) *Amistad*. Like *The Birth of a Nation*, *Amistad* presents itself as history. An analysis of *Amistad*, however, demonstrates that reading a film's ideology to make it visible can move history beyond an examination of the past and towards a greater understanding of history's function as discourse (i.e., as renditions told from particular positions and points of view) rather than as objective truth.

Amistad ostensibly tells the story of an actual slave rebellion in 1839 on the Spanish slave ship "La Amistad." As a means of establishing its story and providing the motivation for the rebellion, the film includes a segment on the Middle Passage, depicting slaves being first herded onto the ship, shackled into its hold, and maltreated throughout the voyage across the Atlantic. These scenes in *Amistad* clearly attempt to portray the depraved brutality and the utter inhumanity of the Middle Passage (and by association, the institution of slavery itself). In this sense, the meaning of the scenes is quite unambiguous, as is the film's condemnation of what it represents. The issue in using this film to teach history, however, is not just what is shown, but *how* it is shown.

The story of *Amistad* is not told chronologically. The scenes of the Middle Passage do not come before the rebellion on the ship, as chronological order would have it, but rather after the bloody and violent overthrow of the ship's crew in which all but two of the whites on board are killed. Instead of the chronological, *Amistad* begins with the visceral. It opens with an extreme close-up centered around the eyes, lower forehead, and bridge of the nose of a black face that, we only later learn, belong to Cinque, the leader of the slave revolt. Darkness fills the shot, and what light does appear accentuates and emphasizes the sweat extruding from every pore of the black man's skin. On the sound track, harried breathing is brought into the foreground to be as up close as the shot scale — sometimes even eclipsing the sound of a thunderstorm. The first shot gives way to another close-up, of fingers scraping at a nail head embedded in wood. These two shots, and the sequence constructed around them, emphasize and heighten the physical. The function, as the bloodied fingers demonstrate, is to convey the physical sense of what is going on in the sequence. This emphasis on physicality then expands into the broader action of the rebellion itself. Here, individual shots are composed, sequenced, and maintained for specific durations in order to emphasize the action of the violence. There is a striking parallel between the blood that emanates from the black fingers desperately working at the nail and the blood that will gush from the white bodies: by comparison, the latter far surpasses the former, in effect, minimizing it. So bloody is this uprising, in fact, that even when the film resorts to implied violence, using one of the sails to block out the action from being seen, blood from the sailor oozes through.

This film's minimal buildup to the rebellion, combined with an emphasis on graphic violence, invites viewers to respond to the violent action, to the display of ruptured bodies. Although the narrative makes clear that this is a rebellion on a slave ship, the minimal context for its action makes it little more than a spectacle of black violence. The manner in which the text withholds, and thus diminishes, the narrative context around the representation of violence heightens the spectacle of graphic black violence. In this respect, the film's opening reaffirms and recirculates the same image of black violence that Griffith chose to highlight memorably for his viewers more than three-quarters of a century earlier. In Spielberg's film, the disparity between the extremity of the graphically depicted violence and the minimum of narrative context to justify it creates an uneasy ambivalence, especially for white viewers, with respect to the acceptability of the retaliation, an ambivalence rooted in the long-standing fear of — and belief in — the propensity of blacks towards violence. This effect is further enhanced by the image of the main character, Cinque, who brandishes a sword and stalks the surviving white characters on the ship. Even though set within the justificatory context of a slave rebellion, the image nonetheless perpetuates the familiar iconography of violent black men. The structure of a film, how it organizes what it represents, inscribes the ideological. By withholding scenes of the Middle Passage until after the rebellion, the film diminishes the justificatory and retaliatory context for the violence and highlights instead the spectacle of black violence. Further, and most important for teaching films about and by African Americans, the ideology inscribed by such reorganization of events can undermine, contradict, or even negate the more progressive ideas in the film.

As with the opening of the film, the abduction and Middle Passage in *Amistad* are positioned to emphasize the physicality of African Americans. The film complicates viewer identification, whose sympathies are aligned with the main character, Cinque, but who necessarily want to detach themselves from the physical suffering he endures during his abduction and captivity. Several film techniques support the viewer's detachment: camera position (which is consistently framed as objective observer with a privileged view), camera movement (the camera is rarely stationary and thus never dwells on any one subject), shot duration (none lasts very long), and shot frequency (the editing rarely returns to any particular shot, cycling instead through the brutality). The viewer's detached position is further enhanced by the plot's distancing of the events. Unlike the rebellion and the trial, the abduction and Middle Passage are framed as past events. They are distanced from the rest of the story as events recounted by the main character telling his story to others. The function of this distanced, detached way of viewing is to encourage a voyeuristic position for the audience. Viewers are encouraged to be repulsed by the suffering and brutality of the Middle Passage but to do so from a detached position. This detachment provides the necessary distance by which the individual viewer does not have to be in a position of culpability for slavery or its aftermath. For students, analyzing this kind of depiction renders visible the manner by which the structure of a film functions ideologically and what is at stake in the way in which history is told. Students learn that film analysis can make visible the process of the telling and provide new insights regarding the ways in which histories are organized and remembered. For teachers, *Amistad* invites this kind of close textual analysis.

A further analysis of *Amistad* and of Michael Mann's 2001 film *Ali* can help students examine how the "Great Man" theory of history offers a structured ideology in historical and biographical films. In *Amistad*, the introduction of John Quincy Adams at the trial — as the man who sways jury opinion to set Cinque and his fellow rebels free with his evocation of American ideals — ellipses viewer identification with the African Americans. The great white man of reason is the American hero with whom Americans can identify with by the end of the film. In *Ali*, the great man is an African American who is represented as a successful product of American celebrity culture rather than a public voice against America's racial ideology. In *Ali*, the great man is Ali the boxer and celebrity personality at the expense of Ali the political activist and, even more significantly, at the expense of the collective struggle for equality that made Ali such a lightning rod figure. The film's selection of events and discreet moments consistently subordinates the political dimensions of Ali to the excitement of his professional and personal lives, a glaring set of choices for the most political of sports figures, despite the fact that within the dynamics of plot, the political consistently swirls around the character, supposedly making him more complex, more dramatic, more enigmatic.

Ali as a political figure is precisely what is selected out of the film. In *Ali*, Muhammad Ali's criticism of racial policies and politics in America is consistently spoken rather than shown, and the spoken is subsumed by nonpolitical action or is removed from America. Whether it is Ali's stinging indictment of the press and white society in conjunction with his refusal to participate in the draft or his second wife's critique of Don King and Joseph Mobutu, the politics of race are consistently relegated to the spoken as a means of subordinating them. The repression and displacement of Ali's political status is nowhere more clearly evidenced than in the representation of the crowds that chant his name. In the scene of the Jerry Quarry fight, the crowd's chant of "Ali" is situated and contained within the context of Ali's victory in the ring. It is merely part of the setting of victory. The film refrains from showing Ali as a political figure—as a political icon—until the plot shifts to Africa, where the racial politics and ideology of the U.S. can be displaced and repressed. It is not until Ali travels to Africa for his fight with George Foreman that the film contextualizes him as a political icon, representing how people identified with him, organized around him politically, and chanted his name as a political act. The politics, however, has been displaced to Africa. The crowd that chants his name struggles against life under a black African dictator, not the racial dynamics of American culture. When it comes to the politics of race in the U.S., the film drops shady suggestions about the FBI and represents the assassinations of Malcolm X and Martin Luther King, Jr., but withholds the representation of Ali's racial politics. We hear about Ali's conversion to Elijah Muhammad's Nation of Islam but not about his differences with Malcolm X. This subordination of the political functions ideologically: it displaces the African-American collective struggle in favor of individual heroes—Ali, Malcolm, Martin. As a result, the film assigns the African-American collective struggle to the margins, diminishing its political potential even as it seems to talk about it.

Examining events in the Civil Rights Movement in documentary films is also an excellent way to illustrate the many ways in which the structure of a film functions ideologically. Examining the structure can reveal the relationship between the subject of Civil Rights and its representation—how that subject comes to us and through what strategies. Besides learning the history of the Civil Rights Movement through its various film representations, students can focus on differences in the representations of one event within the Civil Rights Movement. One such event is the murder of Emmett Till, a fourteen year old from Chicago who was murdered by two white men while visiting his uncle in Mississippi because he spoke "fresh" to or whistled at a white woman. Viewing the same event through different film frameworks can provide students with a basis of comparison to analyze how one event is variously represented. Such differences can be evidenced by comparing the representation of Emmett Till's murder in *A Time for Justice: America's Civil Rights Movement* (Charles Guggenheim, 1992) with *Eyes on the Prize I: America's Civil Rights Years* (Part I: "Awakenings," 1986).

Both films contextualize the murder of Emmett Till within the history of the Civil Rights Movement, and yet each film situates the event within a different framework. The segment on Emmett Till in the "Awakenings" episode of the *Eyes on the Prize* series renders the crime, and especially its aftermath, as a series of important and early events that helped to galvanize the Civil Rights Movement as a collective struggle. The film introduces the event with a voice over narration describing how the Civil Rights Movement started "step by step, ... first, with small acts of personal courage." It then introduces Emmett Till's uncle, Mose Wright, who Till was visiting when he was killed. Till's murder is thus initially placed within the framework of the story of Mose Wright to emphasize Wright's courage in testifying at the trial, where he dared identify the two white men that took Emmett from his house the night of Emmett's murder. The horrific event is then described from various perspectives to emphasize how its tragic injustice, Mose Wright's example, and Till's mother's radical act of having her son's casket remain open at the funeral so everyone could see what was done to him all played a part in mobilizing the collective struggle. Other elements within the film also emphasize the event as an important part of a collective struggle coming into being. Shot selection, for example, is predominantly of large groups of people on the move. Archival footage of individuals speaking is frequently pointedly sociological in its use, as with the Southern sheriff interview, which shows how easily and normally many Southerners made recourse to the term "nigger." All of these elements work to place the event within its larger social context.

A Time for Justice, a film designed specifically for student viewing, briefly chronicles major events of the Civil Rights Movement, highlighting the sacrifices of black as well as white youth to gain the rights of African Americans to eat at lunch counters, to travel freely, to register, and to vote. The film begins and ends by taking viewers to the gravestone of an innocent young African-American man needlessly and maliciously killed during the struggle for civil rights. Within this framework, *A Time for Justice* thus situates the murder of Emmett Till as an early and pivotal event in the larger struggle that took the lives of many innocent youth before America collectively took notice. The film ends with the passing of the Voting Rights Act but then emphasizes in intertitles that "the struggle against prejudice continues" to suggest that the film's goal is to mobilize all Americans, as did news broadcasts of Emmett Till's murder during the Civil Rights Movement, to continue the ongoing struggle for civil rights. While each film documents that Emmett Till's murder is a historical fact and took place within the larger civil rights struggle, their differences demonstrate that the meaning of the event is not self-evident but is determined by its representations. Students can compare different historical approaches, not to determine the truth or the better version of history, but to learn how the meaning of a historical event comes to us via its various representations.

Visual and Multicultural Literacy: Social Studies

In the social studies classroom, lessons about representation can be extended to an exploration of the idea of race itself through the use of films about and by African Americans. Students can examine how race, and especially the meaning of race, is not a biological reality but is determined by representation. Classifications and categories, themselves systems of representation, bring race into being and not vice versa. In this respect, race exists only in representation. In addition, since representations evolve and change, new representations help change ideas about race. Social studies students can trace recurring images of African Americans that reproduce the idea of racial difference, beginning with D. W. Griffith's (1915) *The Birth of a Nation*. Or students can examine a number of films that challenge the concept of racial essentialism (the idea that there are inherent and defining traits shared by all members of one race) and thus open the issue to examination. Two striking examples are independent feature films by African Americans, Robert Townsend's (1987) *Hollywood Shuffle* and Julie Dash's (1991) *Daughters of the Dust*.

A comedy, *Hollywood Shuffle*'s humor is decidedly pointed: it delivers stinging criticism of Hollywood's insistence on constructing and perpetuating black racial stereotypes. The film wastes no time in introducing its subject. It opens with the sound of a 1970s style "street jive" character as a voice over to a black screen. Within a few moments, the character speaking the lines is shown standing in a bathroom, looking in a mirror, as his younger brother holds the script and sits near him. The character (who turns out to be the film's main character, Bobby Taylor) then asks, in a normal voice, "What's my next line?" and then waits for his brother to prompt him from the script. With a little prompting, he then continues by picking up a "street jive" affectation and delivers more lines. The story introduced in this scene is Bobby Taylor's struggle for a career in Hollywood as a black actor. The opening establishes what will be a consistent topic within the film: that traits associated with blackness are constructions by those in the business of representation, in this case the most influential of those businesses— Hollywood. The style of the film reinforces this point. A highly self-conscious film, *Hollywood Shuffle* makes several exaggerated references to Hollywood film genres (especially those involving African Americans) and frequently breaks up the plot for an exposition of the ludicrous lengths Hollywood goes to create ideas about blackness. These plot disruptions are then returned to the story as the main character's daydreams, or nightmares, but only after the pointed critique has been made.

The film's critique is not limited to Hollywood but extends itself into the black community's responses to the effects of racism. By assigning Bobby a day job at the black-owned "Winky Dinky Dogs," the film's plot creates a space where it can criticize African Americans who are content to get by. In stark contrast to Bobby's character, Mr. Jones (the owner) and his employees, Donald and Tiny, are content with making "Winky Dogs" their life ambition. Through the character of "Batty Boy," who comes to visit the hot dog stand, the film also criticizes black performers who sell out by taking the denigrating roles Hollywood constructs for them. In addition, however, the film questions whether the street-talking "home boy" personas that contemporary African-American youths adopt are any better suited at uplifting the race. In one of its plot disruptions, *Hollywood Shuffle* shows Bobby and a friend as homeboys who, in a send-up of the Siskel and Ebert movie-review television show, critique films that they sneak into. The highly comical scene exaggerates the homeboy persona as a means of showing that it is too insular, self-limiting, and ultimately accepting of the stereotypes that Hollywood imposes.

Rather than accepting Hollywood's limited ideas about what it means to be black or discovering any one idea of authentic blackness, the story of *Hollywood Shuffle* insists instead that African Americans need to negotiate identities that are true to their individual selves and responsible to their families and community. In the end, Bobby rejects his chance at Hollywood stardom, refusing to play the role of a black gangster, but he does not go to work in the post office either, as his grandmother suggests. Instead, the film ends with Bobby as the sincere main character acting in a public service announcement for the U.S. Postal Service. It is a compromise between the kind of Hollywood superstardom he dreamed about but rejected, because such stardom comes at the expense of self-respect, and work that is not as glamorous but has a positive impact on his younger brother and his community. The closing scene emphasizes that this compromise is the proper solution for Bobby: he can be true to himself without having to sell out. The film prescribes being true to oneself over an elusive essence of blackness that it repeatedly demonstrates is illusory.

A more challenging but equally important film, Julie Dash's (1991) *Daughters of the Dust* is a seminal film in terms of its challenge to Hollywood classical norms and to Hollywood's ideas about African-American identity. It is the story of an extended African-American family facing migration from their home on the Sea Islands off the coast of Georgia to the mainland at the turn of the twentieth century. Through the splitting up of the family, as some choose to migrate and others choose to stay, the film examines issues of assimilation versus resistance to Euro-American culture, as well as links between African cultural traditions and African-American identity. *Daughters of the Dust* examines these issues while challenging the conventions of the Hollywood style as they relate to the representation of African Americans.

Two of *Daughters of the Dust's* fundamental challenges to Hollywood are particularly significant. The first is its plot structure. One of the things students will quickly notice about *Daughters of the Dust*, when compared to most feature films, is that the plot seems extremely slow. The demonstrably unhurried plot results from the fact that, in many respects, the story is anti-narrative. The plot of *Daughters of the Dust* begins where the story ends: with the migration of the family to the mainland already a foregone conclusion, indeed, as the very basis of the story itself. As a result, the story does not so much build to the actual migration but instead explores the dynamics at stake in such an undertaking. In her discussion of the film, Toni Cade Bambara argues that this anti-developmental plot structure is a means by which the film uses the classic African style of narrative, with digressions and meanderings that are hallmarks of an African oral tradition, rather than an attempt to fit an African-American story into a Hollywood style tale of heroic action.[7]

In addition to its alternative structure, *Daughters of the Dust* consistently challenges ideas about objective realism —chiefly through the character of "the unborn child," the spirit of a child who is about to be born into the family — as part of its challenge to the notion that there is any objectively quantifiable African-American identity. The unborn child, unseen by the other characters in the film, manifests herself within the plot as both a voice-over narration on the audio track and as the image of a small girl wearing an indigo ribbon seen by viewers. As the plot makes clear, this manifestation is not to be assigned to fantasy as much as the presence of the fantastic — as when the child appears through the lens of the photographer Mr. Snead, who has been hired by the family to photograph as many members of this extended family as he can find. The appearance of the child is associated with the family's matriarch, the film's main character, Nana Pazant. Nana offers an alternative to a completely rationalized and objective social reality, insisting instead on the reality of connectedness to the family — living, dead, and yet to be born — and to other cultural traditions. Divisions among family members demonstrate their different identities. Nana's African spirituality does not reject Western empirical objectivism but refuses to be subjugated to it or supplanted by it, as has been the case with some of the Christianized family members who see Christianity and assimilation to Euro-American culture as their only means to salvation and the good life.

The film's consistent challenge to objective realism and its appropriation of a distinctly African-American plot structure function together as a means of redefining the representation of African Americans. Precisely what the film challenges is the definitive manner in which Hollywood films assign objective meaning to race via representation. In a meandering and digressive plot structure that explores the varying lives and differing views of one extended African-American family, *Daughters of the Dust* resists the finalizing of meaning that representation seeks to impose on the category of race. Moreover, by undermining objective realism, the film contests objectivity itself and its credibility to maintain the meaning of race. Reminiscent of the films of Oscar Micheaux, Dash's *Daughters of the Dust* also deals with recurring issues: with white men's rape of black women and with color discrimination within the African-American community. Dash's film resolves these issues, but only within the context of reconciliations between members of one extended family. Similar to films such as Robert Townsend's *Hollywood Shuffle* and *The Five Heartbeats* (1991), Charles Burnett's *To Sleep with Anger* (1990), and Spike Lee's *School Daze* (1988), *Daughters of the Dust* insists that African-American identity comes from the varying ideals and the spirit of a diverse African-American community.[8]

What these films emphasize is that race exists within the realm of ideology, not biology. Race is a social construct whose old meanings (blacks are lazy, uncivilized, and prone to violence, or blacks are happy to serve and to be subservient to whites) have been assigned by the dominant culture of white America for the purpose of marginalization and disenfranchisement. And race remains a social construct in films by African Americans who oppose and resist this process in order to posit new and various representations from the authority of their own experience. No film, and no approach to film, is free of ideology. The aim for students is not to be free from ideology but to be able to consciously discern how it operates through film. Such films as *Hollywood Shuffle*, with its alternatives to Hollywood genres and stereotypes, and *Daughters of the Dust*, with its alternatives to narrative causality and objective reality, offer students a means to understand both the conventional film frameworks that have attempted to determine the meaning of race and independent film alternatives. These independent films help dispel the notion of a racial essence by representing complex individuals in the ongoing process of determining their own African-American identity in the context of their own families, their cultural heritage, and their diverse experiences as African Americans.

2

Using Film and Video to Teach About Asians and Asian Americans Across the Curriculum[1]

by Gina Marchetti

Visualizing racial differences has always been an important part of American culture. Cigar store Indians, blackface minstrels, Mexican bandits, and Chinese coolies all carry with them a visual baggage that testifies to the American ideal of Anglo-Saxon "whiteness" as the norm. Often these images signify who can and cannot "melt" into the great American Melting Pot, i.e., who can be assimilated and who must be excluded for the supposed greater good of the American body politic. In efforts to forge a more genuinely multicultural America, secondary school and undergraduate college educators are at the forefront of efforts to equip young citizens with the tools to analyze and criticize these visual representations and to appreciate the enormous contribution Asian Americans, African Americans, Latinos/as, and American Indians have made to American visual culture. To this end, the critique of visual culture should be woven throughout the curriculum. Relegating a discussion of Asians in Hollywood or the use of Asian American film and video to the film studies classroom, for example, would be a grave error. Rather than arming students with tools to understand how film and other media have helped to shape our history, economy, arts, culture, and society generally, students may be encouraged to discuss film and video as ancillary to a "real" understanding of American culture through historical records, literature, or social science texts. Since students so often rely on images from the mass media to understand their place within American society, it becomes crucial for them to see that these images are an organic part of the curriculum across the disciplines.

This essay serves as a guide to incorporating Asian American film into the history, social sciences, literature, arts, and film studies curriculum at the high school and undergraduate college level. Although I will mention the possible use of commercial Hollywood films in conjunction with Asian American productions, the focus here remains on films and videos produced by Asian Americans to highlight images, issues, and perspectives ignored or marginalized by Hollywood. While students generally have access to commercial films at the multiplex, video store, and on television, they have less exposure to independent film and video. Although many Asians and Asian Americans have had successful careers in Hollywood, the mainstream American film and television industries generally reflect a point of view in which Asian Americans are marginalized, represented from a skewed perspective, or completely ignored. While it is important to understand how racist images inflect American ideology, simply looking for racist representations in Hollywood can actually reinforce the idea that Asians and Asian Americans can *only* be visualized as dragon ladies, houseboys, lotus blossoms, geishas, martial arts gurus, Fu Manchu, or Charlie Chan. In fact, a close examination of Hollywood history shows that these stereotypes have, since the silent era, been contested as well as reinforced within the commercial industry. In order to avoid the trap of spending time and effort looking for, identifying, and condemning these racist Asian stereotypes in American film, it is important to move beyond Hollywood into the realm of Asian American filmmaking.

A Brief Overview of Asian American Filmmaking

Since the silent era, Asians and Asian Americans have been both the objects and subjects of Hollywood film. Sessue Hayakawa, for example, in addition to defining Asian malevolence in Cecil B. DeMille's *The Cheat* (1915), played the romantic lead in many silent films and ran his own studio, Haworth Pictures, which made over twenty feature films. Keye Luke, Anna May Wong, Nancy Kwan, Nobu McCarthy, Philip Ahn, and Frances Nguyen, among others, were familiar faces in front of the camera during Hollywood's Golden Age, and James Wong Howe won two Academy Awards for cinematography during that period. However, these talented filmmakers worked very much within the confines of the studio system that severely limited how Asians and Asian Americans could be represented on the screen. Particularly during the classical era, Hollywood studios

The Cheat (Cecil B. DeMille, 1915). A diabolical Asian American tries to take advantage of a Euro-American couple (Photofest).

operated like factories, and films were highly formulaic. Thus, working against stock characterizations, familiar settings like Chinatown and accepted narrative devices like the "tong war" became particularly difficult.

A series of changes in immigration laws after World War II to 1965 helped to make Asians a more visible and viable part of the American landscape. As other minority groups agitated for greater social justice and the full rights of American citizenship, Asian Americans were among their ranks. Because of their influence on popular thought and public policy, the mass media were among the first institutions scrutinized by Asian Americans interested in social change. To combat exclusion and misrepresentation, Asian Americans took several paths. Some agitated for change within Hollywood; others looked to independent fiction feature films; still others turned to critical documentaries, personal filmmaking, and experimental forms to break with commercial media constraints.

Founded in 1967, Third World Newsreel had an early commitment to making alternative films about the Chinatown community as well as works that agitated against the war in Southeast Asia. In 1970, Robert Nakamura, Eddie Wong, and others started Visual Communications in Los Angeles to promote Asian Pacific American Media Arts. In 1976, Asian CineVision was established in New York, and the National Asian American Telecommunications Association (NAATA) was formed in 1980 in San Francisco. In 1983, Asian American Arts and Media of Washington, D.C. (AAAM), began to run a successful film festival and promote arts events. All of these organizations helped to produce, distribute, exhibit, and promote films made by and about Asian Americans. They helped to nurture a generation of film and video artists committed to presenting an alternative vision and voice for the Asian American community. Feature filmmakers championed by these organizations, such as Wayne Wang and Ang Lee, have gone on to receive accolades for their films. Asian American filmmakers, such as Chris Choy, Rene Tajima-Pena, Rea Tajiri, Loni Ding, and Arthur Dong, have helped to revivify the American documentary tradition with their works on the Asian American experience. Nam June Paik and Yoko Ono are just two of the many Asian American experimental film and video artists who have substantially contributed to the development of American avant-garde media.[2]

Currently, Asian Americans work in all aspects of film and video from feature narratives to animated shorts. While not all their work deals with Asian American issues, their films have made an important contribution to the development of an American visual culture that includes a broader range of images associated with Asians and Asian Americans.

A Note on Nomenclature

Over the years, different words have been used to talk about Asian Americans. Even today, there is considerable controversy surrounding the appropriate language to use when talking about Asian Americans. Although it is a generally accepted term, some people prefer not to be classified as Asian Americans, but prefer Chinese American, Korean American, and so on, to specify their ethnic heritage. There is also a blurry line between Asians and Asian Americans. Some insist on citizenship to be considered Asian American; others consider longtime sojourners, permanent residents, undocumented workers, and even international students as Asian Americans in certain circumstances. While many Asian American families have been in America for several generations, others are children of immigrants or immigrants themselves and have a different feeling about their ethnic and national identity due to their different experiences.

The United States government prefers Asian Pacific Islander Americans in order to include Samoans, Hawaiians, and other Pacific Islanders under the rubric. Some scholars have noted that the political interests of the colonized natives of the Pacific Islands are very different from the interests of immigrant Asian Americans and closer to the concerns of Native Americans and other indigenous peoples. Some prefer Asian Pacific American to include the peoples of the Pacific Rim. However, the range of inclusion varies widely among different Asian American groups. Some groups include the Middle East and Arab world (sometimes referred to as "West Asia"), and others exclude South and Central Asians. Increasingly, Asian Indians (more broadly South Asians to include Pakistanis, Nepalese, Bangladeshis, etc.) are included under the rubric of Asian American. Some organizations include Asian Canadians and people of Asian ancestry who settled in the Caribbean and Latin America, and others limit themselves to the United States.

As the Civil Rights Movement has gained ground, terms used to refer to Asian Americans have changed. While particularly abhorrent terms like "chink" and "Jap" have always been disparaging, other terms that may have seemed more neutral for an earlier generation are now considered offensive. For example, "Oriental" is inappropriate, and noted scholar Edward Said has written a book called *Orientalism* that traces the racist roots of the concept back through the history of European colonial expansion into North Africa and the Middle East. Other terms that may sound offensive, like "hapa," are actually widely accepted. "Hapa" is a Hawaiian word that refers to people of mixed Hawaiian and white heritage that is now used by many to refer to anyone who has Asian and some other ancestry. There has been a great deal of debate within the Asian American community about the use of the hyphen when referring to Asian Americans. The current consensus seems to be that the hyphen is offensive and should not be used even when the term "Asian American" is used as an adjective. Many argue that the hyphen makes Asian Americans into lesser, "hyphenated" citizens and should be avoided at all costs.

A Note on Visual Literacy and Media Analysis

Even when films and videos are used outside of the film or media studies classroom, the importance of availing students of the tools to analyze and critique mass-mediated images cannot be overemphasized. Films and videos should be used in conjunction with other modes of delivering course content (e.g., lectures, textbooks, primary source materials like speeches and legal documents, print media materials such as advertisements and newspapers, etc.) to paint as complete a picture as possible of the aspect of Asian American life explored in the classroom. Visual materials should be used to help the student come to grips with how film and video interrogate the history of American representation of Asians and Asian Americans and how Asian Americans have chosen to represent themselves on screen.

To develop these skills, students should be asked some key questions whether the film is screened in a history, social studies, literature, or film studies classroom. The following questions can be broached virtually with regard to any film, including commercial features, independent films, documentaries, and experimental works.

• Who produced this film/video? What do you think this piece is trying to communicate? Why was it produced (e.g., for commercial purposes, to provide information, etc.)? What do you know about the filmmaker? Does that affect how you view the film/video?

• Who is the intended audience for this film/video? How can you tell? Do you feel you are personally being addressed by this piece? Why or why not?

• Is the filmmaker part of the Asian American community being represented in the film/video? How can you tell? Are you part of the community being represented? If you are or if you are not, how does that affect your perception of the piece?

• Could this same information be presented to you in another form (e.g., print, theatre, radio, etc.)? Why do you think it is being presented to you as a motion picture? Do you get a different picture of the subject matter because of the medium used?

• What are some of the aesthetic techniques used to communicate the film's message? Where is the camera placed? How does it move? How close is the camera to its subject? Does the camera maintain a certain distance? What is the lighting like (e.g., bright, shadowy)? How are objects organized in the frame? Where does your eye move in the shot? Why? How are the shots in the film put together? Do you get a different idea of what you see on screen because of what comes before or after? What is the relationship between the image and the soundtrack? Is there a narrator? Music? Does the subject address the camera, or do experts talk about the subject of the film?

• How are Asians and/or Asian Americans represented in this film/video? How do they dress, act, move, and speak? How does their gender, class, race, ethnicity, accent, age, and body type affect your perception of them? How is their identity communicated visually through dress/costume, make-up, posture, and movement?

• Do you think this film/video communicates its message effectively? Why or why not? What have you learned from this piece? Is the film/video lacking in any way? Does it ignore an aspect of the issue you wish had been addressed? Do you agree or disagree with its point of view?

If an experimental film is being screened, teachers may want to ask students why they feel the filmmaker chose not to make a conventional narrative or documentary film. Does the way in which the film experiments with form enhance an understanding of the subject matter? Does a different vision of this subject emerge because of the film's departure from the usual means of communicating visually? Although some students may resist experimental films, these are sometimes the best films to use in the classroom. They are often short and self-contained, so instructors do not need to take excerpts out of context. Experimental shorts also tend to make their point quickly and efficiently. Moreover, because they can be poetic, ironic, or ambiguous, they provide fuel for discussion. Teachers should feel free to take a chance and include a few more challenging experimental films along with commercial features and documentaries.

Using Film to Look at Asians in American History

Motion pictures have documented virtually every period in the complex history of Americans in Asia, Asians in America, and the emergence of Asian America. Films and videos can be found that deal with everything from American involvement in the Opium Wars to the wars in Afghanistan and Iraq. However, the Spanish-American War and the Japanese American Internment stand out as two events that often do not get the attention they deserve in the history classroom and that have been explored in some innovative ways by Asian American filmmakers.

American cinema begins at the same time the United States acquired its first (and only) major colony in the Pacific, the Philippines, during the Spanish-American War in the late 1890s. The war to suppress Philippine independence followed at the turn of the century, and the Biograph motion picture company sent C. Fred Ackerman to film the colony. In 1904, the

Louisiana Purchase Exhibition, a.k.a. the St. Louis World's Fair, featured an entire "village" devoted to the Philippines that contained people representative of various ethnic groups from across the archipelago, including the Moros, Bagobos, Negritos, and Igorots. Asian American filmmaker Marlon Fuentes used some of the surviving footage of the fair to create *Bontoc Eulogy* (1995), a fictional account of an Igorot warrior on display in St. Louis, told from the perspective of a grandson who searches for his relative's remains in the United States. Biograph's and Fuentes' mingling of fact and fiction about the Philippines frame the history of America's cinematic involvement with Asia over the course of the century, and Fuentes' film provides an accessible and thoughtful entry into a discussion of American expansionism and ideas of Manifest Destiny. As *Bontoc Eulogy* confirms, Asian Americans have mined the history of American film to find something lost, repressed, and/or liminal, like the exhibition of Filipinos at the 1904 World's Fair. For Fuentes, this icon of American innocence — immortalized by Judy Garland in Vincente Minnelli's *Meet Me in St. Louis* (1944) — becomes the search for a missing cinematic record of an Asian American history of exploitation, exhibition, and exclusion.

Increasingly, Asian American filmmakers have engaged in subverting Hollywood's representation of Asians, and they have contested commercial cinema's portrayal of what Edward Said terms "the Orient as a sort of surrogate and even underground self."[3] Over time, Hollywood turned Asia on American screens into an emblem of Euro-American superiority; a validation of racial, gender, class, and ethnic hierarchies; and a rationalization for foreign and domestic policies that affected the United States' relationship to Asian nations as well as Asian Americans. Like many other Asian American films, Fuentes' *Bontoc Eulogy* transforms Hollywood truisms into a narrative about the search for ethnic roots that most students find compelling.

For decades, Hollywood avoided any direct depiction of the Japanese American internment camps. Although anti–Asian violence after Pearl Harbor was mentioned in films like John Sturges' *Bad Day at Black Rock* (1955), starring Spencer Tracy, Hollywood did not fully explore the issue until after the 1988 Congressional apology and restitution put to rest any lingering doubts that the internment was unnecessary, racist, and unconstitutional. In Alan Parker's lumbering love story, *Come See the Paradise* (1990), and Scott Hicks' *Snow Falling on Cedars* (1999), the focus remains on the white protagonist in love with the Japanese American female victim of the excesses of the American government. John Korty's television movie, *Farewell To Manzanar* (1976), based on the book by Jean Wakatsuki Houston, is a notable exception in its depiction of the camps as a racist indignity suffered by over 100,000 Japanese Americans.

Asian American filmmakers have also attempted to uncover the neglected history of the interment in documentaries like Satsuki Ina and Stephen Holsapple's *Children of the Camps* (1999), Loni Ding's *The Color of Honor* (1988), Lise Yasui's *Family Gathering* (1988), Robert Nakamura's *Manzanar* (1971) and *Wataridori: Birds of Passage* (1976), Janice Tanaka's *Memories from the Department of Amnesia* (1991) and *Who's Going to Pay for These Donuts Anyway?* (1992), Emiko Omori's *Rabbit in the Moon* (1999), and Rea Tajiri's *History and Memory* (1991), as well as in fictional accounts such as Robert Nakamura's *Conversations: Before the War/After the War* (1986) and Rea Tajiri's *Strawberry Fields* (1998). All of these films tell a story very different from Hollywood fantasies of Japanese American spies or beautiful victims of false imprisonment. Rather, these Japanese American films show resistance to government oppression, the multi-generational impact of the internment that still affects Japanese Americans today, and the struggles for civil rights prompted by this false imprisonment. Many of the films trace the filmmaker's personal journey to uncover an episode of the family's history shrouded in secrecy and shame in order to come to terms with the unjust imprisonment of parents and grandparents.

By showing three or four of the shorter films with excerpts from the Hollywood films and the longer documentaries, a picture emerges of how varied the experiences of internees were and of the complex ways in which the internment experience continues to affect the children and grandchildren of the interned. *Family Gathering, History and Memory,* and *Who's Going to Pay for These Donuts Anyway?* stand out as gripping portraits of families in pain because of the internment. It may be useful to compare the approach of each filmmaker, look for differences and similarities in their experiences, and talk about how each filmmaker views history and the responsibilities of the historian who also has a personal involvement with the history being depicted. Not only does this exercise give students insight into the internment beyond the history textbooks, it also encourages them to engage with the ethics of being an historian and the challenges faced by those victimized by the internment who feel compelled to expand the "official" history of the event.

Using film to look at the internment as a way of understanding legal history provides another approach. Eric Paul Fournier's *Of Civil Wrongs and Rights: The Fred Korematsu Story* (1999) and the Constitution Project's *A Personal Matter: Gordon Hirabayashi vs. the United States* (1992) examine legal challenges to Executive Order 9066. Steven Okazaki's *Unfinished Business* (1986) documents the struggles of Fred Korematsu, Gordon Hirabayashi, and Minoru Yasui as ongoing court battles. Rea Tajiri and Pat Saunders' *Yuri Kochiyama: Passion for Justice* (1993) presents the absorbing life history of a woman who devoted herself to social justice after experiencing the internment. All of these films introduce students to Asian Americans who have made an impact on the history of civil rights law in American.

Using Film to Teach About Asian Americans in the Social Studies Classroom

The social studies curriculum can be enriched in many ways by the inclusion of Asian American films. Labor issues can be approached through films such as Duane Kubo and Robert A. Nakamura's classic *Hito Hata: Raise the Banner* (1980), one of the first independently produced Asian American feature films, which deals with a Japanese American railway worker as its protagonist. *Dollar a Day, Ten Cents a Dance* (1984) looks at early Filipino laborers, and Arthur Dong's *Sewing Woman* (1982) creates a composite portrait of Chinese garment workers. Kayo Hatta's *Picture Bride* (1995), set on a sugar cane plantation in 1918, presents a convincing picture of what life may have been like for the immigrant laborers in Hawaii at that time.

Violence and crime can be explored by studying the experience of Asian Americans as well. Taggart Siegel's *Blue Collar and Buddha* (1988), for example, looks at the case of a Laotian Buddhist community terrorized in Rockford, Illinois. Trac Minh Vu's *Letters to Thien* (1997) examines the brutal murder of Thien Minh Ly in California. Christine Choy and Spiro Lampros' *The Shot Heard 'Round the World* (1997) documents the murder of Yoshi Hattori in Baton Rouge, Louisiana. In addition, Christine Choy and Rene Tajima-Pena's *Who Killed Vincent Chin?* (1988) looks at the murder of a young Chinese American man in Detroit. Although many of these cases did not provide the justice sought by members of the Asian American community, carefully looking at all these violent crimes helps students to better understand the meaning of "hate crimes" and the necessity for legislation that specifically addresses racist violence.

Immigration can be approached from a number of perspectives. Students may be particularly empathetic to the struggles of other young people. The difficulties young — and often poor — Indochinese refugees have faced in America have been explored in a number of documentaries, including Nick Rothenberg and Ahrin Mishan's *Bui Doi: Life Like Dust* (1994), Nith Lacroix and Sang Thepkaysone's *Letter Back Home* (1994), Spencer Nakasako and Sokly Ny's *a.k.a. Don Bonus* (1995), and Spencer

Nakasako, Kane Ian "Kelly" Saeteurn, and Nai "Tony" Saelio's *Kelly Loves Tony* (1998). *A.K.A. Don Bonus*, a collaboration between veteran documentarist Nakasako and Sokly Ny (a.k.a. Don Bonus), a teenage Cambodian American refugee living in San Francisco public housing and struggling to graduate from high school, presents a particularly intimate, first-person account filmed entirely by Ny himself. This video can be used effectively in conjunction with other films such as Frederick Wiseman's *High School* (1969), Joel DeMott and Jeff Kreines' *Seventeen* (1983), or Steve James' *Hoop Dreams* (1994) to take a critical look at the institution of secondary education in America.

Another fecund topic for discussion in the social studies classroom involves the relationship of various minority groups to each other. A somewhat unconventional approach takes up the interrelationship of African American culture and the Hong Kong/Hollywood martial arts film. Robert Clouse's *Enter the Dragon* (with Bruce Lee, 1973), Stanley Tong's *Rumble in the Bronx* (with Jackie Chan, 1995), Brett Ratner's *Rush Hour* or *Rush Hour II* (with Jackie Chan and Chris Tucker, 1998, 2001), or Andrzej Bartkowiak's *Romeo Must Die* (with Jet Li, 2000) may be worth screening. Rob Cohen's *Dragon: The Bruce Lee Story* (1993) also deals with race relations within the world of American martial arts as well as the Hollywood film industry. A subplot involving one of Lee's African-American students, Jerome Sprout (Sterling Macer, Jr.), provides a different view of African-American and Asian American relations than the other action films listed above. All of these films bring up many of the similar struggles Asian Americans and African Americans have faced, including violence, ghettoization, racial discrimination, poverty, and marginalization within a genre that many students find entertaining. Tony Bancroft and Barry Cook's animated feature *Mulan* (1998) can also provide fertile ground for the discussion of interracial relations within the martial arts genre. The casting of African-American comedian Eddie Murphy as Mushu the Dragon points to a formulaic inclusion of an African-American voice within a martial arts epic, helping to flesh out the multicultural appeal of the film in much the same way *Rush Hour* does with its casting choices.

Given the media coverage of the assault on Korean businesses in Los Angeles' African-American communities at the time of the Rodney King incident, Korean American filmmakers took it upon themselves to give a different picture of Black-Asian relations in the city. Dai Sil Kim-Gibson and Christine Choy's documentary *Sa-I-Gu* (1993), which literally means in Korean April 29, presents the perspective of Korean women shop owners whose voices had not been adequately heard in the mainstream media. In a very different vein, Chris Chan Lee explores the coming of age of a

Korean shopkeeper's son in *Yellow* (1998), a film which does not shy away from the close, but often strained relationships between the Korean and African-American communities. Michael Cho's *Another America* (1996) looks at Korean American and African-American relations in Detroit through the investigation of the circumstances around the murder of one of the filmmaker's relatives.

Certainly, all of these films provide many fruitful avenues for the discussion of race relations in America. One way to approach these issues involves encouraging a discussion of the meaning of the American Dream in the Korean American and African-American communities depicted in these films. Students may be asked to use these films to compare the way in which African Americans and Korean Americans define the American Dream and how that definition may be inflected by gender, class, or immigration status. Further, students may be asked to compare this definition to their own idea of the American Dream or Hollywood's portrayal of it. Students can then begin to explore the flexibility of what may have been a taken-for-granted notion, and how race and ethnicity may influence our most intimate dreams, hopes, and aspirations.

Recent Events

Since September 11, 2001, there has been some urgency in developing course materials on the Middle East, Central Asia, Islam, Arab Americans, American foreign policy in Asia, and related issues of racial profiling and ethnic prejudice. Some films about September 11, such as New York Independent Media Center and Big Noise Films' *9.11: New World Disorder/Another World Is Possible* (2001) and Nikki Byrd and Jennifer Jajeh's *In My Own Skin: The Complexity of Living as an Arab in America* (2001), can promote considerable debate and productive discussion. In addition, many fine films made before September 11 are available. Some that deal specifically with the experience of being Muslim in America include Joan Mandell's *Tales from Arab Detroit* (1995), Jennifer Bing-Canar and Mary Zerkel's *Benaat Chicago (Daughters of Chicago): Growing up Arab and Female in Chicago* (1996), Persheng Sadegh-Vaziri's *A Place Called Home* (1998), and Aysha Ghazoul's *My American Grandmother* (1999). Mehrnaz Saeed-Vafa's *A Tajik Woman* (1994) deals with being an Afghanistan woman in exile in America. Although it does not deal with Muslim characters, Erika Surat Anderson's *Turbans* (2000) deals with Sikh children facing prejudice in early twentieth-century America, and it provides an excellent platform for discussion for younger students. Given the violence that many Sikhs have suffered because of the association of the turban with the Taliban, this film can be used effectively to teach about the relationship between appearance and prejudice.

Rather than isolating the discussion of Arab Americans from other racial and ethnic groups in America, it may also be useful to pair these films with films about the internment mentioned above. This is an excellent way to open students' eyes to the concept of racial profiling from an historical perspective that may change the dynamic of the discussion in the classroom.

Art, Music, and the Asian American Experience on Film

It may not be obvious to include Asian American films and videos in classes devoted to art and music, but, in point of fact, a number of films pay tribute to Asian Americans' contributions to architecture, graphic design, the fine arts, and music. Freida Lee Mock's *Maya Lin: A Strong Clear Vision* (1994), about the competition to choose the design for the national memorial to U.S. soldiers killed in Vietnam, has received numerous awards and is perhaps the best-known documentary devoted to an Asian American artist. A number of documentaries dedicated to Asian Americans' involvement in jazz and rap may also be worth considering, including the classic *Cruisin' J-Town* (Duane Kubo, 1976), Renee Cho's *Jazz Is My Native Language: A Portrait of Toshiko Akiyoshi* (1983), and Nandini Sikand's *The Bhangra Wrap* (1994).

Another way to expose students to Asian American arts is through animation. Not only have Asian Americans made outstanding contributions to commercial animation, they are also at the forefront of experimental animation. Ann Marie Fleming's animated series *The Continuing Adventures of Stick Girl* and Lela Lee's *Angry Little Asian Girl* Web site[4] are worth considering. Troi Pang's *Mochi Monster* (1985) and Kelly Takemura's *Little One Inch* (1985) are perfect for younger students.

Teaching Drama, Speech, and Theatre with Asian American Film[5]

Casting has been a vexing question in the Asian American community for decades. While "black face" has been taboo in mainstream entertainment for decades, white performers continue to perform in "yellow face" or "Asian drag" on a regular basis. The controversy surrounding the casting of the Broadway production of *Miss Saigon* received considerable reportage, for example, well before its premiere in 1991. Talking about casting, acting, and performance can lead to a discussion of the idea of color-blind casting and when it may or may not be appropriate.

Screening Mina Shum's feature film *Double Happiness* (1994) provides an excellent starting point for a discussion of how Asian American actors and actresses face the constraints of racism in the theater and entertainment industries. Jade Li (played by Sandra Oh) aspires to play Joan of Arc and Blanche DuBois but ends up settling for parts in which she is typecast as the Chinese menial. Roughly autobiographical, the film can be shown with Mina Shum's companion documentary *Me, Mom, and Mona* (1993) that gives the filmmaker's own story of juggling the expectations of her traditional Chinese father with her own aspirations to work in the film industry and the roles her sister and mother played in supporting her ambitions. Because it deals with the coming of age of a young girl and her relationships with family and friends as well as her professional objectives, this film may strike a responsive cord for many students facing similar issues. *Double Happiness* carefully places issues surrounding acting and entertainment within the context of how we all "perform" a variety of roles in our daily lives. Jade, for example, performs her race, ethnic, class, gender, and sexual orientation through a range of "roles," including daughter, sister, girlfriend, employee, and Asian American woman. *Double Happiness*, on another level, invites a discussion of cross-ethnic casting as well. Sandra Oh, a Korean Canadian, plays Jade, a Chinese Canadian woman. For some students, this may immediately bring to the fore questions concerning when it is and is not appropriate to cast Asian Americans of various ethnicities in roles that may be foreign to them linguistically or culturally. Although debates surrounding race, ethnicity, authenticity and exploitation seldom find easy resolutions, these points may lead to some fruitful class discussion of how Asian Americans negotiate racial differences in a predominantly Euro-American society in different ways.

Using Asian American Film to Teach American Literature

Several Asian American novels have been turned into fine motion pictures, and looking at adaptations is a logical way to bring the Asian American experience into a literature program. Amy Tan's *The Joy Luck*

Club (1989) is one of the more often taught Asian American novels. The Internet is brimming with innovative ways to approach the book, including a Web Quest by Kimberly Picozzi and a vocabulary list.[6] Screening Wayne Wang's *The Joy Luck Club* (1993) provides an opportunity for students to expand their understanding of the book and look at the way one noted Asian American film director chose to visualize its narrative. One pedagogical approach in analyzing adaptations involves an examination of the way aesthetic techniques and devices translate from one medium to the other. Point of view provides a good starting point, and this discussion can be extended to include how film takes up certain literary devices such as metaphor, irony, characterization, dialogue, recurring motifs, ambiguity, conflict, parallel structure, plot, or suspense in ways different from the literary source in order to highlight cinema's distinctly visual forms of storytelling. It may also be instructive to examine the transformation of a book into a film by looking at how the paths of Amy Tan and Wayne Wang crossed, how the film was financed, and what compromises had to be made to bring the book to the screen.[7] One of the more obvious points for discussion involves the switch from a female author to a male director and how gender may affect the way in which relationships in the same story are presented differently in each medium. To expand on this topic, it might be useful to contrast Wang's interpretation of Tan's novel with his vision of a novel by a male author, *Eat a Bowl of Tea* (1989), based on the novel of the same name by Louis Chu.

Asian American Film in the Film Studies Classroom

Although the film studies classroom may be the obvious location to find Asian American film and video, it might actually be just the place where Asian American cinema may be most difficult to find. Many approaches can be taken to redressing this gap in film education. An instructor can highlight the contributions Asians and Asian Americans have made throughout film history from Sessue Hayakawa to Jackie Chan, focus on the evolution of the representation of Asians and Asian Americans in American film, or provide a history of Asian American filmmaking.

Wayne Wang's *Chan Is Missing* (1982) can provide an entry into a discussion of several of these neglected aspects of American film history. The film establishes an aesthetic dialogue between mainstream Hollywood and the American independent feature that places Asian Americans squarely within the conversation as a major voice of innovation and critique.

Conjuring up visions of Hollywood's Charlie Chan, the missing Chan Hung of the film's title offers no easy platitudes to solve the mystery of Asian American identity. Indeed, as an anti–Charlie Chan mystery, the titular Chan never does show up, and the closure Hollywood offers remains elusive. Indebted to the French New Wave as well as the burgeoning Asian American documentary movement, *Chan Is Missing* offers a look at San Francisco's Chinatown that defies convention and provides plenty of material for discussion of film technique as well as social issues. Wang uses a moving hand-held camera, jump cuts, available light and sound, and variably exposed black and white film stock to present his raw vision of life in the social clubs, cafes, homes, schools, and restaurant kitchens that make up contemporary Asian America.

For any discussion of editing and as a companion piece that directly alludes to *Chan Is Missing*, Rene Tajima-Pena's *My America ... Or, Honk If You Love Buddha* (1996) provides opportunities for students to look at the artistry involved in the documentary form. A tour de force of contemporary documentary techniques, this "road movie" includes interviews, archival material, personal testimony by the filmmaker, and humor edited expertly to highlight the diverse ways in which Asian Americans have become part of the American landscape. *Yellow Tale Blues: A Tale Of Two Families* (1990), by Rene Tajima-Pena and Christine Choy, who did the principal cinematography for *Honk*, is worth screening as well since it takes up many of the same themes of personal filmmaking, community activism, and media culture explored in *Honk*.

Kip Fulbeck's *Some Questions for 28 Kisses* (1994) provides a provocative look at the representation of interracial romance in popular media and the impact it has on Asian American self-perceptions. An educator himself, Fulbeck gives his video a Socratic quality, and it can be illuminating for students to try to answer Fulbeck's questions, pose their own questions back to Fulbeck, and talk about how they may answer their own questions about a film Fulbeck may not have covered. This video gives a "hip" voice to questions of ethnic representation and brings up many questions about the relationship between film images and sexuality that teenagers may find particularly compelling.

A Note on Appropriate Screening Materials

Although I have only mentioned films and videos I feel would be appropriate for use in the high school and undergraduate college classroom, I urge teachers to prescreen any motion pictures they plan to use in the classroom. Some of the films and videos are graphic, may deal with controversial topics (e.g., violence, sexuality), and contain explicit language that may not be within every teacher's level of comfort for his or her own classroom. Teachers should use the information provided here as guides only and should preview chosen films for themselves to find out if they are appropriate for the issues they expect to discuss as well as the maturity level of their students.

A Note on Using Excerpts

Using excerpts from a film can be an excellent way to quickly illustrate a point or highlight some aspect of the larger work. However, excerpts must be used with caution. When taken out of context, an excerpt can give a skewed view of what the overall film may be trying to communicate. A single excerpt may not be representative of the work, and relying on excerpts too frequently can give students the impression that looking at a work in its entirety is not important. This advice should be taken to heart particularly when the work being viewed is not familiar to the students. For example, it may be more appropriate to use an excerpt from *Rush Hour II*, since many students may have seen the film or know about it from reading reviews or talking to friends, than to use an excerpt from *The Cheat*, a film that students are not likely to have seen.

Motion pictures communicate information in a way that cannot be replicated by any other medium. When students think about ethnic difference, they often think about those differences in visual terms or fantasize through narratives that shore up traditional ways of viewing gender, race, and ethnicity. Therefore, educators turn their backs on film culture at their own peril. Not only do students need to develop the necessary tools to critique the images they encounter in commercial media, they also need to be exposed to alternative voices and visions. To this end, Asian American film and video should find its way into every facet of the high school and undergraduate college curriculum. Creative thinking, some background research, a little digging, and a little push in the right direction should place this goal within the reach of every teacher.

3

American Indians and Film in the Classroom

by Jacqueline Kilpatrick

In teaching films depicting American Indians in high school and undergraduate college classes, a major portion of the task is un-teaching what audiences around the world have been learning from Hollywood for more than a hundred years. For most of that time, filmmakers' primary goal was not depicting ethnic minorities in a realistic manner. As a result, both educators and film industry professionals must now put forth a concerted effort to combat the stereotypes of African-Americans, Asian Americans, Latinos/as, and American Indians perpetuated — both intentionally and unintentionally — by Hollywood. However, while the stereotypes of other ethnicities are often as pejorative as those of American Indians, the challenges presented by the image of the "Indian"[1] in mainstream films is in some ways substantially different because the idea of the Indian has, from the beginning, been such an important element in the American nationalist mythology, the very idea of what America is. Teachers can address this challenge by engaging their students in research and critical analysis projects that examine film representations of American Indians in order to enrich, and perhaps even revise, their study of American history, literature, journalism, social studies, and film studies.

Stereotypes and History

Stereotypes of American Indians go back much farther than 1896, when the first films were shown. Their genesis can be traced to the fifteenth and sixteenth centuries, to first contact, when the first explorers from Europe returned with stories of wild savages that fit preconceived notions

58

the Europeans had of what a savage would be. This was the beginning of the *invented* Indian, a fictitious entity that continued to develop through the captivity narratives and other tales of the seventeenth and eighteenth centuries. History students may want to examine this fictional creation in such early reports as Christopher Columbus' fifteenth-century journals of his voyages to America or in John Smith's sixteenth-century *Generall Historie* of his captivity by Powhatan (and of Pocahontas supposedly saving his life). Literature teachers can address the images presented later in captivity narratives such as Mary Rowlandson's (1682) "Narrative of the Captivity and Restauration." Students can explore how such early impressions of American Indians became rooted in America's justification of colonialism and Manifest Destiny and later in hundreds of Western films about early settlers, pioneers, and cowboys and Indians.

By the time James Fenimore Cooper wrote *The Leatherstocking Tales* in the first decades of the nineteenth century, ideas about the Bloodthirsty Savage (a purely violent, soulless, and cultureless impediment to civilization) and the Noble Savage (the untainted embodiment of the land who usually acted as the trusty sidekick or other helper of the white hero) had become firmly engrained in American nationalist mythology. However, Cooper's influential novels did much to establish these stereotypical formulas of what makes an "Indian" in the American psyche. That the expectations Cooper created for audiences regarding American Indians have had staying power is obvious by the fact that his most famous novel, *The Last of the Mohicans* (1826), has been made into a Hollywood film at least seven times, the latest in 1992, a time of supposedly new sensitivity and sensibilities. Among the Huron, Iroquois, and Mohican Indians in Cooper's novel, the Mohicans are absolutely noble, and he evoked a nostalgic longing for the past by presenting them as the last of a vanishing people. By reading the novel and viewing several versions of *The Last of the Mohicans*, literature and film studies students can examine how the written word becomes the visual image and can trace changes in characterizations and film techniques over the years. And history and social studies students can document changes in how the same period of early American history has been imagined differently and determine exactly how stereotypes of Indians have or have not changed according to the times the films were made.

Early American novels, including Cooper's, can initiate student explorations of the way specific traits of American Indian caricatures are repeated or revised and the effect such representations can have. For instance, Cooper's Indians— even the Bloodthirsty Savages Cooper made of the Huron — talk a great deal, a characteristic *not* generally adopted by Hollywood. Other nineteenth-century novelists, such as Robert Montgomery

Bird, made their Indians inarticulate except for savage grunts and pro-
noun-challenged pidgin–English, a characteristic wholeheartedly embraced
by the majority of Hollywood's filmmakers through at least the first eighty
years of film history. Language is a bearer of culture, but the majority of
Hollywood Indians were props, not representatives of any culture, real or
imagined. Because it is easier to depict a character as one-dimensional if
he or she keeps his or her mouth shut, when these "props" talked at all,
their language consisted of "Tonto-talk," a strong suggestion of intellectual inferiority. Most Hollywood Indians have been these one-dimensional,
uncomplicated caricatures.

Cooper, Bird, and other authors creating the American literary tradition also figured significantly in building an American mythology by
identifying its original inhabitants with the natural landscape. While their
work often depicts historical events or characters, the point of view and
the assumptions made in the fiction result in an elaborate fabrication of
myth, a meta-reality that was more readily believed than a reality that was
less flattering to the reading public of their time. The simplified history
presented by Cooper, Bird, the authors of scores of captivity narratives,
and the journalists who took their cues from them rendered the complex
societies of northeastern Indians into mere background for their colonial
stories.

These early colonial stories were filled with characters much like
Cooper's Natty Bumpo, the prototypical Indianized white intermediary
and hero. Students interested in this quintessentially American hero can
investigate how his character later became a buttress of the film industry,
with stars like Gary Cooper, John Wayne, and even Paul Newman playing savvy woodsmen or plainsmen who were raised by Indians. They were,
in fact, generally better at being Indians than the Indians, just as Natty
Bumpo always managed to be a better Indian than either Chingachgook
or Uncus, leading his Indian companions through fields and forests and
proving himself the superior hunter and warrior. History, literature, and
film studies students can compare current historical accounts of the French
and Indian Wars with Cooper's depiction in *The Last of the Mohicans* and
its film adaptations to explore how historians, novelists, and filmmakers
each reflect the thinking of their own times and use the various techniques
of their media. Journalism students can compare early newspaper accounts
of Indian encounters with film portrayals of Euro-American heroes living
among Indians, to trace the repeated stereotype of the Indianized hero
initiated in early American traditions.

In 1860, Irwin P. Beadle and Company published the first in a long
line of dime novels, which were short, exciting stories that took Cooper's

Last of the Mohicans (Michael Mann, 1992). Foregrounding: the Euro-American hero is literally and metaphorically foregrounded to show his superiority.

ideas about woodland and plains Indians—including the spice of danger generated by the bloodthirsty stereotypes and the romance of a shrinking frontier—and blended it all together to perpetuate stereotypes that could work as a sort of shorthand for concepts of nostalgic nobility or terrifying danger. One of the heroes depicted in the dime novels was Buffalo Bill Cody, a prolific self-promoter who had no qualms about exaggerating the story, whatever story that might be. His popularity as a dime novel hero contributed to his remarkably successful Wild West Show and, later, his film company. His Wild West Show, modeled on the fiction of the dime novels, provided the simplified, standardized, and largely erroneous image of an American Indian for American audiences of his time as well as for later film audiences. The Wild West Show lost some of its sparkle before it faded away in the early 1900s, replaced by the moving picture, a large percentage of which were Westerns. Literature, social studies, and film studies students can profitably trace how the dime novel—many of which are still in print—and the Wild West Show lived on in the movies, and how the whooping Bloodthirsty Savage and the unbearably noble Red Man became staples of the new film industry.

The Moving Picture Show: Persuasive Images

In 1894, when Americans—including many immigrants new to the country—poured into Koster and Bial's Music Hall in New York City to see the first moving pictures, they were unprepared to view the images critically. The moving pictures were persuasive and were seen on the same screen as the newsreels that told them of real world events. Though they understood the stories were fiction, they trusted the images. They believed their eyes. Audiences understood that the particular Indian, whether noble or savage, was probably a screenwriter's invention, but they believed in the *idea* of Indianness represented on the screen. And most of the early audiences accepted unquestioningly films presented as documentaries depicting the lives of American Indians.

It seems that the majority of those first filmmakers did not fully understand how powerful a tool — and weapon — they were manipulating. They were interested in entertaining the masses, giving them what they wanted to see, generating excitement, reaffirming ideas already held, and making money. Many considered themselves artists, but most did not initially think of the films they produced as significant agencies of social change or consciousness, nor did they see themselves as producers of anything but art and entertainment. D.W. Griffith, director of such films as *Iola's Promise, or How the Little Indian Maid Paid Her Debt of Gratitude* (1912) and *The Battle of Elderbrush Gulch* (1914), was one of the first filmmakers to understand the powerful influence of the new art form, though even he could not have fully foreseen the lasting impact his films would have. In an article he wrote for *The Independent* in 1916, he referred to his films as "influential" and noted that "last year in twelve months one of many copies of a single film in Illinois and the South played to more people and to more money than all the traveling companies that put out from New York play to in fourteen months."[2] The film images reached an unprecedented number of Americans of all classes, ethnicities, and levels of literacy, something stage plays and written words, even the dime novels, could not do. The lack of critical experience of the huge audience and the persuasive nature of film made the nascent film industry immensely important in forming and perpetuating ideas about America, which included the Indian as part of America's past.

The motion picture is indeed a powerful persuader. As Christian Metz points out in *Film Language: A Semiotics of the Cinema*, film creates an impression of reality much more forcefully than theater, where the audience is generally aware of its own participation, or still photography, where the mind sees the place as "here" but the time as "past." Film gives the audience a place that is here and a time that is present, and, most importantly, it gives motion to the image. According to Metz, "the strict [psychological] distinction between object and copy dissolves on the threshold of motion. Because movement is never material but *always* visual, to reproduce movement is to duplicate reality."[3] The result is that generations worldwide have seen the Hollywood Indian and believed what they saw. As Ana Lopez has noted, "Hollywood does not *represent* ethnics and minorities: it *creates* them and provides its audience with an experience of them."[4] Because most films that include American Indians are Westerns stuck in the time-freeze of the nineteenth century, the images audiences have had of American Indians, even were they in any way realistic,[5] would still be a hundred years out of date. Contemporary American Indian men and women have only recently begun to be seen in Hollywood films.

By the mid-twentieth century, movies had become part of the fabric of American life, and teachers often showed films, without film analysis, in their classrooms and took classes on field trips to theaters. The images Hollywood provided were so accepted that movies were frequently shown to teach children about American history and social studies in public schools. That many of the films were based on "Hollywood History" and built around the stereotypes of American Indians doesn't seem to have been cause for concern among white educators. For instance, after its popularity in theatres garnered attention, King Vidor's (1940) film *Northwest Passage* was chosen by the Department of Secondary Teachers of the National Education Association for study because "Rogers [of Rogers' Rangers] comes to personify man's refusal to bow to physical forces, and the success of this hardy band of early pioneers symbolizes our own struggle against bitter enemies in the modern world."[6] The Indians in *Northwest Passage*, however, are presented as a bloodthirsty bunch of heathen devils who get what they deserve for attacking innocent settlers and are little more than ciphers for the looming "bitter enemies" of America at the time the film was made — Nazi Germany and the Japanese. The general attitudes and ideas about American Indians as enemies in the way of progress are transparent. *Northwest Passage* is worthy of study, especially for generating discussions with students about film as propaganda virtually invisible as such to the target audience.

Students interested in how stereotypes are recycled to fit new situations can juxtapose scenes from *Northwest Passage* with popular written accounts from the same era of American Indian involvement in World War II. For instance, a *Reader's Digest* article of 1943 attempts to reconcile widely accepted stereotypes with contemporary reality, stating

> The red soldier is tough. Usually he has lived outdoors all his life, and
> lived by his senses; he is a natural Ranger. He takes to Commando fight-
> ing with gusto.... At ambushing, scouting, signaling, sniping, [Indians
> are] peerless. Some can smell a snake yards away and hear the faintest
> movement; all endure thirst and lack of food better than the average white
> man.[7]

This is a good description of a Hollywood Indian under the guise of accurate reporting. It must have been very strange for young American Indian
students, many of whom had relatives fighting in the war, to watch films
such as *Northwest Passage*, in which Indians are evil, and then read actual
accounts of American Indian soldiers, in whom the negatives of the Bloodthirsty Savage had temporarily become positives since they were employed
in defense of the USA.[8] The American Indian super-soldier in the news
often became this combination of Bloodthirsty and Noble Savage. Both
images were possible largely because mainstream audiences believed that
virtually all *real* Indians had vanished and that American Indian soldiers
were an anomaly, a remnant of a race still in the process of vanishing. In
1933, *Scientific American* published an article entitled "The Disappearance
of the Red Man's Culture," sadly reporting "the Indian is now a creature
of the past, who can be studied mostly in books and museums."[9] Hollywood writers and filmmakers evidently believed this notion (although
there were American Indians working in the film industry at the time) or
at least found it profitable.

Metaphors

Students interested in how and why stereotypes of Indians have
remained popular can examine how such portrayals continued to generate dramatic excitement and even came to represent contemporary enemies. The bloodthirsty caricature remained a Western movie staple,
immediately conjuring up ideas of glory (in taming the frontier/Indian)
and menace. All it took was the low beat of a tom-tom on the film's soundtrack to signal danger. This stereotype has been particularly useful to writers and directors of Western movies for obvious reasons. A hero must have
something or someone to overcome, and the image of the savage with
blood in his eye made a perfect foil for the Euro-American hero, who protected Euro-American women and children while eliminating the savages
and forging his way across the frontier.

Buffalo Bill Cody's first film, *The Indian Wars* (1914), like the dime
novels and the Wild West Show before it, showed exactly that. It glorified

the American army, particularly the 7th Cavalry, and provided thrilling scenes of soldiers fighting the Sioux at Wounded Knee. Although the film shows a pitched battle, Wounded Knee was in reality a massacre in which over three hundred Sioux, mostly old men, women, and children, died. The film was, however, billed as an accurate representation of the events. Interestingly, it was financed by the United States government and was not only distributed to movie houses across the nation but also placed in the national archives as an accurate depiction of actual events. The idea was

Tonto and the Lone Ranger: Tonto is an American-Indian Sidekick to the Euro-American hero.

apparently to bolster enthusiasm for joining the U.S. Army in case America should go to war against the Kaiser's Germany, which of course it did. Cody's film was one of the first uses of the American Indian people as a metaphor for other enemies to be similarly overcome. While the film is not available for classroom use, scholars' discussions provide key elements in analyzing a plethora of later films that repeat its problematic metaphor and pseudo-history.

In addition to serving as the necessary obstacle / impediment / danger, the Hollywood Indian has long served the role of the sidekick for film heroes, as well as providing a pause for some nostalgic tears for the America of yesteryear. Sidekicks provided reassurance that a white hero, such as the Lone Ranger, was superior to the noble but not-quite-articulate Indian. While the Hollywood Indian was always in the process of vanishing, the Noble Savage's traits of honesty, bravery, and stoicism in the face of insuperable odds could be infused in the white hero who lived with the Indians or who knew them well. In this way, the Noble Indian served as a kind of alter ego, a metaphor for that which America felt it lost once the frontier closed. The Euro-American hero who *becomes* Indian has been a staple of the film industry, with films ranging from *The Last of the Mohicans* (all seven) to *Hombre* (1967), *A Man Called Horse* (1970), and *Dances with Wolves* (1990), among many others. Many of these films include a sidekick-/alter-ego. Even *Windtalkers* (2002), though ostensibly about the Navajo code talkers of World War II, is actually a film about an anguished Euro-American hero and the noble sidekick from whom he learns wisdom.

In the real world of post–World War II America, life became good once more, if individual economic prosperity is the measure of such things. However, by the early fifties, fear that the Communists might provoke a nuclear war prompted bomb drills in schools and backyard bomb shelters. The Cold War was on.[10] Congressional committees led by Wisconsin Senator Joe McCarthy investigated anti–American activities and developed blacklists, resulting in a climate of fear and, in Hollywood, the shock of suddenly finding oneself among the oppressed. Films of the 1950s, therefore, ran the gamut from racist political propaganda to an unprecedented enlightenment. Because making a film that challenged the current oppressive cultural climate was potentially dangerous, some filmmakers found ways to deliver that message by trading on nostalgia for the vanishing American Indians and making them a metaphor for the oppressed.

History, social studies, and film studies students interested in how a film ostensibly about American Indians also criticizes oppression prominent in its own era can study Delmar Daves' *Broken Arrow* (1950), a film consistently cited as an example of a burgeoning cultural awareness in Hollywood. The Euro-American protagonist in *Broken Arrow*, played by Jimmy Stewart, obliquely investigates stereotypes and examines his own cultural norms. In questioning an idea as firmly implanted in the American psyche as the righteousness of Manifest Destiny, Daves opened a door for questioning other ideas and actions, such as blacklisting and even exporting artists for their personal beliefs and ideas. In *Broken Arrow*, Daves envisions Apaches as multi-dimensional human beings—an unusual idea in Hollywood—and Jeff Chandler as Cochise is as noble, articulate, and human as Jimmy Stewart's character. Students will have no trouble recognizing the limits of the film's sympathetic portrayals: a Euro-American actor plays Cochise, it is through the experiences of a Euro-American protagonist that the viewer learns about the Apaches, and miscegenation gets the same treatment as in earlier films—the Apache woman loved by the Euro-American protagonist dies so that the film does not promote inter-ethnic romance. In general, however, the Apaches are shown as intelligent, kind human beings with a sense of humor and a sense of honor just as genuine as the honor exhibited by the best of the Euro-American men. The point of view of American Indians is depicted as having validity.

Another film readily available to students that looks at American Indians sympathetically as a means to making a larger statement is Abraham Polonsky's *Tell Them Willie Boy Is Here* (1969). Blacklisted artist Polonsky chose this film to make his return to Hollywood after two decades, a film that has frequently been recognized as a statement about civil rights. Although the Civil Rights Movement was defined by most Americans as the struggle of blacks to gain equal status with the white majority, many Americans in the late sixties and early seventies were apparently not yet disposed to pay to see a film about an oppressed African American. Pauline Kael, in a *New Yorker* review, insists that Polonsky's Willie Boy is a metaphor for the militant black men of the era, reasoning that "since a Black man (the Indian pretense isn't kept up for long) can't trust any white man ... there can be no reconciliation of the races, so he should try to bring everything down."[11] The stereotypes of American Indians during this time period made them sympathetic subjects because they were seen as not only poor and oppressed but also mystical and natural, to say nothing of slightly vanished. Students can explore the idea that this film makes Indians, en masse and in particular, stand-ins for other people and other ideas, as did many other films of the era.

Students interested in anti-war films will find Ralph Nelson's (1970) *Soldier Blue* an interesting variation on the genre. An anti-war film that combines criticism of the U.S. government's treatment of American Indians with criticism of the Vietnam War by using Black Kettle's Cheyenne as a metaphor for the Vietnamese, *Soldier Blue* received a great deal of criticism for being too violent and too graphic in its representation of the massacre at Sand Creek. Despite the fact that the real massacre was even worse than Nelson depicted, the film's violence against women and children shocked his audiences. His intention was to sensitize the American public to the suffering of the Vietnamese by depicting similar atrocities committed by the U.S. government ninety years before, and Nelson was evidently somewhat successful in getting his message across. From an American Indian perspective, it was appropriate to show the Battle of Sand Creek as the massacre it was, but it was unfortunate that the film's Indians fall once more into the descriptions of savages and victims who lost and then vanished — again.

Another film that uses the treatment of Indians as a metaphor for the Vietnamese is Arthur Penn's *Little Big Man* (1970). Though far superior to *Soldier Blue*, this film is also problematic: besides portraying the Cheyenne to make a point about atrocities in Vietnam, it again features a Euro-American hero to depict the Indian experience for viewers, and his interethnic romance again ends with the Indian woman's death. This is in keeping with attitudes about miscegenation found in Hollywood films from the very beginning. American Indian women were stereotyped as beautiful Indian "princesses" who chose Euro-American heroes over their own people, were willing to sacrifice everything for their men, and who were doomed to die before the film's end, thereby leaving the Euro-American gene pool undamaged. When children *were* born of Euro-American / Indian relationships, whether through rape or love, they were "breeds" and treated with absolute disdain by both Euro-Americans and Indians in the film. However, of all the films made in the sixties, seventies, and eighties that were sympathetic portrayals of American Indians, *Little Big Man* is the one that has received and deserves the most positive response. It, too, has a massacre scene, but although Penn's massacre at the Washita is less graphic and bloody than the scene of the massacre at Sand Creek in *Soldier Blue*, it is more effective. Because *Little Big Man* invites viewers to know and care about the Cheyenne personally, their slaughter is more heartrending than the butchery of unknowns in *Soldier Blue*. Penn's Cheyenne may have been used by the filmmaker to make a point about the Vietnam War, but at least the audience saw them as fully realized human beings.

Soldier Blue and *Little Big Man* are good films to teach in history, social studies, and film studies courses — not because they depict the 1800s with anything approaching accuracy but because they reveal how Hollywood viewed and used portrayals of American Indians during the 1970s and because they can be studied as films that have a clear subtext reflecting the times in which they were made. To explore the question of why films that depict historical events are not more accurate, students can fit these films into the context of the time of their origin and the intentions of the filmmakers. A close examination of scenes in *Little Big Man*, particularly the Washita section, can lead to interesting discussions about making a point with a single image or sound.

The New Hollywood

Although success has been spotty at best, most filmmakers in Hollywood have become more sensitive to depicting characters less stereotypically. There are even a few films that depict American Indians in ways that allow Native people to recognize themselves. One of these films is *Powwow Highway* (Jonathan Wacks, 1989). This film is sometimes funny and sometimes thrilling, slow paced but full of action, and difficult to categorize according to any Hollywood genre because it is a mixture — a road movie that is a bit of a western. It is a good film to use in a social studies class, mainly because the issues and people in the film ring true. One of the two main characters, Buddy Red Bow, is a volatile young man who is in many ways like his cinematic predecessor, Willie Boy. The other initially seems like the opposite: Philbert Bono is a big man with a sweet smile, a soft look, and an open sincerity that seems, at first, very simple. He has chosen the "old way" but is quite at home in the late twentieth century. What makes this film so worthwhile is that the Native people in it are complex, contemporary, and interesting. They also exist in a world that corresponds to real issues of concern to contemporary American Indians: the poverty on reservations such as Pine Ridge, American Indians in the armed services, the 1973 standoff protest at Wounded Knee, the politics of tribal resources, the value of traditional beliefs, and racism are all significant issues for students to explore in this film.

Students will probably have already seen the more mainstream *Dances With Wolves* (1990). When the film premiered, it was lauded for its treatment of American Indians as fully realized human beings, and students can explore how it makes an attempt to do so, as well as where it succeeds and where it fails. Kevin Costner (director, producer, and star of the film) chose to use talented American Indian actors from the U.S. and Canada for the American Indian parts, with the result that they are believable, likable, and interesting. That is the good news, but not the only reason why this would be a good film to show in a high school or college classroom. The film's failures also provide good points for discussion. For instance, every positive trait of the Lakota has an opposite correlative trait in the white world of the film, represented by the Union Army. Whereas the Lakota are individualized, respectable, and intelligent human beings, the cavalry officers almost to a man are misfits at best and psychotics at worst. In short, the film involves itself in white guilt; there is little good in the white world and no bad in the Lakota world, except that brought by the white men. Exchanging one stereotype for another is not the same as respecting differences, and students generally see this clearly. Students also note that the film revitalizes the old stereotypes. The Lakota are depicted as individuals, but also as goodness personified and one tribe of a vanishing race. Also, the Lakota are noble while the Pawnee, the film's Indian villains, are depicted as bloodthirsty as any stereotypes in any earlier movie. Literature students can gain much by reading Michael Blake's novel in conjunction with viewing the film and comparing Blake's treatment of the Lakota (Comanches in the novel) and the Pawnee and to consider how written texts are transformed into films.

Students of all disciplines can consider the idea of responsibility in this and other films. *Soldier Blue*, *Little Big Man*, and *Dances with Wolves* are only three of many films made by filmmakers trying to be more sensitive to American Indians. However, they are films in which white cruelty can be related to madness, thereby releasing the general public from responsibility because the violence and cruelty reflect the insanity of only a few. Students can explore what it means when filmmakers choose to depict Custer in *Little Big Man*, Colonel Chivington in *Soldier Blue*, and the commanding officer at Fort Hayes in *Dances with Wolves* as not only insane but humorously so. The historical Custer and Chivington were not insane; in fact, they were considered at the time heroes and their actions heroic. Students can also attempt to answer why the main character, John Dunbar, in *Dances with Wolves*, is another Euro-American hero who becomes a better Indian than the Indians, even showing the Lakota where to find the buffalo. Students can consider why the woman Dunbar meets and marries in the Lakota camp turns out to be Euro American. Is it so the long outdated restrictions on miscegenation will not be disturbed? And students can also ponder why so many films, including *Dances with Wolves*, are set within a limited fifty-year period. Why is it, as Jan Elliott, editor of *Indigenous Thought*, puts it, that "Indians are the only minority group that the Indian lovers won't let out of the 19th Century?"[12]

John Woo's (2002) *Windtalkers*, a film about a Euro-American soldier during World War II who is suffering from traumatic stress, does portray American Indians of the twentieth century. The soldier is assigned to keep a Navajo code talker safe, if possible, but to kill him rather than let him fall into enemy hands. One of only a handful of feature films that depict American Indian involvement during war time, it shows the enormous contribution the code talkers made to the war in the Pacific, and the Navajos are shown deserving of respect. However, the Navajos in this film are a kind of exotic diversion, a pallet on which to paint the main character's story. That isn't necessarily a bad thing — at least the Navajo characters are believable and likeable, and one of them is allowed to return to his family and culture — but the story of the characters' getting to know and respect one another is drowned in a sea of bloody battle scenes. It seems more of an occasion for director John Woo, renowned for his action films filled with violent special effects, to show off his technical prowess than a meaningful story about men from different cultures learning about one another. However, students can profit from comparing and contrasting *Windtalker* with *War Code: Navajo Code Talkers*, a documentary produced by Navajo filmmaker Lena Carr for National Geographic, to discover how Hollywood's perspective on the code talkers differs from the perspective of an American Indian.

American Indian Filmmakers

The most promising aspect of American Indian depictions in film is the fact that many American Indians are now telling their own stories. Writers such as Tom King, Gerald Vizenor, and Sherman Alexie are writing films that tell the story from a Native point of view and privilege a Native perspective. Directors such as Lena Carr, George Burdeau, Victor Masayevsa, Geraldine Keams, and many more are directing independent films outside of Hollywood with Native actors and writers. The most readily available of these is Chris Eyre's *Smoke Signals* (1998). In January of 1998, *Smoke Signals* premiered at the Sundance Festival in Park City, Utah, and received the Audience Award for Dramatic Films, the Filmmakers Trophy, and a nomination for the Grand Jury Prize. Advertised as the first film written, produced, and directed by American Indians, it deals with issues that confront many Native (and non–Native) people. The specters of alcoholism, injustice, and loneliness form the skeleton upon which the story hangs. However, it is also very funny. Social studies students can examine how it depicts American Indians living on and off the reservation as contemporary humans with contemporary problems and emotions. The film holds much of the tone of Sherman Alexie's book, *The Lone Ranger and Tonto Fistfight in Heaven*, from which it was made —clever, funny, and bleak. Literature and film studies students can explore how the film draws from several short stories in the book to tell the larger story in the film. If students read and discuss the book before viewing the film, it is possible to have excellent discussions about American Indian writing and filmmaking as well as contemporary life on "the Rez."

Documentaries

As noted earlier, a major problem with most films about American Indians is the time-freeze. A few films present contemporary American Indian issues, and some students are aware of current debates over such issues as gambling and efforts to reclaim or to keep American Indian lands and resources. However, most Americans think of the oppression of American Indians as something from the past that no longer requires attention. Fortunately, there are many documentaries, by both Native and non–Native filmmakers, that offer contemporary perspectives. Two that may be especially useful in the classroom are *Broken Rainbow* and *Rocks with Wings*.

Broken Rainbow (1985), by Maria Florio and Victoria Mudd, an Academy Award winner for Best Documentary Feature, is sure to engage students. The topic is the forced relocation of the Navajo so that their land in the four corners region of the Southwest could be strip-mined. Shots of Black Mesa being ripped apart, old men and women forced into government housing and then evicted for not paying taxes, livestock slaughtered by the government, and federal tractors plowing under the scrub grass necessary for sustaining stock fill the film. Students are generally shocked and angry, and the film precipitates animated discussions. For history and social studies students, the film provides a good starting point for research and writing about what has happened to the Navajo and Hopi people involved since the film was made in 1985. It is also a good way to start looking into the history of the Native peoples of the Southwest, including the first removal of the Navajo in 1868 in a forced march across most of New Mexico that caused the death of many, especially the old and the infirm, and their internment at Fort Sumner, a camp reportedly of research interest to Adolph Hitler. A recent documentary, *Rocks with Wings* (Rick Derby, PBS, 2002), was filmed at Shiprock on the Navajo reservation. It is about the 1988 Shiprock High School girls' championship basketball team, coached by a hard-pushing African-American coach, Jerry Richardson. Of particular relevance to social studies students, the film deals with issues of culture, which is particularly apparent in the girls' reaction to Richardson's insistence that they be aggressive, a trait not held in high esteem in Navajo culture. It also offers students an opportunity to talk about Richardson's experiences in the segregated South and his move to the reservation, where he is even more of a minority presence, as well as how the high school girls manage to confront him and cause him to reassess his coaching style. In addition to showing contemporary life on the Navajo reservation, the film raises other issues for student discussion, such as relations between gender and ethnicity, ideas about sports and gender, and depictions of individuals from different ethnic groups working together.

Approaches

Film can be a powerful tool for teachers. Juxtaposing film depictions of American Indians with the representation of a film's events in the popular press of the time, government records about those events, and the way the stories are told by the Native people involved in those events (or their descendents) can build a more interesting and more accurate picture of the nation's history from first contact to the present. Films can also provide a fairly painless way to coax students to think in different ways and engage ideas from a point of view they may not have previously considered. Representations of American Indians that have evolved over the last five hundred years are intricately tied to events and ideas generally discussed in history and social studies classes. For example, a class that viewed and discussed just four films—*Nanook of the North* (Robert Flaherty, 1922), *Allegheny Uprising* (William Seiter, 1939), *Dances with Wolves* (Kevin Costner, 1990), and *Smoke Signals* (Chris Eyre, 1998)—could provide an interesting overview of this evolution. Flaherty's *Nanook of the North* was a nostalgic, staged re-creation of the life of Native peoples of the far north. Although not the documentary it is usually assumed to be (Flaherty had to shoot around modern elements such as telegraph poles), it is generally thought to be a good representation of pre-contact life in the upper latitudes of North America.[13] *Allegheny Uprising* is a film starring the model film hero, John Wayne, in which attitudes about American Indians are not only mixed but confused. Wayne's character is a "blood brother" to the Indians, but he chases down the "red devils." In this way, he assumes the identity of the indigenous people, including their nobility and their right to the land, and also "cleanses" the land of their presence, making it available for white farmers. The film presents the idea still widely held in America that land not "used" is wasted, an idea that made the U.S. government theft of land seem not only appropriate but righteous. *Dances with Wolves* is a good film to study for its attempt to be politically correct and to present the Lakota as fully realized human beings. One point of contrast for students to consider is the way in which Wayne's character in *Allegheny Uprising* is bifurcated compared, on one hand, with Costner's more unified character and, on the other, with the white soldiers who are presented as both Bloodthirsty Savages and saviors who want to "cleanse" the land of the Indian presence in the interest of Manifest Destiny. *Smoke Signals* is a good film to end with because American Indians made it and it stars Native people. It effectively portrays modern Native life and issues and makes it clear to students that American Indians haven't vanished after all.

Another approach especially relevant to literature and film studies students but important for students in history and social studies classes as well would be to view one story in its various representations over the last one hundred years. A good choice for that is *The Last of the Mohicans*, which has been made into a feature film many times. Seven of those were Hollywood films, but the story has caught the imagination of British, French, German, and East Indian filmmakers as well. The Hollywood films are particularly transparent in the connections made by the filmmakers to social and political issues of the day. A cursory glance at a few of the differences between the versions of *The Last of the Mohicans* shows clearly the connection between the films and the socio-political views of the filmmakers and/or the times in which they were made.[14] D.W. Griffith in his version, titled *Leatherstocking* (1909), was interested in making an action hero of Natty Bumpo. Griffith's Natty leaves his Mohican friend behind and goes off with the white characters, leaving Chingachgook to vanish on his own. This fifteen-minute film hearkens back to the nostalgic image of the doomed Noble Red Man and America before the closing of the "frontier," and Natty is a salt-of-the-earth woodsman tied to the land. Bumpo's association with the Mohicans is clearly meant to make him the legitimate inheritor of the North American continent. In 1920, Tourneur and Brown were interested in issues of race and miscegenation, and their film, titled *The Last of the Mohicans,* is clearly a reaction to Griffith's (1915) *Birth of a Nation* primarily, but it is also a reaction to Griffith's *Leatherstocking*, which holds many of the same racist values found in *Birth*. Though the 1920 film focuses on the love story between the Euro-American woman and the Indian man, neither Cora nor Agnes are of mixed blood. An interesting element for students to discuss is the fact that Cooper's Cora was half-black, but in all of the films she is white. In 1936, George Seitz's *The Last of the Mohicans* stars one of Hollywood's super-heroes, Randolph Scott. The main theme of this story is real estate, the taming of the frontier in the interest of Manifest Destiny. Natty's Mohican friends are presented as doomed to vanish from the beginning, which the film invites viewers to see as sad but necessary for the building of a nation. In Depression-era America, Seitz understood the idea that people taking matters into their own hands and making something of their lives with just hard work was sure to appeal to this audience. Michael Mann's 1992 version, also titled *The Last of the Mohicans*, attempts to tell the story in a politically correct fashion, but his Natty, now a ladies' man, is also a better Indian than his Mohican friends. By critically viewing these four adaptations of Cooper's book and relating them to the history and popular culture of the times in which they were made, students can understand the development of the Hollywood Indian as based on repetitions of earlier fictions and films, but with differences that reflect the events and attitudes of the times in which they were made.

Capturing Those Pesky Images

One of the challenges in using films in the classroom is that the very nature of film resists critical assessment. We are accustomed to sitting in a darkened theater with only the sights and the sounds of the film to experience. We go to be entertained. Teachers therefore need to show students, at least once, how to read a film. I give my students a list of terms (such as in the Glossary of this book) that provides them with ways to think about the film. I then ask them to take notes using the following guidelines: 1) Maintain an active, critical perspective and take notes on both the content and the form of the film. Include your initial perceptions, impressions, and reactions while watching the film in class. 2) Add further impressions and your general reaction shortly after watching the film, noting especially any important connections between parts of the film and connections to other films. A good way to get students started taking notes is to show a short clip (fifteen minutes will do) and ask them to take notes on a sheet of paper divided into two columns. The left column is for "content" and the right column is for "form." They will make entries on what is happening in the content column and how it is presented in the form column. This visual literacy exercise is difficult to do because content and form are, of course, tied to one another and separation is sometimes not possible. While not as useful as a standard practice, this exercise does allow students to see how sensitive they are being to the film's modes of representation. It also gives them practice in gathering evidence for their assertions and evaluations.

Evolutionary changes in representations of American Indians are surely far from over. Students' study of films of the past prepares them for future viewing — providing them with the ability to distinguish repeated stereotypes and outmoded ideas from responsible representations of realistic individuals, real events, and real issues — and prepares future filmmakers with the inspiration to learn from the past in order to create realistic images in the future.

4

Changing Faces: Exploring Latino/a History, Culture, and Identity through U.S. Cinema

by Joaquin Alvarado

The history of cinematic representations of Chicanos/as and Latinos/as[1] in the United States has evolved in a complex and dynamic fashion since the beginnings of film in the late 1890s. With disturbing regularity, mainstream depictions of Latinos/as have been predicated on misguided paternalism, racist misconceptions, and economically driven vilification. For a group of citizens so integrally linked to the development of the United States over the last two centuries, Latinos/as have had the dubious distinction of being generally depicted as Greasers, Spitfires, *Bandidos,*[2] gangsters, and lazy dimwits in the dominant media of their own country, a country to which they have committed so much of their labor and efforts. The persistent stereotypes of Latinos/as predate even the Treaty of Guadalupe Hidalgo, which ceded a major swath of Northern Mexico to the United States following Mexico's defeat in the Mexican-American War (1846–1848). Oftentimes demonized, stereotyped, and marginalized in popular media, the image of the Latinos/a population in the United States has been inextricably linked to the sociopolitical conditions of the era in which these images were produced. Traditional Hollywood films of the last hundred years, along with independent films produced during and subsequent to the Chicano/a Movement, have cinematically explored, in divergent ways, many of the issues that continue to confront Latinos/as. By studying the history of Latino/a images in these films, high school and undergraduate college students have the opportunity to examine the lives,

77

cultures, and many histories of the fastest growing segment of the U.S. population.

Changing Demographics of the U.S.

The Latino/a population of the United States is experiencing unprecedented growth in population and geographic distribution. In the ten years from 1990 to 2000, the U.S. Hispanic (the term used by the U.S. Census Bureau denoting both Chicanos/as and Latinos/as) population increased at a rate of 57.9 percent.[3] This is four times the rate of the total U.S. population, which increased at a 13.2 percent rate. As of the year 2000, Hispanics represented 12.5 percent of the total U.S. population, some 35.3 million people. As of the year 2002, Hispanics reached 13.4% of the population, surpassing the African-American population of 13.3%. The social and political dynamics of being the largest minority group in the country are just starting to evolve. In the states of California, Texas, Arizona, and New Mexico, one in three residents is now Hispanic. The trend is not limited to the Southwest, however. Even in states not traditionally associated with large Hispanic populations, such as Connecticut and Rhode Island, nearly ten percent of the population is of Hispanic descent. Based on the demographics alone, it is evident that knowledge of and familiarity with the Latino/a population are going to be necessary components of an educated and democratically organized U.S. population. Considering the population trends, educators must be sensitive to the diversity and distinctions within the Latino/a community. As of the 2000 census, of the total Hispanic population, 58.5 percent are of Mexican descent. This compares with the next largest group, those of Puerto Rican descent, representing 9.6 percent of the Hispanic population. Cuban Americans are the third largest segment at 3.5 percent of the total Hispanic population.

Ethnic Identity, Media Challenges, and New Images

The impact of the increasingly multicultural makeup of the United States must be considered against the development and importance of ethnic identity in the Latino/a community. The very terms "Chicano/a" and "Latino/a" resulted from a political and social struggle to redress some of the historical injustices endured by these respective communities within the United States. The victims of a virulent racism and economic apartheid during much of the nineteenth and first half of the twentieth century, many

Chicanos/as and Latinos/as began to reclaim and renegotiate their traditional cultural identities as a defense against cultural annihilation. In the
face of open hostility from the dominant social groups, Latinos/as in the
first half of the twentieth century began to use identity as a form of resistance. The Chicano/a Movement adopted and catalyzed this effort in conjunction with the larger Civil Rights Movement. As a part of the struggle
for economic equality and social access in the U.S., minority communities began to analyze and deconstruct the many ways that the media had
contributed to and naturalized their status as second-class citizens. This
new media awareness inspired young activists to criticize racist and discriminatory representations and pressure Hollywood to stop such depictions. Nowhere was this new awareness more pronounced than in the
Latino/a community, where the mobilization against the Frito Bandito
advertising campaign, which ran from 1967–71, was an early testing ground
for media accountability. Under pressure from Chicano/a activists, the
campaign was eventually discontinued. The offensive images were not
restricted to caricatures of fictional bandidos, however. Corporate advertising also used images of important Mexican historical figures. A popular media campaign for Elgin watches, for instance, featured the image of
Emiliano Zapata and described him as a lawless thief. These kinds of depictions were not only historically inaccurate but also reflected a deep cultural insensitivity. Students can view a number of Latino/a reactions and
responses to such caricatures in the documentary *Americanos: Latino Life
in the U.S.* (Susan Todd and Andrew Young, 1999).

As activists began to confront the monolithic media companies of the
late 1960s and early 1970s, it became apparent that critiquing the status
quo was not a sufficient response to the decades of damage that date back,
in the case of film, to the early 1900s. Any effective action would have to
include the creation of new and accurate depictions by and for Latinos/as.
Only by providing alternative media representations, these early media
activists reasoned, would the oppressive stereotypes ultimately be shed.
Chicano/a filmmakers such as Luis Valdez (*I Am Joaquin*, 1969), Jesús Salvador Treviño (*La Raza Nueva*, 1969), and Sylvia Morales (*Chicana*, 1979)
were some of the early voices in this movement providing groundbreak-
ing representations of the new and empowered Latino/a identity in the U.S.
From this urgency of action, Latino/a Cinema in the United States was born
and continues to evolve. Helpful to teachers and students for its relatively
short (95 minutes) Latino/a film history, the documentary *The Bronze
Screen* (Susan Racho, Nancy de los Santos, and Albert Dominguez, 2001)
encapsulates a century of Hollywood's failures and successes in representing Latinos/as from the days of silent cinema to 2001.

The challenge for teachers in introducing this important subject is to contextualize the formation of Latino/a Cinema in the U.S. Issues of identity and discrimination in Latino/a cinema are intimately connected with a nexus of subjects ranging from social and political history to the development of the U.S. Southwest, and from contemporary immigration to youth violence and bilingualism. History, social studies (including American cultures and political science), literature, and film studies teachers will find a number of appropriate films.

Many Latino/a films explore the complex intersections of these subjects by attempting to portray accurately the lives and values of Latino/as. In the place of the stereotypical Latino thug, films such as *Stand and Deliver* (Ramon Menendez, 1988) and *American Me* (Edward James Olmos, 1992) expose their audiences to the roots and intricate lives of Latino youth. Students viewing these films may not be aware of the history of racist cinematic depictions of Latinos as hot-blooded heathens incapable of self-control or reason, although specific examples of these stereotypes date back to the silent era in such films as *The Greaser's Gauntlet* (Biograph, 1908) and *Martyrs of the Alamo* (W. Christy Cabanne, 1915). Both of these early films depict their Mexican characters as ignorant, idiotic, and lecherous villains capable of extreme acts of violence and depravity. The trend continues in many later films, such as *Colors* (Dennis Hopper, 1988) and *Training Day* (Antoine Fuqua, 2001).

Independent and Experimental Films

The variety of Latino/a films in the U.S. allows teachers to point out some of the economic and market issues endemic to the media industry, a point that may be particularly interesting to film studies students. Although the concerns of the Latino/a community have an obvious social, political, and cultural relevance to the nation, they have typically gained little response from this country's centers of media power. The large studios and production companies that ultimately determine investments in feature films, television, commercials, and even network news have been slow to support content developed by the Latino/a community. The struggle to gain access and financing has paralleled the larger struggle for equal rights. To this day, few funding opportunities are available for Latino/a-produced media in the United States. While an unfortunate fact, this condition has led to a rich and varied history of experimental and independent[4] productions by and about Latinos/as. Experimental films are important as teaching tools because they challenge the structure and definitions of film that commercial filmmaking promote. As a literacy lesson, experimental films can help teachers demonstrate to students that many of the cinematic elements considered normal are in fact constructed. Close-ups, for example, exploit the emotional tension of a scene. Independent films are crucial in teaching film across the academic curriculum as they often represent the only opportunity for students to see narratives and characters that traditional media does not represent. A few important experimental artists teachers may want to consider are Harry Gamboa,[5] who uses performance art and still photography to assess the role of Chicano cinema in the larger struggle for equal rights and media access, and Lourdes Portillo, whose award-winning films have helped redefine Latino/a media production. Portillo's *Señorita Extraviada — Missing Young Woman* (2002) combines traditional documentary techniques with personal and creative narrative forms.

The New Pachucho

In 1981, Luis Valdez, a preeminent figure in Chicano theatre with his *Teatro Campesino*, released his first feature film, *Zoot Suit*. Adapted from his play of the same name, Valdez's film tells the story of a young Chicano, Henry Reyna, and the infamous Sleepy Lagoon Murder Trial. A narrative device developed by Valdez in Chicano *Teatro* and used again in his film places the common person at the center of the story to show how the issues have a direct impact on the lives of everyday people. The tale of a zoot suit-clad Chicano youth suffering a political and physical attack is an excellent example of the history of discrimination that Valdez wanted to address. During August of 1942, a young Chicano, José Díaz, was found gravely injured in Los Angeles and died in the hospital a few days later. The media and general public were soon convinced that his death was the inevitable result of a war raging between rival Zoot Suit gangs running wild in the barrios. Scores of young Latinos were rounded up by the police and held illegally. Eventually, twenty-three were charged with murder in the case. In June of the following year, mobs of uniformed U.S. enlisted men went on a rampage in downtown and East Los Angeles, seeking a perverse vengeance on Latino youth whom the media had demonized. This week of chaos became known as the Zoot Suit Riots. Though dozens of young Latinos were attacked and brutalized, no servicemen were arrested. Ultimately, twelve of the original Sleepy Lagoon murder suspects were convicted without any physical evidence. The U.S. Court of Appeals overturned the case in 1944. At the time of the appeal, eight of the men had already spent two years in federal prison. Literature and film studies teachers can explore with students how this film at once retains the conventions of the theatre and transforms the play to the language of film. Social studies and American history teachers can compare the film with historical accounts of this event, such as the PBS *American Experience* documentary *Zoot Suit Riots* (Joseph Tovares, 2001) or selections from Mauricio Maxon's 1984 book, *The Zoot Suit Riots: The Psychology of a Symbolic Annihilation.* Students can focus on how Valdez uses a personal story to explore larger issues of racism, culture, and politics while representing an actual event.

Throughout Valdez's film, viewers see the problematic relationship between the criminal justice system and Latino urban youth. Social studies and history teachers can use this film to discuss the alarming incarceration rates in the Latino community that persist today. El Pachuco, played by a young Edward James Olmos, narrates Valdez's *Zoot Suit.* He acts as a mischievous, but always critical, conscience for Henry's character. Literature and film studies students can analyze the effectiveness of this narrative point of view, and students from all disciplines can discuss how and why the actual testimony of Los Angeles Police Edward Duran Ayres is incorporated verbatim into the dialogue of the film. During the film, Ayres suggests that people of Mexican descent, in his opinion, continue to embody the blood lust of the "cannibalistic Aztecs." Although some students are certainly aware of the continuing tensions in U.S. cities between the police and minority communities, all students will benefit from being exposed to this sad chapter of American history. Film studies and literature teachers can ask students to discuss the way violence is handled in a sophisticated manner in this film, stylizing most of the action to avoid any graphic treatment. *Zoot Suit* offers an effective starting point for any discussion about violence in America. A central theme of the film is the role of the *Los Angeles Times* and other media outlets in stigmatizing Latino youth as violent gangsters. Journalism students can explore the critical role of newspapers in constructing the popular image of Latinos during this era. Valdez's *Zoot Suit* is a microcosm of this world, interpreted by a Chicano filmmaker who developed his filmmaking skills in the heart of the Chicano Movement.

Mi Vida Loca (*My Crazy Life*) (Allison Anders, 1993) is also a film about Latino/a youth but with a decidedly different thematic and narrative concern. This film, about members of a Chicana gang in the Echo Park neighborhood of East L.A., was the first mainstream film dealing with Chicanas as well as female gang activity. After becoming pregnant by the same man, best friends are pitted against each other in the film. When the father of their children is gunned down in a botched drug deal, the women must confront the harsh reality of raising fatherless children and surviving in East LA. This film is atypical in its reliance on female solidarity to drive its narrative. The women in this film take action to affect their lives, in this case cooperating to sell the dead father's low-rider truck to help support their babies. Students studying challenges to stereotypes will note how this depiction of female friendship is rare in the history of Latina representation in film, a history that overwhelmingly portrays them as Spitfires, loose women, or docile victims. The film is also important for the authenticity of its portrayals of the nuances of life in East LA. When Anders was writing the film, she consulted with local gang members to insure accuracy and cast one of the main characters from that gang.[6] Teachers will find many of the issues experienced in all American high schools, ranging from violence to teen pregnancy, broached in this film with a unique honesty and insight. However, individual teachers should screen this film to judge its appropriateness for their particular classes. It contains some violence, sexual content, and mature language.

The U.S.-Mexico Border

The U.S.-Mexico border is a highly contested political, social, cultural, and economic space with incredible importance for the United States and for all of its southern neighbors. Many populations in the Western Hemisphere have historically been identified by and linked to the colonialism that began with the first European incursions in the "new world." The U.S.-Mexican border represents one of the few examples in the hemisphere where the conquering and defeated countries have continued to coexist intimately since the war that established the current borders. From the mid–1800s, the border has been anything but a stagnant geographic boundary. The U.S. annexation of a huge territory[7] after the Mexican-American War created a new class of citizens from those who were already living there: the first Mexican Americans. Despite the fact that provisions in the Treaty of Guadalupe Hidalgo provided for the protection of the Mexican Americans' rights as citizens and landowners, the first decades after the war saw many of these provisions ignored and violated. A film that effectively addresses this situation is *The Ballad of Gregorio Cortez* (Robert Young, 1983). In the film, a man of Mexican descent, Gregorio Cortez (played by Edward James Olmos), is falsely accused of a crime — resulting from a Euro-American translator's poor command of Spanish and his assumption that all Mexican Americans are *bandidos*— and must go on the run to protect himself. The film is not only an engaging depiction of life along the border early in the twentieth century, but also an excellent resource for examining issues of bilingualism and the history of U.S. expansionism, as well as cross-cultural awareness.

While the issue of Latino/a, especially Mexican, immigration into the U.S. is still hotly contested in many social and political circles on both sides of the border, it is important to consider some of the factors that have continued to make it a vital part of Latino/a cinema. Students are often unaware that the United States has sponsored numerous immigration programs to bring Mexican laborers to this country. Most notable among them is the Bracero Program, which coordinated the infusion of Mexican workers into U.S. farms from 1942 to 1964. Mexican immigration continues to provide the U.S. with a critical source of cheap labor. Factories, known as *maquiladoras*, in the border region of Mexico are the manufacturing bases for many consumer goods in this country. News reports about the deaths of people crossing into the U.S. along the California and Arizona border regions heighten national awareness of some of the issues confronting the region.[8] Social science and history teachers can choose between a number of films as effective ways to teach these topics.

Students will find that U.S. films dealing with the U.S.-Mexico border treat it in ways as distinct as the filmmakers and times that produced them. Orson Welles' noir classic *Touch of Evil* (1958) portrays the border as a murky world of nefarious activity and people. Marijuana-crazed Mexican hoodlums pounce on the Anglo wife (played by Janet Leigh) of a Mexican narcotics agent (played by Charlton Heston in brown-face) who is battling a drug ring and a crooked Euro-American cop (played by the director himself). Students can investigate how the border in this film represents a place of dubious morality that compromises everything it touches. Right and wrong are difficult to define in Welles' film. Welles uses the interracial marriage of Heston and Leigh as a flashpoint for the film's consideration of the mixed racial heritage of the border region. Their relationship as newlyweds is physically and thematically contested by the drama played out in the film as she is kidnapped and their lives endangered, thus providing a cautionary tale of the perils of interracial commingling. In Chicano/a cinema, the border has been engaged both geographically and economically in different ways. Films such as Jesús Salvador Treviño's *Raices de Sangre* (1977) and Robert Young's *Alambrista!* (1978) explore the economic and social pressures faced by the people who live on the border, as well as those who must cross it for work. *Alambrista!* focuses on the migrant farm worker experience, while *Raices de Sangre* is concerned with the lives of people who are more settled in the border milieu.

Other films have focused on the living culture that thrives on both sides of the border, making them an excellent resource for teachers of American culture. A popular example of this is *Selena* (Gregory Nava, 1997). In this biographical film about the young *Tejano* music star, the vibrant and close relationship between Chicanos/as and their Mexican neighbors is presented as a key element in the success and support that Selena received before her untimely murder. *Selena* raises the issue of bilingualism in the Latino/a community when the film reveals that Selena is not proficient in Spanish but learns to sing in the language in order to connect with her core audience. The ease with which she switches between the two languages and cultures significantly characterizes the border region. The life and impact of Selena is also the subject of two documentary films by Lourdes Portillo: *Conversations with Intellectuals about Selena* (1999), in which Portillo gathers Chicana scholars to discuss the life of the young performer, and *Corpus: A Home Movie for Selena* (1999), a film that goes to the source of Selena's popularity and speaks to the young women who keep her alive as a cultural icon. In these two films, students can recognize the importance of non-traditional role models in the lives of young people. The music and culture of the border has been explored in other films as well. Independent filmmaker Les Blank's *Chulas Frontera* (1976) is a documentary about Border music. Shot largely at various border venues, this film captures the energy of the music and its importance to the community.

A comical, yet politically biting, film on border dynamics is Richard "Cheech" Marin's *Born in East LA* (1987). Useful for teaching the absurdity of stereotypes, this film follows the exploits of a U.S. citizen, played by Marin himself, mistakenly deported to Tijuana while minding his own business in East Los Angeles. Marin, whose popularity began in the 1970s with the seminal comedy duo Cheech and Chong, satirizes many of the stereotypes that have plagued Latino/as in cinema since its inception. The accidental deportee must use a series of unexpected and cunning maneuvers to return to the U.S. To earn money to return to Los Angeles, he helps a group of Asian immigrants stranded in Tijuana learn what they need to know to gain entry into the U.S. In a particularly ironic and insightful segment, Marin's character teaches them how to be a stereotypical Latino, including walk, hand gestures, and dress, in order to avoid detection in the U.S. This sequence alone explodes the myth of what the mainstream media has portrayed as Latino/a culture.

The border has also developed into a major metaphorical device in Latino cinema. Films ranging from *El Norte* (Gregory Nava, 1983) to *La Bamba* (Luis Valdez, 1987) to *My Family /Mi Familia* (Gregory Nava, 1995) have ascribed importance to the border as a place of transition and transformation. In John Sayles' *Lone Star* (1996), the border becomes both a literal and figurative division, splitting the different social and ethnic groups in a small rural Texas town. This film develops many themes in both its characters and narratives that demonstrate the often-ignored ethnic and cultural connections of the region. The town itself is named Frontera, which literally means Frontier. This name is poignant in a film that looks to both sides of the border as well as to past and present divisions in order to tell its story of this multicultural region and its people.

Latino/a Individual and Family Identity and Community Issues

Students can explore a number of issues important to the Latino/a community in one of the most commercially successful Latino/a films: *La Bamba*. This tale of the rise and tragic death of music sensation Ritchie Valens (born Richard Valenzuela) was a huge personal and financial success for director Luis Valdez. Released in 1987, *La Bamba* benefited from a resurgent nostalgia for the 1950s and the birth of rock and roll. Lou

La Bamba (Luis Valdez, 1987). Portrayals of Ritchie Valens and his brother Bob.

Diamond Phillips' portrayal of the young musician made the actor a star. While all of the ingredients of a traditional Hollywood movie are present (e.g., a handsome leading man in a tale of triumph and tragedy, a budding interracial love affair, a troubled family life), Valdez is able to infuse the film with a discourse on the nature of identity, assimilation, and culture in the Latino/a community. In the film, Valens must constantly work to maintain his own sense of identity against the tide of discrimination he faces. Never forgetting his humble farm-worker beginnings, Valens is able to maintain an honest and personal dignity in the face of mounting family and commercial pressures. Valdez uses Valens' relationship with an Anglo girlfriend to examine racial attitudes and prejudices of the time. Valens' girlfriend Donna is pressured by her father to stay away from the Latino rock singer and refers to his music as "jungle music." The film also features Latino actor Esai Morales as Ritchie's alcoholic and turbulent half-brother Bob, who is a steady reminder that, for every miraculous success story in the Latino community, there are many more who cannot enjoy such success. For all his negative characteristics, Bob is also a catalyst for Ritchie remaining connected to his roots, challenging Ritchie for his perceived assimilation with the dominant Anglo community and attempting to keep him grounded in his version of the Latino community. In one memorable scene, Bob takes Ritchie to a house of ill repute in Tijuana, where Ritchie becomes infatuated by the music of a Mexican mariachi band (played in the film by the popular Chicano rock group Los Lobos). This scene, literally set on the border, can initiate discussion about assimilation and, again, about how intricately the cultures of the U.S. and Mexico are connected. This film, however, was not Valdez's only incursion into the musical history of Latinos in the U.S. His widely regarded *Corridos: Tales of Passion and Revolution*, which premiered on PBS the same year of *La Bamba*'s release in 1987, explores the history and influence of traditional Mexican songs during the Mexican Revolution and its aftermath.

In 1988, another surprise hit came to U.S. theatres: *Stand and Deliver*, a story about Latino/a high school teachers and students. Directed by Ramon Menendez, *Stand and Deliver* tells the story of a group of under-achieving Latino/a students attending Garfield High School in East Los Angeles who flourish when a new math teacher arrives at the school. The film is based on the true story of Jaime Escalante, who left a lucrative job and his suburban existence to teach math at a barrio school. Edward James Olmos' performance as Escalante earned an Oscar nomination. In many ways *Stand and Deliver* is an extremely effective traditional story of under-dogs overcoming incredible odds, in this case high school students preparing for and passing an AP Calculus exam. While this conventional structure certainly contributed to its general audience appeal, *Stand and Deliver* is important for its honest depiction of Latino/a characters and the challenges they experience in the educational system. In the film, both the students and the faculty of Garfield suffer from low expectations and the even lower effort that results. Menendez effectively portrays the poverty and violence permeating the school grounds and the students' everyday lives in East Lost Angeles. The academic issues raised in the film continue to resonate with students and teachers from all disciplines, particularly in the math and sciences, where Latino/a students continue to perform below the national averages.

What is exemplary in *Stand and Deliver* is the realism it invests in the student ensemble. Many of the usual Hollywood characters appear in the film: the tough *cholo*, the struggling student who must juggle work responsibilities with school, and the quiet girl whose family does not value education. All of these and more are sitting in the class into which Escalante walks on the first day. As the film develops, however, a rich texture of detail and motivations begins to emerge. The hardened cholo (played by Lou Diamond Phillips) is shown caring tenderly for his grandmother. A female student, Raquel, is shown attending to her many siblings while her mother works nights. When Raquel sits down to study, her mother returns home and asks her to turn the lights off so she can rest, a moment that explains the earlier classroom scene when Escalante calls Raquel out for not being prepared for that day's quiz. This level of detail in creating characters and depicting family situations provides this film with an accuracy not often found in Hollywood films about Latino/a characters. Since its release, teachers have consistently used *Stand and Deliver* to demonstrate a positive example of change and achievement that challenges the usual Hollywood stereotypes.

In an historical sense, *La Bamba* and *Stand and Deliver* mark a certain apex in the popularity of Latino/a cinema in the U.S. Few subsequent films have realized their promise of studio-produced and marketed Latino-driven content. This trend mirrors closely the community's continued stagnation in economic and social development from the late 1980s to the start of the twenty-first century. While Latino/a figures in cinema — such as director Gregory Nava and actors Edward James Olmos and Jennifer Lopez — continued to experience growth in their professional careers, there was a general lack of development for Latino/a film in the U.S. market.

An exception to this trend is Gregory Nava's 1995 film, *Mi Familia/My Family*, which enjoyed considerable attention and support from its initial release. This Chicano/a epic follows the multi-generational members of the Sanchez family living in East Los Angeles. Nava stresses the family bond in this film, reflective of the importance of generational interaction in the Latino community. The family in this film is capable of surviving any hardship, from deportation to death. The film is also an ode to the world of East Los Angeles and to the family home where family members live, die, and are literally buried. Of special note is the brooding and disaffected youngest brother, Jimmy Sanchez, played by Jimmy Smits. After seeing his older brother Chucho gunned down by the Los Angeles police, Jimmy becomes unreachable and turns to a life of crime. Nava is successful in matching the stark reality of Smits' character with the harshly lit scenes in prison, contrasted with the more active camera work that follows him down the bustling streets of East Los Angeles upon his release. Smits' performance evokes many of the lingering frustrations and contradictions of the Latino/a community in the United States. Betrayed by the institutions of his country and unable to relate to any real tradition, Jimmy Sanchez finds redemption through social engagement. He succeeds in saving himself only when he marries a young Central American immigrant to save her from the death squads that await her if she returns home. Reluctantly, he falls in love and they have a son together, though she dies during childbirth. Jimmy's ensuing attempt to connect with his son is a potent commentary on the relationship between fathers and sons in the Latino community. The themes of *Mi Familia* can be a catalyst for social studies teachers wishing to explore the generational violence that plagues many communities in the U.S., particularly the Latino/a community. While not specifically dealing with the issue of gangs that is so prevalent today, it provides a multifaceted perspective on some of the underlying causes of violence in the community and the effects on the families involved.

Interethnic Romance, Assimilation, and Gender Identity

While many of these films take place in the Los Angeles area, contributions by filmmakers working in the other major center of Latino/as in the United States, New York City, are significant. According to the 2000 Census, more people of Latino/a descent — 2.1 million — live in New York than in any other city in the country. The largest group among them is the Puerto Rican community. Not surprisingly, many of the films to come out of the city are focused on the plight of Puerto Ricans and other Caribbean American populations, such as Cuban Americans and Dominican Americans. The most famous of these from traditional Hollywood is *West Side Story* (Robert Wise, 1961), in which non–Latina Natalie Wood plays Maria, a young Puerto Rican woman in an interracial romance doomed by ethnic rivalries between Latino and Euro-American gangs. Literature students can analyze this film as an ethnic update on Shakespeare's *Romeo and Juliet*, and literature and social studies students can explore how it compares with other films as a reflection of changing ideas about inter-ethnic romance.

Films that dramatize choices between assimilation and tradition can be an effective means to initiate discussion about these issues in the social studies classroom. *Crossover Dreams* (Leon Ichaso, 1985) relates the story of Rudy Veloz, a popular local Salsa musician. Though he enjoys modest success in the local scene, Rudy, played by Rubén Blades, yearns for success in the commercial market. This is Rudy's coded attempt to assimilate into the larger Anglo community with his music — to cross over. Though he enjoys brief success, it is short-lived. The film successfully captures the experiences of Latino/as living in New York by showing the places where they live, work, and relate to each other. It also dramatically communicates the choices for Latinos between assimilating and maintaining their culture, one bringing expected financial rewards and the other ascribed with personal integrity.

Assimilation and the New York landscape get further treatment in *Hangin' with the Homeboys* (Joseph Vasquez, 1991), a film that follows a night out spent by four interethnic friends, two African Americans and two Puerto Ricans. The film's depiction of the relationship between the four friends highlights both identity and education issues. One of the friends, Vinny (whose real name is Fernando), tries to pass as an Italian American and receives consistent ridicule from his friends about it. Another of the group, played by John Leguizamo, is faced with the challenge of applying for college as a way out of his dead-end grocery clerk job. Throughout the film, we see his character struggle with this decision and ultimately make the necessary effort to apply for a college scholarship. The film offers a unique look at young urban men. It is as much about the emotional life of its characters as it is their macho-infused pretenses, which makes it an important film when dealing with the stereotypes of young urban men, so often maligned and feared by the popular media. Teachers should preview this film and may choose just to show excerpts, as it includes drinking, explicit language, and scenes with some sexual content.

Karyn Kusama's film *Girlfight* (2000) made a remarkable debut by winning two major awards at the 2000 Sundance Film Festival for best film and best direction. This story of a troubled teenage girl, Diana Guzman, whose frustrations lead her to boxing, subverts a number of common cinematic expectations. The character of Diana (played by Michelle

Rodriguez) is a refreshing new take on a young Latina who takes control of her life and succeeds against great odds (e.g., an abusive father, life in the projects, trouble at school). American culture and social studies teachers will find the film useful in providing a window into many of the issues confronting the urban Latino/a community. The success of Rodriguez's character in a sport traditionally associated with male dominance provides teachers with a good film for discussing gender issues and ethnic stereotypes. Rodriguez's little brother in the film is a good example of a Latino not interested in the macho ethic represented by boxing that his father attempts to instill in him. Kusama tells this story in a personal and intimate way that focuses on the life of the character and the world in which she lives. The cinematography is as stark as the buildings and environment Rodriguez's character lives in and around. Kusama also uses a number of extreme close ups to further reveal the emotional arc of Rodriguez's character. The result is a film about an unexpected subject that can initiate explorations of characterization, Latina identity, and film techniques for literature, social studies, and film studies students.

Students viewing these films will gain insights into the issues of assimilation and Latino/a identity, as well as the urban experience. Many of the films that take place in Los Angeles have an obvious nostalgia for the city and its history, as well as a preponderance of Mexican-American characters. The films set in New York tend to be entrenched in a contemporary urbanism with characters of Puerto Rican and Caribbean descent. The differences in the two locations are important to explore as a way of gauging some of the regional variations of culture, language, and heritage within the Latino/a community.

The Latino/a Working Class

History, social studies, and film studies teachers have a number of films to choose from as historically accurate and culturally sensitive representations of Latino/as as laborers in the U.S. This is a crucial concern since so much of the politics, culture, and history of Latinos/as in the U.S. has been driven by their membership in the working class. "The Struggle in the Fields," one of four episodes from the documentary *Chicano! History of the Mexican American Civil Rights Movement* (Hector Galon, 1996), chronicles the struggles of migrant farm workers to obtain decent living and working conditions with period photographs, film footage, and recollections from many of the farm labor leaders themselves. Feature films particularly worthy of study include *Salt of the Earth* (Herbert Biberman,

1953) and *El Norte* (Gregory Nava, 1983), which were made some thirty years apart and feature widely different lead characters and narratives. What each of these films share is their commitment to telling the stories of people driven to extreme measures to secure a basic level of dignity as workers.

Salt of the Earth is a film of historical importance appropriate for film studies, literature, history, and social studies students. Film studies teachers will want students to discuss the effectiveness of this feature film's documentary style and to place the film in its historical context. It was written by Michael Wilson and directed by Herbert Biberman, two members of the Hollywood community blacklisted for their resistance to the congressional inquiry into Communist activity in Hollywood. Deborah Silverton Rosenfelt and Michael Wilson's book *Salt of the Earth* contains Wilson's screenplay as well as background essays on the blacklisting of Hollywood figures and the making of the film as a representation of an actual miners' strike. Film studies and literature students can consider how the words of the screenplay become visual images. History students can explore the film as an empathetic representation of the true story of striking Chicano mine workers in New Mexico. And history and social studies teachers may want to have students discuss the film in terms of first amendment freedoms denied during the McCarthy era. The film depicts actual strike events: after a court injunction forces the men off the picket lines, the women in the community take up the strike. This film is an early example of feminist themes being seriously incorporated into any film. For this feature alone, it deserves study in the film studies, literature, history, and social studies classroom. As the women begin to walk the picket lines, the men in the community start to realize the amount of work involved with maintaining a household and raising children. There are few examples in the history of film that so poignantly express the dynamics of gender in the Chicano/a community. *Salt of the Earth* also enjoys the distinction of being a film about a labor struggle produced in collaboration with the community involved in the real events. Most of the actors in the film were actual members of the community and the mineworkers' union who had been directly involved in the strike.

The history of American labor and labor economics is incomplete without an examination of undocumented Latino/a laborers. *El Norte* follows the migration of Rosa and Enrique Xuncax, Mayan siblings from Guatemala who migrate to the U.S. after their father is murdered for attempting to organize the indigenous workers against the repressive government. Their tale is rife with the ironic realities of life in el Norte (the North), where things are not always what they seem. The trip itself almost gets them killed as they are forced to fend for themselves in the wasteland of Tijuana and then to make a harrowing journey through an abandoned sewage line to get to the U.S. side. The fact that these are Central American indigenous Indians provides a fertile juxtaposition with the Mexican and Latino/a characters with whom Rosa and Enrique come into contact. The protagonists, like their real-world counterparts, are differentiated from the larger community twice over. Not only is their first language not Spanish, but both the Mexicans and the Anglos in the film treat them as inferiors. This film, the first feature from director Gregory Nava, is a major achievement in many ways. Separated into three sections, *El Norte* employs a different visual and editing aesthetic in each of the sections. The first section is set in the lush countryside of Guatemala, and the cinematography reflects its brilliant colors and spare architecture. The editorial pacing is slow and considered. When the siblings start their trek north and arrive in Tijuana in the second section, the framing of the shots becomes tighter and the editing quicker. Finally, in the third section, the U.S. is shown in diametrically opposed visions: the serene wealthy neighborhoods and restaurants in which the siblings temporarily work contrasted with the crowded, rundown area of East Los Angeles where they live. For teachers wishing to introduce the issue of immigration into the U.S., there is no better and complex example than this film. The terrible tragedy of this film is that, by the end of the film, Enrique finds himself doing the same exploitative labor in the U.S. that his father was killed for resisting in Guatemala. The many mythical and cultural references layered throughout the film are invaluable examples of a culture that typically gets little coverage in mainstream media outlets.

Toward a New Media

Teachers intending to use films about Latino/as should be aware of several recent technological advances. Many of the films discussed in this essay resulted from an articulated effort on the part of their producers to tell stories that have traditionally been ignored or exploited by cinema in the U.S., stories that reflect the contributions and complexities of the Latino/a community. Some of the films deal with explicit historical injustices, such as *The Ballad of Gregorio Cortez*, while others focus on contemporary culture, such as *Selena*. Much of the effort of independent Latino/a media producers has been dedicated to basic issues of access to the production resources and distribution networks necessary to make a project creatively and financially viable. With the onset of the digital video explosion and the rapid promulgation of Internet access, some alternatives are appearing on the horizon. The combination of affordable production tools, in the form of DV cameras and desktop editing capabilities (many new computers such as Apple's IMac come with editing software preinstalled), and new Internet distribution channels is leading to a democratization of the kinds of media produced. Distribution may yet be the most critical front, as even today, many good films are shot yet will never be seen due to a lack of network or theatre distribution opportunities, which remain the domain of large corporations and are driven by tight market economics. The Internet is already home to many independent films streaming on various sites.[9] As technologies continue to get better and cheaper, video is becoming a truly accessible and affordable means of communication. As the tools become more available, it is critical that students be adequately equipped to analyze critically the visual media that surrounds them. It is also vital that students come to see themselves as participating in the construction of the media messages that are relevant to them. These young producers will one day create the images, texts, and narratives that define the nation. It is a responsibility that must begin with the teachers in the classrooms who educate them.

PART II

METHODS FOR TEACHING ETHNIC FILM IN AMERICAN HISTORY, SOCIAL STUDIES, LITERATURE, AND FILM STUDIES

5

Methods of Film Analysis

by Carole Gerster

In familiarizing themselves with the methodologies practiced in cinema studies and selecting those they find most useful in their own classrooms, teachers can educate their students to read films as carefully constructed texts and to respond critically to film representations of ethnic minorities. These methodologies include an examination of films as

- historical documents that (accurately or inaccurately) reflect the events, eras, and peoples they depict, and as products of the times in which they were made;
- cultural documents that reflect the customs, values, beliefs, anxieties, fears, and fantasies of the ethnic cultures from which they derive;
- adaptations of literary works that transform the written word into the visual image, and as film narratives that form the popular literature of our age;
- products of auteurs that reflect the particular ideas, concerns, and style of their directors;
- specific types of films—feature films, documentaries—compared with written literary, historical, or social analysis texts on the same topic or theme to understand that all texts are products of their times, use the conventions of their medium, and offer varying kinds of evidence and persuasions;
- creatively crafted products that adhere to or revise genre conventions and use the techniques of film to invite specific viewer response.

Whole Films and Film Excerpts

The question of whether to teach whole films or film excerpts often depends on the time it takes to show an entire film in class, especially if it requires several successive class days to complete because additional screening times are not feasible. Based on a number of assumptions — that the value of film is entertainment rather than information, that teachers are not actively engaged in teaching and students are not actively engaged in learning while viewing a whole film, and that class time is not being as well spent as it could be if students were involved in reading about or discussing a topic or practicing a skill — teachers are often reluctant to show whole films. Teaching students to read films critically, however, as they should be taught to read any text, actively engages them throughout the film screening. When students are given viewing guides to complete while watching — to which they can refer for text comparisons and writing assignments — and there are no completely darkened rooms, students must use critical thinking and viewing skills. Viewing guides can help students understand both the content and the form of a film by asking them to note such elements as plot details in feature films and chronology in documentaries, point of view in feature films and voice over in documentaries, and the distinctive techniques of each film type to convince viewers that what they are seeing is believable, such as reactive characters in feature films and the testimony of experts in documentaries. Teaching visual and multicultural literacy is an active process for both students and teachers and makes showing whole films a worthwhile learning experience.

A good guideline is to show a film in its entirety when teaching the film as a film and to show excerpts when teaching specific aspects about the medium of film. Just as anthologies contain excerpts (from literary works, from historical and cultural documents, and from social commentary texts) gathered under a particular topic, teachers can create an anthology of film excerpts on video to illustrate a topic of study in the history of film or to illustrate important film techniques. Creating a collection of film excerpts complies with copyright law if each excerpt is within a three-to-five minute length and is strictly for classroom use.[1]

Teacher-created collections of film excerpts serve a number of aims. Film excerpts are useful for reviewing a selection of scenes from a whole film already taught to encourage close readings of content, point out film techniques, and spark detailed discussions about specifics in a film that students are already familiar with. Or, combining comparable excerpts from a number of documentaries on the same topic (Japanese American Internment, for example) or on one incident in history (from the Civil

Rights Movement, for example) can initiate good discussions about how one event can be approached from a number of perspectives or how one incident can be represented in a variety of ways. Also, a video of excerpted scenes from a number of feature films is an excellent way to illustrate the film history of stereotypes for a particular ethnic group as well as challenges to those stereotypes. For example, excerpts can illustrate how some films simply repeat the stereotype of Latinos as gangsters and how other films repeat the stereotype to challenge it. Excerpts depicting scenes of the South American *bandido* in F. Richard Jones' (1928) *The Gaucho*, the Mexican *bandido* Gold Tooth and his shiftless men in John Huston's (1948) *Treasure of the Sierra Madre*, the Puerto Rican-American gang members in Robert Wise's (1961) *West Side Story*, the Cuban-American drug dealer in Brian DePalma's (1983) *Scarface*, and contemporary Latino gang drug dealers in Antoine Fuqua's (2001) *Training Day* can illustrate for students how Latinos have been stereotyped repeatedly as bandits since film beginnings. Additional excerpts— of the Mexican-American farmer mistaken for a bandit in Robert Young's (1983) *The Ballad of Gregorio Cortez*, the opening spoof of gang activity by Puerto Rican and African-American youth in Joseph Vasquez's (1991) *Hangin' with the Homeboys*, and the Mexican-American drug lord who cannot break the cycle of gang violence in Edward James Olmos' (1992) *American Me*—can further illustrate how both Latino and non–Latino independent filmmakers (operating outside the required profit-making formulas of Hollywood) have attempted to challenge the stereotype by dismissing it as a mistaken (or mistakenly chosen) identity. The same kinds of film history excerpts are equally useful for educating students about stereotypes of African Americans, Asian Americans, and American Indians, and about attempts to dismiss such blanket caricatures as false to reality.

Teaching students to both recognize and interpret the meaning of standard film techniques is yet another excellent use of video and film excerpts. Students are quick to learn that if they can read these techniques, they can know what a film is directing them to think. A viewing guide that lists film techniques and definitions (such as those in this book's Glossary) accompanied by film excerpts illustrating each technique is an effective way to teach students to recognize the techniques and interpret their use in a variety of films. For example, a teacher can help students understand the purpose and varying uses of a match cut, which is an editing technique where two shots with matching shapes (objects, people, or actions) are shown in immediate succession. Film excerpts illustrating instances of the match cut from early to recent films allow students to interpret its various uses, understand its effectiveness, and realize its continuing importance

The Birth of a Nation (D.W. Griffith, 1915). The first half of a Match Cut: The empty South Carolina Legislative Hall.

in creating meaning. In D.W. Griffith's (1915) *The Birth of a Nation*, viewers see a still photograph of an empty room from an 1870 South Carolina newspaper, identified by intertitles (words on the screen) as the place where the South Carolina state legislature met. Viewers then see history come alive via a match cut showing the exact same room but now filled with newly elected African Americans in 1871. The still photo part of this match cut serves as a historical document to convince viewers of the film's accuracy. What follows are scenes of African-American legislators eating chicken, drinking liquor, and going barefoot, scenes designed to discredit African Americans as incapable legislators that rely on the earlier match cut for believability. In Gregory Nava's (1983) *El Norte*, a brother and sister travel from Guatemala to Mexico to the United States. A match cut shows a truck in which they are traveling turn into a bus. Here viewers are encouraged to believe that they are watching reality: to understand that the trip is a long one and that they have witnessed some of the vehicles the immigrants traveled in. In Edward James Olmos' (1992) *American Me*, a match cut showing boys playing handball in reform school turns

The Birth of a Nation (D.W. Griffith, 1915). Scenes of African Americans as inferior and incapable legislators follow the Match Cut.

into a shot of the boys, now grown men, playing handball in Folsom Prison. The match cut suggests that the transition from reform school to prison is seamless for those who choose gang life. Mike Gabriel and Eric Goldberg's (1995) *Pocahontas* opens with a match cut: a drawing of England and a ship waiting to go to America turns into an animated drawing of birds flying across the landscape of England and the same ship. The drawing-to-animated drawing match cut invites viewers to think they are seeing history come alive. In Chris Eyre's (1998) *Smoke Signals*, a match cut ends a flashback scene of the protagonist being abused by his alcoholic father. It shows the protagonist as a young boy who enters his mother's house but turns into a teenager as he comes through the front door. Here the match cut suggests that the young man's life is built on memories of his now absent father. Asking students first to identify a basic technique, such as the match cut, in particular scenes and then to interpret how the technique is used to create meaning and invite viewer response initiates lively discussion and helps students to practice their visual literacy skills in order to make these skills a part of their everyday viewing habits.

Viewing whole films by and about ethnic minorities allows students to learn about both content and form, and thus to practice their multi-cultural and visual literacy skills. Studying whole films allows teachers to explore with their students how to read films about and by America's eth-nic minorities as texts that portray an event or an era, depict a cultural event, examine an idea or social issue, or convey a compelling story, and also to read films as texts that reflect the times in which they were made, promote the ideas of the filmmakers who made them, and use the tech-niques of the medium to persuade viewers to think likewise. For exam-ple, a good film to study gang life in 1990s America, violence in America, Latino life in East L.A., or representations of Latinos and violence in the gangster film is Edward James Olmos' (1992) *American Me*. The film was created during a time of increasing gang-related drive-by shootings in East Los Angeles. Olmos depicts Latino gang life from the point of view of a gang leader — with whom viewers are encouraged to identify — who learns that it is dangerous, self-destructive, and destructive of Latino/a families, community, and heritage, and who cannot escape the fatal consequences of his actions. To persuade viewers, *American Me* employs such film tech-niques as the match-cut described above to give visual expression to the

American Me (Edward James Olmos, 1992). The first half of the Match Cut shows boys playing handball in reform school.

American Me (Edward James Olmos, 1992). The second half of the Match Cut shows the boys, now men, playing handball in Folsom Prison.

all-too-common transition from reform school to prison for gang members. Also to persuade viewers, scenes of violence repeatedly focus on the aftermath of death and, with the use of reactive characters, the pain for families and loved ones. The usual thrills of gangster film violence remain but are challenged throughout with depictions of overwhelmingly negative consequences. Here, a typical gangster film becomes an anti-gang, social-message film ripe for student analysis and a means to teach multicultural and visual literacy.

6

History: Teaching Ethnic-
American History with Film

by Carole Gerster

Films are part of our nation's historical record. Films help create our (sometimes accurate, sometimes inaccurate) collective historical memories, and they are part of our nation's historical record of what was thought and felt at a particular time. In the history classroom, feature films and documentaries about and by ethnic minorities can help students to understand historical events and eras by experiencing vicariously what they cannot experience firsthand, to realize that all history is told from an interpretative point of view, and to learn how changing representations (including revisionist history) reflect and affect changing times.

Feature films and documentaries can be used in a number of ways to teach multicultural and visual literacy. Screening film versions of specific eras, events, and peoples in American history important to the ethnic groups studied and to the unfolding history of the nation at large can offer new perspectives and illustrate the numerous ways history can be told and visually experienced. Students are interested in whether historically based films are accurate and how they convince viewers to care about and identify with the people and events represented. A good analytical starting point is to have students consider how feature films invite viewers to empathize with the protagonist's point of view and how documentaries encourage viewers to identify with the voice over (off-screen voice) that explains what viewers see. Students can also examine the means by which conventions of realism (such as the use of authentic historical detail in costumes and settings) serve to suggest historical authenticity in general and the ways in which intertitles (words on the screen) attempt to establish historical authority. When teachers ask students to compare a feature film or documentary with what they have read about an historical event or person in their textbook or in supplemental readings, they encourage students to develop their analytical skills and to become careful readers of both visual and written texts.

Films are an important and appealing way to learn history, as dramatic stories in feature films and chronological overviews in documentaries give shape and meaning to historical events and eras. In "Movies as the Gateway to History: The History and Film Project," Paul Weinstein acknowledges that "film and television [are] the great history educators of our time," citing Robert Rosenstone's corroboration that "visual media have become arguably the chief carrier of historical messages in our culture."[1] In teaching ethnic films, teachers can engage students in current debates about the problems as well as the values of learning history from historical films. In a special supplement on "Film and History" in the film journal *Cineaste*, leading documentary and feature filmmakers, historians, and educators discuss both the commonalities and differences between written history and history on film based on their agreement about "the increasing role of the cinema in shaping the public's perception of historical events and processes." In discussions regarding what constitutes historical accuracy, these filmmakers and scholars consider the ideas that even eyewitness accounts do not provide consensus, that skewed history can occur in written as well as filmed accounts, that historical accounts in all mediums are subject to reevaluation based on the latest data, and that all history is a matter of interpreting that data and making choices in how it will be presented.[2] Teaching ethnic films as primary texts invites students to directly explore how the makers of historical documentaries and Hollywood and independent feature films make such choices. A survey by the American Historical Association showing that most Americans prefer historical films to written history[3] suggests the importance of studying films in the classroom as a preferred — and thus effective — means for students to learn American history and as a prelude to lifetime learning.

Teaching ethnic films and multicultural and visual literacy offers additional benefits. Examining films about and by America's ethnic minorities is not only a means to explore how films create history for the majority of Americans but also what constitutes American history at any a given time, whose perspectives prevail, and what additional perspectives come from those who do not represent the dominant Euro-American culture. By studying ethnic films as a medium that reaches millions of Americans, not just students of history, students can learn to appreciate the presence of the past, exploring how public memories of the past are as important as the past itself because they shape the future, and how public memories of the past come most frequently from film images.

Historical Films as Reflections of Their Times and Tellers

Studying films that disparage the role of ethnic minorities in American history can help students explore how films are historical documents that are — like other historical documents, including historical novels and history textbooks— affected by the circumstances of their time, the views of their tellers, and the conventions of the medium in which they are told. One of the first historical films ever made, D.W. Griffith's (1915) *The Birth of a Nation*, a silent film version of the antebellum, Civil War, and Reconstruction periods, is a film adaptation of Thomas Dixon's (1905) novel *The Clansman* but also includes Griffith's historical research of the era. Griffith's film includes quotes in intertitles of several passages from Dixon's novel and from President Woodrow Wilson's (1902) history text, *History of the American People*. Dixon's novel, Wilson's history text, and Griffith's film each contend that the Ku Klux Klan saved the South from threatening African-American predators, a popular belief at the time in the South (Dixon was from North Carolina, Wilson from Virginia, and Griffith from Kentucky), since refuted as fantasy prompted by fear in changing times. The film was made during one of the most violent periods in the history of race relations in the South and at a time when new Asian immigrants brought fears of social and political change in the North.[4] In a filmed interview that accompanies one print of *The Birth of a Nation*, Griffith reveals how his family history (his father was in the Confederate army and his mother sewed KKK costumes) influenced his beliefs.[5] Griffith included passages from President Wilson's history text to lend historical authority and legitimacy to his images, insisted on authentic detail in costumes and settings to suggest a more general historical accuracy, and created reenactments he labeled "historical facsimiles" to suggest that his characterizations and enactments were based on reality. Students can individually analyze and then discuss how Griffith's attempts at authenticity with costumes, props, settings, facsimiles, and intertitle quotes affect viewers' attitudes. After reading about the same eras in their textbooks, and perhaps also reading how Griffith's film differs from current understandings of the same events in historian Leon Litwack's essay in *Past Imperfect: History According to the Movies*, students can discuss differences between the techniques of realism and ideological accuracy.

History students can also examine films that are sympathetic to ethnic minorities as historical documents of the times in which they were produced and received. Background information about when a film was made and, if available, the filmmaker's intentions, can help students to

understand the ideas and attitudes from which it originated and to realize its (sometimes multiple) purposes. Ostensibly, Arthur Penn's (1970)
Little Big Man and Ralph Nelson's (also 1970) *Soldier Blue* are simply about
the U.S. government's early genocidal Manifest Destiny policies against
American Indians. Penn said that in *Little Big Man* he wanted to "challenge the glorification of the gunfighter and the simple proposition that
the cavalry was the good guys and the Indians the bad guys."[6] Penn's film
attempts to reverse the savage Indian stereotype by making the white soldiers the true savages. *Little Big Man* and *Soldier Blue*, however, were both
made during the time of widespread protests in America against the Vietnam War. Inspired by these protests and by their own anti-war beliefs,
both directors include atrocities against Indians as a metaphor for U.S. government actions in Vietnam. When Penn was asked if he intended any
parallels between his characterization of General George Armstrong Custer
and President Lyndon Johnson, he answered, "Possibly," and admitted that
historical accuracy in his portrayals of Native Americans wasn't a concern
beyond "transgressing violently or too egregiously" and wanting to avoid
getting "the wrong costume or something."[7] That filmmakers in general
pay more attention to the material details of historical representation than
to what actually happened is echoed by director John Sayles when he
says, "I probably use historians the way most directors use them: I tend
to use people who are well versed in historical details, very specifically in
the details, but not in the big picture" and he adds that "preserving the
spirit of what happened is really up to the filmmaker's abilities and intentions."[8]

Studying selected excerpts from *Little Big Man* and *Soldier Blue*, students can investigate how films reflect their own times and also come to
an understanding of the complexities of envisioning and analyzing history
on film. Armed with a textbook or other written and film accounts—such
as selections from Dee Brown's *Bury My Heart at Wounded Knee* and perhaps documents from Steven Mintz' edited collection *Native American
Voices*,[9] along with selections from a film documentary such as *The American Experience*'s (1992) *Last Stand at Little Big Horn* or the History Channel's *Little Big Horn: The Untold Story*, which are relevant for *Little Big
Man*—students can critically evaluate the accuracies and inaccuracies in
important scenes. Open to historical analysis are Penn's depictions of the
1868 Washita River, Texas, massacre and the 1876 Battle of Little Bighorn
that led to George Armstrong Custer's legendary status, as well as Nelson's
representation of the 1864 Sand Creek, Colorado, massacre. Students can
also discuss how the particularly graphic violence serves the anti-war message in both films. In considering these films as products of a particular

historical era, students can discuss audience reception in terms of whether or not Americans would have been receptive to the revisionist ideas in Nelson's and Penn's films—which characterized American Indians as victims rather than aggressors and criticized American's doctrine of Manifest Destiny as continuing in Vietnam — because they understood the movies' parallels with their own time. Juxtaposing John Wayne's (1968) *The Green Berets* with *Little Big Man* offers students an opportunity to explore how movies can be inspired by other movies. *The Green Berets* is a (pro–Vietnam) War film staged much like Wayne's Westerns and is filled with enough inaccuracies (including the sun fading into the east) to provoke a filmmaker like Penn to create a Western as a (anti–Vietnam) War film.

Teachers can also help students recognize the similar and reciprocal influence of film and other visual media as an important element of visual literacy. Before Penn's and Nelson's films were made, Eddie Adams' 1968 Pulitzer Prize–winning photograph of South Vietnamese General Nguyen Ngoc Loan executing a prisoner (alleged to be a Viet Cong captain) at point-blank range in Saigon had turned a number of Americans against the war. Both films echo this photograph with graphic scenes of U.S. Army officers shooting innocent Native Americans at extraordinarily close range. Nelson's depiction of the historical Sand Creek massacre includes a particularly brutal scene of a U.S. Army officer shooting a Native American child right beside him. Following the release of Penn's and Nelson's films, anti–Vietnam war imagery that captured the horrific nature of the war for Americans began to resemble images from their films. The child shot in Nelson's film has clear parallels with Nick Ut's famous 1972 (also Pulitzer Prize-winning) photograph of nine-year-old Kim Phuc running naked down the road screaming in agony from burns suffered in an aerial napalm attack on suspected Viet Cong hiding places. Also following Nelson's and Penn's films, a newly acquired sympathy toward what was largely assumed to be a Native American way of life forever lost was soon evident in a widespread media image of film star Iron Eyes Cody (who was actually an Italian immigrant rather than a Cherokee, as he identified himself[10]) as a crying Indian throughout the 1971 Keep America Beautiful campaign.

While Nelson's and Penn's were not the first history-based films depicting American Indians to have a political subtext, earlier films were not such sympathetic portrayals. John Ford's (1939, re-released in 1947) *Drums Along the Mohawk* takes place during the American Revolution and concludes with the news of Washington's defeat of Cornwallis at Yorktown, ending the war. Students can explore connections between the time Ford's film was made and its patriotic message. Ostensibly a film about ordinary people living through the Revolutionary era of the 1770s, Ford attempts to demonstrate that the colonists had faced and overcome hardships even more challenging than those of the Great Depression and had survived because of their belief in the American Dream. The protagonists are a young couple who settle successfully in New York's Mohawk Valley until barbarous Indians attack, burn their crops, and, aligning themselves with the British, threaten to destroy the settlement and the budding new country along with it. The film resolves everything simultaneously: the settlers emerge victorious over the Indians, the young couple inherits the prosperous farm they have been working on, and the colonists declare victory in the Revolutionary War. The film's conclusion reinforces the patriotic theme as its one African-American character, depicted throughout as an obedient and submissive house slave, and its one good Indian, depicted as a friend of the settlers and the enemy of other Indians, join a gathering of Euro-American colonists as reactive characters in admiration of the new American flag as "My Country 'tis of Thee" plays on the soundtrack.[11] The reassuring message to Euro Americans in *Drums Along the Mohawk* is not only about economic and wartime hardships; it also puts American Indians and African Americans in their supposedly happy-to-serve place in American history.

World War II Films

Students who trace representations of ethnic minorities in World War II movies will find both ethnically segregated and ethnically integrated platoons. Stanley Kramer and Mark Robinson's (1949) *Home of the Brave*, created in response to discrimination against African-American soldiers both during and following their service in World War II, depicts a black hero who suddenly finds himself in a white World War II combat platoon (a necessary fictional plot device since there were no platoons integrated with African Americans until the Korean War).[12] Students can analyze how this film challenges racial stereotypes, blatantly expressed by some of the Euro-American soldiers and internalized by the African-American protagonist, and then foresees a future of at least token racial integration in postwar America. The made-for-television film *The Tuskegee Airmen* (HBO, 1996) dramatizes the lives of African-American fighter pilots of the 99th pursuit Squadron, later incorporated into the 332nd Fighter Group, who were trained at Tuskegee Army Air Field in Tuskegee, Alabama. The 442nd all-–Japanese American unit is honored in a number of documentaries, but no feature films. In Hollywood films with ethnic minorities, Latinos occasionally played secondary characters, such as Desi Arnaz in Tay Garnett's (1943) *Bataan*. Anthony Quinn is a stereotypical Latin Lover in Lewis Seiler's (1943) *Guadalcanal Diary*, while Irving Pichel's (1945) *A Medal for Benny* shows a small town hypocritically honoring one of its Latino war dead after he is gone. In *The Outsider* (Delbert Mann, 1961) Tony Curtis plays Ira Hayes, the Pima Indian who helped raise the U.S. flag on Iwo Jima. A Euro-American actor playing the role of an American Indian adds another dimension to the issue of authenticity for history students to consider. More recently, Hollywood's *Windtalkers* (John Woo, 2002) includes a Navajo code talker as a secondary character. Students can analyze these depictions variously: as Hollywood's attempt to show how all Americans needed to band together to win the war, or to provide both new and old ideas about American diversity.

Historical Films as Social Influence

Some feature films offer a means to teach ethnic–American history as American history that helped reshape the conscience and the laws of the nation. Films about Japanese American Internment during World War II include John Korty's (1976) *Farewell to Manzanar*, a made-for-television movie based on a memoir of personal internment, and Alan Parker's (1990) *Come See the Paradise*, Hollywood's only direct depiction of internment. And films about the Civil Rights Movement include Alan Parker's (1988) Hollywood feature *Mississippi Burning* about the government's investigation into the deaths of three young Civil Rights Movement workers, and Roger Young's (1990) *Murder in Mississippi*, a made-for-television film about the lives and deaths of these three young civil rights workers who were killed in 1964. These four films all have something in common. As did the historical events of Japanese American Internment and the Civil Rights Movement, these films bring to light the inequities of ethnic discrimination in America for all Americans to understand, inequities that caused the internment of Japanese Americans and the need for equal rights laws sought by the Civil Rights Movement.

But simply viewing such films as history come alive for later review is insufficient since it promotes passive viewing that does not involve critical analysis. Teachers can help students understand how these and other films have educated and continue to educate the nation about the internment and the Civil Rights Movement and how they continue to act on the nation's conscience. Although largely about Japanese American Internment, Parker's *Come See the Paradise* features a Euro-American male protagonist with whom viewers are invited to identify and focuses on a love story between this besieged labor leader and his interned Japanese American wife. As a big budget, high production film, it offers both vast panoramic scenes and authentic details to give viewers the perception that they are actually witnessing the internment evacuation and resettlement of some 120,000 people. But it also adheres to the Hollywood convention of providing a white male protagonist to usher Euro-American viewers into a story supposedly about Japanese Americans. The same is true of Parker's *Mississippi Burning,* in which white male FBI investigators become the focus of the film, and of Penn's *Little Big Man* and Nelson's *Soldier Blue* (although the latter shares the spotlight with a white female protagonist, which students should note breaks with Hollywood convention but is appropriate for a film made during the one of the most vocal periods of the Women's Movement in America). Korty's and Young's made-for-television films, on the other hand, focus on the interned and the civil rights workers themselves so that viewers can learn their stories. Pairing Korty's and Parker's internment films, or Parker's and Young's Civil Rights Movement films, can help students to see how different points of view on the same events reveal that history, in film as well as in other media, is understood differently because of the multiple perspectives from which events can be seen.

Learning history through competing visions is a good exercise for students. In this case, a comparison of Parker's *Mississippi Burning* with *The American Experience* documentary *Freedom on My Mind* (Connie Field and Marilyn Mulford, 1994), made partially as a corrective to Parker's film, quickly reveals its distortions of history. Parker's depiction of the two white FBI agents, as dedicated to and successful in investigating the case of the missing civil rights workers and in fighting for black civil rights, ignores black activism and the FBI's actual obstruction of civil rights workers.[13] Beyond historical accuracy, there is another issue at stake here. When asked to determine "What is gained?" and "What is lost?" students can debate the effectiveness of Hollywood's white male protagonist convention to best inform a Euro-American audience about such events as the internment and the Civil Rights Movement against the argument that Hollywood tends to homogenize and limit the ways Americans think about U.S. history by ignoring the events of ethnic minority history until they are turned into heroic stories about Euro-American males.

Revisionist History

Students can understand the importance of revisionist history by exploring how key historical events are recast in feature films and documentaries that add previously unseen perspectives, include previously ignored people, and update historical understanding. Edward Zwick's (1989) *Glory*, for instance, is the first feature film to add the perspective of African-American soldiers to earlier film accounts of the Civil War. Although the film is narrated with the voice over of Colonel Robert Shaw, the youthful white abolitionist who led the all African-American volunteer unit of the 54th Massachusetts Infantry, the story highlights the injustices suffered and the steadfast heroics of the African-American troops. Instead of stereotypes, the film's central African Americans are character types: a country innocent, a northern intellectual, an angry runaway slave, and an intervening wise old man. Viewed in conjunction with Marlon Riggs' (1987) documentary *Ethnic Notions*, which traces the history of African-American stereotypes in popular culture, students can determine how the characterizations in *Glory* challenge such stereotypes by depicting black soldiers as individuals from a variety of backgrounds and with a variety of beliefs. Because historical films have a wider audience than written texts—as Mark C. Carnes bluntly observes, "For many, Hollywood is the only history"[14]—*Glory* quickly disseminated what was new information to a large public audience. With an awareness that *Glory* is generally acclaimed by historians for its historical accuracy despite some dramatic discrepancies,[15] students can compare written accounts, such as Louis Emilio's *A Brave Black Regiment: History of the 54th Regiment of Massachusetts Volunteer Infantry-1863–1865*, with the film to understand how the film has translated written historical records into a visual record. Practicing their visual literacy skills, students can note how the pageantry of period costumes recreates the appearance of the Civil War, how an exciting rush-to-combat long-shot vista dramatizes the bravery of the 54th, and how a visual metaphor (something natural to the scene that also serves a larger meaning) shows the dead bodies of the Euro American Colonel Shaw and his African-American soldiers falling into the same common grave to demonstrate for viewers the men's equality in death. A comparison of *Glory* with Jacqueline Shearer's (1991) film documentary *The Massachusetts 54th Colored Infantry* can help students consider how different film types portray the same topic and issues differently.

Revisionist history also includes films about previously ignored or misunderstood historical figures. Spike Lee's (1992) film biography *Malcolm X* has garnered both praise —for bringing the life and ideas of a pivotal and controversial figure in the Civil Rights Movement, black nationalism, and black pride politics into a wider consciousness than Malcolm X reached during his lifetime — and blame for its selective recounting. To decide for themselves the value of the film to inform viewers about

Glory (Edward Zwick, 1989). The Visual Metaphor suggests black and white equality in death.

the life and significance of Malcolm X, students can also view the PBS *American Experience* documentary *Malcolm X: Make It Plain* (Orlando Bagwell, 1993) and read Alex Haley's *The Autobiography of Malcolm X*, the told-to memoir on which the film was based, or various other accounts of Malcolm X's life, ideas, and influence, as well as historical critiques of the film.[16] Assigning a number of students to different viewing and reading tasks and then engaging them in a debate on the relative merits of Lee's *Malcolm X*— regarding authentic details included or omitted, accuracy and balance in presenting or omitting events and people in Malcolm X's life as well as Malcolm X's own changing ideas throughout his life, and the use of film techniques to guide viewer response — can bring students to a new understanding of how the life and ideas of one historical person have been presented or could be better presented to the American public. Debates could involve detailed comparisons. For example, short passages from Haley's autobiography and from Lee's screenplay compared to an excerpt of the same scene from Lee's film can yield fruitful discussions about point of view, historical accuracy, and the way the written word becomes the visual image. Students can discuss the film's *mise-en-scène* positioning of actor Denzel Washington (as Malcolm X) in specific places where Malcolm X actually spoke and the film's juxtaposition of black and white with color shots to give viewers the impression they are watching both old newsreels and the real life of Malcolm X, as just two of Lee's sev-

Malcolm X (Spike Lee, 1992). *Mise-en-scène*: Denzel Washington speaks in the same spot where Malcolm X spoke in Harlem.

eral attempts to convince viewers of his film's accuracy. These kinds of multifaceted, multicultural and visual literacy discussions can help students acquire portable skills for similar close analyses of other historical films.

By studying films depicting historical events, students can also learn that revisionist history involves more than adding previously neglected perspectives and persons. Like revisionist feature films, several documentaries serve to correct fictionalized versions of Manifest Destiny misrepresented in the Wild West images of popular Westerns. Joel Geyer's (1996) PBS documentary *In Search of the Oregon Trail* challenges commonly held notions about America's westward expansion found in such films as James Cruz's (1923) *The Covered Wagon*, Ford Beebe's (1939) *The Oregon Trail*, and countless Hollywood films thereafter. According to testimony from the documentary's experts, many of America's myths and misconceptions about relationships between pioneers and American Indian tribes along the Oregon Trail have come from Hollywood Westerns. Featured historian Patricia Limerick points out that, contrary to such films, "whites injured themselves more than they were injured by the Indians," "encounters of violence were quite rare," and Indians not only still exist but still suffer from the erroneous notions and ill treatment of the past. Students

The Covered Wagon (James Cruz, 1923). *Mise-en-scène*: Hostile Indians surrounding and attacking circled wagons suggest that American Indians are part of the landscape to be conquered.

can discuss the plausibility of Limerick's explanation of why such fictional film *mise-en-scène* images as circled wagons and Indians surrounding and violently attacking innocent pioneers proliferated and helped to form many Americans' beliefs about Manifest Destiny. Limerick suggests there is a Euro-American need to feel justified in the conquest, to make it appear that the Indians attacked and the settlers simply had to defend themselves. Both Euro-American and American-Indian experts in the film address the important need to remember the past accurately and to educate students about its complex realities—including both the hardships of the pioneers and the self-defense actions of American Indians.

Stereotypes and Controversial Representations in Revisionist Films

Hollywood history, including its revisionist history, often still relies on stereotypes that have little to do with historical reality. In comparing popular (and thus influential) early films with more recent ones, students can discover how ideas about Manifest Destiny and American Indians have and have not changed over the years. In John Ford's (1939) *Drums Along the Mohawk*, the protagonist is a Euro-American settler whose farm is destroyed by savage Indian antagonists in league with the British and whose family is rescued by the U.S. Army. In Kevin Costner's (1990) revisionist western *Dances with Wolves*, the Euro-American protagonist prefers the culture of noble Indians to serving in the U.S. Army, whose soldiers are now as savage as the savage Indians. Ideas about Manifest Destiny have changed. Both films, however, include the supposed positive stereotype of the Noble Savage Indian who befriends the hero: in *Drums Along the Mohawk*, the Noble Savage is one lone Indian named Blue Back; in *Dances* they are one band of Lakota Sioux. And both have Hostile Savages who attack both the hero and the good Indians: in *Drums*, the hostile Indians are the Iroquois; in *Dances*, the Pawnee. Recognizing these recurring and oversimplified portrayals of Indians can bring students to the understanding that stereotypes, whether positive or negative in terms of the film story, are still caricatures that deny full humanity to entire groups of people.

Controversial historical representations can challenge students to engage in discussions about how such representations could or could not be better imagined. Students can explore how feature films have created public memories of historical events that, even though they do not mindlessly repeat old stereotypes, are troublesome to historians. For instance, Steven Spielberg's (1997) *Amistad*, which depicts an 1839 slave revolt, offers students an opportunity to examine, discuss, and perhaps even debate its controversial representations and historical distortions[17] and to speculate how the slave revolt could be depicted so that the slaves are not the most frightening people on board the slave ship. Students can also discuss ways this film may, in spite of its inaccuracies and controversial images, help the American public understand some of the basic social, political, economic, and psychological aspects of slavery, especially during the period before the U.S. government outlawed the importation of African slaves.

Historical Allusions in Revisionist Films

Fictional feature films that do not claim to be historical depictions, yet allude to actual historical events, people, and even the iconography from earlier films, can also invite historical research and foster critical viewing. Michael Apted's (1992) *Thunderheart*, a film loosely based on 1970s events on the Pine Ridge Reservation, provides an occasion for students to research recent Lakota history through its allusions and to analyze the meaning of the allusions in the story the film tells. These include references to the Dawes Act of 1887, an allotment program which led to the loss of millions of acres of Indian land; to the beating death of Raymond Yellow Thunder by white vigilantes in Gordon, Nebraska, in 1972 and a subsequent court ruling of death by suicide, which brought protests of more than 1,000 Sioux from Pine Ridge Reservation, resulting in a new manslaughter verdict; to the American Indian Movement (AIM) referred to as the Aboriginal Rights Movement (ARM); and to the shooting death of AIM leader Anna Mae Aquash on the Pine Ridge reservation in South Dakota in 1976, for which Arlo Looking Cloud was convicted only in 2004. Analysis of a film's allusions helps students to understand how history informs films and how films can incorporate history to promote ideological sympathies, in this case, Apted's sympathies for American Indian land rights. Students can discuss how Apted's film includes a visual allusion to earlier films and how revisionist films such as this are often reactions to earlier films in order to change the way Americans have been shown to think. A pan shot (where the camera moves from left to right, or vice versa, along a horizontal plane) near the end in *Thunderheart* invites a new public memory of American Indians and settlers. An oft-repeated image of Indians in Hollywood Westerns, established in James Cruz's (1923) *The Covered Wagon* and repeated in hundreds of Westerns thereafter, shows them the first time they are seen in the film as suddenly appearing on a plateau as part of the menacing landscape to be conquered. Conversely, in *Thunderheart* the pan shot shows familiar Lakota characters from throughout the film suddenly appearing in large numbers on a high bluff in solidarity to ward off contemporary thieves of their land. Here, Apted achieves a reversal of both visual expectation and ideological message.

Historical Documentaries

Historical documentaries shown frequently in history classrooms across the nation are too often expected to be and too readily accepted as objective, factual documents simply because they are labeled documentaries and adhere to the conventions of the documentary. Students need to be aware that documentaries, like feature films, are products of their times, tellers, and techniques and that they are made to entertain and persuade as well as inform. Historical documentaries employ trusted faces or voices to introduce and narrate events, and voice-over explanations typically derive from a person not identified until the final credits, to suggest an unbiased authority. Documentaries provide other authorities through the testimony of some combination of experts in the field (their credentials identified in intertitles), participants, eyewitnesses, or descendants. And documentaries always show selected evidence in the form of documents (often archival photos, home movies, newscasts, or excerpts from feature films), collaborative artifacts, and geographical location shots to create a detailed yet coherent overall picture in a limited time. Documentaries, like any other historical account, are the result of someone selecting whose story to tell and how to tell it. Historical documentaries are, as John Grierson once called them, "the creative treatment of actuality."[18]

Revisionist Documentaries and World War II

Students can read a documentary as a documentary and learn about an often-neglected aspect of World War II — its domestic front — by analyzing Connie Field's (1980) *The Life and Times of Rosie the Riveter*. Field's film chronicles the personal lives and the discrimination faced by women factory workers during World War II, while also celebrating the women's spirit and resolve.[19] Students can discover how the film is revisionist history with a persuasive point of view, as they note how it juxtaposes period newsreel footage with more recent interviews of five women (two Euro-American and three African-American) "Rosies" to reveal discrepancies between official period media depictions and how actual public policy discriminated against women workers of other than European ancestry — with low wages, more dangerous jobs, and exclusion from child care and even shower facilities. Students can explore how documentaries can include and discredit earlier newsreel documentaries in order to revise historical understanding, in this case, by including the ethnic minority women workers' point of view. As with any historical account, students should be encouraged to ask, "With whose point of view am I being asked to identify?" and "What, if anything, is missing from this account, and why is the omission important?" to ascertain historical accuracy. Comparing Field's film with Sherna Berger Gluck's (1987) book *Rosie the Riveter Revisited*, to determine how each presents and privileges certain kinds of information, can help students become better critical viewers and readers.

Other revisionist documentaries of World War II also offer neglected ethnic perspectives and provide students with sources of new information, critical viewing, and American history discussion topics. William H. Smith's (2000) documentary, *The Invisible Soldiers: Unheard Voices*, chronicles the contributions of African-American soldiers in World War II and their battles after the war against continuing racial discrimination at home. *The Invisible Soldiers* notes that segregated units of African Americans have fought in every American war up to and including World War II and that some of the first D-Day combat units in the allied invasion of Normandy were African American, although in the popular movie *The Longest Day* (Ken Annakin, 1962) only a few black soldiers appear in the background for a few seconds after the fighting scenes are over, and in the box-office hit *Saving Private Ryan* (Steven Spielberg, 1998) there are no African Americans at all. A number of documentaries—Loni Ding's (1984) *Nisei Soldier: Standard Bearer for an Exiled People* and (1987) *The Color of Honor*, Joan Saffe's (1995) *Honor Bound: A Personal Journey*, and Steve Rosen's (1997) *Beyond Barbed Wire*—recover stories about World War II Asian American soldiers, focusing on Japanese Americans who left their families in America's internment camps to fight for a world free from such discrimination. And Lena Carr and Amy Wray's (1996) documentary *War Code: Navajo*[20] recounts Navajo Indians' vital role in World War II in devising a secret code from their native language that was used in the Pacific theater, from Guadalcanal to Iwo Jima to Okinawa, and was never broken. Knowing the conventions of the documentary, students can determine how these documentaries have chosen to portray ethnic minority contributions to winning the war and ending discrimination at home. Students can evaluate their effectiveness in informing, persuading, and even entertaining viewers with personal stories of individual heroism.

Comparative Analysis

War Code: Navajo can also serve as a comparison piece with John Woo's (2002) Hollywood feature film *Windtalkers,* about one Navajo code talker and his Euro-American companion and protector, who provides the conventional Hollywood white male perspective. The comparison (What's the same? What's different? What's missing? What's expendable as pure entertainment?) should involve form as well as content to ascertain some of the ways documentaries and feature films include different materials and present some of the same materials differently. To be critical viewers, students need to know what they are learning and how they are learning it. Adding the images and ideas of these revisionist documentary filmmakers to already familiar images of the World War II era at home and abroad, students can discuss the ironic complexities of a nation that fought for and promoted democratic principles abroad that were not yet achieved at home. Students of American democracy can explore how film helps viewers to understand that U.S. democracy is an ongoing process of inclusion visible in the changing representations in feature and documentary films.

A comparative analysis of how different film types depict the same topic can help students to understand similarities and differences in film forms and aid in reading history-on-film on their own. Mexican-American labor history offers examples of the comparative potential of the historical documentary and historical feature film. Hector Galan's (1990) documentary *Los Mineros* and Herbert Biberman's (1954) independent feature film *Salt of the Earth* are both about the history of and life within Mexican-American mining communities as seen through the eyes of the miners and their families. Both films point to contributions by Mexican Americans to America's economic growth, and both depict the hardships and discrimination they faced in gaining safety and sanitation rights granted other American laborers. Created by McCarthy-era blacklisted director Herbert Biberman, *Salt of the Earth* portrays an actual New Mexico strike by Mexican-American miners, chosen as subject matter that Hollywood would never approve. The film has the visual style of a documentary, achieved by employing features typical of the documentary — a hand-held camera, black and white film stock, actual striking miners as central characters with only a handful of professional actors, and voice-over narration to explain what viewers are seeing — to create a historical document in the form of a feature film. Similarities between the films' contents are striking, but so are their differences in form: *Los Mineros* uses the voice-over narration of an unseen authority and includes period photographs that focus on an entire community. *Salt of the Earth* uses the voice-over narration of Esperanza, the Latina protagonist, and focuses

Salt of the Earth (Herbert Biberman, 1954). Voice over: Esperanza narrates the story.

on her immediate family to dramatize their story and elicit viewer identification and empathy. Determining what they learned and how they learned it, students can discuss the individual merits of the documentary and the documentary-like feature film to provide historical information, hold viewer interest, and include memorable images and ideas.

Secondary sources provide an historical context for *Salt of the Earth*. Michael Wilson and Deborah Rosenfelt's book *Salt of the Earth* contains a record of how the film was made despite a number of hardships: the producer, screenwriter, director, and a major actor in the film were blacklisted by Hollywood, the filmmaking process was often seriously disrupted by Hollywood conservatives, the leading actress was deported to Mexico before the film was finished, and the film was immediately banned, all as a result of the U.S. government's 1947 HUAC (House on Un-American Activities Committee) hearings to root out any Communists that had infiltrated Hollywood. HUAC had decided that movies examining America's social problems served the Communist cause and could not be permitted. Students can screen *Salt of the Earth* to study the kinds of film images that, during this historical era of the Red Scare, HUAC feared would persuade Americans to accept Communist ideas. Christopher Koch's (1995) documentary *Blacklist: Hollywood on Trial* shows the HUAC Chairman announcing the committee's intent to expose "subversive elements" in movies "because the industry offers such a tremendous weapon for education and propaganda." Koch's documentary also shows *Salt of the Earth* director Herbert Biberman and others attempting to testify in defense of free speech. The documentary helps students understand both the historical context in which the feature film was made and the kinds of public and political fears that keep film representations of America's working class ethnic minorities off the silver screen.

Comparing different documentaries on the same topic can sensitize students to the numerous ways history is recounted on film and the varieties of the documentary form itself. Current written history of Japanese American Internment teaches students that President Franklin D. Roosevelt signed Executive Order 9066 authorizing the mass incarceration of 120,000 Japanese Americans during World War II, that two-thirds were American citizens and over half were children or infants, and that forty-six years later the U.S. government officially apologized for what it recognized as a "grave injustice" and paid reparations to those still living. But internment documentaries also provide individual faces and experiences to capture the human history that lies behind the facts.

Films about Japanese American Internment most often focus on personal histories, as Japanese American internees and their children and grandchildren tell their own stories to come to terms with their past and share it with viewers. Lise Yasui's (1988) documentary *Family Gathering: A Search for a Japanese American Past* is told from the perspective of a third-generation Japanese American who grew up with little understanding of her ethnicity or awareness of the traumas of prejudice and internment her family experienced. Yasui's film focuses on her grandfather Masuo Yasui who, after thirty years in the U.S., was arrested by the FBI as an enemy alien after the attack on Pearl Harbor. Her film reflects her research into the lives of her family members prior to, during, and after Pearl Harbor and internment, using photographs, home movies, and interviews to reconstruct her personal family history. Rea Tajiri's (1991) experimental documentary *History and Memory: For Akiko and Takashige* juxtaposes fragments of memory from family photos and footage of her own visit to the site where her mother had been interned with government and Hollywood films of the period. The juxtapositions explore how media images create public memories and suggest ways in which private histories can create new media images and new public memories of Japanese American Internment. Stephen Holsapple's (1999) *Children of the Camps* features roundtable discussions with unrelated Japanese American adults who were interned as children to show the lasting consequences of their internment and their efforts to come together to heal their lives.

Japanese American Internment's relation to legal history and to the aftermath of 9/11 in 2001 are the focus of other documentaries. John De Graaf's (1992) *A Personal Matter: Gordon Hirabayashi vs. the United States* retains the personal story format, chronicling Hirabayashi's forty-two-year struggle to overturn his conviction for refusing to be interned on the grounds that Executive Order 9066 violated his constitutional rights, and discusses basic protections of the U.S. Constitution. Students can discuss the importance of civil rights activists such as Hirabayashi and internment filmmakers such as De Graaf in exposing the unconstitutionalities of internment to ensure that it does not happen again — to any Americans. A more recent documentary, Lois Shelton's (2003) *After Silence: Civil Rights and the Japanese American Experience*, focuses on Frank Kitamoto, who spent three and a half years of his childhood in an internment camp, and looks at Japanese American Internment through the lens of 9/11. Kitamoto and five students discuss the need to safeguard our constitutional rights, especially in times of uncertainty and fear. Jason DaSilva's (2003) documentary *Lest We Forget* also connects violations against Japanese American's civil liberties with the aftermath of 9/11, while Sharat Raju's (2003) short narrative *American Made* explores issues of cultural assimilation and national identity for a South Asian American (Singh) family stranded in an Arizona desert when their car breaks down and the son remarks that his father won't get a ride because his turban makes him look like a terrorist. If a reason to learn history is to avoid past mistakes, internment history — especially in light of the U.S. war against terrorism — is a relevant example of the need for Americans to understand their past.[21] From a point of view very different from all of these documentaries, The Department of War Information's (1942) newsreel documentary *Japanese Relocation* presents the government's 1942 position on internment, claiming that Japanese Americans willingly abandoned their businesses and homes for their own protection and were being treated well.

Students can easily determine how each of these documentaries on Japanese American Internment has a point of view. The perspective defending internment in *Japanese Relocation* is from the government official, Milton Eisenhower, in charge of explaining the government's actions as positive. Students can discuss the government film's historical accuracy based on the "What's missing?" question, comparing what it says regarding its motives for the internment and how internment was accepted by Japanese Americans to accounts in classroom textbooks, in individual books such as *Japanese Americans: From Relocation to Redress*,[22] and in film documentaries researching the reasons behind the mass incarceration such as Emiko Omori's (1999) *Rabbit in the Moon*. Teachers may want students to discuss the war panic that rekindled old Asian stereotypes (often replayed in movies as inscrutable Asians embodying the Yellow Peril stereotype who want to take over the world) and hearsay evidence of Japanese Americans spying for Japan, compared to how *Japanese Relocation* defends the internment decision on other grounds to the American public. Students can contrast the government's official position with the perspectives of those who experienced and suffered the consequences of internment as represented in the documentaries. Contrasting the two positions can help students to understand the importance of adding Japanese American images and voices to the historical record in order to set the record straight.

Slavery is another topic appropriate for a comparative analysis. Documentaries, feature films, and history textbooks and other written accounts allow students to discover various perspectives, discern similarities and differences in different accounts, and analyze the variety of ways slavery has been represented. The (2004) HBO documentary *Unchained Memories: Readings from the Slave Narratives* draws on personal accounts from and photographs of ex-slaves gathered during the Depression by the Federal Writer's Project, when about 100,000 of the four million slaves freed by the Civil War were still living. Whoopi Goldberg narrates and prominent African-American actors read from narratives in the vernacular of the time. Students can discuss how these direct accounts reveal the physical, mental, and moral violence of slavery. Orlando Bagwell's (1989) PBS *The American Experience* documentary *Roots of Resistance: A Story of the Underground Railroad* describes slave life, shows escape routes, depicts the subversive actions of slaves who ran away, and includes personal recollections of descendants of fugitive slaves, slaveholders, and network activists. Jonathan Demme's (1998) feature film *Beloved* depicts fugitive slaves, slaveholders, and network activists; recounts an escape; and features a fictionalized version of a an actual escaped slave (Margaret Garner) who, when about to be recaptured, killed one child and attempted to murder two others to keep them from the horrors of slavery. Teachers can select and students can examine comparable excerpts from the films to determine how the history of slavery is taught differently for the audiences of different mediums and can discuss the effectiveness of each in providing them with new information. Placing one or more of these films alongside a written memoir, such as the *Narrative of the Life of Frederick Douglass* (1845) or Harriet Jacobs' *Incidents in the Life of a Slave Girl* (1860) or written historical accounts such as John W. Blassingame's *The Slave Community: Plantation in the Antebellum South* or Charles Blockson's *The Underground Railroad*[23] provides students with a range of films and written materials to examine how the history of slavery can be told in numerous ways and from various perspectives to reveal new insights.

Another approach to provide students with a better understanding of both slavery and its representations is to compare feature films on the subject. Charles Burnett's (1996) *Nightjohn* and Jonathan Demme's (1998) *Beloved* each invite viewer identification with the perspectives of those who were enslaved and illustrate a variety of ways in which the horrors of slavery can be represented. Burnett's *Nightjohn* presents a number of differing perspectives, including those of a nine-year-old slave girl who learns to read and a slaveholder's son who befriends a slave his own age and refuses to whip him when his father orders him to do so. Students can discuss, and even debate, the necessity for film violence in depicting the brutalities of slavery by comparing the efficacy of scenes in Burnett's *Nightjohn* and Demme's *Beloved*. In *Beloved*, intercuts (shots of something outside the locale or time typically inserted in a scene as a flashback to show what a character is thinking) show the physical violence of slavery as residual psychological horrors that continue to haunt the protagonist's thoughts. In the scene where Sethe (Oprah Winfrey) describes her successful escape to another former slave, she remembers in brief and audience-jarring intercuts what she saw and experienced, including her visualized memories of other slaves caught, tortured, and hung, and her own breast milk stolen by the overseer's sons. In *Nightjohn*, a match cut (where two shots with matching shapes, objects, people, or actions are shown sequentially to suggest a relationship) depicts a young man lying face down to have his back whipped for leaving the plantation without a pass that suddenly becomes the young man in the same prone position having his back wounds treated by fellow slaves. Here the match cut allows viewers to learn about the violence used to maintain slavery without having to see it. Demme and Burnett agree that to understand slavery is to understand its physical and psychological brutalities, and their films open for discussion the issue of how to represent that violence. If the topic of discussion is the issue of what film violence teaches viewers about historical violence, excerpts from these two films provide students with specific evidence to compare.

History as Representation

That multiple versions of any one historical event coexist is evidence that history (in textbooks, personal memoirs, and novels as well as historical documentaries and feature films) cannot mirror that event but consists of constructions from what facts are available. Charles Burnett's film about Nat Turner, the leader of the notorious 1831 slave revolt, demonstrates that history is reconstruction. Burnett's *Nat Turner: A Troublesome Property* (2002) is about Nat Turner as a troublesome piece of property for slave owners and as a troublesome property for historians to explain. Little is known about the man, and the earliest written account, *The Confessions of Nat Turner*, was assembled from a series of jailhouse interviews by a white Virginia lawyer rather than written by Turner himself. Burnett's independent and experimental film is both a documentary, with historians presenting various ideas about Nat Turner, and a series of dramatic representations with different actors playing the role of Nat Turner. The film establishes that the figure of Nat Turner became a metaphor for discussion whenever racial tensions flared. In the case of this slave and this revolt, history is clearly uncertain; because historians cannot establish a definitive past, they struggle in their attempts at historical reconstruction. Students easily discern that this film is about the multiple ways that Nat Turner and his violent slave revolt have been remembered, interpreted, and represented. And students can just as easily understand that Burnett's multiple representations tell viewers that, although the man actually lived and the revolt actually took place, historical meanings come only through representations that reflect the times and perspectives from which they were created. History is its representations.

Multiple film versions of another historical event known as "the Alamo" continue to generate public debate about the meaning of the event itself through the meanings its film representations offer. Debates over the details of the 1836 thirteen-day siege and its aftermath have occupied both historians and filmmakers for decades, but it is the film representations that create and recreate meaning for the American public. This event has been depicted on film many times, beginning with the early silent (1911) *The Immortal Alamo*, followed by *Martyrs of the Alamo* (a 1915 epic produced by D.W. Griffith and echoing the racism of his 1915 *The Birth of a Nation*), and continuing with a siege of films that present unblemished Americans as patriotic heroes: *Davy Crockett at the Fall of the Alamo* (1926), *Heroes of the Alamo* (1936), *Davy Crockett, King of the Wild Frontier* (1955), John Wayne's ultra-patriotic *The Alamo* (1960), and *Alamo: Thirteen Days to Glory* (1987).

Students can analyze the latest version, John Lee Hancock's (2004) *The Alamo*, as revisionist history when compared to any of the earlier films. Erick Hoover's article "Myth Understood" describes how Hancock's desire to avoid an ahistorical film (with romances and subplots and guns from a different era in earlier Alamo films) led him to consultations with historians and adherence to history texts that helped him to get the details — down to the dialogue, the set, and "the buttons on the soldiers' uniforms" — right. Some details, however, such as the design of the Mexican helmets and the accuracy of the historical account that says Davy Crockett did not die fighting but was executed after the siege, were matters left to the director. Choosing to depict Crockett's death as an execution signals Hancock's film as revisionist history that attempts to get the history right by following an early (but disputed) written account. Students can view the earlier films as well as this latest version as reflections of their directors' intentions and the times in which they were created. Since historical accuracy has come to mean that the same event can be seen differently from different perspectives, Hancock's *Alamo* nods to perspectives other than Euro-American ones. Hoover's article reports that, unlike earlier films, Hancock's *The Alamo* reflects the "perspectives of diverse characters, including that of Juan Seguin, a Mexican-born soldier who fought against the Mexican army," to suggest "that the Mexican side of the story was many faceted," and Hancock not only includes the fact that "[Jim] Bowie and [William Barrett] Travis both owned slaves" but adds these slaves as "characters who discuss their plight." But Hoover's article also makes it clear that Hancock "did not want to turn the movie into a history lesson" and thus decided to "embrace" both the "mythology of the Alamo" and "the new facts historians have learned" and thus once again made the Americans the heroic focus. Hoover describes a scene revised from earlier films: as the men in the Alamo turn to Davy Crockett for inspiration, "instead of delivering a pep talk, Crockett, haunted by his experiences fighting in the Creek War, recalls the sight of Indians burning alive in their houses."[24] Realistic? Probably not. Heroic? Certainly. Although the new Davy Crockett is a flawed hero, he remains a hero, a somewhat reformed man with a conscience, much like today's America. The new Crockett is the old Crockett sanitized in a new way to allow today's viewers to continue to believe in the glory of their old heroes and their own flawed past in light of what this film suggests should be their own newly reformed conscience.

The Interdisciplinary Nature of Film

Films, including those about historical eras, events, and peoples, are inherently interdisciplinary. All films invite historical analysis because they are the products of and reveal attitudes of the times in which they are made, and films about historical topics can easily move beyond the history classroom. Films used to study slavery in history courses can also be taught in social studies, literature, and film studies courses. The documentary *Roots of Resistance: A Story of the Underground Railroad* provides written study questions and follow-up activities appropriate to social studies topics and issues, including suggestions for researching Supreme Court decisions, to learn the impetus for and impact of legal decisions; ideas for researching slave songs, to learn how they were used to protest slavery and as paths to freedom; and actual maps of routes and refuges, to learn which were slave and which were free states and which routes were more frequently used because of geographical features. The feature film *Beloved* is an adaptation of the (1987) novel by Toni Morrison and *Nightjohn* is a film adaptation of the (1993) adolescent novel by Gary Paulsen.[25] Novel and film comparisons are especially appropriate in literature and film studies classrooms, where students can discover how the written word becomes the visual image — how, for instance, written descriptions of the protagonist's memories in Morrison's novel become sound-enhanced visuals seen in flashback intercuts in the film to allow viewers to experience for themselves what the protagonist is thinking and feeling. While the specific fields of study differ in their goals for students, the historical background, social and cultural issues, and fictionalized and documentary versions of real events and people can combine in ethnic film study in each field to give a more complete picture of any ethnic studies topic.

Students' film and video productions need not be limited to film production courses, as the less than ten-minute (1996) Minnesota History Day video *Cultivating the Wildflower: Indian Boarding Schools* demonstrates. This student-made video records their prize-winning History Day presentation, which was inspired by Bruce Pittman's (1989) *Where the Spirit Lives*, a feature film about children brought to a government-initiated, church-run boarding school for Indians in Canada. In Pittman's film, while working in his garden, The Reverend who runs the school explains to a new teacher his educational philosophy regarding acculturating Indian children with a visual and verbal metaphor about cultivating the wildflower. "Wildflowers," he says, "are nothing but weeds.... I must scrape every trace of the old soil from their roots ... and cut them back often or they will return to the wild." The new teacher, who serves as a reactive character (a character who guides viewers to respond likewise), is shocked that he would treat "living, breathing human beings" as if they were weeds. Using the Reverend's words as the central metaphor of their project, the high school history students re-dramatize the misguided philosophy of both Canadian and U.S. governments to remove American Indian children from their homes in order to be assimilated into the dominant culture. These History Day students clearly responded to the reactive character as the filmmaker intended, demonstrating the power of film to affect viewers emotionally as well as intellectually. As the editor of *Past Imperfect: History According to the Movies* says, many of the historian authors of *Past Imperfect* essays "acknowledge that movies were what attracted them to history as youngsters."[26] In-class as well as History-Day presentations can benefit from creative history students who have learned specifics of history from film and can demonstrate their historical knowledge and visual literacy with their own productions.

7

Social Studies: Teaching Ethnic-American Topics with Film

by Carole Gerster

In the social studies classroom, feature films, short narratives, docu-dramas, and documentaries about America's ethnic minorities allow students to temporarily enter and virtually experience contemporary cultures other than their own, often from ethnic minority perspectives. For students who do not know firsthand about American ethnic cultures other than their own, films can invite identification with otherwise unfamiliar faces and can provide background information and understanding of otherwise unfamiliar cultural practices. From films, students can also learn about their own cultures and cultural histories, often from perspectives they may not otherwise encounter and often highlighting issues they may not otherwise have the means to consider. For high school and undergraduate college students, issues of ethnic identity, acculturation, and assimilation dramatized in film are of particular interest in providing ways to imagine their own roles in American society. Feature films and documentaries also offer a pictorial and attitudinal record of stereotypes as well as challenges and alternatives to stereotypes. This film record is essential to understanding the ways ethnic prejudice has been practiced in America, and it offers students the chance to experience vicariously the harm it can do to individuals, communities, and the nation itself. In studying how ethnic minority representations are defined by their time even as they help to define it, social studies students can explore the ability of films to educate — to change minds, attitudes, and social policies— and even to enact social justice.

Ethnic Heritage and Identity

Films that attempt to establish and record an ethnic–American identity can take students into ethnic minority cultures and illuminate ethnic issues. Although Latino/a communities are themselves diverse, films about shared cultural practices demonstrate a shared ethnic heritage even as they highlight individual issues. Non-Latina Susan Orleans's essay about and titled "Quinceanera,"[1] provides other non–Latino/as with background reading from the perspective of someone learning about cultural practices outside her own experience, while several films provide an insider perspective. In Victoria Hochbert's (1990) *Sweet 15*, a made-for-television, after-school special, a Mexican-American girl in California who is eagerly planning her *quinceanera* (the traditional Latin-American fifteenth-year birthday mass and celebration that ushers a girl into adulthood) discovers that her father is an undocumented Mexican-American immigrant seeking amnesty. This knowledge interrupts her plans and changes her sense of self. Viewers learn as she learns of the difficulties for undocumented workers to become U.S. citizens, and viewers celebrate as she celebrates her *quinceanera* and her successful efforts to help her father. Students can examine how this feature film invites them to understand Latino/a heritage and issues of Mexican-American immigration and amnesty citizenship from the point of view of a young Latina. Elizabeth Schub's (1997) short narrative *Cuba 15* takes viewers to Cuba for the same celebration and includes a two-minute interview with the filmmaker explaining the importance of the *quinceanera* for the entire family. *Home* is the title of another fictional film that depicts a *quinceanera*, this time in New York City, in one of four short narrative segments in David Riker's (1998) *La Ciudad (The City)*. Here the focus is on a young man from Mexico who is new to and lost in the city and happens upon the familiar cultural ritual. *Home* is filmed in black and white and a documentary newsreel style to give viewers a you-are-there experience of alienation and confusion in an unfamiliar land of tall buildings and complex regulations that often accompanies the immigrant experience. This film allows students to experience the *quinceanera* from the young man's point of view as a familiar one that evokes the feeling of home. Films such as these about the same cultural event can take students into an ethnic culture, even when that culture is spread out across and beyond America, and reveal different perspectives and a multitude of social issues worthy of discussion in the social studies classroom.

Some films provide this kind of cross-country, inter-ethnic coverage, while others focus on differences within just one community or even one family. Films about the diversity of Asian American experiences and identity work to counter stereotypes, as viewers learn about the various backgrounds, experiences, and views of people within different Asian American communities as well as from different people within the same community. Renee Tajima-Pena's (1998) documentary *My America ... or honk if you love Buddha* is an on-the-road journey across America to discover what constitutes Asian American identity. This documentary also provides students with a you-are-there experience, as viewers discover along with Tajima-Pena the diversity of Asian Americans. Viewers travel with her, for example, to New Orleans to visit with eighth-generation Louisianan Filipinos who describe growing up as "honorary whites" in the Jim Crow South, to Mississippi to talk with Yuri Kochiyamato who was incarcerated in a World War II internment camp for Japanese Americans and became a civil rights activist, and to Seattle to meet Korean rappers known as The Seoul Brothers. Students can discuss how *My America* provides them with firsthand experience of both Asian American ethnic and generational diversity. The film ends with Tajima-Pena's own marriage to a Latino, showing how diversity within Asian America is taking on new meaning. From Christine Choy and Renee Tajima's earlier (1990) documentary *Yellow Tale Blues: Two American Families,* students can also learn about diversity among Asian Americans. Here, the filmmakers turn the camera on their own families: the Choys, an immigrant, working class family, and the Tajimas, a fourth-generation middle-class family, to demonstrate their differences. *Searching for Asian America* (Donald Young, Sapana Sakya, and Kyung Sun Yu, 2004) is a series of three short films, including *Oklahoma Home,* which is about two Filipino American doctors practicing medicine in the same small town who disagree about whether the Philippines or America should be considered their home. Centering on differences between family members, Alberto Justiniano and Roger Schmitz's (1996) *Portraits from the Cloth* is a narrative about Hmong immigrants, based on stories by Xiong Vang, that reveals how family members disagree about the value of retaining cultural traditions or assimilating into the dominant culture. These films bring viewers into Asian American communities and families to reveal both ethnic diversity and individual differences.

Teaching Documentary Films to Identify Stereotypes

Documentaries are particularly useful in developing an important aspect of multicultural literacy: helping students recognize recurring ethnic stereotypes in films and other mass media. When unrecognized and unnamed, these repeated caricatures can easily slip by unnoticed as natural to the situation, the stories, and (when there are not enough alternative images available to contradict them) even to reality. Once identified and thus made identifiable, stereotypes can be challenged as such. Students can use these documentaries as starting points to recognize stereotypes in films of the past and present and to discover how a number of filmmakers are challenging such caricatures and attempting to envision a viable ethnic identity in their stead. And students can also examine the documentaries themselves to discover how they offer their own challenges to stereotypes in their attempts to move images of ethnic Americans from object and victim to self-defined subject.

Identifying African-American Stereotypes, Challenges, and Alternatives

Marlon Riggs' (1987) documentary *Ethnic Notions* identifies, defines, and illustrates six demeaning stereotypes of African Americans, including the seemingly benign Mammy and Uncle. As described in *Ethnic Notions* and depicted in popular culture and hundreds of Hollywood feature films, the Mammy stereotype is a heavy-set and very black African-American woman who generally has no family of her own and is always happy to serve Euro Americans. The Uncle Tom stereotype is the male equivalent to the Mammy. According to *Ethnic Notions*, he, too, is happy to serve whites and recognizes the supposed superiority of Euro Americans and Euro-American culture. The Mammy and Uncle are so-called positive stereotypes (not positive depictions) because they were seen by Euro Americans as commendable. As *Ethnic Notions* demonstrates, these caricatures were repeated in songs, drawings, cartoons, games, children's books, advertisements, household notions, and films to promote the idea of African Americans as happy slaves and then, following slavery, as contented servants.

Students can note definitions of and identify the Mammy and Uncle in *Ethnic Notions* and then find these stereotypes for themselves in a number of Hollywood films. In D.W. Griffith's (1915) *The Birth of a Nation* all of the African-American stereotypes defined in *Ethnic Notions* appear in readily recognizable form. In Griffith's film, the faithful Mammy and Tom slaves (ironically) save their white master from arrest for his role in helping form the Ku Klux Klan. Students can find the Mammy and Uncle again in mid-century films. In David Butler's (1935) Shirley Temple plantation film, *The Littlest Rebel,* the faithful Uncle takes care of his white master's child when her Confederate father is imprisoned by Yankees during the Civil War. He is not interested in his own freedom: he says he just doesn't know what emancipation is all about. And in John Ford's (1939) *Drums Along the Mohawk,* the faithful Mammy slave looks admiringly at the newly raised American flag, following the revolutionaries' victory at film's end, to signify her belief in the Euro-American settlers' supposed superiority in the new slave-holding nation. To help students understand the pervasive nature of such stereotypes, teachers can point to current packages of Aunt Jemima pancake mix and Uncle Ben rice, both of which continue to showcase (modernized) pictures of smiling African Americans seemingly still happy to serve. Reviewing the segment of *Ethnic Notions* where Aunt Jemima is shown in successive updates, each change giving her a more contemporary appearance, can highlight for students how updated versions make old stereotypes appear natural to the times.

To become aware of the lingering and pervasive use of these stereotypes in film, and of how specific films repeat or challenge them, students can trace recurrences from early films to the present. Versions of the docile

Drums Along the Mohawk (John Ford, 1939). Reactive Character: The Mammy slave admires the U.S. flag.

Black Mammy not only appear in early and mid-century films, including Victor Fleming's (1939) still popular *Gone with the Wind*, but also continue into our own times. The stereotype is updated to match the social mores of the times in such popular films as John Stahl's (1934) *Imitation of Life* and Douglas Sirk's (1959) *Imitation of Life* remake, is stubbornly intact even in films designed to negate other stereotypes such as Robert Mulligan's (1962) *To Kill a Mockingbird* and Stanley Kramer's (1967) *Guess Who's Coming to Dinner*, is significantly revisioned in Richard Pearce's (1990) *The Long Walk Home*, is completely dismissed in Julie Dash's (1991) independent film *Daughters of the Dust*, is reinstated with a revised romantic ending twist in Jessie Nelson's (1994) *Corrina, Corrina*, and is again simply repeated in Roland Emmerich's (2000) *The Patriot*. The acting talents of Hattie McDaniel in her role as Mammy in *Gone with the Wind*, which won her the first Motion Picture Academy Award for an African American, problematize the issue of why actors would agree to play such roles. Excerpts of McDaniel's performance can serve to initiate a nuanced student discussion about actors' attempts to humanize the stereotyped roles offered them and about the kinds of roles that Hollywood considers worthy of recognition and reward. Students who trace the Uncle Tom stereotype will also find stereotyped depictions continuing to merit Hollywood rewards. Bruce Beresford's *Driving Miss Daisy* (1989), with Morgan Freeman playing an obliging chauffer, won the Academy Award for Best Picture, and playing a self-sacrificing, happy-to-serve-whites role in Frank Darabont's (1999) *The Green Mile* won Michael Clarke Duncan an Academy Award. These films were followed by Robert Redford's (2000) *The Legend of Bagger Vance*, where Will Smith plays a role somewhere between an Uncle Tom and a Sambo, a new combination of old caricatures given new life.

Other popular stereotypes identified in *Ethnic Notions* include the Sambo and the Coon. These are both buffoon caricatures, distinguished one from the other by ambition or lack thereof. The Coon attempts to adopt and adapt to white culture, but he soon demonstrates that he is an inferior being incapable of assuming a place of equality in a white man's world. The Sambo is lazy and irresponsible and, when he has one, is ruled by his wife. Students can recognize both caricatures in Griffith's depiction of the Reconstruction era in *The Birth of a Nation*, where a bi-ethnic (the "mulatto") character named Silas Lynch rises to the position of Lieutenant Governor of South Carolina, tries to usurp power from whites, and decides to marry a white woman to create an empire. Whites find Lynch guilty of abusing his power, strip him of his position, and save the white woman from his clutches. Other Coon stereotypes in *The Birth of a Nation* include the newly elected African-American legislators, who spend their time eating chicken (and tossing bones on the floor), drinking liquor, and putting their bare feet on their desks, and other anonymous characters who stuff the ballot box and keep whites from voting. They, too, are ousted from office and town. Sambo caricatures can be seen dancing throughout Griffith's depiction of the slavery era and thus are made to seem happy, carefree slaves. In later films, Stepin Fetchet played the role of the Sambo buffoon to great laughs. Students can speculate about whether he was right when he said he opened the door for other kinds of roles for African Americans. Willie Best, who plays the buffoon slave in *The Littlest Rebel,* is a good example for students to explore how this comedic role can be both amusing (when he says and does funny things) and demeaning (because the joke is always on him). Students can find more recent incarnations of these demeaning stereotypes in Jessy Terrero's (2004) *Soul Plane,* which Spike Lee has renounced as "coonery and buffoonery" and Anne-Marie Johnson (the national chair of the equal employment opportunity branch of Hollywood's Screen Actor's Guild and actor in Robert Townsend's [1987] *Hollywood Shuffle*) has denounced as worse than the stereotypes parodied in *Hollywood Shuffle.*[2]

Ethnic Notions also identifies the popular culture and film stereotypes of the Pickaninny and the Black Brute. As its name suggests, the Pickaninny stereotype of African-American children portrays them as inferior to white children, as ninnies. They are depicted as unkempt and are kept outdoors, suggesting that they are no better than little animals. *Ethnic Notions* shows numerous depictions of Pickaninnies being eaten by animals as if they were no more than little animals themselves. The Black Brute, also depicted as animal like, is often considered the most pernicious of all the stereotypes. This caricature depicts African-American men as vicious threats to civilization, and often to white women in particular, in order to justify the idea that black men need to be kept under the control of white men. Learning about the Black Brute stereotype can help students understand how ethnic stereotypes reflect and shape Euro-American attitudes at specific times in our country's history. As *Ethnic Notions* explains, the Black Brute stereotype is absent from the slavery era and from later plantation films because such a depiction would not reinforce the idea that slaves were content. The Brute appeared during the Reconstruction era, when Jim Crow laws were enacted to enforce the idea of white superiority based on the supporting idea that Black men were so dangerous that they must be kept in their inferior place. Later reincarnations of the stereotype continue to be harmful because they serve to renew the old ideas.

Students who trace stereotypes from early films on will discover that both the Pickaninny and the Brute also find a place in film representations as early as *The Birth of a Nation*. In Griffith's film, Pickaninnies fall off a wagon and are simply tossed back on, as if they had no human feelings. Students can also discover Pickaninnies as part of the panoply of stereotypes in *The Littlest Rebel*, where the black children are kept in their place outside the plantation's big house and display an obvious intellectual inferiority compared to the bright white heroine, Shirley Temple. In *The Birth of a Nation*, the Brute merits a prominent role as Gus, a newly freed slave and now captain in an all-black army, shows his new-found power by commanding the sidewalk so that whites must move into the street, by taking over and terrorizing the town with his black militia, and by relentlessly pursuing a white girl to marry despite her refusal. After chasing Flora, a genteel white Southern girl, through field and forest until she jumps off a cliff rather than be defiled by a black man, Gus is subsequently caught and lynched. Gus serves as the film's justification for the formation of the Ku Klux Klan and for the lynching of African-American men accused of lusting after white women. As the conclusion of *Ethnic Notions* points out, the old stereotypes have not disappeared; they are simply repeated in new ways. The Black Brute stereotype has been updated for the times in the numerous contemporary gangster roles created for African Americans, such as Allen and Albert Hughes' (1993) *Menace II Society*, an anti-violence, anti-gang movie where black violence and mayhem are still shown as disrupting white civilization and the young black killer is never caught. Students can discuss why Hollywood continues to create and reward such roles, for example in presenting an Academy Award to Denzel Washington for a role in *Training Day* (Antoine Fuqua, 2001) that reinforces rather than challenges the idea of African-American men as brutal, hypersexual, destructive of the social order, and a foil against which white moral superiority can be defined.

Steven Spielberg's (1985) adaptation of Alice Walker's novel *The Color Purple* provides students with an opportunity to analyze what seems to be an updated confluence of African-American stereotypes. Students can discuss and even debate whether or not the brutality of Mr. qualifies him as an updated Black Brute; whether or not the bumbling actions of Harpo qualify him as an updated Sambo; and whether or not the children, who are not in other scenes but suddenly appear as outdoor onlookers when Mr. brutally throws his wife's sister Nettie out of the house, qualify as updated Pickaninnies. Such discussions can help students to move beyond identification of blatantly depicted stereotypes to a recognition of more subtle depictions and to address theoretical questions such as why so prominent a filmmaker as Steven Spielberg could create demeaning caricatures from the characters in Walker's novel.

Readings to accompany *Ethnic Notions* add information, trace recurring stereotypes, and offer answers as to why such images recur in films. Donlad Bogle's (2001) edition of *Toms, Coons, Mulattoes, Mammies and Bucks: An Interpretive History of Blacks in American Films*[3] adds the stereotype of the Tragic Mulatto to those specified in *Ethnic Notions* and traces African-American stereotypes throughout the twentieth century, well beyond the 1987 release date of *Ethnic Notions*. The Tragic Mulatto is a woman whose dual ethnicity allows her to pass for white and to love and be loved by a Euro-American male, but dooms her to lead a dual cultural life that often comes to a tragic end. This stereotype appears in Griffith's *The Birth of a Nation* in the character of Lydia Brown, servant to the powerful Northern statesman, Austin Stoneman, who is sympathetic to the newly empowered African Americans until he learns of their savagery. Griffith's Tragic Mulatto is unstable and oversexed; in one scene she sits on the floor and tears at her blouse.[4] The Tragic Mulatto reappears most notably in Elia Kazan's (1949) *Pinky* and in John Stahl's (1934) and Douglas Sirks' (1959) versions of *Imitation of Life*. Halle Berry's Best-Actress Oscar-winning performance in Marc Foster's (2002) *Monster's Ball* updates the stereotype for a twenty-first century audience: despite her discovery that the white man with whom she is having an affair turns out to be her African-American husband's prison executioner, the unstable light-skinned African-American woman continues the relationship. Patricia Turner's (1994) *Ceramic Uncles and Celluloid Mammies: Black Images and Their Influence on Culture* focuses on what she sees as images more dangerous than blatant caricatures: the more subtle distortions that continue to dominate films and other forms of popular culture. Turner attempts to answer the question particularly relevant for social studies students of why, "when confronted with blacks in the real world, do whites rely upon expectations generated by the reel world?" Students can discuss the merits of her answer: that Western culture and education have shaped the ideology of Euro-Americans and that it is the concentration of Euro-American filmmakers that determines whose stories and whose largely uncontested perspectives dominate.[5]

Using whole films or film excerpts, teachers can help students recognize how both documentary and feature filmmakers directly challenge stereotypes of African Americans. *Ethnic Notions* itself includes a number of African-American experts who offer their own lives and bodies to counter distorted images of household notions and film stereotypes. For example, as Jan Faulkner shows her collection of African-American artifacts, she compares herself to them, noting that "My lips don't look like large pieces of liver. My eyes aren't snow white or bulging in a frightening appearance." Offering herself as proof, she dismisses demeaning representations of black features. Faulkner's appearance provides students with an example of how documentary films can create space for authoritative African Americans as subjects defining themselves in the midst of objects proven false to reality. An angry Melvin Van Peebles, in Mark Daniels' (1998) documentary *Classified X*, shows excerpts from and dismisses as false Hollywood's treatment of black characters throughout the history of American cinema. Van Peebles' visible anger during his assessment of Hollywood films helps to demonstrate for students how the struggle for accurate representation remains an essential part of the African-American struggle for equality.

Feature films that challenge film stereotypes emphasize for students both their prevalence and the importance of dispelling them. Robert Townsend's (1987) *Hollywood Shuffle* focuses on and dismisses the stereotype of the Black Brute as gangster as a Hollywood invention and as one of the few roles available to African-American actors, but rejected by Townsend's protagonist. Other feature films tell stories that invoke stereotypes in order to challenge them as a skewed perspective on the lives of real people. John Singleton's (1991) *Boyz 'n the Hood* offers an insider view of the lives of young men with dreams and aspirations living in East L.A. amidst gangs, drugs, and shootings. This anti-gang film reveals the social neglect and temptations that draw young men into gang life but focuses on community activism and a college education as viable alternatives. Richard Pearce's (1990) *The Long Walk Home* dismisses the caricature of the Mammy with its examination of the life of a woman who works as a nanny and maid during the Civil Rights Movement. The film not only gives this servant a life and family of her own but makes her the protagonist and shows viewers from her point of view how segregation and then the Civil Rights bus boycott affects her life and her own family compared to the life of the white family she works for. Parodies also work to dismiss the old caricatures. Mel Brooks' (1974) *Blazing Saddles* makes fun of and invites viewers to laugh out of existence the idea that black men are Black Brutes lusting after white women. Spike Lee's (2000) *Bamboozled* satirizes contemporary television programming. It tells the story of how a television show filled with old buffoon stereotypes could again be popular based on the lack of African-American executives allowed to make decisions, on African Americans' lack of knowledge of their own entertainment history, and on a general lack of respect for black culture in favor of what is deemed humorous and highly profitable entertainment.

Identifying Asian American Stereotypes, Challenges, and Alternatives

Another documentary about stereotypes, Deborah Gee's (1988) *Slaying the Dragon*, chronicles Hollywood's recycling of one-dimensional images of Asian American women and the impact these stereotypes have, both psychologically and socially, on the real lives of non–Asians as well as Asian American men and women. One influential image is that of the evil Dragon Lady, such as the villainous women played by Anna May Wong in *The Thief of Baghdad* (Raoul Walsh, 1924), in *Shanghai Express* (Josef von Sternberg, 1941) and in Fu Manchu films where she is the villain's equally diabolical assistant. Students who trace the stereotype from early to recent films can find the Dragon Lady in full force as late as Lee Tamahori's (2002) James Bond film *Die Another Day* and Quentin Tarantino's (2003) *Kill Bill, Vol. I*. Gee's film also finds recurring images throughout Hollywood film history of the subservient Geisha Girl/Lotus Blossom and the seductive Susie Wong, such as the newly arrived immigrant who wishes only to please her man played by Miyoshi Umeki and the nightclub singer/dancer who attempts to seduce more than one man played by Nancy Kwan, both in Henry Koster's (1961) *Flower Drum Song*. *Slaying the Dragon* notes that depictions of Asian women — as love interests for Euro-American men in such war films as *Teahouse of the August Moon* (Daniel Mann, 1956) and *Sayonara* (Joshua Logan, 1957), where American soldiers fall in love with supposedly subservient Japanese women, and in *The World of Suzie Wong* (Richard Quine, 1960) where a Euro-American artist falls in love with a sexy Hong Kong prostitute played by Nancy Kwan — originated the Geisha Girl and Suzie Wong stereotypes that have come to dominate film portrayals of Asian American women. The film notes that a particularly demeaning version of the stereotype of an exotic Asian American woman who is subservient to a Euro-American male appears in Michael Cimino's (1985) *Year of the Dragon*. Here a former Vietnam veteran continues his own private war in America by ill-treating his Chinese American girlfriend and battling an underground world of Yellow Peril gangsters. Gee's film also shows how updated replications of subservient, exotic Asian women as love interests for American soldiers continue to perpetuate the stereotype in such war films as *Rambo: First Blood Part I* (Peter Macdonald, 1988), where the hero finds temporary love when he enters Cambodia searching for Americans missing in action.

Slaying the Dragon suggests that these stereotypes affect how non–Asian American viewers see Asian American women as well as how Asian American women view themselves. Testimony from a number of

Euro-American men, including a filmmaker, confirms that many view real Asian American women as naturally passive, exotic, sex objects of male pleasure. On the other hand, testimony from Asian American women themselves reveals that their experiences with such expectations have forced them to question their behavior — as not conforming to stereotypical subservient and sexually exotic images and the expectations of others or having to internalize such imposed expectations in order to be accepted. Students can determine how the number and variety of women in the film who claim the stereotype has nothing to do with them or their upbringing yet often defines them in the eyes of others reveals how *Slaying the Dragon*, like *Ethnic Notions*, uses the self-defining technique of juxtaposing real people against stereotypes. The film also emphasizes the power of film representations. An Asian American expert's reading of then-current statistics suggests that Japanese American women increasingly tend to marry Euro-American men because of the preponderance of influential film images that endorse such relationships. Claims such as this can inspire students to explore how the films referred to in the documentary go about endorsing specific kinds of romantic relationships (with stereotypes of Asian American women, storylines, and standard film techniques such as reactive characters and crosscutting comparisons) and to examine how later films with Asian American women — perhaps Wayne Wang's (1995) *The Joy Luck Club*, McG's (2003) *Charlie's Angels: Full Throttle*, or Eric Byler's (2003) *Charlotte Sometimes*— do or do not fit the stereotypical models.

While focusing on film images of Asian and Asian American women, *Slaying the Dragon* does not ignore film stereotypes of Asian and Asian American men. Of particular interest to social studies inquiries about social influences, Gee's film reveals how the frequent recurrence of Asian and Asian American movie characters as Yellow Peril imperialist villains reflect our nation's fears at any given time. For example, Gee's film recounts how when an influx of Chinese immigrant workers to America was seen by Euro Americans as an economic threat, Chinese and Chinese Americans served as movie villains. But when Japan launched an attack on the Chinese in 1937, popular films such as Sidney Franklin's (1937) *The Good Earth* switched characterizations to make the Chinese into admirable characters. Japan's December 1941 attack on Pearl Harbor seemed to cement the image of the Japanese villain as a ruthless imperialist lusting after Euro-American women. But then, reflecting the United States' role in Japan's post–World War II economic recovery and U.S. fears regarding the 1949 Communist takeover of China, the Japanese once again became the good Asians, the Chinese the bad Asians, and Japanese women desirable love interests for Euro-American soldiers. Gee's documentary can inspire students interested in changing political ideologies in American films to trace how the ethnicity of villains in war films and action films reflects U.S. foreign policy at the time of a film's making. Such efforts can help students determine how and why pervasive ethnic stereotypes recur and to note (or imagine) new film villain alternatives that do not seek to demonize entire ethnic groups.

Another stereotype noted in Gee's film, of Asian Americans as the model minority, is also identified as originating from a particular time. One of the film's experts finds the model minority stereotype emerging as the result of African-American Civil Rights Movement initiatives demanding equal rights. He notes that Asian Americans were often promoted in the media, in contrast to African Americans, as passive but hard-working assimilationists who made it on their own, quietly and successfully, in American society and as role models for other minorities to emulate.[6] Gee's film can foster non–Asian American student understanding that the model minority and the passive and exotic Asian American women stereotypes, often deemed positive depictions, are not positive to Asian Americans who want to see themselves represented on film as complex characters that reflect the diverse reality of diverse Asian American lives. Students can examine the model minority issue from a variety of perspectives offered in films. Justin Lin's (2002) feature film *Better Luck Tomorrow* portrays the lives of five contemporary Asian American high school students in ways that clearly reject the model minority myth. These honor students do not question the need to get into elite universities, but they use their status as honor students as both reason and excuse for criminal activity. Lin's film can open discussion for students about the goals, pressures, and self-expectations of Asian American students. The third part of Bill Moyers' (2003) three-part documentary *Becoming American: The Chinese Experience* includes a segment with a college student who testifies how the model minority role is fully endorsed by her own and other first-generation Chinese American parents as the only means by which their children can succeed in America, how these parents pressure their children to get straight As in school and become doctors and lawyers, and how the children often internalize such expectations. Students can also view and discuss the model minority assimilation emphasis for Chinese Americans in Henry Koster's much earlier (1961) *Flower Drum Song* (which depicts first-generation Chinese Americans as comically old fashioned and bewildered by their children's immediate assimilation) and for Vietnamese Americans in Louis Malle's later (1985) *Alamo Bay* (the story of a Vietnamese refugee who follows all the rules and even eludes the Ku Klux Klan in his determination to have American opportunities). Films such as these can help students to explore whether the model minority/assimilationist stereotype in film can be detrimental in itself in its implication that this image represents all Asian Americans, or detrimental as a role model that inhibits individual expressions of ethnic culture and creates undue pressures, or detrimental only when it is used to silence civil rights demands from other ethnic minority groups.

A stereotypical male Asian American film character also worth student discussion is Charlie Chan. Like the Model Minority, Charlie Chan, the Honolulu Police Department's ace detective in over forty films from the 1930s and 40s, has often been considered a positive stereotype: he is smart and humble, he always solves tough cases that seem to be beyond the Euro-Americans' ability to figure out, and his Oriental fortune-cookie philosophy makes him appear wiser than everyone else. Students can explore how Chan is an early version of the non-threatening Model Minority — with additional baggage. Chan was always played in yellow face by Euro-American actors who exaggerated their features, behavior, and speech to look, act, and talk like caricatures of Asians. Chan was assimilated into American culture, but his Oriental looks, his mysterious ways of solving cases, and his peculiar accent (never using articles or pronouns) suggested his foreignness, all of which contributed to the idea that all Asian Americans are foreigners. He was also desexualized: pudgy and unmanly, he is the stereotyped asexual Asian American man. In addition, as the National Asian American Telecommunications Association (NAATA) points out in a response to Fox Movie Channel's plan for a summer 2003 Charlie Chan Movies Festival (using restored versions of the films, now also released on VHS and DVD), Charlie Chan was created by a Euro American and "is a white man's fantasy of what a Chinese man should be. To the extent that this image remains in the public consciousness, the Chan series only reinforces it." NAATA also notes that in some of the films Chan is called "chop suey" and "egg foo yung" and in some of the films an African-American character named Birmingham Brown is a wide-eyed, perpetually scared chauffeur who plays a Sambo buffoon for comic relief. NAATA does not advocate censorship but instead suggests that the series "be set in [its historical] context with commentary about why some people believe the films are offensive" as well as why others do not see them as racially insensitive. Students can consider the viability of contextualizing the Charlie Chan series and restored VHS and DVD releases, and, by extension, all movie channel television rebroadcasts of old classics with ethnic stereotypes. The central question is whether or not showing the old films along with this kind of open dialogue would help audiences come to a "greater understanding of racism" and of stereotyping in particular.[7]

Gee's *Slaying the Dragon* goes beyond identifying Asian American film stereotypes and placing them in their historical contexts; it also promotes film representations of ordinary Asian Americans as alternatives to stereotypes. The documentary recommends Peter Wang's (1986) *A Great Wall* and Wayne Wang's (1985) *Dim Sum: A Little Bit of Heart* as two independent feature films offering such alternative depictions. These films illustrate for students how Asian American filmmakers who concentrate on the lives of ordinary people challenge ideas that lead to misunderstandings and stereotyping. *A Great Wall*, the story of a Chinese American family's trip to visit relatives in China, focuses on the similarities between them as human beings and on their differences as Chinese Americans and Chinese. Students can easily note the similarities in extended crosscutting scenes: how, for example, the Chinese American high school student has not bothered to learn Chinese in after-school classes he has attended for years and the Chinese student has also not bothered to learn English in her after-school classes, as well as how the men and women have similar (humorous) complaints about their spouses. The film, however, stresses that socially constructed ethnic differences are as important as the similarities. Cultural differences about privacy, about being demonstrative in public, about appropriate clothing, and about how students qualify for advanced education serve to show that Chinese Americans are related to, but not identical with, Chinese. Students can discuss how the distinctions between cultures demonstrated in this film are important to deconstruct the stereotypical idea in America that all Asian Americans are foreigners[8] and to avoid the similar conflation that identified Japanese Americans with Japanese following Pearl Harbor and helped to promote Japanese American Internment. Wayne Wang's *Dim Sum* counters stereotypes with ordinary Chinese Americans. Wang's film promotes understanding of Chinese American culture from the sometimes conflicting, sometimes complementary, perspectives of a Chinese American mother and daughter, played by an actual mother and daughter rather than professional actors. While this film focuses on differences between generations, like Wang's later (1995) film *The Joy Luck Club*, it remains respectful of older immigrants' ideas.

Teachers need not screen both a documentary to inform students about Asian American stereotypes and a feature film to examine the counter-stereotyping technique of depicting the lives of ordinary people. Instead, they can accomplish this dual goal with a single video or film. In her (1987) part narrative, part documentary video *New Year Parts I and II*, Valerie Soe begins with storybook drawings of her childhood in San Francisco, filling in the drawings with details as she delivers the specifics of her autobiographical narrative via voice over. Her personal story dismisses stereotypes, as she explains that she did not particularly like Chinese food and that her parents made "terrible rice" and chronicles her unique experiences during one year of her life. The caricatured images that fill the screen in Part II are not an extension of Soe's story. What has taken its place are representations of Asian Americans from TV and movie screens. Soe uses a series of five intertitles to label the caricatures as she documents them: "Japs, Sloops, and Gooks," "Fortune Cookie Philosophers," "The World Wide Empire of Evil," "Geisha Girls and Dragon Ladies," and "Masters of Kung Fu." *New Year* invites students to confront their own misconceptions, to see the sources of these misconceptions, and to compare them with Soe's story of growing up as a fourth-generation Chinese American in San Francisco. Soe's experimental video can help students recognize how stereotypes make ordinary people invisible and to see how Asian American filmmakers are choosing to move beyond invisibility and victimization by depicting their own personal lives. Another film to aid student thinking about a common stereotype is Soe's (1986) short (one and one-half minute) video, with the humorously ironic title *All Orientals Look*

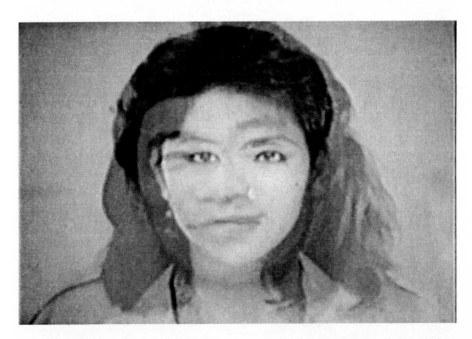

All Orientals Look the Same (Valerie Soe, 1986): Changing images challenge the stereotype.

the Same, which focuses on physiognomy. In just seconds, dozens of faces appear on the screen to reveal dozens of distinct Asian American features that blend into one only if viewers are not paying attention.

A number of Asian American documentaries also juxtapose stereotypes with the diverse personal lives of ordinary people. Renee Tajima and Christine Choy's (1990) film *Yellow Tale Blues: Two American Families* includes excerpts from Hollywood movies—from a 1910 silent film to the scene in Blake Edwards' (1961) *Breakfast at Tiffany's* where Mickey Rooney appears as a bumbling buck-toothed Asian American admirer of the Euro-American protagonist — to disclose Hollywood's history of disparaging images of Asians. But *Yellow Tale Blues* also juxtaposes via crosscutting sequences these too familiar images with portraits of actual families: the Tajimas and the Choys. The uniquely personal again counters the stereotypical as viewers hear the differing histories and see the individual identities of the two filmmakers' own families. In a similar manner, Rea Tajiri's (1991) experimental documentary *History and Memory* juxtaposes Hollywood images of Japanese Americans and World War II propaganda with stories from the videomaker's own family, to remember her story of Japanese American Internment as the story Hollywood chose to ignore. The idea that all Asian Americans are foreigners and the often-revived Yellow Peril stereotype are both effectively dismissed in Christine Choy and Renee Tajima's (1988) film *Who Killed Vincent Chin?* This film confronts the confusion of two Euro-American Detroit autoworkers at the height of the auto industry crisis of the 1980s who beat Chinese American Vincent Chin to death with a baseball bat because they thought he was Japanese. Due to their assumptions about a Yellow Peril threat to their livelihood in the American car manufacturing industry, they felt justified — and two juries concurred — in killing a man based on his Asian American ethnicity. *Who Killed Vincent Chin?* documents real anti–Asian scapegoating and violence, but it also includes interviews with Vincent Chin's mother, who laments the senseless loss of her son. Students can assess the effectiveness of these videos and films according to the filmmaking method Asian American filmmaker Loni Ding describes as her "preferred approach," which is "to displace stereotypes by creating vital images of Asian Americans as real human beings, with individual faces, voices, and personal histories that we come to know and care about."[9]

Identifying American Indian Stereotypes, Challenges, and Alternatives

Phil Lucas and Robert Hagopian's (1979) five-part documentary series *Images of Indians* identifies stereotypes and raises important issues regarding representations of American Indians in feature films. It informs viewers how Hollywood's gross misrepresentations — including inauthentic costumes, muddled languages, erroneous geographical locations, misinterpreted customs, and misrepresented history — and its stereotyped portrayals of American Indians as Hostile Savages, Noble Savages, Squaws, and Princesses have led to serious misconceptions about American Indians. As the film's on-screen narrator, American Indian actor Will Sampson, explains at the beginning of each segment, for people raised on Hollywood movies, Native Americans are invisible unless they look like the Hollywood Indian — in buckskin, war paint, and feathers. Like *Ethnic Notions* and *Slaying the Dragon*, *Images of Indians* offers real people, particularly Will Sampson himself, in counter distinction to stereotypes. Each segment of the series includes a montage of film images where non–Indian actors have played Indian roles, to demonstrate that until recently Indians have not been allowed to participate in the own representation, and several segments conclude with excerpts from more recent films that represent the reality of contemporary American Indian life from an American Indian point of view.

Students can explore the origins of film misrepresentations of American Indians and their effect on viewers. As *Images of Indians* Part I "The Great Movie Massacre" notes, Hollywood stereotypes of American Indians can be traced to dime novels (beginning with *Seth Jones* in 1860) and Wild West Shows (popular from 1870 to 1900). Both portrayed American Indians in some combination of primitive victim (the Noble Savage) or villain (the Hostile Savage) who stood in the way of Euro-American civilization and thus, in the words of Will Sampson, "as not quite human." *Images of Indians* focuses on the effect of such images on non–Indians as well as American Indian children. Indian children, Sampson says in Part III, are influenced by Hollywood Westerns and root for the cowboys because they do not recognize themselves as related to the Indian caricatures they see onscreen and because, like everyone else, they are encouraged by films to have sympathy for the good guys and hatred for the bad guys. As the character Crow Horse reveals about his childhood in the feature film *Thunderheart* (Michael Apted, 1992), "When we played cowboys and Indians, I was always Gary Cooper."

The most prevailing and pernicious film stereotype of American Indians is the Hostile Savage. Sampson states that innumerable films have "shown the Indian as a savage warrior, a renegade, a killer of innocent pioneer women and children, and a merciless scalper who used the most cruel means of torture in his vicious attacks against the white men." In literally thousands of Westerns, American Indians are depicted as Hostile

Savages who viciously obstruct Euro-American settlers and civilization, not as members of Indian nations protecting themselves, their lands, and their cultures from invasion and occupation. As Part I of *Images of Indians* shows, early films—including James Cruz's (1923) *The Covered Wagon* and John Ford's (1924) *The Iron Horse*—and later Western classics—including Ford's (1939) *Stagecoach*, (1949) *She Wore a Yellow Ribbon*, and (1956) *The Searchers*, in addition to Raoul Walsh's (1941) *They Died with Their Boots on* and John Huston's (1960) *The Unforgiven*—portray Indians as Hostile Savages who variously sneak up on, surround, kidnap, rape, torture, and mercilessly kill innocent white settlers, including women and children. The Indians' savage nature and the need for western settlers and the U.S. cavalry to exterminate them go unquestioned, as each of these films serves to justify historical attempts at physical and cultural genocide in compelling dramas about America's past. American Indian historian Vine Deloria, Jr., explains in *Images of Indians* that, contrary to Hollywood plotlines, American Indians won many battles, and the popular Hollywood image of the savage warrior seen from the perspective of white settlers is a fantasy created by filmmakers who have made no attempt to understand history.

Hostile Savage caricatures have not been limited to drama. Norman McLeod's (1948) Western Comedy *Paleface*, as *Images of Indians* Part III points out, stars American comedy icon Bob Hope playing a tenderfoot hoping to impress his girlfriend. He thinks he is shooting the attacking Indians so skillfully that they fall into a pile, although (as viewers see in a crosscutting sequence) she is actually doing the sharp shooting. As a final comic touch, when his gun seems to fail, he climbs out of his shelter and hits an Indian over the head with his gun barrel to complete what he calls a "neat pile" of dead Indians. A topic for student discussion is whether or not the comic genocide in *Paleface* and its sequels (*The Son of Paleface* and *The Shakiest Gun in the West*) would be thought humorous without the residual effect in viewers' minds of images of Indians as Hostile Savages who, within the context of movie after movie, are justifiably killed.[10]

If Indians are not Hostile Savages, they are stereotyped as Noble Savages. As early as D.W. Griffith's (1911) *The Squaw's Love*, Indians are depicted, according to *Images of Indians* Part II, as "quaint" and "romantic children of nature" from a time long past. Noble Savages in films are primitive beings whose way of life is appealing—because it is simple and in harmony with nature—but is also doomed to extinction in the face of the oncoming, and superior, civilization brought by hard-working settlers who know how to work the land. As *Images of Indians* Part IV argues, the popularity of the Noble Savage film stereotype can be traced to film adaptations of early novels, such as Zane Grey's (1922) novel *The Vanishing American* and George Seitz's (1925) and Joseph Kane's (1955) film adaptations and James Fenimore Cooper's (1826) novel *The Last of the Mohicans* and its many (1909, 1911, 1920, 1936, 1946, 1955, 1977, and 1992) film versions.[11] *Images of Indians* stresses that the stereotype is a Euro-American fantasy. Students inspired to watch the whole of Seitz's *The Vanishing American* will discover its prologue of vignettes depicting Herbert Spencer's Social Darwinism in which only the fittest survive and will note how the Navajo are portrayed as vanishing Noble Savages conquered by the Euro Americans, who are apparently more fit to survive and rule. Students can interpret how the *mise-en-scène* at the end of Seitz's film, where a funeral procession for the dead Indian hero fades into the sunset, provides the visual image of a tribe literally vanishing. As each of the film adaptations demonstrates, the Noble Savage is a friend to Euro Americans and — like the Uncle Tom stereotype who gladly serves his Euro-American superiors — is represented as a positive stereotype. Depictions of Noble Savages are abundant in films about the establishment of the colonies and in Westerns but do not often fit into twentieth-century stories. In a more recent Hollywood depiction, however, John Woo's (2002) *Windtalkers,* ostensibly about the role of Navajo code talkers in World War II, the Navajo code talker character takes on familiar characteristics of the Noble Savage in juxtaposition to the Euro-American hero. Students can compare the depiction in this Combat film to depictions of Noble Savages in Westerns to determine how far Hollywood is willing to go beyond its standard caricatures of American Indians in relation to white heroes.

Stereotyped images of American Indian women take on the same major traits as the Hostile and Noble Savages, as Part IV of *Images of Indians* shows: they are either unfriendly or friendly to the Euro-American hero, and frequently neither type survives to the end of the film. The Squaw stereotype is most often an older, heavy-set woman who is either unfriendly to the white hero or is the target of his rejection and laughter. When married to an Indian, the Squaw is supposedly subservient to him and is a mere workhorse. In John Ford's (1956) *The Searchers,* after the hero's young companion inadvertently marries an older, heavy-set Cheyenne woman while merely attempting to trade goods, he rejects her by literally kicking her away from his bedroll. An object of comic relief in a highly dramatic film, the Cheyenne woman rolls down a steep hill to the great laughter of the John Wayne hero. Wayne's role here as a reactive character gives students a chance to discuss how he guides viewer response. Without his laughter, would the scene be humorous? An excerpt from *The Apache Kid* (1941) shows how Indians are again misrepresented, as an

The Searchers (John Ford, 1956). Reactive Character: John Wayne's laughter directs viewer response.

Indian man and woman agree that she should "not speak her mind in family matters" and should "not object to being beaten." Countering such images, the American Indian women experts in *Images of Indians* explain that, in Hollywood films, the Squaw stereotype makes Indian women seem servants of men, but in real Indian societies women are powerful members who (unlike other American women) have always had the vote and who, in a number of tribes, were in charge of deciding matters of life and death, including whether or not the tribe went to war.[12]

The supposed positive stereotype of the Indian Princess/Indian Maiden, as *Images of Indians* Part IV explains, is often the daughter of a chief; she is young and thin, conforms to Euro-American female standards of beauty, and inevitably chooses the white hero instead of her Indian suitor, though their love is most often doomed. Similar to many films about Euro-American men's romances with Asian and Asian American Lotus Blossom/Geisha Girls, the Princess/Maiden often kills herself or is killed so the films do not promote the idea of interracial marriage. The romance provides a brief and exotic love affair or even marriage, but not a lasting relationship. Arthur Penn's (1970) *Little Big Man* even depicts the Euro-American hero having to decide which one of his wife's sisters to make love to first as they giggle and eagerly await his advances, and his Cheyenne wife and their baby are murdered during Custer's attack. Delmar Davis's (1950) *Broken Arrow* shows the wedding ceremony of the Euro-

American hero to his Apache bride as a complete distortion of Apache tradition, according to the experts in *Images of Indians*, as if a European secret society ritual of mingling blood were authentic to the Apache ceremony. The relationship in *Broken Arrow* is inevitably ended as the Indian woman is killed before the end of the film. The death of the Indian bride in *A Man Called Horse* (Elliot Silverstein, 1970), like others before and after her, makes her a temporary mate. The Indian Princess/Maiden is obviously friendly to the white man, serving as an object of his sexual pleasure, until he returns to his own people. The caricature of the Indian Princess/Maiden continues through films about Sacajawea (in Rudolph Mate's 1955 *The Far Horizons*) and about Pocahontas (in early shorts of 1908 and 1910 and in Lew Landers' [1953] *Captain John Smith and Pocahontas*). The Indian Princess in Hamilton Luske, Clyde Geronimi, and Wilfred Jackson's (1953) animated *Peter Pan* is another link in the chain that leads to Mike Gabriel and Eric Goldberg's still-popular animated (1995) *Pocahontas*. In this latest manifestation, the Indian Princess rejects her current Indian suitor in favor of Captain John Smith, but they are separated when he must return to England. From the perspective of a Euro-American male looking for romance, the Indian Princess/Maiden is the positive stereotype and the Squaw is not. However, to the Native American women experts in *Images of Indians*, both stereotypes are completely negative, and they lament that these are the Hollywood film roles offered to Indian women.

Students interested in tracing recurrences of American Indians stereotypes will most often find them together in the same film. As early as D.W. Griffith's (1912) Western *Iola's Promise*, or *How the Little Indian Maiden Paid her Debt of Gratitude*, stereotypes of the Hostile Savage, Noble Savage, and Indian Maiden define the Indian characters. John Ford's (1939) *Drums Along the Mohawk* is a good film for students to recognize how the Hostile and Noble Savages are differentiated by who befriends the white hero and how both are clearly marked as savage. Hero Gilbert Martin's attempt to build a successful farm is thwarted by the savage Iroquois, allies of a wicked Royalist who burn the settlers' crops and cabins as they whoop wildly. In contrast, the Christianized Indian Blue Back, the hero's friend and ally, warns the colonists of impending Iroquois attacks. The savage Iroquois are defeated, and Blue Back remains friendly with the hero, but — similar to the African-American stereotype of the Coon — he does not become part of the Euro-American community. He joins them in church, but his misplaced shouts of "Hallelujah" show that he only goes through the motions without following the service or understanding the religion. He is not civilized, for he advises the hero to beat his wife, strongly suggesting that even good Indians beat their wives into submission. Including both friendly and hostile Indians in the same film became conventional. In Kevin Costner's still-popular Academy award-winning (1990) *Dances with Wolves*, the hostile Pawnee are contrasted with the peaceful but threatened Lakota, who befriend the hero. And in Michael Mann's (1992) *The Last of the Mohicans*, the brutal Huron, Magua, is contrasted with the kindly but doomed Mohicans, Uncas and his father Chingachgook, who are friends and companions of the white woodsman hero, Hawkeye.

Images of Indians ends Part I with a selection from Harvey Hall's (1977) *Standing Tall*, a story of Indian ranchers that explores contemporary American-Indian identity, and students can find more recent films about contemporary American Indians that depict Indian life and current issues. Noteworthy films include Jonathan Wacks' (1989) *Powwow Highway*, Chris Eyres' (1999) *Smoke Signals* and (2002) *Skins*, and Sherman Alexie's (2002) *The Business of Fancy Dancing*. *Powwow Highway* is especially useful in the classroom as a film that counters stereotypes and stands in direct and playful contrast to the formulas of Hollywood cinema. It has no white hero. Instead, it is about contemporary American Indian life on a Cheyenne reservation in Montana called Lame Deer and has two American Indian protagonists: Buddy Red Bow and Philbert Bono. Rather than seeing Indians in and as part of grand vistas of the American landscape, viewers learn about contemporary reservation problems, such as unemployment, poverty, and corporate and government attempts to exploit tribal resources—all from an American Indian perspective. The plot is an on-the-road journey of self-discovery where tribal traditions are used to reclaim Indian identity and help solve recurring problems. Students can explore how the film evokes the familiar stereotype of the Hostile Savage in the character Buddy Red Bow, the Noble Savage in Philbert Bono, and the plot of Manifest Destiny as the government, police, and a mining company attempt to take tribal resources, only to reimagine these Hollywood conventions from an Indian point of view. Buddy is hostile — hot tempered, confrontational, and smart, managing to outwit his antagonists—but he is not a savage. He is an educated political activist who is trying to stop the collaboration between a mining company and the government from taking reservation resources under the guise of helping the tribe. Buddy's anger against white society is justified in the film. His sister, Bonnie, and her children are jailed on false charges, forcing him to leave Lame Deer and miss voting against the mining company, and an electronics salesman stereotypes him, saying, "No gettum special deal on this one, Chief." And while Philbert may be attached to traditional tribal ways, which he is gradually learning about and attempting to live by, he also lives in the present and is far from being doomed to extinction in the face of a superior civilization.

Students can also explore how the plot of *Powwow Highway* reverses the familiar plot lines of many Westerns. Instead of Indians capturing innocent white females (as occurs in *The Searchers*, in repeat versions of *The Last of the Mohicans*, and in *Dances with Wolves*), in *Powwow Highway*, the federal government and police capture Buddy's innocent Indian sister and children. And instead of the usual short-lived inter-ethnic romance between a Euro-American hero and an Indian Maiden, Buddy and his sister's Euro-American friend, Rabbit, strike up a romance that is still in progress at film's end. Students can also explore the humorous plot reversal of typical Hollywood cowboy and Indian chase scenes. In this film, the Indians are not chasing innocent settlers and pioneers; instead, the cowboys are chasing the innocent Indians. As the Santa Fe police, FBI agents, and mining company officials all join together in chase to catch Buddy, Philbert, Buddy's sister, her friend, and her children with the rallying cry, "Let's cowboy up," viewers expect the worse, except this time they are on the side of the Indians. And finally, this time, the Indians win by simply escaping rather than getting shot or fading into the sunset. Students can discuss the significance of the film both in light of the earlier Westerns it critiques as well as its commentary on the situation of today's American Indian. Many will note that *Powwow Highway* tells the story of Manifest Destiny from a contemporary American Indian perspective to reverse the mindset of viewers about Hostile and Noble Savages and to expose the reality that battles against Manifest Destiny are not yet over.

In Chris Eyre's *Smoke Signals*, two contemporary American Indians again partially discover and partially create their ethnic identity as they come to respect each other's differences on a road trip. The protagonists, Victor Joseph and Thomas Builds-the-Fire, are considerably younger than those in *Powwow Highway*, but their characterizations and the plot again challenge Hollywood stereotypes. Students can explore how the film responds to the vanishing Noble Savage stereotype in its direct allusions to *The Last of the Mohicans* and *Dances with Wolves* and how it replaces the popular plot of a vanishing race with the real problem of a vanishing alcoholic father. Students can also examine how other movie allusions subvert Hollywood's images of marginalized Indians. For example, when the two young men help save a young woman injured in a car accident, they respond to a thank you and a compliment that they are like "the Lone Ranger and Tonto" with Thomas's correction that they are more like "Tonto and Tonto." Their song about whether or not John Wayne's teeth are real or fake invites viewers to consider what is fake in what has been accepted as realistic depictions in Hollywood Westerns. In conjunction with Will Sampson's contention in *Images of Indians* that movies about

Indians affect Indians and non–Indians alike, students can discuss how even Victor, who chides Thomas for watching *Dances with Wolves* multiple times, must also shed his movie-made image of the stoic Indian who has just returned from a buffalo hunt, which is not only a stereotyped look but is especially inappropriate, as Thomas points out, for their salmon-fishing tribe. This film, like *Powwow Highway,* encourages viewers to discard Hollywood Indian images and to discover contemporary American Indians learning new respect for their heritage while living in the present. Thomas, for instance, like Philbert in *Powwow Highway,* tells traditional stories relevant to contemporary life. Like Victor's mother, whose fry bread recipe comes from her mother's mother and who watches Julia Child, the young men retain their heritage and live in the present.

Complementary film and print sources for both teacher and student research on the Hollywood Indian are numerous. Victor Masayesua's (1992) *Imagining Indians* is a more recent but less comprehensive documentary on Indian images from Hollywood films than *Images of Indians.* Lorraine Norrgard's (1988) documentary *Indian Princess Demystified* chronicles images of and myths about Indian women, focusing on Pocahontas. A useful reading to accompany *Images of Indians* is Michael Hilger's (1995) *From Savage to Nobleman: Images of Native Americans in Film.*[13] Hilger provides a good discussion of Indian stereotypes and films made about and by Indians since 1979 when *Images of Indians* was released. The book effectively describes film techniques, such as camera distance and angles in specific scenes so that students can understand how viewers are being directed to respond.

Identifying Latino/a Stereotypes, Challenges, and Alternatives

Susan Racho, Nancy de los Santos, and Albert Dominguez's (2001) documentary *The Bronze Screen: 100 Years of the Latino Image in America Cinema* identifies Latino/a stereotypes and reviews a century of Hollywood and independent film attempts to capture Latino/a American identity and culture on the silver screen. The film chronicles the repeated use of Hollywood stereotypes—the Greaser/ *Bandido* (updated as the gangster and drug dealer), The Loose Woman, the Latin Lover (with both male and female versions), and comical Buffoons—and it provides historical contexts for their origins and recurrences. Written scholarship on Latino stereotypes to complement *The Bronze Screen* includes Charles Ramirez Berg's (2002) *Latino Images in Film: Stereotypes, Subversion, Resistance* and

David J. Weber's (1988) *Myth and the History of the Hispanic Southwest*.[14] Like the other documentaries on ethnic minority images, *The Bronze Screen* also recommends films that challenge stereotypes and attempt to give viewers accurate representations of the diversity, in this case, of Latino/a American experiences and cultures.

Two major Latino/a stereotypes recur from the beginning of film history: the Greaser and the Loose Woman. The Greaser—probably so named, as film historian Chon Noriega explains, after the term used to describe Mexican shipyard laborers who greased their backs to unload cargo—is labeled Hollywood's "first bad guy." Early films such as *Tony and the Greaser* (1911), *Licking the Greasers* (1914), and *Bronco Billy and the Greaser* (1914) presented Latinos as dark, dangerous, dirty, and violent thieves who caused mayhem and tried to kidnap white women. The Greaser was the absolute villain in simple good-versus-bad dramas. For social studies students interested in the sociology of film villains, a comparison of the Latino Greaser with other ethnic minority bad guys—the Black Brute for African Americans, the Yellow Peril Imperialist for Asian Americans, and the Hostile Savage for American Indians—would expose their similar traits (they all, for example, attempt to impede or disrupt Euro-American civilization in some fashion, and they all attempt to kidnap Euro-American women). The Greaser and the other stereotyped ethnic film villains raise important questions for either a group project or a debate: each group of students could investigate one stereotypical ethnic-minority villain across a number of films and then decide or debate whether or not they function as interchangeable others set up against Euro-American heroes or whether their recurring appearance has more to do with an ethnic group's relation to the social conditions of the times. Students could decide, in other words, if filmmakers generally use ethnic villains indiscriminately, picking from among available stereotypes that fit the drama, or whether specific ethnic villains express the filmmakers' and the dominant Euro-American population's fears about possible social, cultural, and economic change. Either way, students will no doubt find these villains provide a foil for Euro-American heroes to prove themselves and their social values most worthy, and to get (or keep or rescue) the girl. *The Bronze Screen* finds that women were not immune from the villainous category of characters and that the Loose Woman Latina matched the poor morals of the Greaser.[15] In films such as *Bronco Billy's Mexican Wife* (1912), she has a violent nature and is unfaithful to her husband. For students, this Loose Woman stereotype also invites comparison with other ethnic female stereotypes and the similar purposes they serve in numerous repetitions. If the Greaser stereotype served as the antithesis of what Euro-

American males thought they should be, the Loose Woman stereotype provided Euro-America women with their negative model.

Students can trace the evolution of these two major stereotypes in relation to various social pressures and changing social conditions. As *The Bronze Screen* chronicles their history, after Latin countries complained about the Greaser caricature and threatened to boycott and then, in 1922, to ban such offensive movies, the stereotype lost its prominence for a time. While the image never completely disappeared, it returned more prominently at the beginning of the Civil Rights Movement, when filmmakers found it impolitic to feature African-American villains and replaced them with the less politically visible Latinos. The Greaser appears in the well-known *Treasure of the Sierra Madre* (John Huston, 1948) in the Mexican character Gold Tooth and his fellow *bandidos*, who prove to be both ruthless and stupid in failing to recognize as valuable the gold they have stolen and in trying to sell stolen burros that are clearly branded. The Loose Woman reappears as a somewhat different character in the still-popular *High Noon* (Stanley Kramer, 1952). In this film, a Mexican-American woman, the secret owner of local businesses, proves herself to be strong-minded, strong willed, and independent; however, she has also had as lovers all the main characters in the film, including the villain, the sheriff, and the deputy sheriff. *The Bronze Screen* questions whether this portrayal is simply a repetition of the old stereotype or a significant departure, a question that students can also engage. In *The Bronze Screen*, Rita Moreno recalls her Academy-Award winning Loose Woman role as Anita in *West Side Story*, Robert Wise's (1961) film about Puerto Rican gang members, and notes that she refused to appear in another film for seven years because the only roles she was offered were the same stereotyped gang roles in lesser quality films. Students can find the Loose Woman stereotype replayed, this time as a Cuban refugee by a non–Latino, in Mira Nair's (1995) *The Perez Family*. What *The Bronze Screen* calls "the Urban Greaser" marks the replay of the Greaser/*Bandido* caricature in the updated form of urban gangsters and drug dealers in movies from the 1950s to the present, such as *Blackboard Jungle* (Richard Brook, 1955) with its Puerto Rican punk, *Touch of Evil* (Orson Welles, 1958) with Mexicans hoodlums harassing the Euro-American female, and then *Boulevard Nights* (Michael Pressman, 1979) and *Colors* (Dennis Hopper, 1988), along with films not mentioned in *The Bronze Screen*, *Scarface* (Brian DePalma, 1983) and *Training Day* (Antoine Fuqua, 2001)— with hard core Latinos lacking any moral standards. Students with a tolerance for on-screen violence can evaluate the success of Edward James Olmos' (1992) anti-gangster, anti-drug film *American Me* in its attempts to show the Urban Greaser not as the villain but as the protagonist who serves as a model of the lifestyle and attitudes that real-life Latinos should not emulate.

The sensual and sexual Latin Lover, described in *The Bronze Screen* and in written scholarly studies[16] as an on-and-off replacement for the Greaser/*Bandido* beginning in the 1920s, remained popular during the Great Depression fantasy movies of the 1930s and throughout the 1940s and 1950s. A more recent reincarnation is played by Antonio Banderas in Martin Campbell's (1998) *The Mask of Zorro*, a replay of earlier Zorro and Latin Lover roles. Unlike the lowly Greaser, Latin Lovers were consistently portrayed as South American aristocrats with whom wealthy Euro-American women would fall in love. Although it is deemed a positive stereotype (even Ricardo Montalban, who played the role of many Latin Lovers, says in the documentary that there is nothing detrimental about this caricature), students tracing film stereotypes may decide otherwise. It was a popular role for light-skinned actors, whereas only dark-skinned actors or actors in brown face makeup played underclass Greaser roles. The South American location and upper class status of the Latin Lover were chosen, according to *The Bronze Screen*, for escapist fantasy films, as real Mexicans and Mexican Americans were being deported in large numbers as threats to Euro-American workers' jobs. Many of the early Latin Lovers were not even Latin: Rudolph Valentino was Italian, and Jacob Kranz became Latinized by changing his name to Ricardo Cortez. For women, a Latin identity was not desirable. Dolores Del Rio, Rita Hayworth (born Margarita Consino), and Rachel Welch (born Raquel Tejada) became "de-Latinized," or what *The Bronze Screen* also calls "Europeanized." Hollywood changed their names and their looks to fit a white standard of beauty and paired them with Anglo men, assuming they would only then appeal to a Euro-American audience. A number of actors who refused to Anglicize their names and deny their ethnicity — Ricardo Montalban, Cesar Romero, John Leguizamo, Elizabeth Pena, and Lupe Ontiveros — appear in *The Bronze Screen* to mark a more recent insistence on Latino recognition and self-pride. The double standard (of the Latinized man and de-Latinized woman) was reversed for men and women when sound came to motion pictures and silent film stars had to speak. Men who spoke with a Latin accent were relegated to secondary roles while women with accents gained in popularity. Latina Lovers who did not change their names or their looks but instead capitalized on them for laughs include Lupe Velez, who helped create the stereotype of the hot-blooded, hot tamale Spitfire who spoke with an accent and got into lots of comedic mischief. Velez and Carmen Miranda used their accents as part of their comedic charm.

Comparable to stereotypes of other ethnic groups that embody racist

assumptions about Euro-American superiority, Dim-Witted Clowns/
Buffoons are noted in *The Bronze Screen* as recurring caricatures in come-
dies and as comic relief in dramas, often used to discredit historical Mexican leaders (such as Poncho Villa) in fictional portrayals. Although she
does not exactly compare with caricatures of Latino cowpokes without a
clue, with lazy Latinos napping under sombreros, or with backwards Latinos ineptly commanding troops against Anglos, students can debate
whether or not the happy, carefree, and often childlike Spitfire also qualifies
as a (female) Buffoon.

As with other ethnic groups, Latinos/as are concerned about the ways
they have been misrepresented and that they have not been able to represent themselves. *The Bronze Screen* notes, for example, that the lead Mex-
ican character in *Touch of Evil* is played by a Euro American (Charlton
Heston) in brown face and that the two lead Puerto Rican characters in
West Side Story are not played by Puerto Ricans or even Latinos/as (Natalie
Wood is Maria, and George Chakiris is Bernardo). This, according to *The
Bronze Screen*, suggests to Latinos/as that they cannot be lead actors even
in stories about themselves. And, while Luis Valdez discusses *Giant*
(George Stevens, 1956) as a rare Hollywood movie about racism against
Mexicans and Mexican Americans, he also laments that such a film has
only been done with a Euro-American protagonist.

The Bronze Screen recommends a number of films as important for
displacing Latino/a stereotypes with portrayals of diverse individuals and
families with distinct cultural backgrounds. Among these films, Anthony
Mann's (1949) *Border Incident* exposes abuses of the Bracero program that
brought Mexican farm laborers into the U.S. to fill labor needs during
World War II. Herbert Bieberman's (1953) *Salt of the Earth* chronicles a
real-life labor strike by Mexican-American miners to again show the dignity of working class men, as well as the critical role played by women.
When the men are prohibited by the Taft-Hartley Act from continuing
their strike for safer working conditions and wages equal to Anglos, the
women take over and add sanitary conditions (such as running water)
equal to Anglos to the demands. Although they are treated like and are
called a Greaser and a Hot Tamale, the husband and wife protagonists and
other Mexican-American strikers prevail, striking blows against stereotyping as well as corporate greed at the expense of Latino/a workers. Luis
Valdez' (1987) *La Bamba*, a feature film biography of rock and roll star
Ritchie Valens' rise to stardom and early death, is also the story of his
Mexican-American family, including the older brother whose dreams were
never fulfilled. Gregory Nava's (1983) *El Norte* and (1995) *My Family/Mi
Familia* chronicle the immigrant histories and lives of Latino families in

America. *El Norte (The North)* begins in Guatemala, where a brother and sister must leave their village or be killed by the same people who killed their father and kidnapped their mother: rich landowners who refuse to return land to the peasants (who are now forced to work the land they once owned) and military and government officials who profit from the exploitation. The siblings make their way across Mexico and into the United States, only to find the North is not the paradise they expected. As in Guatemala, they are again part of an exploited underclass of laborers, but they are now also subject to deportation. Nava's *My Family/Mi Familia* tells the story of the Sanchez family, from the father's arrival from Mexico in the 1920s through his children's (and grandchildren's) lives in East Los Angeles in the 1980s. The story encompasses much of Latino history in California, including the deportation of Mexican Americans during the Depression and the immigration of South Americans for political asylum during the 1980s. The Sanchez children themselves represent the diversity of Mexican Americans: one joins the military, one graduates from college and becomes a lawyer, one becomes a nun and then a political activist, one runs a restaurant, and two become gang members. As in the earlier *American Me, My Family* details the discrimination and limited opportunities that can tempt young men into gang life and highlights its deadly consequences. And — as in *Border Incident, Salt of the Earth, La Bamba*, and *El Norte—My Family* traces family histories and celebrates cultural traditions for non–Latinos/as to understand and so Latino/a Americans can recognize themselves.

Comparing Stereotypes of Ethnic Minorities

Students should understand that identifying stereotypes and recognizing them in films of the past and present is only a beginning. The study of ethnic caricatures includes dispelling those images as false to reality and understanding how such misrepresentations have ill served both the ethnic groups themselves and the nation's efforts to define and create itself as a democracy with equal opportunity and equal justice for all. Dismissing ethnic stereotypes also involves recognizing more accurate depictions of ethnic history, culture, and diverse individuals within each ethnic group and using these depictions to understand each other and to understand the actual basis on which our ever-changing multicultural nation exists. Comparing stereotyped representations of different ethnic groups can help students to understand the dominant culture's tendency to prejudge and stereotype in order to justify unjust actions, especially during eras when historical, cultural, and economic circumstances seem to threaten that dominance. There are, for example, similar derogatory representations of African-American slaves and former slaves, of American Indians and Mexican Americans during periods of Manifest Destiny, and of Japanese Americans during World War II as uncivilized, inferior, and unworthy of full citizenship. And there are similar so-called positive stereotypes that are positive only to those who perpetuate them. These representations are becoming part of America's past and how the dominant culture saw itself in relation to ethnic minorities. They need to be recognized as snapshots of past errors that can serve as guides to a different future.

Education Issues

Films about education issues are an effective means for students to learn about past and ongoing issues of segregation and assimilation and about the variety of film forms that depict individual case studies. Frank Christopher's (1985) *The Lemon Grove Incident* is about a California school board's 1930 attempt to segregate Mexican-American students from Euro-American students. This docudrama (part documentary and part feature film) provides a unique combination of both mediated facts and emotion-evoking fictions, using the techniques and persuasive evidence of both film types. *The Lemon Grove Incident* combines archival photos, interviews with now-adult former students, and reenactments of the events that made Lemon Grove the nation's first successful desegregation case. Students can examine the validity of dramatic reenactments and note how match cuts (that replace archival photos of groups of former students with groups of actual former students) and sound bridges (where period background music played to accompany archival photos becomes foreground music played on the piano in a reenactment scene) serve to create a seamlessly realistic representation. Comparing depictions, issues, and film techniques in *The Lemon Grove Incident* with those in a more traditional documentary, "Taking Back Our Schools" (part three of Hector Galon's 1996 four-part *Chicano! History of the Mexican American Civil Rights Movement*), can foster students' familiarity with Latino/a issues of desegregation and with the techniques and evidence that docudramas and documentaries use to persuade viewers.

The ongoing topic of desegregation for African-American students is addressed in several films on the important Civil Rights legislation known as Brown v. Board of Education. William Elwood and Mykola Kulishm's (1989) documentary *The Road to Brown*, George Stevens' (1991) made-for-television feature film *Separate But Equal,* and the (2004) documentary *Black/White and Brown: Brown Versus the Board of Education of Topeka* each focus on the legal assaults on segregation that led to the Supreme Court decision of equality under the Constitution. Given comparable scenes to analyze, students can come to understand different aspects of the case, how even documentaries on the same topic approach that topic differently, and how documentary and feature film representations differ substantially in the ways they present the same information. The films cover a variety of topics that can lead to supplemental student research for individuals or groups, such as the Jim Crow segregation that led to the Brown decision, the combined legal cases in the Brown case, the deliberations and wording of the Supreme Court decision, the immediate and continuing backlash in response to legal desegregation, the immediate effect of the decision on all students and on the Civil Rights Movement itself, and the continuing legacy of the Brown decision today for students of all ethnicities. Following the 2004 fifty-year celebration and analysis of the successes and failures of Brown v. Board of Education, books, websites, and lesson plans on Brown became available for teachers.[17] Films on Brown v. Education offer overviews of this pivotal moment in the Civil Rights Movement as a means for students to understand how and why the Civil Rights Movement began, how and why the work of desegregation is not yet over, and how the issue is directly relevant to students of all ethnicities today.

Another topic addressed in films on education is past and ongoing issues of assimilation. One such issue is whether students from Spanish-speaking homes should be taught in Spanish, English, or some combination. The (1998) documentary, *The Merrow Report: Lost in Translation: Latinos, Schools and Society*, looks at the controversy over bilingual education in the context of high school dropout rates among Latino youth. A narrative short, *Victor,* Dianne Haak Edson's (1989) adaptation of a Clare Galbraith book of the same title, shows how a Mexican-American youth struggles to live in two separate worlds: his English-only speaking school and his Spanish-only speaking home. Students can discuss how neither film successfully resolves the issue but both bring varying perspectives to this multi-perspective issue. Bringing the topic of Latino/a education into a contemporary urban setting, a narrative segment from David Riker's (1998) *La Ciudad (The City)* offers a contemporary view of the effects that a bureaucratic requirement (that all students enrolled in New York City schools must have a home address) has on a homeless Latina child, preventing her from attending school. On the topic of assimilationist schooling for American Indians, students can pair for comparison Bruce Pittman's

(1989) made-in-Canada feature film *Where the Spirit Lives* with Christine Lesiak and Matthew Jones' (1991) *American Experience* documentary *In the White Man's Image*, about Canadian and U.S. government boarding schools designed to eliminate Native American customs, religions, languages, and family ties in order to force Indian assimilation into a subservient place in white culture. Both films take viewers into North American Indian communities of the past, and both examine government and church attempts at cultural genocide from both well- and ill-intended patrons and educators. These films, alone or in combination, provide students with an abundance of discussion material for the topic of how even good intentions in deciding what is best for unfamiliar and unconsulted others can have unintended and often disastrous results.

Immigration Issues

Immigration stories on film can provide social studies students with insights into assimilation issues and ethnic relations in America. Pairing a Hollywood feature and a documentary film can give students different information and a variety of perspectives on a single issue. On the topic of immigrant employment and civil rights, teachers can pair for comparison viewing and discussion Louis Malle's (1985) feature film *Alamo Bay* and Spencer Nakasako and Vincent DiGirolamo's (1982) documentary *Monterey's Boat People*. Both films are about new Vietnamese American refugees attempting to use their fishing skills in American waters previously controlled by Euro Americans. Comparing *Alamo Bay*, which includes a love story and is meant to entertain but is based on a real event, and *Monterey's Boat People*, which is meant to inform as well as engage interest, students can discuss both what they learned and how they learned it in order to come to a better understanding of labor disputes in areas where there are scarce resources (in this case in over-fished waters) and ethnic discrimination based on which group was there first. Discussions should include comparing the film forms and techniques that convince students to adopt or question the positions the films advocate. Students can also discuss how *Alamo Bay* challenges the usual white male perspective in Hollywood films by adding both a Vietnamese male and a Euro-American female protagonist to divide viewer interest among the three and, at the film's end, by eliminating the white male as someone uninterested in the professed American values of fair play and equal opportunity. After learning about the Asian American Model Minority stereotype, students can note how *Alamo Bay* creates sympathy for the Vietnamese male

In the White Man's Image (Christine Lesiak, Matthew Jones 1991). This archival photograph of an Indian Boarding School appears in the documentary.

by making him a model minority character who is eager to follow the rules, decides to rock the boat in the interest of equal opportunity when he wants to own his own boat rather than work for Euro Americans, and is on his way to fulfilling his wish by film's end.

Other immigrant experience films challenge the idea of acceptance and reward for model minority behavior that *Alamo Bay* relies on. The (1996) documentary *From a Different Shore: The Japanese American Experience* exposes assumptions underlying the stereotype with stories of how difficult and how fraught with discrimination the Japanese American road to assimilation has been. The (1990) documentary *The Iron Road*, about the building of the transcontinental railroad by Chinese immigrants after gold was discovered in 1849 in California, also speaks to the continual dangers and discrimination they faced. And Erika Surat Anderson's (1999) short narrative *Turbans* tells the story of an Indian American Sikh family (the parents born in India and the children in California) in Oregon. When the boys are abused because they wear turbans and school officials refuse to protect them, the price they must pay for their safety is reluctant and distressful cultural assimilation: removing the turbans and cutting the boys' hair.

Cultural Appropriation

Documentary films identifying ethnic social and cultural issues offer students informative content and a means to examine how that content is presented — to critically examine point of view, what filmmakers offer as compelling testimony and relevant evidence, and to decide what may be missing — in order to become both informed and critical viewers. Jay Rosenstein's (1996) documentary *In Whose Honor?* looks at both sides of the controversy surrounding the use of Indian names, logos, and mascots for high school, university, and professional sports teams. The film includes still-photo and video accounts of the real-life attempts of American Indian Charlene Teters to stop the controversial practice, including her struggles as a graduate student to persuade the University of Illinois-Champaign to eliminate their Indian mascot and then to educate the nation about this widespread appropriation and misuse of her cultural heritage. Students can examine the film as a point-of-view documentary that aims to present both sides of the issue fairly — as it includes interviews with university administrators and alumni who favor keeping the mascot and logo based on the argument that it honors Indians— even while persuading viewers to accept Teters' position. The issue and the film itself are particularly relevant for high school and college students, whose own high schools, colleges, and favorite professional teams often have Indian names and whose practice in weighing evidence in documentary films is minimal.[18]

Land Rights Issues

Documentaries, as students can quickly discern, do not always present both sides of an issue equally, as a variety of films about American Indian land rights demonstrate. Native American battles over Black Hills land rights are presented solely from a Native American religious perspective in Mel Lawrence's (1993) documentary *Paha Sapa: The Struggle for the Black Hills*. Students can discuss how this limited but compelling perspective can be effective in educating others as Native Americans testify how the sacred Black Hills are being desecrated and how they are frequently prevented from worshipping in their sacred space because the hills are open to anyone who wants to hike, picnic, and camp while, ironically, the faces of U.S. Presidents on Mount Rushmore are legally off limits to anyone because they are set apart as a sacred space within the Black Hills for Euro Americans. The contrary is true in Randy Croce's (1987) *Clouded Land*, where the conflicting perspectives of both Euro Americans who are farming Minnesota land and American Indians who want to move back to their native lands (illegally taken by the U.S. government and sold to the farmers) are given equal time and weight. Interviews with individuals on both sides of the disputed lands issue encourage viewers to sympathize with all of them as victims of poor government policies of the past. Students can discern and discuss the kinds and amounts of information these documentaries provide to help them understand both Indian land rights issues and the variety of ways documentaries present information to get their point of view across.

Civil Rights Issues

The social studies classroom is an ideal place to discuss civil rights issues on film and films as a means to inspire social justice. While the (1986) PBS documentary *Eyes on the Prize* remains the definitive film series on the Civil Rights Movement, Charles Guggenheim's (1989) documentary *A Time for Justice: America's Civil Right's Movement* provides an abbreviated chronological overview useful for shorter classroom viewing time. This film offers students an opportunity to analyze how some documentaries not only attempt to show viewers what actually happened but also provide a virtual experience of those events. *A Time for Justice* often documents important events with black and white still photographs, as it explains the events with voice-over narration and adds realistic sound effects. Viewers experience the horror of a burning Freedom Rider bus, for example, by seeing a still photograph and hearing the sounds of a crackling fire, the screams of people in and surrounding the bus, and the background sirens of a fire truck. This documentary offers viewers a mediated, and persuasive, perceptual-reality, you-are-there experience, with added sound effects akin to those in feature films. From this film, students can also realize how documentaries present much information in a short period of time and are thus valuable overviews that invite viewers to learn more about specific events.

A Time for Justice can provide the impetus for students to examine fictionalized versions of civil rights events and issues in feature films in order to understand more about the civil rights era from narratives that tell personal, behind-the-scenes stories. John Korty's (1973) *The Autobiography of Miss Jane Pittman* traces the life of a black Louisiana woman from her childhood as a slave to the birth of the Civil Rights Movement. Richard Pearce's (1990) *The Long Walk Home* depicts white and black perspectives on the 1955 civil rights bus boycott. Roger Young's (1990) *Murder in Mississippi* recounts the murders of three young civil rights workers in 1964 from their perspectives. George Stevens' (1991) *Separate But Equal* tells the story of NAACP lawyer Thurgood Marshall's fight for desegregation after black children are denied a school bus in 1950s South Carolina. Rob Reiner's (1996) *Ghosts of Mississippi* chronicles the 1963 murder of civil rights leader Medgar Evers and the Euro-American lawyer who reopened the unsolved case thirty years later to finally convict the killer in 1994. And Phil Robinson's made-for-television (2000) *Freedom Song* is a coming-of-age story of a black teen who joins the crusade to desegregate his small Mississippi town. Two feature films by Spike Lee bring civil rights events and issues up to date and remind viewers that the struggle for civil rights is far from over. Lee's (1989) *Do the Right Thing* presents a day in New York's Bedford Stuyvesant that erupts into violence when African-American patrons confront the owner of an Italian pizzeria about his promotion of Italian-American culture in their African-American neighborhood and the confrontation results in the police-induced death of one of the protestors. The film ends with intertitles quoting the opposing philosophies of Martin Luther King, Jr., and Malcolm X, inviting viewers to interpret the story in terms of the need to continue the work of the Civil Rights Movement and in terms of the two very different philosophies to end discrimination as possible solutions. Major issues in the film are clear — African Americans are still fighting for representation and the lives of African Americans are still being lost to needless police brutality — but the solutions are not, and that is the real issue of the film. Students can also analyze Lee's (1996) *Get on the Bus*, a story about the journey of very different black men all going to the 1995 Million Man March who discuss what it means to be a black man in today's America as a civil rights film with both ongoing and new civil rights issues.

For students exploring the social impact of visual images and the ability of films to inspire social justice, the ongoing story of the death of Emmett Till provides the means to do both. While the Supreme Court's 1954 Brown v. Board of Education decision to end segregation was the landmark legal beginning of the Civil Rights Movement, the death of Emmett Till one year later and the legal injustice of the court system that acquitted his murderers (who, shielded by double jeopardy, later confessed in a story they sold to Look magazine for $4,000) was clearly the spark that ignited the nation emotionally. Part I of the documentary *Eyes on the Prize: America's Civil Rights Years* tells the story as it was known in 1986. Fourteen-year-old Till, an African-American boy from Chicago visiting his Southern relatives in Money, Mississippi, was murdered for whistling at a white woman named Carolyn Bryant while buying candy at the

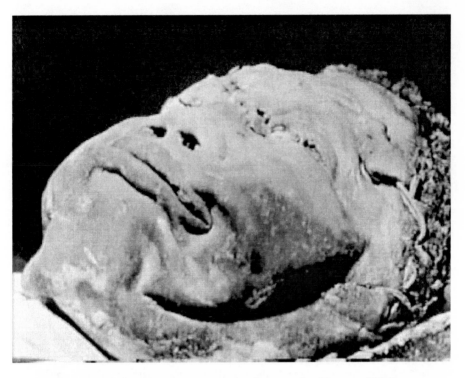

Eyes on the Prize (Henry Hampton, 1986). Photograph of Emmett Till in an open casket.

Bryant's grocery store. His uncle, Mose Wright, testified at the trial that Till was taken from his bed during the night, and Till's corpse was found at the bottom on the Tallahatchie River a few days later, a bullet hole in his head, and his mutilated body weighted down with an old cotton-gin fan. Along with the lack of justice during the trial, a photo of Till's mutilated body in the open casket that his mother insisted upon — shown in *Eyes on the Prize*— both offended and awakened the nation. Thousands saw Till's body for themselves as they passed by the casket, and thousands more saw the visual image in the pages of *Jet* magazine and other publications. A little more than three months after Till's murder, Rosa Parks chose not to give up her seat to a white man on a bus in Montgomery, Alabama.

The power of film to enact belated social justice is evidenced in two documentaries— Stanley Nelson's (2003) *The Murder of Emmett Till* and Keith Beauchamp's (2004) *The Untold Story of the Murder of Emmett Louis Till.* In May of 2004 the Justice Department announced that it was reopening the criminal investigation into the almost fifty-year-old murder of

Emmett Till on the basis of new information provided by these documentaries.[19] The documentaries show that several people (in addition to the two men acquitted) still living may have also participated in Till's murder. Each of the documentaries captures on film the testimony of witnesses who were harassed or too frightened to testify originally and the testimony of witnesses who did testify but were ignored. In an age where video images of the police beating of Rodney King have become part of our nation's collective consciousness and part of our nation's historical record of the racism embedded in our criminal justice system, the two Emmett Till documentaries send the clear message that film images have the power to inform and influence — in this case to confront rather than ignore and silently condone our racist past, to expose the disastrous effects of racism and inspire viewers to work to eradicate it, and to give our criminal justice system the documentary evidence it needs to enact social justice.

8

Literature: Teaching Ethnic-American Literature on Film and as Film

by Carole Gerster

Film narratives are the popular literature of our age. In the nineteenth and the early twentieth centuries, when the novel was the dominant narrative medium, cultural critics worried about the novel's power to affect the attitudes and actions of impressionable readers. With film now the dominant narrative medium, cultural critics write of the demise of the book and the ascendancy of the image, as they worry about the power of film to affect the attitudes and actions of apparently even more impressionable film viewers.[1] On the negative side, Hollywood films still too often ignore ethnic minority stories, or they pander in stereotypes or focus on the adventures of Euro-American male protagonists venturing into ethnic communities. On the positive side of films' influence, ethnic literature on film can provide students of all disciplines with the opportunity to learn about ethnic minorities in America's past and present in well-crafted, memorable stories that engage attention and rouse emotions in ways that non-narrative texts cannot. Narrative is an essential element of human activity; we tell stories about ourselves, and we absorb stories about others to help us make sense of the past as well as the world we currently live in. Because viewers become involved with the characters they see in front of them — we come to dislike the antagonists and to identify with the protagonists, care what happens to them, and root for and remember them —film stories have the power to shape viewers' ideas about people of their own ethnicity as well as people of ethnicities other than their own. For literature students, ethnic literature on film can be defined according to its origins: as film adaptations of written literary works and as original film stories.

Film Adaptations of Written Literary Works

Pairing written narratives and their film adaptations allows students to compare the two, not to ascertain fidelity or lack of fidelity to the original, but to understand their differences. If for no other reason, film adaptations differ from their written originals because the two are different media. Rather than simply reducing a film narrative to what is missing from the original story, students can discover what is missing, what is changed, and what is added and can then develop their analytical and interpretative skills by asking of the film content "What is gained?" and "What is lost?" in the transformation. Students can also compare similar and differing narrative techniques of prose fiction and feature films in order to understand how the written word is transformed into the visual image, and, ultimately, to become better readers of both media.

Film Adaptations of Non-Fiction Texts: The Memoir

The memoir is a literary genre. Although based on lived realities, memoirs follow fictional narrative conventions in giving order and meaning to individual experiences, and they arise from (sometimes faulty and always reconstituted) memories that need to fit into that order and meaning. Film adaptations (whether faithful or loose) most often condense the story to fit the time limits of the feature film, and filmmakers always make changes to the story to fit an order and meaning that will be visually experienced. Pairing for comparison a written and a filmed memoir invites students to explore not only plot and structural differences but also similarities and differences in how written and visual narrative techniques provide information, emphasize themes, engage emotions, and encourage reader and viewer identification with central characters.

Pairing Jeanne Wakatsuki Houston and James Houston's (1973) memoir *Farewell to Manzanar* with John Korty's (1976) made-for-television film adaptation of the same name provides students with a specific task: to compare written memories of Japanese American Internment with film visualizations.[2] Wakatsuki Houston's account of the three and a half years she and her family spent in California's Manzanar internment camp when she was a child, beginning at age seven in 1942, was composed with the aid of the memories of family members and friends, with the findings of researchers (see the memoir Foreword), and with the help of her writer husband to choose material and help shape the whole into story form.[3] The resulting memoir is not fidelity to memory almost thirty years after the fact but an attempt to record some of the historical realities of the internment and share some of the experiences of, and effects on, one family. In comparing the written and film versions, students can discover and discuss both structural and storytelling differences to develop critical reading skills for both types of narrative.

After reading the memoir and viewing the film, students answering the "What is lost?" and "What is gained?" questions will notice that the film version has omitted events in the memoir. Gone is the chronicle of the family's struggles to reenter society after internment, recounted in the book from about the middle of Chapter 19 to the middle of Chapter 22. Although the film includes the voice over of Jeanne Wakatsuki and a conversation between Jeanne's mother and father (Misa and Ko Wakatsuki) before they leave Manzanar in 1945 — informing viewers of lingering racism in the society they are about to reenter and of the problems the family will have starting over without a home or employment — the missing part of the Wakatsuki's story constitutes a significant omission in the film. Film viewers do not learn about the after effects of the internment on Jeanne Wakatsuki. Missing is the way she is made to feel — that she is a foreigner in the country of her birth (114), that she must assimilate to become "invisible" and "acceptable" (114), that she is somehow to blame when she is discriminated against (115), that to be accepted, she must look like an exotic "Oriental female [who] can fascinate Caucasian men" (117, 124), that her wish to fit in conflicts with her parents' ethnic traditions (120), and that she cannot quite fit in even as she strives to be a model minority (122–23, 133). Because these are the stereotypes and lingering issues that Japanese American written and film texts still confront, students who have studied stereotypes or other Asian American literature will insist that the omission of this part of the memoir is an important loss. The reason for the omission is clear: the film focuses on Wakatsuki Houston's memories of her father's story rather than her own and on the internment itself rather than the aftermath. Students not only interpret literatures differently; they also bring different levels of expertise to discussions. In this case, some students, especially those for whom Japanese American Internment is a new subject, may decide that an answer to "What is gained?" in the page-to-screen transformation is that the film's focus further informs them about the internment experience and that to include the family's reentry into California society would dilute that story.

The beginnings and endings of the memoir and the film are worth comparing. The film ends as the memoir ends, with Jeanne Wakatsuki Houston's memory flashback to Ko Wakatsuki's triumphant, if shaky, practice exit from Manzanar in a newly purchased old car that he insists the family use to leave Manzanar instead of being relegated to a bus like the other interned families. The purpose of the scene in the memoir is the same, but heightened, in the film: both serve to return Ko Wakatsuki's dignity and self-respect. In the memoir, Wakatsuki Houston recalls how she and other family members hung on for a bumpy ride past the firebreak and out into open country, and how she now thinks of the firewall area as the "invisible barrier" that once kept the family interned (144). In the film, Ko Wakatsuki and his family again drive beyond the firewall, but he also drives the car into, and knocks down, a sign reading "Manzanar Limit: War Relocation Area" that marked their imprisonment. If asked to make a page-to-film scene comparison, students can discover that, since crossing an "invisible barrier" is not a viable option in a visual medium, the sign serves as a visual metaphor of internment for Ko Wakatsuki and for viewers to (vicariously) destroy. It is a defiant act of liberation shared as a memorable experience by viewers.

While the memoir begins with an announcement of the bombing of Pearl Harbor, the film begins with a voice over of Jeanne Wakatsuki Houston explaining that Manzanar is where she spent her childhood years. Korty's film begins as both it and the memoir end: with Wakatsuki Houston, accompanied by her husband and children, returning to Manzanar thirty years after her internment so that she might come to an understanding of an experience she has tried to forget and they can begin to learn about. The film's beginning borrows from the memoir's ending to establish that the story to follow is a flashback from the point of view of a former internee, Wakatsuki Houston. Showing a scene from Deborah Gee's (1988) documentary *Slaying the Dragon*, where director John Korty appears as one of the experts, can help students understand why the film begins this way. Korty explains that he was asked to film the memoir story from the point of view of a Euro-American male, perhaps a teacher or visitor to Manzanar, to give viewers someone to identify with. Although he is a Euro-American male, Korty insisted that the story should be told from the perspective of an internee and that the old Hollywood convention of a white male protagonist/narrator is not necessary in a film where there is an entire family of a mother, father, children, and grandmother for viewers to identify with. Korty's remarks also explain why he immediately follows the opening with the voice over of Wakatsuki Houston describing and the camera depicting her parents' silver wedding anniversary: although the same scene doesn't appear until Chapter 6 of the memoir, Korty moved it near the opening to invite viewers to identify with the family enjoying a well-known family celebration. Exemplifying the filmmaker's intention to depict victims of internment as Japanese Americans rather than Japanese, the scene shows a typical American family for audiences of all ethnicities to identify with and have empathy for. Students can analyze the scene as an introduction to Japanese American life for non–Japanese American viewers and a realistic representation of pre–World War II life for Japanese Americans. The dinner is a combination of American and Japanese foods, and the after-dinner celebration includes a daughter and a daughter-in-law singing both popular American and Japanese songs. Invited guests include an Italian-American fishing buddy of Ko Wakatsuki, Tony, and his wife, and Granny shows them how to use chopsticks and eat sushi.

This family celebration scene, with the Italian Americans included as good friends of the family, and a later scene in which a sympathetic German-American internment camp director explains that his sons are currently at war in Germany and may be killing or killed by their own distant relatives, are additions to the film that students can discuss as important gains in the memoir-to-film translation. Teachers who isolate these scenes — and perhaps also the scene where two Wakatsuki sons, Woody and Rich, try to visit their father in jail and wonder aloud why Italian and German Americans are also not being arrested — can guide their students to and through a discussion of important issues highlighted in the film. Teachers can provide information about the little-known, short-term relocation of a number of Italian and German Americans who were not U.S. citizens[4] and can open for discussion the question of why Japanese Americans were singled out for internment from February of 1942 until the end of the war in 1945, even though no cases of Japanese American spying were ever discovered. Students guided to find and analyze these and other additions to the film — such as the information added to the film that Ko Wakatsuki provides in his answers to his interrogator regarding the legal discrimination against Asian Americans — can discuss and better understand the racial prejudice that led to, maintained, and persisted after the internment of Japanese Americans.

Students can compare a number of similar representations in this memoir and film, including the arrest and interrogation of Issei (first-generation Americans, born in Japan) men as suspected spies for Japan, the evacuation and internment of Issei and Nisei (second-generation children of the Issei, American citizens by birth), the unlivable camp conditions made more livable by internees, and the disagreements among internees over the loyalty oath they were required to take.[5] Specific scenes invite specific comparisons. For example, in both memoir (Chapter Seven) and film, Ko Wakatsuki is arrested by the FBI, sent to Fort Lincoln in North Dakota, and interrogated to determine whether he should be sent back to Japan as a spy who has been "delivering oil to Japanese submarines off the coast of California." Much of the dialogue exchanged between Ko Wakatsuki and the interrogator is similar. In both memoir and film, Wakatsuki explains that FBI photos of containers in his boat are not drums filled with oil but barrels filled with chum (fish bait). He also complains that the photos are over a year old, suggesting that the FBI has been spying on Japanese Americans long before Pearl Harbor.

A topic for student analysis is why some of the depictions and dialogue in the two media are significantly different. In both memoir and film, when the interrogator asks, "Do you feel any loyalty to Japan or to its Emperor?" Ko Wakatsuki answers with the question, "When were you born?" The answer, "1913," elicits Wakatsuki's response that he has been living in the United States nine years longer than the interrogator has been alive, yet he is prevented by law from owning land because he is not a citizen and is prevented by another law from becoming a citizen. The difference is in the interrogator's response. In the memoir he says, "Those matters are out of my hands." In the film, before this line, he says, "In America, anyone can become a citizen," and Wakatsuki responds, "Anyone but Orientals. Look it up, Captain. The government can do anything it wants to me. I have no rights." Students who analyze the subtle but important difference will notice that, in both instances, the interrogator is naïve regarding what he knows about Issei life in America and Wakatsuki educates him, but also that his naivete is emphasized in the film and he is admonished to "look up" what he does not know. Students can respond to the idea that the additional lines suggest that the FBI, the young interrogator and, by extension, viewers who do not know the facts can and should "Look it up" to get them right.[6] As his final question in both memoir and film, the interrogator asks, "Who do you want to win the war?" and Ko Wakatsuki answers, "When your mother and father are having a fight, do you want one to kill the other or do you just want them to stop fighting?" The memoir chapter then abruptly ends, inviting readers to react to the powerful metaphor Wakatsuki has provided as his answer. Film viewers hear the same question and the same answer, but then watch the interrogator react with embarrassment as he lowers his eyes to his desk. The film's point is clear: the interrogator realizes he knows little about Japanese American (Issei) identity and has asked a foolish question. Readers and viewers are expected to recognize the foolishness of the question and to empathize with Ko Wakatsuki in knowing that those involved in internment policies were operating without adequate knowledge, but film viewers are guided to the response via the interrogator as a reactive character. The novel begins a new chapter, but the film then includes a visual metaphor: viewers see the U.S. flag being lowered, suggesting that the United States internment policy is not a matter of national pride. Students can easily learn to recognize and distinguish literary and film techniques, such as the literary metaphor, the reactive character, and the visual metaphor in these film scenes. Whether or not readers come to the same conclusions without the film's additional visualizations of a reactive character and a visual metaphor is a topic for student discussion.

Additional Memoirs

Memoirs offer personal points of view and sustained accounts of individual lives for students to identify with and understand that other nonfiction texts lack. Akin to *Farewell to Manzanar*, an African-American and an American-Indian memoir, in both written and filmed versions, also involve students in the larger picture of the eras in which the individuals lived. The African-American film biography, Spike Lee's (1992) *Malcolm X*, based on Alex Haley's (1964) *The Autobiography of Malcolm X*, invites students to follow the awakening of a petty criminal to the racist society in which he lives and to learn how he forms and reforms his ideas of ways to change that society. Following Malcolm X's transformation helps students to explore what it meant then to live in a racist society compared to what African Americans experience today, the need for civil rights then compared to needs for social and economic justice today, and Malcolm X's varying solutions of separation and integration that are still being debated today. Comparing Lee's film to Haley's book, or to selected scenes from Haley's book, offers students a means to judge a book by its film in terms of what is lost and what is gained in the word-to-image transformation.

Students can discuss and even debate the importance of Lee's changes as a means to simplify complexities, emphasize memorable events, and involve viewers in the drama in ways that the written word cannot. Additions include images in the prologue opening (continuing as background as the opening credits roll) of the beating of Rodney King to alert viewers that the story of Malcolm X is still relevant. An important episode in both the memoir and the film, of Malcolm X exposing an instance of police brutality and insisting on medical assistance for the man beaten, connects back to this opening. For students interested in thinking about how people and events of the past are relevant to the present, this opening is a significant gain. Changes involve beginning the film story with a more dramatic scene from later in the memoir but omitting the commentary that originally accompanied the scene. The film story begins with Malcolm

Little getting a conk (getting his hair straightened) and being pleased because it makes him look "white." Haley's memoir describes the same scene but also includes Malcolm X's commentary that "This was my first really big step toward self-degradation: when I endured all of the pain, literally burning my flesh to have it look like a white man's hair, I had joined that multitude of Negro men and women in America who are brainwashed into believing that the black people are 'inferior'—and white people 'superior'—that they will even violate and mutilate their God-created bodies to try to look 'pretty' by white standards" (54). Here, as elsewhere, the film story unfolds so that what viewers see is always in the present, while the memoir is told in retrospect with Malcolm X's informative hindsight commentary. Students can discuss whether or not the film is effective in presenting insights from the commentary in the book via a visual metaphor. In the film, when Malcolm Little is getting another conk and discovers the water (necessary to wash out the caustic lye used to straighten his hair) has been shut off in the apartment, he must degrade himself by putting his head in the toilet. Commentary about self-degradation is replaced here with a visit to the toilet and is postponed until the point in the film where Malcolm Little is in prison and actually did learn that his efforts to look white were self-degrading.

Film additions, omissions, and a change of emphasis invite student analysis. Additions to consider as significant gains include a fantasy sequence where Malcolm Little is a waiter on a train serving with a big smile while imagining himself smearing food in his customer's face in response to the customer's remark, "I like you, boy." Students can discuss the effectiveness of this scene as a visual metaphor for the "double consciousness" W.E.B. DuBois described as the condition of African-American life—the inescapable sense of living in both a black and a white world, of being a divided self, and of having to forever see oneself through the eyes of whites. As a waiter, he must smile rather than retaliate while being insulted. While the film omits much, including the influence of Malcolm X's relatives on his life and ideas, a perhaps even more important issue is Lee's emphasis. A large portion of the film is devoted to Malcolm Little's "Detroit Red" period while giving short shrift to the important changes Malcolm X experienced after his break with the Nation of Islam when he learned that true Islam included people of all ethnicities and revised his claim that all white men are devils. Students can compare the latter part of Malcolm X's autobiography with Lee's attention to the post–Mecca period to judge the final impression the filmmaker gives the viewer of Malcolm X.

An American Indian memoir and its film adaptation also offer students a page-to-screen comparison for analysis. Comparing Mary Crow

Dog and Richard Erdoes's (1990) written memoir *Lakota Woman* and Frank Pierson's (1994) made-for-television feature film adaptation *Lakota Woman: Seige at Wounded Knee*, can help students understand contemporary Lakota life in the context of American-Indian history and explore how film adaptations both remove from and add to their originals. Akin to Malcolm X's differences with the Nation of Islam, this memoir and film reveal how violent disputes between Indians themselves can be seen as the result of different responses to Euro-American racism rooted in the past but continuing in the present. Both memoir and film focus on the 1973 American-Indian protest at Wounded Knee, the site chosen as an alternative to Pine Ridge (where the Lakota Tribal Chief Dick Wilson dismissed traditional Indian culture and beliefs, aligned himself with the federal government in exchange for guns and ammunition, and eliminated Indian protests against his corrupt government by creating a police state) and as the place where George Armstrong Custer and his 7th Cavalry massacred three hundred unarmed Lakota Sioux in 1890, eighty-three years earlier. It is a sacred site that could draw public attention to recurring problems. Memoir and film both depict Mary Crow Dog's life before, during, and after the seventy-three-day protest at Wounded Knee, and both place Wounded Knee events in the larger context of Lakota life.

In comparable scenes about Indian boarding schools, both memoir and film show how the U.S. government's earlier attempts to eliminate American-Indian culture and beliefs and to make Indians into second-class citizens continue and are the basis of the Wounded Knee protests. In Crow Dog's memoir, Indian boarding school education (aided first by religious groups and then by the government's Bureau of Indian Affairs) is indicative of contemporary Indian problems. She writes that the Indian schools "were intended as an alternative to the outright extermination seriously advocated by generals Sherman and Sheridan, as well as most settlers and prospectors over running our land." The schools tried to turn Indians "into useful farmhands, laborers, and chambermaids" who would work for low wages. After their boarding school education, "when they found out — and they found out quickly — that they were neither wanted by whites nor by Indians, they got good and drunk, many of them staying drunk for the rest of their lives" (30). Crow Dog concludes that whites "retreated from this position only step by step in the wake of Indian protests" (31). Her memoir describes in some detail her life and the lives of others at the boarding school, her eventual protest of their treatment, and her leaving the school. Her life is then filled with heavy drinking until she meets American Indian Movement activists and, retracing the Lakota history the boarding school had tried to erase, she rediscovers her past and her pride. The film version's elimination of Crow Dog's commentary about the basis for and the aftermath of the boarding schools is a decided loss, but the its addition of a you-are-there scene offers viewers an understanding of the trauma of the experience itself. The film shows what the memoir does not describe: the arrival of frightened young girls immediately doused by nuns with flea powder and forced to have their hair cut short while a background voice over recites a Christian prayer (beginning "Angel of God, my guardian dear, to whom God's love commenced me here") that they girls must repeat over and over until memorized, heard over the background sounds of the children crying. Then, accompanying a class photo of seemingly well-trained youth, the voice over of Crow Dog explains that "They took our language, our history, our memories." The sensory overload for viewers—seeing the trauma, hearing the indoctrination over the children's cries, and then learning from Crow Dog about her deep sense of loss—offers viewers an experiential sampling of the boarding school experience.

Both memoir and film attempt to show that American Indians need to remember Indian history and that the U.S. government and the country at large need to know that history in order to understand that racism, reservation poverty, alcoholism, and the need for Indians to be reconnected with their culture and their land are related and ongoing problems. Students can also note that both memoir and film are filled with details about Lakota life and culture (including the importance of women in tribal counsels and tribal affairs in general) missing from, or misrepresented in, hundreds of Hollywood Westerns.

Film Adaptations of Novels: The Western

Many students read novels, but most students know the stories in novels through their film adaptations, and most student conversations focus on a non-critical recounting of the memorable characters and scenes in the film versions. They share a visual memory. Comparing the written word with the visual image to discover what and how they learn from films is an appropriate topic of study and a means for all students to become critical viewers. Because film narratives have become the popular literature of our age, tracing ideas and characters in film narratives to their origins in novels or, conversely, following ideas and characters in novels to their transformation in film adaptations, are especially appropriate tasks for literature students. Student research projects can go one step further by comparing the film adaptation to one or more earlier films (which are often more readily available than the novels and are often re-shown on television) in the same genre. Comparing a fictional novel and its film adaptation helps students understand how both are more often reflective of their time of creation than accurate representations of the era they depict, and placing the film beside other films in the same genre helps students discover how often the later film relies on earlier ones for its form as well as its content. As with comparing a memoir and its film adaptation, the goal is not to determine the film's fidelity to the novel but to compare similarities and differences in the transformation from page to screen and to analyze "What is lost?" and "What is gained?" in that transformation. Students who include an analysis of how the film adaptation compares with earlier films in the same genre can ask the additional questions "What is the same?" and "What has changed?"

Michael Blake's (1988) novel *Dances with Wolves* and Kevin Costner's (1990) Academy-Award winning film adaptation of the same name both portray U.S. Army Lieutenant John Dunbar's extended encounter with Plains Indians (Comanche in the novel, Lakota Sioux in the film[7]) during the final days of the Civil War. American Indians did not create either text (Michael Blake, in fact, wrote both the novel and the screenplay), but the film won seven Academy Awards as a highly entertaining revisionist Western that depicts Indians in a new light and, because it is frequently shown on television, it continues to reach millions of new viewers every year. Both texts represent American Indians in ways similar to how viewers have been encouraged to view Indians throughout the twentieth century and, for that reason alone, are worth student analysis. Blake's novel and Costner's film are also good examples of how novels and films differ even when their content is almost identical. In addition, when students discover Costner's repetition of earlier Western conventions and representations, they are often inspired to seek out contemporary films made by Indians about Indians as alternative representations.

Students can begin their comparative analysis by exploring how Blake's novel and Costner's film are products of their time, rather than accurate representations of the era and the Indians they depict, and deciding why this is important. Designed to appeal to a late twentieth-century audience, Blake's novel is filled with anachronisms that students can discuss as one indication that the story is not a serious reflection of a historical era. For example, the omniscient narrator in the novel (who is not a character in the story and thus tells the story from a third-person perspective) compares the dirt stirred by the gallop of Lieutenant Dunbar's horse to the wake of a speedboat (32). The descriptive anachronisms are not repeated in the film, but the protagonist in each has late twentieth-century ideas, values, and sensibilities. In both novel and film, Lieutenant Dunbar thinks, looks, and acts more like a handsome movie-action figure with late twentieth-century American values and beliefs than a Civil War officer. In both, Dunbar is a "lethal machine" (Blake 18) ready for any enemy as well as an environmentalist (who cleans up the polluted river and camp debris left by the Army personnel who were there before him) with a sensitivity to women, children, and animals and a reverence for Plains Indians as Noble Savages whose life in nature he sees as laudable yet doomed to extinction. Akin to a New Age imitator of American Indian ways transported to the nineteenth century, Lieutenant Dunbar joins a band of Lakota and participates in their lifestyle. As a late twentieth-century novel and movie protagonist must, he outdoes the Lakota, letting them know that the buffalo they have been earnestly seeking are so close by that he can hear them even if the Lakota cannot (Blake 154–59), saving a Euro-American woman the Lakota took in as a child when her mourning rituals threaten her life (89–103), and saving the village during a raid by Pawnee while the Lakota warriors are away by supplying them with rifles and instructing them when to shoot (265–70). Both novel and film encourage readers and viewers to identify with the hero during his daring adventures, and the film adds his rescue of a Lakota boy at the end of the buffalo hunt to keep the focus on the Euro-American hero.

Students who compare Costner's *Dances with Wolves* with earlier Westerns will discover other Euro-American and European heroes who are also imaginative reflections of their own time dropped into an imagined nineteenth-century western frontier. In *A Man Called Horse* (1970), for example, an English hero who was initially captured by a band of Sioux while on a hunting trip proves himself worthy of their admiration when he outperforms them at a Sun Dance ritual which not only has little to do with the actual ritual but can only be described as akin to a 1960s hallucinogenic experience. This movie hero also saves the Sioux from other Indians by instructing them how and when to shoot their arrows during a battle. Comparisons can alert students to be aware that Westerns are fictional representations, even when they advertise their historical accuracy, and that repeated misrepresentations of American Indians and their cultural rituals, as well as the focus on superior non–Indian heroes, are all conventions of the Western novel and film genre.

Blake's novel and Costner's film differ more in form than in content. Some novel scenes are left out of the film, and the film adds some and changes some scenes, but students will have difficulty finding any significant gains or losses in the content. Blake's novel begins with the omniscient narrator describing Dunbar's first awe-struck (spiritual) reaction to the great open "empty space" of the west (1). Costner's film opens instead with a highly dramatic scene (described by Blake's narrator as a flashback some thirty pages into the novel), with Dunbar in a makeshift Army hospital about to have his leg amputated. He decides he would rather die, so stuffs his bloody leg into his boot, sneaks on a horse, and rides through enemy fire (twice). Instead of being killed, Dunbar rouses the Union army into action so that they beat back the Confederates, and he is then mistakenly considered a hero. After being given medical aid, he is rewarded with a horse and granted his request for an assignment to a wilderness frontier post before the frontier is gone. Both openings establish Lieutenant Dunbar as the Euro-American protagonist who will usher readers and viewers into American Indian country. To answer "What is lost?" and "What is gained?" in the translation from novel to film, students can discuss how the differences are mostly a matter of visual drama. In the novel, Dunbar is impressed with the magnificently dramatic landscape he finds himself in; in the film, Dunbar is himself impressive and earns viewer empathy with his dramatics and his adventuresome desire to experience the wild frontier for himself. Students can consider how the opening descriptions in both novel and film of a magnificent frontier about to close would differ if the story were told from an (additional or alternative) American-Indian point of view. And students who link *Dances with Wolves* with other films about American Indians with a Euro-American hero — *Broken Arrow* (1950), *The Searchers* (1956), *Little Big Man* (1970), *Soldier Blue* (1970), *A Man Called Horse* (1970), *Return of a Man Called Horse* (1976), and *The Last of the Mohicans* (1909–1992), to name a few of the more famous — can compare how they, too, command the point of view so that viewers learn about the West and American Indians from the perspective and experiences of a dramatically interesting but non–Indian hero.

How the novel and the film evoke and direct reader and viewer responses to the narrative is a topic for student analysis and discussion. The difference in how the stories are told in *Dances with Wolves* is typical of differences between novels and films, as students can explore in comparing how Blake's novel and Costner's film each characterize the Pawnee as dangerous savages. While Blake's omniscient narrator describes everything except the dialogue between the characters and the written entries made by Dunbar in his journal, the film story is told by Dunbar himself via voice over, by dialogue between the characters, and by what the camera shows in long shots, medium shots, close ups, reactive characters, and dramatic crosscutting. In both novel and film, when the wagon driver Timmons leaves Dunbar at his frontier post and travels back to the Army Fort alone, the savage Pawnee appear for the first time. The novel's omniscient narrator explains how Dunbar goes to bed, then depicts the Pawnee as vicious savages, describes how Timmons makes a fire for his morning breakfast, how the Pawnee see the smoke from Timmons's fire and follow it to kill him, and then how Dunbar gets up and makes his own fire (Blake 20–25.) The sequence reveals the viciousness of the Pawnee and suggests that Dunbar could be in danger in the future. The film differs by inviting viewers to fear for Dunbar's life before they realize that it is Timmons' life that is in danger. The film shows Dunbar piling dead animals and rubbish left by his predecessors and lighting the pile on fire. Dunbar then serves as a reactive character: he recoils in fear, and viewers recoil in fear for him, as both see the smoke from his fire rise high into the sky and realize, with the help of a long shot, that the smoke can be seen for miles. Viewers then see and hear the Pawnee having a dialogue about how the smoke they are looking at "could only be from a white man's fire" and connect their discussion with Dunbar's fire. Only with the subsequent crosscutting — between shots of Timmons eating his breakfast beside his smoky fire and the Pawnee continuing their dialogue about whether or not to kill the man who made the fire — do viewers realize that it is Timmons, not Dunbar, who is in immediate danger. Timmons' brutal death then firmly establishes that the hero with whom viewers have come to identify is clearly in danger from savage Indians. Here, as elsewhere, the novel provides readers with the pleasure of imagining the descriptions in their mind's eye and analyzing their purpose while the film offers viewers the pleasure of seeming to be in the scene and seeing and experiencing for themselves both fear and danger as if they were actually there. A comparative analysis of the novel and the film offers students both kinds of pleasures and develops students' critical thinking (visual and multicultural literacy) skills.

As in the novel, in the film, the Pawnee are mere repetitions of Hostile Savage stereotypes with no redeeming characteristics.[8] Novel and film both attempt to mitigate their own stereotyping by slightly differentiating one of the Pawnee men (there are no Pawnee women or children represented) as even more savage than the others, but neither provides any interaction other than showing Pawnee warriors as ready killers of both Euro Americans (first Timmons and then, in flashback, Stands With a Fist's parents) and Comanche/Lakota. Comparing depictions in *Dances with Wolves* with depictions of savage Indians in earlier films reveals many similarities and one difference: that different Indian nations were chosen as savages in different depictions— the Iroquois in *Drums Along the Mohawk* (1939), the Apache in *Stagecoach* (1939), the Comanche (who are the good Indians in Blake's novel) in *The Searchers* (1956), the Pawnee in *Little Big Man* (1970), and the Huron in *The Last of the Mohicans* (1992), to cite just a few of the more famous films.

The endings in the novel and the film differ slightly, but both predict extinction for the Comanche/Lakota that Lieutenant Dunbar comes to know. In both novel and film, the Comanche/Lakota are stereotypical idealized Indians: the Noble Savages who befriend the hero, who live in complete harmony with nature, and whose lives are doomed to extinction in the face of a more technically advanced Euro-American civilization (with such things as the telescope and the rifles Dunbar brings with him) and a ruthless U.S. Army following the ruthless policies of Manifest Destiny. Blake's narrator describes the Comanche from Dunbar's perspective when he first sees them with "everything in such magnificent harmony" (74), and as he later sees them, as "a primitive people ... who lived and prospered through service ... to the simple, beautiful spirit of the way they lived"(177). In the film, viewers hear from Dunbar himself via a voice over about the Lakota: "I'd never known a people so eager to laugh, so devoted to family, so dedicated to each other, and the only word that came to mind was harmony."[9] Both endings begin in the winter camp of the Comanche/Lakota and, in both, Dunbar decides to leave them because he is considered a traitor for dressing like and living among Indians. When the Army comes looking for him, Dunbar reasons, they will also find and destroy the Comanche/Lakota. In both novel and film, Ten Bears tells Dunbar that he is wrong, that he should stay with them because the man the Army is looking for no longer exists; Dunbar is now the Indian Dances With Wolves, as they have been calling him. In the novel, Dunbar takes Ten Bear's advice, and he and his bride Stands With a Fist move with them to a new summer camp, but the omniscient narrator ends with a prediction of the Comanche's extinction: "The good times of that summer were the last they would have. Their time was running out and would soon be gone forever" (313). In the film, Dunbar decides that he and Stands With a Fist must leave to save the Lakota. The film ends as it begins, with high drama. Here Dunbar is established as a potential savior: he leaves to find and talk to whoever will listen to him explain that there are worthy Indians. Viewers see that he was right to leave in crosscutting scenes between the Army traveling closer and closer and Dunbar leaving and then the Army reaching the winter encampment, only to find Dunbar gone and the winter camp moved. As in the novel, however, the Indians are doomed. The film's ending intertitles explain that "Thirteen years later, their homes destroyed, their buffalo gone, the last band of free Sioux submitted to white authority at Fort Robinson, Nebraska. The great horse culture of the plains was gone and the American frontier as soon to pass into history." The demise of the Comanche/Lakota is in line with the stereotyping of the Noble Savage, suggesting that these good but primitive Indians did not survive past the nineteenth century.

Students whose comparative analysis is based on the questions "What is lost?" and "What is gained?" in the novel-to-film translation can be asked to consider why an important gain in the film is having the Lakota actually speak in Lakota language. Contrary to how the novel's anachronistic late twentieth-century analogies reflect the author's late twentieth-century understandings, the film's Lakota language is important in its opposite attempt to reflect historical accuracy and cultural understanding. Because language is an essential element of culture and of cultural differences, the bilingual conversation late in the film between the Lakota medicine man Kicking Bird and John Dunbar speaks to their (and the general importance of) bi-cultural understandings. Students can also react to the idea that presenting Lakota in English subtitle translations is an honest effort to suggest that everything else that viewers learn about Indians in this film is also by means of Euro-American translations and from a Euro-American point of view.

Asking "What is the same?" and "What has changed?" in comparing *Dances with Wolves* with other Westerns opens student explorations to a wide range of similarities and few differences. Students can discover that white male protagonists who take viewers into Indian country, out–Indian Indians, and offer their perspective as the guiding authority on Indians are a film norm; that Hostile Savage and Noble Savage stereotypes have been repeated since film beginnings; and that a great number of film adaptations of novels have ended with the defeat of one and the demise of the other. What is different in *Dances with Wolves* from most Westerns is Costner's attempt to individualize Indians. Students can focus on how the Lakota, even though stereotyped as Noble Savages, are given distinct personalities. In both novel and film, the Comanche/Lakota, like the Pawnee, have "a fierce one" (Blake 119) who argues for killing Dunbar immediately. With the Pawnee, "the fierce one" easily prevails over the others and they immediately murder Timmons; with the Comanche/Lakota, the fierce Wind in His Hair is overruled in a council, and he soon becomes a good friend of Lieutenant Dunbar. His fierceness is a differentiating characteristic when compared to Dunbar's other close friend, Kicking Bird, whom Dunbar describes as "the quiet one." Kicking Bird also has a wife, who often chides him when he is not as attentive as he could be to what is happening with his adopted daughter Stands With a Fist. Few other films attempt to give Indians a family life; here *Dances with Wolves* compares most favorably with Arthur Penn's (1970) depiction of the Cheyenne in *Little Big Man,* a film adaptation of Thomas Berger's (1964) novel, where the Euro-American protagonist also lives off and on among the Sioux. The most significant change from earlier films is Costner's addition of Lakota language and English subtitles to authentically differentiate cultures and to suggest that, in the Hollywood Western, viewers see a Euro-American perspective on American-Indian life.

Alternatives to Westerns

Literature students learning about point of view, and its importance in determining whose story and what story is being told, can explore how Manifest Destiny tales of certain annihilation for American Indians in Westerns change to tales of Indian survival when told from an American Indian perspective. Students seeking alternatives to the popular Western epitomized in *Dances with Wolves* can find them in a number of film adaptations and the novels from which they originate. Jonathan Wacks' (1989) film *Powwow Highway*, an adaptation of David Seals' (1988) novel *The Powwow Highway*, is a depiction of how late twentieth-century Indians successfully battle the continuing consequences of Manifest Destiny. Survival stories of today's urban Indians include Greg Sarris' (1994) novel *Grand Avenue* and the (1996) made-for-television film adaptation of the same title wherein families deal with single-parenting problems and inner-city teen violence, battle unemployment, poverty, and alcoholism, and care for a child with cancer. Other literature and film adaptation survival stories focus on efforts to establish a contemporary Indian identity. Chris Eyre's (1998) independent feature film *Smoke Signals*, based on several short stories by Coeur d'Alene author Sherman Alexie from his (1993) collection *The Lone Ranger and Tonto Fistfight in Heaven*, signals an American Indian attempt at self-representation outside of Hollywood. Students can discuss how pointed allusions to General Custer and the U.S. Cavalry, to John Wayne, and to Hollywood movies (*The Last of the Mohicans, Little Big Man,* and *Dances with Wolves*) define this film as an alternative to Hollywood's Manifest Destiny stories. Akin to Wind in His Hair and Kicking Bird in *Dances with Wolves*, the film features two very different kinds of protagonists to show the diversity of Indian identity, even among young men who have grown up together on the same reservation, but in this film they are not Noble Savages and they are not doomed to extinction. One creates his contemporary Indian identity from his warrior heritage and his love of basketball, and the other tells traditional stories that incorporate contemporary life.

Additional Novels and Film Adaptations

Immigration stories and generational conflicts between mothers and daughters are the focus of another novel and film adaptation. Amy Tan's (1989) novel *The Joy Luck Club* and Wayne Wang's (1993) film adaptation of the same title both tell first-generation Chinese immigrant survival stories that become stories about how the immigrant mothers' hopes and expectations for their daughters seem to conflict with their daughters' own desires. Students of all disciplines can generally relate on a personal level to generational conflicts and can thus identify with protagonists from their own as well as from other ethnic groups whose stories involve such struggles. Tan's novel and Wang's film each address issues for students to explore, including how mothers prove their worth to their daughters, how daughters prove worthy of their mothers' expectations, and how both prove themselves worthy individuals to themselves. In addition, literature students can explore how the stories of four mothers and four daughters are combined in each work to form a whole (through parallels and through the anchoring story of one mother's death and her daughter's preparation to visit China in her mother's place), analyze from the parts that not all

The Joy Luck Club (Wayne Wang, 1993). The Chinese American mothers and daughters.

mothers and daughters from the same ethnic group share the same conflicts, and discover how multiple plot complications can be resolved by the end.

Comparing a scene in the novel to the same scene in the film can help students understand not only what might be lost and what gained in the adaptation, but why the scene is important to this story and even to Asian American storytelling in general. In one comparable scene, Tan's novel and Wang's film both offer the conventional Euro-American male excursion into an ethnic community. Here, however, it is not to see and understand that community through his perspective, but to demonstrate how his perspective can be decidedly wrong. In both novel and film, Waverly Jong is not sure how best to introduce her Euro-American fiancé to her parents, especially to her mother, who thinks no one is good enough to marry her daughter. Waverly brings Rich to dinner so he can praise her mother's wonderful cooking and "win her over" (194). He acts and responds, however, according to his own Euro-American upbringing and makes a disastrous impression. The novel describes the dinner scene in the past tense as it occurred from Waverly's point of view. Waverly's descriptions detail Rich's errors from how he made the mistake of drinking two glasses of wine when everyone else had "just a taste" (196) and then, refusing a fork, thinking he can easily master eating with chopsticks, dropping food onto his lap. Other mistakes follow: as with the wine, he took a large portion of one dish, which did not leave enough for others, and he then refused even a taste of a dish that did not appeal to him. Waverly then describes how Rich inexcusably refused seconds when "he should have followed my father's example" in taking small portions as if they were too good to pass up. The final and "worst" mistake comes when Rich inadvertently criticized her mother's cooking and "didn't even know what he had done." As Waverly explains, "As is the Chinese cook's custom, my mother always made disparaging remarks about her own cooking. That night she chose to direct it toward her famous steamed pork and preserved vegetable dish, which she always served with special pride." She complained that the dish was "not salty enough, no flavor," and Waverly notes that "this was our family's cue to eat some and proclaim it the best she had ever made." But, in Waverly's words, Rich made the mistake of saying, "all it needs is a little soy sauce" and proceeded "to pour a riverful" of it onto the dish, "right before my mother's horrified eyes" (196–97).

Students can analyze differences in terms of how the film scene translates the words of the novel into the language of film with the techniques of voice over and reactive characters. Instead of reading Waverly's assessment of Rich's errors, viewers hear them via voice over while watching a silent, but anxious-looking Waverly react to Rich from across the table. And instead of reading Waverly's descriptions of how Rich should have followed her father's example, viewers see her father and mother as reactive characters who serve as guides for viewer responses, but whom Rich ignores. Waverly's mother says, in response to Rich's mistake of taking so much of a dish that there is not enough left for everyone else, "He has good appetite." Had Rich been alert to those around him, he would also have noticed that Waverly's mother smiles as she explains how her last dish is not worth eating and adds (words missing from the novel) "but try, please," and he would have noticed also that Waverly's father exclaims his disdain with a loud "ahhhh" all during the several seconds it takes Rich to pour soy sauce all over the best dish. In both novel and film, Waverly describes the scene as it happened in the past, but viewers also see and hear it happening to make them part of the dinner experience and to see it through the additional perspectives of Waverly's parents. The novel's descriptions remain, but the added visual and verbal reactions to Rich in the film make the dinner a humorous experience for Chinese American viewers and a learning experience for any inexperienced others. Literature students studying narrative techniques can analyze how this scene functions in both media as comic relief among otherwise serious stories of survival and hope for the future. The scene has no serious repercussions since Rich is accepted into the family, in spite of his culture-ignorant *faux pas*, by Waverly's mother, who, above all, wants her daughter to be happy. Students can also react to the idea that the scene has importance beyond the individual novel and the film to make a statement about point of view. It humorously turns the tables on numerous other stories told from Euro-American perspectives where Asian Americans have served as the butt of humor and where Euro Americans take viewers into and are instant experts on Asian American communities.[10]

Other fiction-to-film comparisons can engage students in ongoing controversies about what is and what isn't a racist depiction. Mark Twain's (1884) *Adventures of Huckleberry Finn* has been made into at least seven films, several of which are available in video form, and several of which are discussed in documentaries, such as the Discovery Channel film *Great Books: Huckleberry Finn* (1995) and the PBS film *Culture Shock*, with a segment called "Born to Trouble: *Adventures of Huckleberry Finn*" (1999). Reading Twain's novel (which is variously praised or banned in high schools across the nation) in conjunction with one or more of the documentaries can help students understand the recurring controversies about racism and representation it elicits.[11] Reading scenes from the novel in conjunction with comparable scenes from one or more of its film adaptations can ignite student discussions about how each one attempts to depict racist attitudes without becoming a racist depiction itself and deciding which succeed, which fail, and why. Students investigating how the novel is a reflection of the time when Twain wrote can also explore how the film adaptations reflect the times in which they were made in the ways they depict (or revise, or simply delete) the novel's most controversial statements and scenes.

William Armstrong's (1969) novel *Sounder* and Martin Ritt's (1972) film adaptation of the same name also provide students with controversies to explore. Both novel and film depict the suffering and resilience of an African-American sharecropping family in Louisiana in the 1930s and suggest that a racist criminal justice system helps to maintain their impoverishment. The film is an important depiction of an African-American woman on screen as it focuses on the mother. Novel and film, however, were both created by Euro-American men, and both have been criticized for their portrayals. Students can join the discussion by noting how Armstrong names none of the major characters except the dog (Sounder), and Ritt changes the novel's ending to a happy one, with the son (David Lee) returning to school and the family situation hopeful. Engaging students in a comparative analysis allows them to decide for themselves what is gained and lost in the film's changes, to consider the recurring question of whether or not being Euro American can make a difference in telling a story about African Americans, and to become both careful readers and active viewers.

Narrative Film as Literature: Coming of Age Stories

Because narrative film is the popular literature of our time, the classroom is the appropriate place to teach the feature film as literature with its own narrative conventions. Most high school and college students enjoy fictional stories on a regular basis by watching feature films in theatres and on television, and this early-cultivated pleasure continues throughout their lives.[12] Fictional films (sometimes based on real-life people or events) affect viewers in much the same ways as short stories and novels (also sometimes based on real-life people or events) affect readers. Readers and viewers are invited to suspend their disbelief that what they are reading or seeing is fiction and to identify with protagonists and disassociate from antagonists as if they are reading about and seeing real people. Films, however, invite identification and encourage dissociation via narrative techniques particular to film, and students studying film as literature have the opportunity to identify those techniques and interpret their use in individual films. Coming-of-age stories in independent films— some particularly relevant for high school students and some only appropriate for college students— often depict individuals coming to terms with how the dominant culture tends to stereotype ethnic groups and being challenged to determine their own sense of ethnic identity. Independent films telling contemporary coming-of-age stories invite students to identify with young protagonists like themselves on a personal level, even as the stories deal with, and students learn about, stereotyping and other issues specific to a particular ethnic group that may be different from their own.

Ramon Menendez's (1988) *Stand and Deliver* dramatizes the real-life efforts of Los Angeles high school teacher Jaime Escalante to lead his Mexican-American high school seniors from chaos and troublemaking to calculus and a well-earned sense of self-worth. How they undergo this transformation and how viewers are invited to experience it with them is a topic for student investigation. To determine how the film invites viewers to suspend their disbelief and to identify with the lives of the protagonists, students can discuss how *Stand and Deliver* opens with a visual driving tour that serves as an establishing shot (a shot that identifies the

Stand and Deliver (Ramon Menendez, 1988). Establishing Shot: An East L.A. barrio.

location where the action takes place) of an East Los Angeles barrio rather than the usual easily recognizable national or city landmark. Viewers virtually experience the sights and sounds of the place and the people living there. And to determine how and why the film encourages viewers to continue to care about the Mexican-American protagonists and even the unseen Mexican-American students at Garfield High School who continue their legacy of success for years to come, students can discuss how the film ends with intertitles (words on the screen offered as the voice of authority) that here inform viewers what took place since the time of the film story's ending and provide further inspiration regarding what can be achieved by motivated students.

The plot focuses on how one math teacher in an under-resourced high school motivates his students to boost their sense of self-worth. He connects their identities to their Mayan ancestors who first conceived the concept of zero, and he challenges them to become good students by telling them that "there are some people who will assume that you know less than you do because of your names and your complexion, but math is the great equalizer." He also motivates them to challenge themselves in order to pass the Advanced Placement Calculus Test, for which they will receive college credit and strengthen the school's accreditation application. The opening verisimilitude continues throughout, inviting students to analyze its effect on viewers as, for example, the film takes them into the homes of individual students to reveal that their desires to achieve academically are often thwarted by poverty and family situations beyond their control. The *mise-en-scène* (all the elements in a scene, including the physical setting and props, and how the actors are arranged and move within that environment) in one female student's home shows her packing her father's lunch as he leaves for work; playing with, feeding, and putting to bed her younger brothers and sisters; and then being asked to turn out the light when her mother comes home exhausted and wants to rest while she tries to study. When all the calculus students pass the test but the Educational Testing Service accuses them of cheating on the basis that barrio kids couldn't possibly achieve high scores, they are again challenged to prove their worth. After Escalante protests what he sees as blatant racism, the students again make individual sacrifices to retake the test and achieve even higher scores, proving to the Educational Testing Service, to themselves, and to viewers that they, as individuals and as Mexican Americans, can overcome personal obstacles as well as stereotyping by the very system that should be rewarding them for their hard work and success.

A film that brings viewers on an all-night tour of the South Bronx and Manhattan that includes crashing a party and a car, Joseph Vasquez'

(1991) *Hangin' with the Homeboys* depicts the concerns of young men — two Puerto Ricans and two African-Americans—coming to terms with their ethnicities. Students can discuss how the film story begins with another establishing shot tour — moving from aerial long shot views to medium shots of people and kids on the sidewalks of a neighborhood identified by sights, sounds, and intertitle as "The South Bronx"— to orient viewers to the lives of the protagonists. The four young men attempt to find girlfriends (one young woman deemed "innocent and virginal" turns up in a peep show video they watch, much to the disappointment of the innocent and virginal young man who mistook her as being like himself), two of them are unemployed while two others put up with low-paying jobs, and three of them question whether or not a college education offers any advantages for ethnic minorities. Students can analyze the importance of the first scene as a detached episode that sets the tone for the rest of the story: *Hangin' with the Homeboys* begins with a challenge to stereotypes of African-American and Latino young men as gangsters, as the four young men act out a subway scuffle to the horror of onlookers and then announce that they are merely acting. Intertitles then identify each of the characters by name and what they do, or don't do, to make a living. Johnny, a Puerto Rican with low self-esteem, stacks grocery shelves and delays applying for a Latino scholarship to college, even though he has been out of high school for two years, because he does not think he is "the college type." Willie, an unemployed African American who dismisses all of his problems with the idea that "It's because I'm black," is seen at an unemployment office where he protests that his unemployment checks are about to end "because I'm a black man," even as the unemployment officer notes that he refuses to attend any job programs. Tom, an African-American magazine salesman with a college degree who aspires to be an actor, has money, a car, and ambition but is stood up by his girlfriend and crashes his car while out with his friends. Fernando, an unemployed Puerto Rican who goes by the name of Vinny so that people will think he is Italian, fashions himself a Latin lover and lives off the food his girlfriends bring him and the money he borrows from them. Their night out on the town is a wake-up call to reassess their lives.

Interpreting any number of scenes can help students to understand how the film is about the absurdities of stereotyping and of assuming an ethnic identity that has nothing to do with ethnic heritage or belonging to an ethnic community. At a Puerto Rican party the young men successfully crash for a short time, Tom declares that he enjoys Latino music but that he dare not dance to it because that is the first step to becoming Latino and having "to wear polyester pants with bellbottoms and eat rice and beans." His Puerto Rican friend Johnny serves as a reactive character (whose reactions invite viewers to respond in the same way) by calling the remark racist and but also insisting that he can teach Tom how to dance to the music. While Tom never does seem to understand that stereotyping is racist (He says, "No [it isn't racist], I just don't look good in bellbottoms"), the *mise-en-scène* shows viewers that stereotyping is out of sync with reality. Tom learns to dance to Latino music and forgets his remark, and medium camera shots show the room filled with Puerto Ricans, including Johnny and Vinny, who are wearing a variety of outfits but nothing akin to polyester pants with bellbottoms. When the four young men jump over turnstiles into the subway instead of paying and are caught, an Italian-American policeman insists on knowing Vinny's nationality and why his friends don't call someone named Fernando something like "Furball" instead of Vinny. In response to his friends revealing that Fernando wants to be called Vinny "because he thinks he is Italian," the policeman says, "I'm Italian. No matter what you do or say, you'll never be Italian. Scum like you could never be Italian." While students can quickly recognize the policeman's remark as ethnocentric and racist, those who identify the next shot of Vinny as a reactive character can also analyze how this film technique complicates the viewer's response. Vinny's obvious embarrassment about being revealed as a Puerto Rican trying to pass as Italian reveals to viewers that, like the policeman, he wrongly disparages his Puerto Rican ethnicity. With no basis other than that others do so, Vinny has accepted and internalized his society's prejudices. Unlike Vinny, Johnny identifies as a Puerto Rican and decides that it qualifies him as a "college type." The film ends with Vinny continuing his charade and Johnny filling out the Hispanic scholarship application for college.

African-American identity gets the same kind of scrutiny. Willie, an African American who has decided that none of his problems are of his own making but are the result of him being discriminated against "because I'm black," gets his comeuppance when he declares to a young African-American woman in a pool hall that she "is perpetrating a fraud." When Willie tells her that she shouldn't dress like white people or hang out with white people, the young woman, who serves as a reactive character, responds by asking Willie about his commitment to African-Americans' rights. Willie has to admit that he has never been to a demonstration and that he did not even vote in the last election. The scene ends with Willie silenced and the young woman telling him that he is the one "perpetrating a fraud." Near the end of the film, when the two African Americans', Tom and Willie, stop at a restaurant on their way home in the wee hours of the morning, Willie, as always, has no money and expects Tom to pay.

When Tom finally refuses and Willie calls him an Uncle Tom because he works for whites and won't pay Willie's way, Willie is left in the restaurant with two unkempt, disheveled older men who seem to have no home to go to. As the three stare at each other, the *mise-en-scène* suggests that the younger man is seeing himself in the older ones. Students can debate the meaning and effectiveness of the film's ending, which eliminates the neat resolution in most Hollywood movies. Johnny decides to go to college and Tom renews his commitment to become an actor, both understanding that they need to act out their own futures, but Vinny and Willie are, literally, left out in the cold with only a wake up call.

Narrative Film as Literature: Coming to America and Returning to Roots

While reports about illegal alien Mexican/U.S. border crossings, or thwarted crossings, have occupied nightly newscasts and created newspaper headlines off and on for decades, depending on the state of the nation's economy and the vacillating needs for temporary low-cost labor, few accounts attempt to present the perspective of the border crossers themselves. A topic for students to explore is how Gregory Nava's (1983) *El Norte (The North)* not only tells the story of illegal aliens from their point of view but invites viewers to identify with them as human beings worthy of respect and to share their wish to find a home and happiness in the U.S. Nava's film brings a Mayan brother and sister out of their violence-torn village in Guatemala, through a terrifying (and illegal) Mexico/U.S. border crossing to a new life in Los Angeles, where they face the difficulties of maintaining communal and family ties in the face of individualistic and material incentives. The journey of brother and sister Ricky and Rosa from Tijuana to San Diego through a long, abandoned sewer tunnel entails their crawling on hands and knees for miles with only bandanas to shield their noses from the lingering smell. As they are attacked by rats within the tunnel, repeated crosscutting (editing cuts that move viewers back and forth between independently shot scenes to create the illusion that the events are occurring simultaneously) between the rat attack and border patrol helicopters waiting outside to capture them should they make it to the end, heightens the tension. Students can discuss how this crosscutting scene engages viewer emotions, elicits identification with the protagonists, privileges the protagonists' point of view, and constitutes an important dramatic device in the film.

Students can also consider how otherwise unrelated scenes in *El Norte* attempt to give U.S. viewers a sense of Mayan culture and a corresponding sense of how strange the technological culture of the United States can be to new immigrants. Scenes that include butterflies, a dead fish, white flowers, and Ricky and Rosa's deceased parents as if they were alive are scenes of magical realism (akin to magical realism scenes in written literature, where visions, dreams, mythic symbols of a culture, and deceased ancestors appear as inseparable aspects of the world we all recognize as real). Students can analyze the effectiveness of these scenes in visualizing the importance of Mayan traditions and family ties in the minds and lives of the young protagonists to a U.S. audience largely unfamiliar with Mayan culture. The film also depicts U.S. culture from a Mayan point of view. Viewers learn that, before she arrives, Rosa gets most of her ideas about life in the United States from her godmother, Josefita, who collects old *Good Housekeeping* magazines given to her by a cook who works for a wealthy landowner. While intercuts showing U.S. suburban homes and manicured lawns comprise the bulk of Josefita's and Rosa's ideas, working for a wealthy Los Angeles suburbanite provides Rosa an unexpected alien

El Norte (The North) (Gregory Nava, 1983). Intercut: Rosa's ideas about America come from glossy photographs in magazines.

culture experience. The scene where Mrs. Rogers gives Rosa and her house-keeping partner Nacha (also an undocumented worker) a quick lesson in how to run a multi-function washer and dryer—for a variety of types of clothes of varying fabrics and various wash load sizes, by pushing multiple buttons that include short soaking and long soaking, medium dry and very dry, and false starts and restarts—ends with Rosa reverting to hand washing and spreading the clothes on the lawn to dry. Students can analyze how the washer and dryer multi-function buttons scene provides a visual metaphor that can give even the most sophisticated U.S. mechanic a sense of alien-culture panic. Students can also discuss the scene's importance as a means to evoke viewer empathy for Rosa and Nacha, who are expected to be efficient, low-cost workers in a new country where they are still learning the language and the technology.

Links between *El Norte*'s beginning in Guatemala and its end in Los Angeles provide students with the means to consider the plight of these illegal workers in light of a recurring theme. Ricky and Rosa leave Guatemala because their lives are in danger. Their father dared to organize fellow peasants to challenge rich landlords who took their lands and, as he tells Ricky before he is killed, now the landlords want the strong arms of the peasants to do their labor. Students can discuss the means by which Ricky's life in Los Angeles ends in a similar predicament. Rosa and Ricky both get work right away, and crosscutting scenes between them shows their hard work and their belief that anyone can be successful in America seeming to pay off. Rosa works at a sweatshop factory until an immigration raid and then does domestic work for the wealthy suburbanite until she dies from typhoid she contracted from the rat bites in the sewer tunnel. Ricky gets picked up as the last one left in a line of day laborers to fill in as a busboy at a French restaurant and does so well that he gets promoted to waiter's assistant until he barely escapes from immigration officials. Offered a "chance to be legal" with a green card if he agrees to work in Chicago for several years, he is tempted but decides he cannot leave his sister, the only family that he now has. Following his sister's death and his lost prospects, Ricky starts over as a day laborer in a line of men waiting to be picked for whatever jobs they can get. As he recalls his father's words, Ricky raises his arms and says, "Take me; I have strong arms" in order to get work digging a ditch on a construction site. His life in the U.S. at the end of the film parallels his father's life in Guatemala. In light of the story Nava tells, students can assess the words of Monte, manager of the motel where Rose and Ricky live and supplier of cheap illegal labor to employers, when he says, "The whole economy would collapse if it wasn't for the cheap labor we bring in."[13] *El Norte* provides no happy ending to send viewers off thinking that all that ends well in the movies is well; instead, viewers are invited to empathize with Ricky and Rosa as examples of the ongoing plight of the undocumented worker in the U.S. economy.

Peter Wang's (1986) *A Great Wall* follows a Chinese American family who journeys back to their roots in China and returns home with new understandings of their Chinese American identity. Like *El Norte*, this film attempts to reveal cultural differences, in this instance between Chinese and Chinese Americans, in ways that viewers can readily understand not as right or wrong, but simply as cultural differences. Students can examine any number of scenes in which Chinese reactive characters and crosscutting between the Chinese and Chinese American families visually demonstrate that Chinese and Chinese Americans are related but not identical. When Chinese Americans Leo Fang, his wife Grace, and their son Paul first arrive at the home of the Chinese Chao family — Leo's sister, her husband, and their daughter Lili Chao — in Beijing, their greeting humorously reveals obvious differences. Leo hugs his sister and, even though she reacts by not hugging him back, pulling back, and smiling awkwardly at his physical demonstration of brotherly love, when it is Paul's turn to greet her, he hugs her even harder, and she expresses even greater embarrassment. Her reactive discomfort with public demonstrations of affection are apparent to viewers, but it is the additional reaction shot of the Chao's Chinese neighbors that points out how different the Fangs are from their Chinese relatives. Crosscutting invites viewers to observe these neighbors observing the behavior of the Chinese Americans as they remark: "Who are these strange people? Japanese? No. Filipinos maybe." Students who note how the layers of reactive characters, beginning with Leo's sister and ending with her neighbors, are interspersed between crosscutting shots, can analyze how these film techniques suggest that what seems normal to Americans seems very strange to Chinese. Students can also analyze how reactive characters reveal different ideas about privacy — in the scene where Paul reacts to the idea that Lili's mother reads her letters before Lili reads them and in the scene where Lili's mother reacts to Lili's new ideas about privacy with her own ideas about protective love — as well as differing ideas about fashion and higher education in both countries.

Students can also consider how the dominant U.S. culture views the Chinese Americans and how their ideas about themselves change following their journey to China. *A Great Wall* depicts members of the Fang family as having different backgrounds and different attitudes and shows how they are confronted with assumptions about them that are inconsistent with the way they see themselves. Leo Fang came to America as a child and considers himself a Chinese American. Denied the promotion at work that every one expects him to get because, in his words, the company president doesn't "think a Chinaman is good enough to be the director," he quits and takes his family to visit China. He does not tolerate the glass ceiling that keeps ethnic minorities out of executive positions. Upon his return home from China, he becomes a devotee of tai chi, which he learned from his brother-in-law, and values the practice enough to keep his former boss waiting to offer him the promotion he was earlier denied. Grace Fang was born in America and considers herself an American, even though others see her as Chinese. When a woman next to her in the gym assumes Grace can speak Chinese, she responds that she cannot and says, "I thought you knew. I'm an American." She is not pleased with being thought of as a foreigner. She is pleased, however, to learn some Chinese while in China, and, although she prefers more tailored clothing than the dress Leo's sister makes for her in China, she compromises between Chinese fashion and her American tastes to wear a Chinese peasant blouse after she returns home. Paul Fang, their thoroughly acculturated high-school-age son, is more interested in his girlfriend and sports than in his schoolwork, his ethnic heritage, or his father's expectations. When Paul spends quite a bit of time with his Euro-American girlfriend, Leo asks him, "Whatever happened to that nice Chinese girl you were dating?" And when Paul's after-school Chinese classes do not show results, Leo asks him why, since he has been going to Chinese classes for years, he has never learned to speak Chinese. Paul, in turn, asks why they always have to "do everything the Chinese way" because "it gets you nowhere. This is America, you know." Students can also assess changes in Paul. After his return from China, viewers see and hear Paul correcting his Euro-American girlfriend's pronunciation of a Chinese word, demonstrating that he is now interested in, and interested in sharing his knowledge of, the Chinese language. His final remarks to his girlfriend open the underlying issue (which includes the glass ceiling and the forever foreign issues) of the whole film for student discussion. Paul's struggle is no longer to be American in spite of his Chinese American father but to realize his ethnic identity in light of, and in spite of, the ways many other people view him. Paul concludes that "in America I am too Chinese, and in China I am too American." With his new appreciation for his dual heritage, it is up to Paul to forge a viable ethnic identity for himself.

9

Film Studies:
Teaching Representations of
American Ethnicity on Film

by Carole Gerster

Film studies students in both critical studies and production courses
need background in the variety of ways films can represent accurate history, elucidate multifaceted social and cultural issues, depict individualized rather than stereotyped characters, and adapt written literary works
to the screen. While much of this is also relevant to, and has been covered
in earlier chapters on film study in history, social studies, and literature
courses, there is much about film that is specific to film studies.

Studying the history of films about and by ethnic minorities allows
students to examine an increasingly large and important segment of American filmmaking today. Including films by and about African Americans,
Asian Americans, American Indians, and Latinos/as in already existing
secondary and undergraduate college film studies curricula can bring new
perspectives to familiar topics such as American film history and film genres. Hollywood films provide a visual record of how America's ethnic
minorities have been represented by the Euro-American dominated industry since the inception of film. Hollywood film history also provides a
record of how ethnic minority filmmakers have entered, joined, and even
altered mainstream filmmaking, setting new precedents in representation
and adding their images and ideas to genres that previously ignored them.
And the film history of independent filmmaking — the venue most often
allowed and also often chosen by ethnic minority filmmakers — offers an
ongoing record of alternative histories, social issues, and stories told from
ethnic minority perspectives in both feature and documentary films. Ethnic inclusion can also bring new topics to old perspectives in courses on

film techniques and film appreciation, such as evaluating the effectiveness of film types and techniques to record, inform, and engage viewers in ethnic minority stories and issues. And, while critical studies of ethnic minorities in film are essential, courses in film production can take visual and multicultural literacy to a new level, moving students from critical viewers to creators of their own responsible ethnic representations.

Film History: Movies Come from Movies

American film history is incomplete without an examination of how ethnic-minority representations have and have not changed since the inception of films in the 1890s as a source of public information and entertainment. Essential knowledge for film studies students includes how ethnic-minority filmmakers and Euro-American filmmakers sympathetic to the cause of accurate ethnic representations have challenged stereotypes and created new kinds of representations. Film documentaries that chronicle the early and repeated use of stereotypes and also mark a number of important changes in ethnic representations include *Ethnic Notions* (Marlon Riggs, 1987), *Slaying the Dragon* (Deborah Gee, 1988), *Images of Indians* (Phil Lucas and Robert Hagopian, 1979), and *The Bronze Screen: 100 Years of the Latino Image in American Cinema* (Susan Racho, Nancy de los Santos, and Albert Dominguez, 2001). As each of these documentaries show, early Hollywood films are filled with depictions of ethnic minorities as different from, and in a variety of ways inferior to, Euro Americans. With their ideas originating from such sources as Euro-American fiction and Wild West shows, early Hollywood films didn't even attempt accurate representations of ethnic minorities, and many later filmmakers simply repeated the plots and characterizations of films that proved successful at the box office. While it is essential for film studies students to recognize ethnic stereotypes in order to dismiss rather than accept or repeat them, more profitable than studying repeated stereotyping is to examine the dynamics of change. One way students can measure changing representations is to consider how movies come from earlier movies. Not just sequels and prequels and new versions of old movies, but plots, characterizations, and even whole scenes can come from earlier films. Students can explore how a number of important changes in ethnic representations are the result of films not just repeating but also reversing and re-contextualizing borrowed plot elements and characterizations from earlier films.

D.W. Griffith's silent (1915) film *The Birth of a Nation* serves well as an early film from which to trace changing depictions of African Americans.

Students can explore how varying responses to this film are products of their times and the corresponding ideas of the filmmakers who created them. Griffith's film was and still is powerfully influential. Because it drew large audiences with its highly dramatic story and contains blatantly racist caricatures, it became the center of controversy about racist depictions in films,[1] prompting a number of filmmakers to respond with films of their own. *The Birth of a Nation*, which depicts the antebellum, Civil War, and Reconstruction periods from a Southern Euro-American point of view, is a compendium of stereotypes of African Americans that filmmakers have been variously repeating and reacting against ever since. The stereotype of the Black Brute appears in Griffith's film as a vicious threat to Euro-American civilization and to Euro-American women in particular. Gus, played by a Euro-American in blackface, is a former slave who becomes a captain in an all-black army regiment, terrorizes the townspeople of Piedmont, North Carolina, and literally chases a genteel Euro-American girl until she jumps to her death from a cliff to escape because he refuses to take no for an answer to his demand that they be married. As if Gus was not enough villain for one film, Griffith adds Silas Lynch to his cast of African Americans who want to marry white women. Lynch, who is part Euro American and part African American, has been helped by Austin Stoneman, an influential white northern Reconstruction legislator, to become Lieutenant Governor of South Carolina. When Lynch decides he wants to marry Stoneman's daughter and, like Gus, won't take no for an answer and kidnaps the young woman, the legislator has his liberalism tested and decides Lynch has overstepped his bounds and that he was even wrong to promote black rule in the South. The Ku Klux Klan, formed on behalf of the young woman who jumped from a cliff to avoid Gus, finds and hangs Gus and rids the town of all African Americans (including Silas Lynch) who have not remained subservient. Consequently, KKK members become the saviors of the town and the film. Within the film's story, Gus and Silas Lynch serve as reminders of the supposed good old days when slaves knew their place and justify both lynching and the idea that freed black men need to be kept under strict control. Another stereotype in Griffith's film, repeated in hundreds of films thereafter, is that of the Mammy. In *The Birth of a Nation*, the Mammy, a large, asexual, very black woman is the family caretaker who values the lives of her slave masters and then, after emancipation, her employers, above her own life. Griffith's Mammy, played by a Euro-American woman in blackface, remains faithful to the white family, even saving her former master from being arrested for his participation in forming the Ku Klux Klan. The Mammy is the model of subservience.

Griffith's film incensed filmmakers then — and still incenses filmmakers today—causing many to respond to his caricature of the Black Brute. Oscar Micheaux, an early African-American independent filmmaker, was perhaps the first to do so. Students can explore how, in the earliest surviving feature directed by an African American, *Within Our Gates* (1919), Micheaux reverses Griffith's characterizations with his depiction of a white man attempting to rape a black woman. The film reminds viewers that black women were raped by white men — most often slaves by their slave masters— throughout the history of slavery and encourages them to see Griffith's film of a black man attempting to rape a white woman as a fantasy reversal of reality. Micheaux's film is a reaction to Griffith's by then infamous film by reversing Griffith's reversal in the ethnicity of his characterizations.[2]

In the 1960s, two Civil Rights era Hollywood films by sympathetic Euro-American males re-envision the Black Brute stereotype by arguing against its existence as anything more than a stereotype. Students can examine Robert Mulligan's (1962) *To Kill a Mockingbird* and Stanley Kramer's (1967) *Guess Who's Coming to Dinner* as the products of changing times and a new awareness that how African Americans are treated by the dominant culture is based on how they are imagined. *To Kill a Mockingbird* re-conceptualizes the Black Brute stereotype as a recurring caricature that can be recalled at will and believed when convenient even though it has no basis in reality. Students can compare this film to both Griffith's stereotypes and Micheaux's response techniques. Akin to Micheaux's *Within Our Gates*, *To Kill a Mockingbird* engages in plot and character reversals. Instead of Griffith's hypersexual black men chasing white women, in *Mockingbird* a white woman is attracted to a black man, and, instead of proving the stereotype to be true and then lynching or riding its brutes out of town, the stereotype itself is exposed as deadly. As Atticus Finch, the lawyer who defends a man falsely accused of rape in 1935 Alabama, makes clear, the young Euro-American woman, Mayella Ewell, who accuses an African American, Tom Robinson, of rape is acting according to the social mores of her time. Finch explains to the jury that since it is not socially acceptable for a white woman to be attracted to black man, Mayella could not even admit to herself her attraction to Tom and relies on a fiction she knew people would believe: that black men want to rape white women. Finch dismantles the Black Brute stereotype for the jury and for viewers when he tells them not to go along with the assumption that all black men lie, are immoral, and are not to be trusted around white women because it is a lie. When Finch proves to the jury that Tom Robinson could not have beaten and raped Mayella, the jury's guilty verdict proves to viewers that the stereotype remains a convenient means to scapegoat

African Americans. Tom Robinson is neither a rapist nor interested in white women. Although he is the antithesis of Griffith's Gus, many men in town want to lynch him, and some succeed in killing him when he attempts to escape from jail.

Another Civil Rights era film, Stanley Kramer's *Guess Who's Coming to Dinner*, provides an even more direct response to *The Birth of a Nation* even while it builds on the characterization of *To Kill a Mockingbird*'s Tom Robinson. Students can analyze how Kramer's film replays the plot and characters in Griffith's film but re-contextualizes them in order to change the message and dismiss the stereotype. Like Griffith's Gus and Silas Lynch, Kramer's John Wade Prentice wants to marry a white woman. But, akin to Tom Robinson, John Prentice is a docile black man, not a rapist, and, unlike Griffith's anti-miscegenation message, Kramer's film promotes the idea of interethnic marriage. In *To Kill a Mockingbird*, Robinson has a wife and children and only stopped to help Mayella do a few chores, not because he was attracted to her but because he felt sorry for her. Similarly, Prentice is not interested in white women per se. He has been previously married to an African-American woman and they had a son; these plot details make it clear to viewers that he has not been looking for a white woman. After his family is killed in a car crash, he happens to meet and fall in love with a white woman and she with him. Their mutual attraction and love is the striking difference between this film and Griffith's as well as most other film responses to Grifffith. Kramer's depiction of Prentice's sexuality also builds on the character of Tom Robinson. Unlike Gus and Silas Lynch, both men are restrained rather than hypersexual. While Robinson describes himself during his trial as having had to rebuff Mayella's advances, Kramer's Prentice refuses to have sex with his white fiancée, Johanna Drayton, before they are married. She reveals in a conversation with her mother that "We haven't been to bed together. He wouldn't." *To Kill a Mockingbird* and *Guess Who's Coming to Dinner* both characterize African-American men involved with Euro-American women as antitheses to Gus and Silas Lynch.

Similar characterizations and plot details in *The Birth of a Nation* and *Guess Who's Coming to Dinner* invite students to determine the exact nature of Kramer's response to Griffith's film. Griffith's Silas Lynch rose from slavery to become Lieutenant Governor of South Carolina while Kramer's John Wade Prentice, the son of a mailman, graduated summa cum laude from Johns Hopkins, became an assistant professor at Yale Medical School, then head of the London School of Tropical Medicine, and serves as assistant director of the World Health Organization. Neither film characters nor film viewers can object to these male suitors on the basis of their socioeconomic status. In Griffith's film, the liberal Northern statesman, Austin Stoneman, who has facilitated Lynch's rise to power, has his liberalism tested when Lynch says he wants to marry a white woman. Stoneman passes this test, agreeing that it is a good idea, but when Lynch says, "It's your daughter I want to marry," he quickly changes his mind. Stoneman is intent on preserving what he considers the purity and superiority of the white race within his own family. In Kramer's film, the liberal father, Matt Drayton, in discussion with his wife, agrees that they raised their daughter not to discriminate against any person of color and did not tell her not to fall in love with a black man. The white father again has his liberalism tested and, although it takes him the length of the film to decide, at the end he agrees to the marriage. For him, the only problem the couple will have is "a problem of pigmentation." In its response to *The Birth of a Nation, Guess Who is Coming to Dinner* attempts to change ideas about racial difference. Griffith's white characters think of racial difference in terms white superiority; Kramer's liberal protagonists see only a difference in skin color.[3] Students can explore how a more recent film, *Guess Who?* (Kevin Rodney Sullivan, 2005), whose title directly references Kramer's film, uses Oscar Micheaux's method of plot and character reversal to join *Guess Who's Coming to Dinner* in promoting the idea of interethnic love. Here, the Euro-American suitor falls for and must win the approval of his African-American fiancée's father in order to marry her.

Stereotyped minor characters and a Euro-American point of view in both *To Kill a Mockingbird* and *Guess Who's Coming to Dinner* invite further student analysis of how films can reveal both change and stasis in their representations of ethnic minorities. Both were breakthrough films in dismissing the stereotype of the hypersexual, civilization-destroying Black Brute, but both merely update the stereotype of Griffith's Mammy to that of the maid who serves the same role the Mammy served. In *To Kill a Mockingbird*, Atticus Finch's African-American maid Calpurnia seems to live to serve the Finch family, agreeing to spend the night when Atticus needs her to stay with the children, having no opinion about or interest in the case of Tom Robinson even though it occupies everyone else in the family, and being a fixture in the Finch household on whom everyone can count on for their care and safekeeping. In *Guess Who's Coming to Dinner*, Tilly, the African-American maid, again lives to serve the Drayton family and also sees her role as protector of Johanna Drayton from the possible ill will of John Wade Prentice. Tilly's objection to John marrying Johanna, that she does not want "to see a member of my own race getting above himself," and her calling John "boy" and "one of those smooth-talking Niggers out for all you can get" to his face reveals her own internalized ideas about black inferiority. Students can analyze the importance of Tilly's allusions to the Civil Rights Movement. Tilly's response to Johanna's question, "Guess who's coming to dinner?" is "The Reverend Martin Luther King?" and her response to seeing Johanna and John together is, "Civil Rights is one thing; this here is something else." She is obviously aware of and announces the Civil Rights Movement as an impetus for change but, since she has no ideas about Black Nationalism, she seems only to have internalized white society's pre–Civil Rights ideas about interracial marriage. For a black maid to object to the marriage on the basis of black inferiority is to strain credulity, but it is a position opposite all the black characters in Griffith's film (who wish to legalize black/white marriage) and serves the plot: Tilly invokes an old stereotype, and viewers realize that she is wrong to do so. But Tilly herself is the embodiment of a stereotype. Although Mr. Drayton makes a point of announcing that she has been a member of their family for twenty-two years, she does not address any of them by their first names and stays in her place as a servant. The Draytons' lifestyle, including inviting more and more people to dinner, depends on Tilly's faithful service. While dismissing the Black Brute stereotype, this self-announced Civil Rights film seems oblivious of the Draytons' and its own brand of institutionalized racism in its uncritical repetition of the Mammy stereotype.

The Euro-American protagonists in *To Kill a Mockingbird* and *Guess Who's Coming to Dinner* provide film students with an opportunity to analyze point of view in films about ethnic minorities in order to discuss what, if anything, has changed since Griffith's *The Birth of a Nation.* Griffith's white male protagonist, Ben Cameron, is a young Southern man whose antebellum plantation life is depicted as idyllic. Ben then fights gallantly in the Civil War, even showing compassion to Union soldiers. During Reconstruction, when Ben's youngest sister chooses to die rather than be defiled by the newly freed slave Gus, Ben forms the Ku Klux Klan to take revenge. And when Silas Lynch kidnaps Ben's fiancée, Ben leads the Klan to meet out vigilante justice to save victimized Southern whites from what the film portrays as African Americans ruining white civilization and taking white women for themselves. The Euro-American protagonists in both *To Kill a Mockingbird* (which, as a film adaptation of Harper Lee's 1960 Pulitzer prize-winning novel retains the novel's protagonist) and in *Guess Who's Coming to Dinner* each have the final word on ethnic relations, and their civil rights efforts make them the films' heroes. These films directly challenge the ideology in Griffith's film with their Euro-American male protagonists and can spark student debate about the effectiveness of their re-use of the white male protagonist convention. The positions of Atticus Finch and Matt Drayton are the opposite of Ben Cameron; they are champions of civil rights for African Americans.

Students can compare the three Euro-American protagonists in other ways. Ben Cameron's vigilante rescue makes him a hero for a Euro-American audience convinced by the film that, during Reconstruction, Euro Americans had to circumvent their own legal system to get justice while the later heroes use reason, not violence, and must argue their cases. As a lawyer, Atticus Finch argues to an obdurate all-white jury, and an off-camera jury of viewers, that they should find Tom Robinson not guilty of the rape charges. And, as a father, Matt Drayton argues to those already convinced (his wife, daughter, John Prentice, and John's mother), to convince others (Tilly and John's father), and to the film's mixed-opinion viewers, that John and Johanna should be married. In *To Kill a Mockingbird*, Atticus Finish is defeated but remains the film's hero, having easily convinced viewers, if not the jury in the film, of Tom's innocence. After the guilty verdict is announced and Finch is leaving the courtroom, the African Americans in the segregated balcony rise to honor him; the Reverend who is watching over Atticus's children tells them to rise also, making this defeated champion of civil rights a hero for still-powerless blacks and a role model for whites. With Finch, and the reactive characters who rise to watch him pass, the film invites Euro-American and African-American viewers to retain their belief in a legal system proven ineffectual in attaining justice for African Americans. Unlike *The Birth of a Nation*, *To Kill a Mockingbird* asks viewers to be patient and to work within white hegemony: for African Americans to wait for more men like Finch and for more Euro Americans to become like Finch. In *Guess Who's Coming to Dinner*, John has asked his fiancée's parents for approval and will stand by their decision whether or not he can marry their daughter. With Johanna's mother firmly for the marriage, viewers must wait for Matt Drayton's closing arguments at the end of the film. Everyone except Tilly and John's father happily receive the good news that the couple can proceed with their marriage plans, and Matt Drayton is confident that he can convince even them. Both of these films argue in favor of equal rights and justice for African Americans; however, as in *The Birth of a Nation*, Euro Americans are still given the power to decide what justice is and how it should be attained. African Americans have their power taken away in *The Birth of a Nation*, are given no power in *To Kill A Mockingbird*, and give their power away in *Guess Who's Coming to Dinner*.

Juxtaposing two segregated balcony scenes— one from *To Kill a Mockingbird* and one from the more recent *Nightjohn* (Charles Burnett, 1996)— can help students see the difference a film's point of view can make. *Nightjohn* follows a twelve-year-old slave girl, Sarny, as she takes the risk of learning to read and write, illegal acts of rebellion that can bring the

Nightjohn (Charles Burnett, 1996). Reactive Characters: African Americans in the segregated church balcony honoring Sarny.

punishment of a beating, dismemberment, or being sold. Nightjohn, a slave who escaped to freedom but returned to teach other slaves to read, finds a willing pupil in young Sarny, who becomes empowered by literacy. She and Nightjohn write passes for a newly married slave couple so they can escape together and, working in her master's house, Sarny reads her master's ledger book recording the names of the slaves he has bought, sold, or bred and their monetary worth. Because her mistress assumes she cannot read, Sarny is entrusted to carry love messages between her mistress and the owner of another plantation. When the two escaped slaves are discovered missing and Mr. Waller, the slave owner, obtains their forged passes, he barges into a church service demanding to know who wrote each of the passes and threatening to shoot all the slaves in the balcony one by one until the writers confess. Sarny, who sits below with the slave owner's young son, tells those in the balcony not to worry, that Mr. Waller will not shoot them, and she calls out each of their names, reciting their value according to Waller's account book. As she tells the slaves, "He won't shoot you. You are his wealth," she reminds Waller that they are all he has, and he puts down his gun. When Waller threatens to kill her, Sarny hints to his wife that she had better take Sarny's side because otherwise she has something to reveal "about the Mrs." In the segregated courtroom balcony scene in *To Kill a Mockingbird*, the African Americans in the balcony rise, as reactive characters, to honor Atticus Finch for attempting to get justice for Tom Robinson through an unjust legal system, and the film becomes a salute to one white man's efforts. In *Nightjohn*, the African-American reactive characters in the balcony honor Sarny with a song sung on her behalf for helping two slaves to escape and for saving their lives as well as her own because she defied the unjust law prohibiting slaves' literacy. In *Nightjohn*, a story from an African-American perspective, African Americans take credit for their own hard-earned accomplishments in the face of an unjust legal system and are not patronized by the film with a message to be patient and wait for more good white men to come along. While *Nightjohn* does not attempt to convince Euro-Americans to work for civil rights, it does expose the supposed inferiority of slaves as a fiction designed to justify economic greed, and it shows that African Americans did not just wait to be saved.

Spike Lee has responded to Griffith's *The Birth of a Nation* in a number of films, and students can consider their place in the history of films that rewrite Griffith's racial ideology. In Lee's (1991) *Jungle Fever*, Angie, an Italian-American woman, and Flipper, an African-American man, have an affair. Flipper alludes to Hollywood movies and sexual stereotypes, saying that their affair is different from depictions in the movies where "love will overcome everything" (as it does in *Guess Who's Coming to Dinner*), and began only because both were curious about the sexual stereotypes (exemplified in Griffith's *The Birth of a Nation*) that black men are hypersexual and white women are the epitome of womanhood. Their curiosity satisfied and the stereotypes dismissed, Flipper sees no reason to continue the affair. Flipper's wife Drew provides another reason for the affair, and it too points to Lee's repudiation of Griffith's film: she accuses Flipper of marrying her because of her light skin and of now finally attaining what he has wanted all along: a white woman. Following Drew's line of reasoning, students can connect Flipper's affair with a white woman to Silas Lynch's wish to have a white wife beside him in his rise to power in *The Birth of a Nation*, to signify his acceptance by and equality with white men. Flipper's own rise to power has recently hit the glass ceiling, having been rejected for equal status as partner by the two Euro-American partners in his firm. They give him what the film visualizes as a run around where they talk circles around him — in a pan shot that twirls the three of them in circles— in their refusal to acknowledge Flipper's role in their success. Flipper wishes to be like them, to be one of them, to be equal to them, and his affair with a white woman could give him the sense of equality he cannot get from them. Flipper, however, ends his affair and does so highlighted in an iris shot — a circle of light around the protagonist — a shot used by Griffith throughout *The Birth of a Nation* but otherwise not used by Lee or any other recent filmmakers, in a cinematic allusion to the film Lee here and elsewhere reconfigures. In realizing his error, Flipper earns his wife's forgiveness and returns home. Using white women as status symbols is not what Lee's film is about and not how his hero creates his sense of self in a white man's world. Flipper ends not trying to be like or be accepted by white men, but trying to be successful on his own by starting his own business and returning to his wife and daughter. Reacting against both the over-sexualized African-American men in *The Birth of a Nation* and the desexualized John Wade Prentice in *Guess Who's Coming to Dinner,* Lee re-sexualizes Flipper, making the point that African-American men have normal sex lives by showing that sex with his wife is frequent and enjoyable for both. Lee's more recent (2000) film, *Bamboozled,* includes excerpts from *The Birth of a Nation* interspersed among the racist caricatures in his ending montage to show how African Americans have been grossly misrepresented. *The Birth of a Nation* is, to Lee, a film not to be forgotten so that it will not be repeated.

Parodies that preceded Lee's *Bamboozled* also target Griffith's film, and students can analyze their effectiveness as parody. Mel Brooks' (1974) Western spoof *Blazing Saddles* invites viewers to laugh old stereotypes out of existence. In an obvious allusion to Griffith's film, a new African-American sheriff disrupts complacent ideas as he taunts Ku Klux Klan members by peeking around a corner and asking, "Where's your white women at?" while he shows no actual interest. Robert Townsend's (1987) independent feature *Hollywood Shuffle* includes a parodic segment called "The Black Acting School" that shows African-American actors being taught how to act in the stereotypical ways Hollywood films, ever since Griffith's Black Brute caricature, have regularly depicted them: as rapists, gangsters, and drug dealers. In this segment, actors are taught how to walk, talk, and act like rapists and gangsters by Euro-American Hollywood filmmakers. The clear intent is to dismiss these stereotypes as the limited roles created and perpetuated by Hollywood.

Movie villains, servants, and buffoons have long served as foils for Euro-American protagonists, and Griffith's caricatures haven't been the only ones alluded to, reversed, reconstituted, and parodied. Blake Edwards' (1961) *Breakfast at Tiffany's* contains a scene with Mickey Rooney playing a bumbling, buck-toothed Asian American photographer who is enamored of the film's lovely Euro-American female protagonist. He is only one of many admirers of the free-spirited Holly Golightly, but he alone serves

Hollywood Shuffle (Robert Townsend, 1987). Intercut: The protagonist imagines a Black Acting School where Hollywood teaches actors to "act black."

as a comic relief foil to the Euro-American male with whom she eventually falls in love. As Holly Golightly repeatedly rings his bell to let her into the apartment building because she can never find her key, his attitude changes from anger to delight when she promises that he can perhaps photograph her someday. In a direct response, Rob Cohen's (1993) fictionalized film biography of Bruce Lee, *Dragon: The Bruce Lee Story*, repeats this scene. The protagonists, Chinese American Bruce Lee and his Euro-American girlfriend Linda, watch it in a movie theatre and serve as reactive characters to what they see on the screen after Linda recommends *Breakfast at Tiffany's* as one of her favorites. The theater marquee announces a comedy film festival, suggesting (accurately) that the film is considered a classic, is re-shown frequently, and draws both repeat and new viewers. Viewers are directed to watch Bruce and Linda watching the scene: Bruce watches Mickey Rooney's yellow face impersonation in humiliation while Linda laughs, but she then reacts to Bruce's reaction, learning how offensive such stereotyped characterizations are to Asian Americans, and suggests that they leave the theatre. The scene repetition illustrates how stereotypes have been perpetuated and then deconstructed in films of different eras and allows students to examine how the film technique of the reactive character guides viewer response — to different ends— in both films. In *Breakfast at Tiffany's*, viewers see the heroine through the eyes of the Asian American buffoon as every man's dream girl and realize that he hasn't a chance with her. As he reacts positively to her beauty and false promises, viewers also see her beauty and accept her false promise from her perspective as her means of passifying men she is obviously not interested in. In *Dragon: The Bruce Lee Story*, the reaction of the Bruce Lee character invites viewers to see Rooney's performance as offensive rather than funny, and Linda's reaction to Bruce Lee invites viewers to learn that one way to protest is to leave the theatre. Students can discuss the chain reaction of reactive characters in *Dragon: The Bruce Lee Story*— moving from a passified Asian American buffoon on the screen to an offended Chinese American to a newly aware Euro-American — to gauge how effectively viewers are being guided to react. *Dragon: The Bruce Lee Story* also undercuts the stereotype that Asians and Asian Americans have a special claim to martial arts expertise when Bruce Lee teaches martial arts to a group whose members consist of various ethnicities and especially when he is easily overpowered by one of them: the Euro-American woman, Linda, who later becomes his wife.

Film History: The Interethnic Romance

Films that focus on an interethnic romance, or include an interethnic romance in a subplot, provide a record of our nation's changing ideas about interethnic relations. Students can discover how the outcomes of possible relationships both reflect and attempt to affect viewers' ideas and attitudes of the time in such films as *Guess Who's Coming to Dinner* (1967) and *Jungle Fever* (1991) for African Americans[4] and *Breakfast at Tiffany's* (1961) and *Dragon: The Bruce Lee Story* (1993) for Asian Americans.[5] Interethnic romance films depicting American Indians[6] and Latinos/as[7] also invite historical overview comparison viewing. Students who investigate how these films protest or endorse interethnic relationships in their attempts to shape viewer attitudes will also note that there has been no straight-line progression from condemning to condoning interethnic romance. In Rob Cohen's (1993) *Dragon: The Bruce Lee Story*, Chinese American Bruce Lee easily wins the heart of his Euro-American girlfriend Linda, but they face discrimination as a mixed race couple in restaurants and by their parents. Viewers are invited to follow the changing attitude of Linda's mother as a reactive character, from her rejection of Lee as a foreigner, "not an American," and as someone with whom Linda will have "yellow babies" to her acceptance of him and their children when she first encounters her first "beautiful" grandchild. On the other hand, in Joel Cohen's (1996) *Fargo*, the Euro-American female detective protagonist, Marge Gunderson, must fend off the (non-threatening) advances of a stereotypical Asian American buffoon, reminiscent of the Asian American buffoon admirer of the heroine played by Mickey Rooney in *Breakfast at Tiffany's* thirty-five years earlier. A new dynamic occurs in *Harold and Kumar Go to White Castle* (Danny Leiner, 2004) as the Korean American Harold (John Cho) begins a romance at film's end with the girl of his dreams, a Latina (Paula Garcés). It continues in *Hitch* (Andy Tennant, 2005) where the African-American Hitch earns the love of his dream woman, who is also a Latina (Eva Mendes). Films such as Mira Nair's (1991) *Mississippi Masala*, with a romance between an African American (Denzel Washington) and an Indian American (Sarita Choudhury), have become less of an exception, as interethnic couples increasingly reflect an increasingly diverse America.

Recent Film History: The Buddy Film

Buddy movies are a film genre that often focuses on relationships between men (and occasionally women) of different ethnicities. Beginning with Stanley Kramer's (1958) *The Defiant Ones*, where the buddies are escaped convicts, students can investigate how the pair interacts in order to gauge how these films attempt to shape, or reshape, viewer attitudes about interethnic relationships. In *The Defiant Ones*, an African American and a Euro American (played by Sidney Poitier and Tony Curtis) are chained together and must look out for each other to avoid recapture and survive. At first, each despises the other but, after overcoming numerous hardships together and learning of each other's past, they each save the other's life even though it means allowing themselves to be recaptured. Kramer's point is clear: getting to know someone of another ethnicity changes people's ideas. Students can debate Kramer's idea as plausible or as an overly easy solution to the complex problems of racism. A similar relationship between African-American and Euro-American buddies is the focus of a number of films where at least one of the buddies is a policeman or detective. In Walter Hill's (1982) *48 Hours*, essentially repeated in Hill's (1990) *Another 48 Hours*, a former convict (Reggie Hammond, played by Eddie Murphy) helps to solve a crime and save the career of a detective (Jack Cates, played by Nick Nolte). In the process, the detective does not hesitate to call his convict assistant racist names, such as "watermelon" and "spear chucker," but he also stands up for him when their African-American boss calls Hammond "a dumb nigger." As in *The Defiant Ones*, the buddies actually become buddies, and students can again debate the plausibility of the premise that familiarity is the solution to racism, as well as the idea of having an African American use a racial epitaph against another African American to cement the relationship between the black and white buddies. Also open for student analysis is the characterization of Hammond as an oversexed buffoon who often melds the old stereotypes of the irresponsible Sambo and the oversexed Black Brute into one character for the sake of comic relief. Student investigation of similar ideas and characterizations can include numerous other interethnic buddy films,[8] but students can also explore new twists. In Amy Heckerling's (1995) *Clueless*, the Euro-American protagonist Cher (Alicia Silverstone) and her African-American best friend Dionne (Stacey Dash) are high school buddies in a film where there are no racist comments and the ideas of race and ethnicity are never brought up. In *Napolean Dynamite* (Jared Hess, 2004), the high school buddies are a Euro American (Jon Heder) and a Latino (Efren Ramirez). And a new dynamic appears in Brett Ratner's (1998) *Rush Hour* and (2001) *Rush Hour 2* (with Chris Tucker and Jackie Chan) where neither of the buddies is Euro American. Students can explore whether any Hollywood buddy film successfully provides a model of equality, or if they instead serve to relieve (or reinforce) racial tensions, as well as the companion idea of whether or not ignoring racial issues suggests to viewers that equal relations between people of different ethnicities is the norm and that a struggle for equality is no longer necessary.

Film Techniques that Direct Viewer Response

Important information for all students, and essential for film studies students, is how films invite viewers to suspend their disbelief that they are watching a staged production and encourage specific viewer responses to characters, actions, and ideas. Students learn from films both inside and outside the classroom and, like all viewers, easily accept what they see as a source of experiential knowledge because established film techniques create a perceptual reality (promoting the illusion that viewers are witnessing and even experiencing reality) and guide viewers to specific responses. Understanding these film techniques empowers students to think critically about what they see and are invited to believe and ensures that film studies students understand the power of the medium. D.W. Griffith's early (1915) silent *The Birth of a Nation* offers a means to examine the language of film at its inception. Griffith has been labeled "the father of film technique" and "the man who invented Hollywood" for his development of techniques still in use today, but he is also known as "a muddleheaded racial bigot."[9] *The Birth of a Nation* is worthy of study as a means for students to explore how ethnic minorities have been represented and how they are representing themselves with the same film techniques. Teachers who give students a list of standard techniques (such as in the Glossary of this book) and compile excerpts of film techniques, beginning with techniques from Griffith's film, can help students recognize how the same techniques that promote racist ideas can also be used to promote ethnic understandings.

Reactive Characters

Reactive characters react to other characters, often the protagonist or other main characters, or to situations to guide viewers to react in the same

The Birth of a Nation (D.W. Griffith, 1915). Reactive Character: A hospital guard admires Elsie Stoneman for her beauty and virtue.

way. Teachers can ask students to identify this technique in a variety of film excerpts and to analyze how it is being used to guide viewer response to specific ends in each instance. In Griffith's *The Birth of a Nation*, the Euro-American heroine, Elsie Stoneman, is established as admirable for her beauty and her virtue. In a hospital scene, this Yankee woman is caring for wounded Civil War soldiers and even helping the mother of a Confederate soldier appeal to President Lincoln to save her son's life. When she pauses for a moment, a hospital guard stares at her. Students can analyze how and why viewers are invited to watch the guard watching Elsie Stoneman and to react as he reacts. He reacts to her by staring in admiration and, as she notices him and quickly steps away, he heaves two heavy sighs. His staring clearly indicates that he is smitten with her beauty and his two heavy sighs — after she reacts to his stare by quickly stepping away from him, suggesting that she too is on guard, for her virtue — that he also admires her as virtuous and knows that she is to be respected as out of his league. As the heroine of the film, Elsie represents the ideal of white womanhood that, like the South, needs to be protected from any who would attempt to despoil it. Griffth's establishment of the reactive character to direct viewer approval, or disapproval, of what they see on the screen has been repeated ever since.

An excerpt to show the use of a reactive character by a contemporary African-American filmmaker is from Robert Townsend's (1987) independent film *Hollywood Shuffle*. Here Townsend himself plays an African-American actor, Robert Taylor, who is chosen for the lead role in a Hollywood gangster movie. Though initially pleased to get acting work, he changes his mind in the midst of shooting a scene because of the reactive characters. Students can identify, differentiate, and analyze the effect of the reactive characters. As he is told by the director to "act more black" and to "stick his ass out" and attempts to act the stereotyped role, his girlfriend, younger brother, and grandmother — who have been invited to the set and serve as an on-set audience — each look on with disapproval and humiliation. Then, when he says he cannot play the role because it isn't the kind of acting he wants to do, each of the reactive characters nods and smiles to approve his refusal and to guide the film audience to do the same. The reactive characters prevent viewers from assuming the gangster scene is meant to be funny or realistic and invite viewers to see it as demeaning (to both African Americans and Latinos, who are also given gangster roles). Students can easily note that the most important reactive character is the little brother. As the protagonist is repeating a line about a slain gang member being his "only brother," he glances at his own real brother, who is looking back with an expression of disappointment. The protagonist rejects the black gangster role in order to establish a realistic African-American

Hollywood Shuffle (Robert Townsend, 1987). Reactive Character: The protagonist's younger brother smiles his approval.

identity on the screen that he and his family can be proud of and that his younger brother can emulate.

Crosscutting

Crosscutting, sometimes also called parallel action, is an editing technique where two or more independently shot scenes are edited together to create the illusion that the various actions are happening simultaneously. *The Birth of a Nation* epitomizes Griffith's development of dramatic crosscutting for chase and rescue scenes that are standard fare in films today. It also reveals his racist inclinations in using such techniques to misrepresent African Americans as predators after white power and white women. In the film's famous chase scene, an African-American man (Gus, played by a white man in black face) pursues an innocent Euro-American girl (Flora), who he wants to marry, until she is so anxious to escape that she jumps from a cliff to her death. As Gus gets closer and closer to Flora,

The Birth of a Nation (D.W. Griffith, 1915). Crosscutting sequence that shows the KKK as saviours. Elsie Stoneman is kidnapped by Silas Lynch.

The Birth of a Nation (D.W. Griffith, 1915). Crosscutting sequence that shows the KKK as saviours. The Ku Klux Klan comes to her rescue.

the editing cuts create increasing dramatic suspense. Students can analyze how crosscutting between the girl escaping in panic, the man in chase gaining on her, and the girl's brother (Ben) in futile pursuit to rescue her clearly directs viewers to identify with the girl and her brother. Griffith's crosscuts give viewers the impression they are witnessing reality (from an omniscient point of view where they can see the whole picture) and involves them emotionally in a sensory experience as they are directed to empathize with the girl being chased and her would-be rescuer. Gus is visualized as a literal threat to white womanhood as viewers see him from Flora's perspective of the threatened and from her brother Ben's perspective of her failed savior who then seeks revenge. In *The Birth of a Nation*'s other famous crosscutting sequence, near the end of the film, viewers vicariously experience multiple threats to Euro-American characters they have been encouraged to admire. Here, the protagonist's (Ben Cameron's) newly formed Ku Klux Klan rescues his fiancée, Elsie Stoneman, and other helpless groups of whites besieged by blacks, and viewers are directed to

The Birth of a Nation (D.W. Griffith, 1915). Crosscutting sequence that shows the KKK as saviours. The Camerons cower in fear of African Americans.

The Birth of a Nation (D.W. Griffith, 1915). Crosscutting sequence that shows the KKK as saviours. The Ku Klux Klan comes to their rescue.

identify with the (this time successful) saviors: the KKK. Students can examine how these scenes create visual rhythms to involve viewers in the excitement of the chase and the rescue. With careful viewing of the increased speed of the editing cuts in the climaxing multiple-rescue crosscutting sequence, students can test for themselves Griffith's idea that in such scenes "the pace should build like an excited pulse"[10] and consider the effect on viewers. With practical knowledge of film techniques such as crosscutting, students can understand the power of dramatic films like *The Birth of a Nation* to persuade — without being persuaded themselves.

For a crosscutting excerpt from a film that takes the perspective of an ethnic minority, one choice is Herbert Biberman's (1953) independent film *Salt of the Earth*. The scene includes crosscutting between the Latino/a husband and wife protagonists and exemplifies another use of the technique. Here, students see how crosscutting can effectively involve viewers in the drama without depicting a chase or rescue. *Salt of the Earth* dramatizes Mexican-American miners striking for better wages and safer working conditions, in a story based on a real 1950 New Mexico strike that lasted for almost two years. When the mining company invokes a Taft-Harley injunction to end the strike and force the miners back to work, the miners' wives take over the picket line, add sanitation (they want hot running water and indoor plumbing in the houses they must rent from the mining company, to match what the Euro-American workers already had) to the list of conditions, and eventually win the strike. The film plot focuses on the family dynamics of Esperanza and Ramon Quintero when the strike necessitates their gender role reversals. When the men must pump the water and chop the wood to heat the water to wash the clothes as well as take care of the children while the women plan strike strategies and walk the picket line, the men understand their wives' demands for better sanitation but (Ramon especially) resent giving up their macho roles as breadwinners in charge, and the women (especially Esperanza) get a taste of being the ones on whom their families' livelihoods depend. Students can assess how the crosscutting scene between Ramon and Esperanza directs viewers to experience for themselves how the couple comes to an understanding. The scene crosscuts between Esperanza, who is in childbirth labor, and Ramon, who is being beaten by local sheriffs. Esperanza is in pain; she is unattended by a physician because no company doctor will see the wife of a striking miner. Ramon is also in pain; the sheriff's men beat him in the stomach in their attempt to get the strike leaders to capitulate. As the crosscuts take viewers from one to the other, Esperanza cries out "Ramon," Ramon cries out "Esperanza," and the scene ends with a superimposed image of the two. Viewers see for themselves that the couple shares a bond of pain and love and learn, as the couple learns, that their struggle against the company's oppression of Mexican Americans is the same and that they must work together.

Intercuts

An intercut, sometimes referred to as an insert shot, is a shot outside the locale and/or time of the main story, inserted in a scene as a flashback, a flash forward, or simply a visual of something to provide a heightened sense of reality by letting viewers know what a character is thinking. D. W. Griffith claimed that "film can photograph thought"[11] without dialogue and, in his silent film *The Birth of a Nation*, he showed that film can convey a character's thoughts through the intercut. Griffith's intercut scene shows Margaret Cameron, a Southerner, in love with Phil Stoneman, a Northerner, after the Civil War. She loves him but has serious reservations when she remembers that he was in the Union army that killed her brother. After a shot of Margaret staring into space, the intercut is a flashback to an earlier scene of her younger brother lying dead on the battlefield. Her memory, as shown in the intercut, is actually the viewers' memory of a shot that occurred earlier in the film and provides another kind of experiential reality for viewers. Viewers see her memory as something they remember and thus experientially understand the psychological barrier she must overcome in order to marry Phil. The intercut has been used effectively to convey thought ever since.

Students can analyze how a film about American Indians, Jonathan Wacks' (1989) independent feature *Powwow Highway*, uses an intercut to show a character's thoughts as important to his ethnic identity. Philbert Bono and Buddy Red Bow, the film's protagonists, have come to different conclusions about Cheyenne traditions even though they have both been raised on the same reservation. Philbert is learning the details of his heritage in order to make it relevant in the present. Buddy considers powwows and the old stories as ineffective against corporate and government exploitation of reservation resources and seeks political solutions as more practical than relying on what he dismisses as "beads and feathers." As the title indicates, the film takes the two men on a journey and, before it is over, traditional ways merge with political moves toward a successful, if temporary, solution to current problems. A mining company, backed by the F.B.I. and local police, has lured Buddy off the reservation to keep him from voting against a contract to allow the company to take reservation resources at the expense of the tribe. When Buddy and Philbert attempt to return home, the police pursue them. Buddy removes a broken window from Philbert's car (which Philbert calls "Protector, the war pony") to throw at a police car in chase, while an intercut shows Buddy as a Cheyenne warrior throwing a tomahawk, causing the police car to crash. Viewers literally see for themselves that Buddy imagines himself as a Cheyenne warrior involved in the political act of saving his people from exploitation. By seeing what Buddy is thinking and how it fosters his suc-

Powwow Highway (Jonathan Wacks, 1989). Intercut: Buddy Red Bow imagines himself as a Cheyenne warrior.

cessful getaway, viewers identify with him, his plight, and his joint efforts with Philbert to maintain their Cheyenne heritage.

Intertitles

Intertitles are words on the screen — offered as expert authority to convince viewers to accept the film's visuals as fact or as based on fact that should be taken seriously. In *The Birth of a Nation*, Griffith uses intertitles in a variety of ways. Because this is a silent film, he occasionally includes intertitles as dialogue. For example, when he has a freed slave refuse to register to vote, the intertitle reads, "Ef I doan' get 'nuf franchise to fill mah bucket, I doan' want it nohow," inviting viewers to come to the conclusion, by means of comic relief, that African Americans do not understand what it means to vote and are incapable of responsible citizenship. Griffith's intertitles also include quotes from President Woodrow Wilson's book *History of the American People* to lend authority to his own version of the Reconstruction era. Intertitles from Wilson's text claim that African

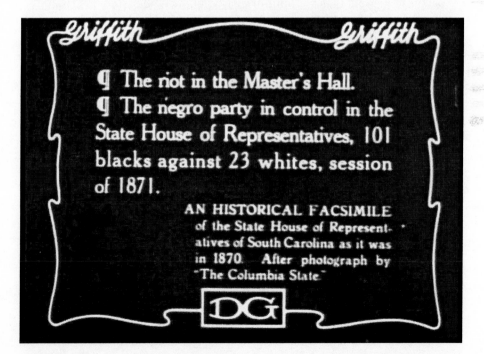

The Birth of a Nation (D.W. Griffith, 1915). Intertitle: Statistics from an omniscient authority.

Americans elected to the South Carolina legislature attempted "to put the white South under the heel of the black ... until at last there had sprung into existence a great Ku Klux Klan, a veritable empire of the South, to protect the Southern country." And Griffith also uses intertitles as they are conventionally used today, as an omniscient source of information that often includes statistics, as in the intertitle that reads, "The negro party in control in the State House of representatives, 101 blacks against 23 whites, session of 1871" that precedes a visual of African-American legislators creating havoc in the legislative hall by eating, throwing chicken bones on the floor, and drinking. Griffith's intertitles lend authority to his visuals in his repeated attempts to prove that Southern whites were besieged by the incapability and irresponsibility of emancipated slaves and created the Ku Klux Klan as their only defense.

Teachers will find intertitles that include the same kind of omniscient statistics (without an author or source cited) used again at the beginning of John Singleton's (1991) *Boyz 'n the Hood*, at the end of Mario Van Peebles' (1993) *Posse*, and throughout most documentaries. Students can analyze how Singleton's and Van Peebles' intertitles attempt to inform and persuade viewers that the films are based on facts. But students should also be aware that many conventional film techniques, particularly intertitles, are essential features of documentary films. To demonstrate the folly of stereotyping, Michael Cho's (1991) documentary *Animal Appetites* makes fun of those who stereotype rather than the stereotypes themselves. The film is a humorous look at how American xenophobia blocks understanding when faced with the unknown customs of new Cambodian and Vietnamese immigrants. The film encourages American viewers of all ethnicities to examine their prejudices and (especially from the perspective of new Cambodian or Vietnamese immigrants) their own strange customs. After the film chronicles one case of refugees accused of killing and eating a stray dog in a California town, and how it caused an uproar about letting uncivilized others live in a civilized Euro-American community, it presents intertitle statistics regarding the American practices of using dogs, cats, and rabbits to test cosmetics, of killing dogs and cats abandoned in animal shelters, and of burying pets in special pet cemeteries. Cho's film offers students the chance to examine the use of satiric humor — via image, voice-over, and especially intertitle explanations — to inform the uninformed. By reading the intertitles, viewers learn for themselves how alike in strangeness everyone's customs are from the point of view of outsiders.

Visual Metaphor

A visual metaphor is something natural to a scene that also serves a metaphorical purpose, inviting viewers to think about the film story in a specific way. The first part of Griffith's *The Birth of a Nation* shows the antebellum South as a paradise that was interrupted by the Civil War and emancipation. In one scene, viewers see a happy Southern family, the Camerons, with a supposedly happy Mammy waiting to serve them and a puppy at the feet of the plantation owner, enjoying life on their front veranda. All is well until a visual metaphor warns viewers that trouble is ahead: a kitten is dropped onto the puppy, and an intertitle announces "Hostilities." Since viewers can anticipate the ensuing cat and dog conflict, they are called on to draw their own conclusions that this paradise is about to be interrupted. For Griffith, the North's imposition on the Southern way of life was a mistake. At the end of his film, Griffith includes another visual metaphor, one that students can analyze as drawing on his viewers'

The Birth of a Nation (D.W. Griffith, 1915). Visual Metaphor: Hostilities between a dog and cat/the South and the North.

visual memory from previous to viewing the film. As the leader of the Ku Klux Klan, Ben Cameron, and his bride-to-be, Elsie Stoneman, lead the Klan triumphantly through the town and beyond, a commonly reproduced image of a Euro-American Christ with white skin and long hair appears in the background behind them. Viewers recognize the unidentified image of Christ, this time with his arms outstretched, as part of their own visual memory and provide the link between what they already know and the film image. The image of Christ serves as a visual metaphor that offers Griffith's moral evaluation: it suggests that Ben and Elsie are blessed as saviors of the white nation from above by this heavenly savior.

Visual metaphors in films by ethnic minorities are equally expressive of the filmmakers' ideas. The first scene of John Singleton's (1991) *Boyz 'n the Hood* also includes a warning metaphor. After the opening intertitles, which read, "One out of every twenty one Black American males will be murdered in their lifetime./Most will die at the hands of another Black male," and the identifying intertitle that follows, "South Central L.A. 1984," the opening scene shows several children walking to school, discussing the

Boyz 'n the Hood (John Singleton, 1991). Visual Metaphors: Street signs indicate that the children are heading in the wrong direction.

gunshots they heard the night before and the people they know who have been shot. One of the boys asks the other children if they want to see something and, as they follow him to look at a dead body lying in an alley, the street signs serve as visual metaphors; they read, "Stop," "One Way," "Wrong Way." Combined with the intertitle statistics, the street signs indicate the wrong direction children are taking, both literally and figuratively, and suggest that the film will attempt to provide alternatives. Comparing them, students can discuss how, like Griffith's visual metaphors, Singleton's street signs are already part of viewers' visual memory and are reproduced to suggest the film's theme. Documentaries occasionally use extended metaphors to make a strong point. Phil Lucas and Robert Hagopian's (1979) *Images of Indians* has another example of how what seems to insiders to be normal practices can seem very strange when viewed from the perspective of another culture. The documentary includes a scene where Martians observe such typical Euro-American practices as men shaving their faces and women sitting under hair dryers at a beauty shop and quickly conclude that Euro-American men lacerate their faces and Euro-American women bake their heads on a regular basis. The point of this extended visual metaphor, as the narrator Will Sampson points out, is that the customs, costumes, religion, and history of American Indians have been misinterpreted and misrepresented in film after film by Hollywood filmmakers.

Other commonly used film techniques, such as the match cut (discussed in Chapter Five), *mise-en-scène*, the long shot, medium shot, and close up, as well as the pan shot, establishing shot, and many more can easily become part of students' film vocabulary. Besides teacher-chosen excerpts of techniques to discuss, film students can bring in their own (or production students can create their own) examples from films about and by ethnic minorities to demonstrate their knowledge and to practice recognizing, analyzing, and interpreting what they see and are encouraged to think.

The Auteur Theory

Film studies can include examination of the auteur theory by looking at one influential director's films. The auteur theory includes the ideas that some directors have a body of work with a distinctly recognizable style or significantly repeated themes and that these directors have both represented and influenced the thinking of their era and have introduced an influential shift in filmmaking practices. Spike Lee is one such director whose films are readily available in VHS and DVD format in video stores for students to study. Lee has, by all accounts, opened doors for other

African-American filmmakers and created an expansive repertoire of films designed to inspire new thinking about African-American history and issues. His films about the Civil Rights Movement include his (1992) feature film biography of the Civil Rights leader *Malcolm X* and his (1995) documentary *Four Little Girls*, about the children killed in their Birmingham, Alabama, church by Ku Klux Klan bombers. In this documentary, interviews with the girls' families and friends, as well as ministers, reporters, political activists and lawyers, reveal the immediate and continuing aftermath of the tragedy from both private and public perspectives. Film studies students can see how close ups and extreme close ups invite viewer intimacy with family members. Lee's (1989) *Do the Right Thing* ends with intertitles of the words of Martin Luther King, Jr., and Malcolm X as a reminder that their alternatives still exist in the continuing struggle for civil rights. Students can apply these civil rights leaders' ideas to the film itself to judge whether Lee's story advocates one position or the other, suggests that we need to reactivate both philosophies, or invites viewers to find other solutions to current cultural conflicts.

Lee's variety of work includes his (1995) film adaptation *Clockers*, based on a Richard Price novel, and his (1994) semi-autobiographical feature *Crooklyn*, which Lee wrote with his brother and sister. The topics of jazz, the struggles of the African-American musicians who create it, and the (often mostly white) audiences who enjoy it are featured in *Crooklyn* and in Lee's (1990) *Mo' Better Blues*. Controversial issues, such as drugs, interracial romance, and color prejudice within the African-American community — triple topics in his (1991) feature *Jungle Fever* — are part of Lee's larger intent to provoke new thinking on continuing concerns rather than provide pat answers. Lee's films provide students with room to interpret and invite new solutions for the problems he raises. His (1996) *Get on the Bus*, a feature film about black men traveling to the Million Man March in Washington, D.C., raises issues of fatherhood, black-on-black violence, homophobia, sexism, African-American and Jewish relations, skin color discrimination, white oppression, Hollywood, black leaders, drugs, gangs, Uncle Toms, and use of the word "Nigger." Lee's well publicized battle with studio heads (he raised the necessary money to complete *Malcolm X* when told he was beyond budget and had to quit filming) and his exposé of ill-informed and money-motivated producers responsible for film images of African Americans on television, in his (2000) *Bamboozled*, have made behind-the-scenes issues of who decides what representations the public will see a matter of public record. Students can trace the title for the satiric *Bamboozled* to a speech by Malcolm X about how African Americans have been tricked into second-class citizenship by white racism and have been co-opted into perpetuating stereotypes of themselves. Students can also analyze how the montage of ethnic stereotypes that closes *Bamboozled* reviews for viewers the message of the film: caricatured images of African Americans continue to permeate and entertain America at the cost of everyone's humanity.[12]

Sports Films and Bi-Ethnic Identities

Analyzing genre films is a productive way for film studies students to understand how the formulas that signal a favorite kind of story to film viewers can be used or challenged to offer entertaining and newly informative images. Sports films are formulaic in how the protagonists most often come from underprivileged backgrounds, encounter seemingly insurmountable obstacles and odds, and triumph with personal and public victories by the end of the film. LaVar Burton's (1998) *The Tiger Woods Story* follows this familiar plot but, in doing so, includes informative segments on how Woods overcame the obstacles of skin-color discrimination and the stereotyped beliefs that resulted in creating and maintaining segregated golf courses, club houses, and tournaments. Burton's film is also a real-life sports-hero biography, based on John Strege's book, and a coming-of-age story. Portraying the actual Tiger Woods' combined African-American and Thai-American ethnicity, *The Tiger Woods Story* includes a protagonist with, and discussions about, a bi-ethnic identity. Both are rare in film history except in passing films, such as Elia Kazan's 1949 *Pinky* and Robert Benton's 2003 *The Human Stain*, where the protagonists' bi-ethnic heritage is African- and Euro-American, and in films about discovering one's heritage, such as Michael Apted's 1991 *Thunderheart*, where the protagonist recovers his mixed Lakota and Euro-American ancestry. Hiroka Tamazaki's (1989) independent film *Juxta*, about the psychological effects of racism on the bi-ethnic children of two Japanese women and two (one African American and one Euro-American) U.S. servicemen, is an earlier exploration of mixed race identity. These representations are important to understand the varieties of ethnic identity that comprise today's America and America's future and to understand the importance of such representations on film. As many testify, to be unseen is to be invisible and unimportant in a culture. To begin a discussion, or to extend a Tiger Woods-inspired discussion, about bi-ethnic identity, teachers can screen the (1994) documentary *Domino: Interracial People and the Search for Identity*, wherein six bi-ethnic people confront the question, "Which race do you consider yourself?" and demonstrate how living intimately within two ethnic cultures can be a source of strength and enrichment.

Boxing and basketball films also offer popular sports and coming-of-age genre stories. A film that challenges the gender expectations of a sports-enthusiast audience accustomed to male African- and Latino-American protagonists is one way to introduce new images and to suggest that females can share spaces once reserved for males only. *Girlfight* is the telling title of Karyn Kusame's (2000) coming-of-age feature film about boxing, this time with a teenage Latina in the title role. As she learns to find an outlet for her aggressions in amateur boxing, the film reveals the source of her frustrations, including gender expectations from her father and school mates, and shows her winning a match with her boyfriend, who remains her boyfriend at film's end. Steve James, Frederick Marx, and Peter Gilbert's (1994) *Hoop Dreams*, a documentary that follows the conventions of a coming-of-age sports-hero story, chronicles the lives of two high school basketball stars who have professional aspirations. The difference here is that the filmmakers' four years of following and filming the lives of the two young African Americans in urban Chicago brings in unexpected reality: a father fighting drug use, a mother finally getting a nursing degree, and neither of the young men fully realizing their dreams of basketball stardom. Examining this documentary as a mediated experience, because the filmmakers chose what to include and how to present it, students can learn about the real-life obstacles of fellow students at once recruited and frustrated by high school sports programs and the educational system they function under, and can discuss the filmmakers' choices.

Video Shorts as Models for Film Production Students

Video shorts of thirty minutes or less can also serve as models for students to learn filmmaking possibilities. The (1994) animated short *Whitewash*, scripted by Ntozake Shange, is the story of an African-American school girl who is the victim of a hate crime. With no live actors to play the parts of teenage bullies or the young girl who gets white paint thrown on her face, this video demonstrates how animation and storyline can depict a hate crime without having to portray the violence of the actual experience. The story focuses, instead, on the consequences for everyone involved. Valerie Soe's (1987) video short *New Year, Parts I and II* combines a variety of forms and techniques to tell a story that contrasts lived experience with media representations. *Part One* uses voice-over narration to share the experiences of an elementary school, fourth-generation Chinese American girl living in the San Francisco area from her now-adult perspective. Viewers see only the arm and hand of the narrator drawing sim-

New Year, Parts I and II (Valerie Soe, 1987). The first half of the Match Cut shows a drawing of Soe in her Chinese New Year costume.

ple storybook pictures that match her narration. *Part One* depicts her home life and how she often felt out of place at school among Euro Americans. Intertitles twice scroll down the screen at a slow pace, forcing viewers to read and think about the words. The intertitles are schoolyard rhymes ("Ching Chong Chinaman/Sitting on a Fence/Trying to make a dollar/Out of five cents") that interrupt her narrative to show viewers how they interrupted her life. After telling and showing how every year she got Valentine cards with caricatured Asian faces drawn on them, Soe's real face, with her hands pulling her eyes and mouth into slits, appears on the screen. Here, Soe again disrupts her narrative, but this time to challenge the passive, model-minority stereotype by making a face back at viewers. *Part One* ends with a match cut. A drawing of Soe in her grade-school classroom, still wearing the special costume she wore to school that day to demonstrate Chinese New Year customs to her classmates, changes to a still photograph. Because viewers see photographic images as evidence of reality, the drawing-to-photograph match cut invites viewers to understand that this experience and the earlier drawings and voice-over narration are depictions of actual events mediated by the filmmaker. *Part Two* juxtaposes

New Year, Parts I and II (Valerie Soe, 1987). In the second half of the Match Cut, the drawing becomes a photograph.

media stereotypes with the real-life experiences of *Part One*. Clips from television programs, U. S. government newsreels, Hollywood movies, advertisements, and comic books show images (labeled under five categories in intertitles) that foster anti–Asian prejudice: "Geisha Girls and Dragon Ladies," "Fortune Cookie Philosophers," "Masters of Kung Fu," "Japs, Slopes, and Gooks," and "The Worldwide Empire of Evil." Simple drawings, a photograph, intertitles, Soe's own face, and clips from media productions combine to create a video (which, like *Whitewash*, was not a film transferred to video, but was created as a video) that tells a personal story of real experiences to juxtapose against, and dismiss as false to reality, popular media stereotypes.

Students Exploring Their Own Ethnic Identity on Film and Video

Students interested in exploring their own ethnic identity on film or video can find variations on the topic in a number of coming-of-age films about high school age students to serve as models of storytelling techniques for their own ideas. John Singleton, who at age twenty-four was the youngest person, and the first African American, to be nominated for a Motion Picture Academy award for best director for his (1991) *Boyz 'N the Hood*, employs a number of film techniques worthy of study. Singleton's film is about parenting, peer pressures, and living with violence in a gang-infested neighborhood in South Central Los Angeles. Besides intertitles and visual metaphors directing viewers at the film's opening, Singleton's film includes an interesting answer to the question of how to present violence in an anti-violence film so that it will not provide viewers with titillating pleasure. The scene where Ricky, the high school star who wants to attend college on a football scholarship, is shot to death invites viewers to feel first pleasure and then displeasure. The shooting scene includes typical Hollywood sound enhancements (additions to a sound, so a small gun sounds more like a canon, for example) for the gunshots and heart-wrenching music, but it also contains sweetened sounds (such as pig squeals for example, that have nothing to do with the original sound). Here, the gunshots are enhanced to make them sound much louder and more powerful than a real gunshot sounds in order to excite and shock viewers. But before the deadly gunshot, the scene also includes the sweetened sound of a baby laughing, subtly and probably honestly suggesting that gunshots are exciting. To turn viewer excitement into the horror following the fatal shot, the baby's laughter turns to crying. The scene in its entirety invites viewers to feel the initial thrill of the gunshot but then immediately deflates that thrill with a reactive character, Ricky's best friend Tre, looking on helpless and horrified, with music designed to make viewers feel saddened, and with the sweetened sound of a baby's cry to make viewers feel uncomfortable and helpless. Students can analyze the effectiveness of the scene to express Singleton's antiviolence theme in the context of the whole film.

For students who want to star in their own productions, Sokly Ny and Spencer Nakasako's (1994) *a.k.a. Don Bonus* can serve as a model. Under the guidance of filmmaker Nakasako, Cambodian-born teenager Sokly "Don Bonus" Ny turns the camera on himself. His film is about his coming of age in San Francisco and confronting the reality of the American Dream, a topic ripe for reinterpretation and re-imaginings by high school and college students of all ethnicities in all United States locales.

Films in the High School and College Classroom

Predictions about the future use of visual images include D.W. Griffith's remarks. "The time will come," he said in 1915 (the same year he filmed what is generally considered one of the most racist films ever made, *The Birth of a Nation*), "when the children in the public schools will be taught practically everything by moving pictures. Certainly they will never be obliged to read history again." He later expanded his idea of visual education to include adults when he added that moving pictures will take the place of books in general and advised his readers that in watching films, "You will merely be present at the making of history."[13] While Griffith failed to see any bias in the perspectives that necessarily accompany, and often motivate, filmmaking, few today would disagree with his assumption that films give viewers the impression that they are seeing reality and that films provide us with our collective historical and cultural memories. Students educated to be visually literate (who understand how film techniques direct viewer response and create viewer attitudes) and educated to be multiculturally literate (who can recognize inaccurate history, misrepresented cultures, and stereotypes, understand the horrific effects they can have, and who expect to see or can create an interesting variety of accurate and diverse perspectives and characters) are the natural heirs of an American filmmaking tradition that is changing with a changing America.

PART III

HIGH SCHOOL CLASSROOM–TESTED CURRICULUM UNITS

10

Teaching American History: The American Dream and the History of Latinos and Latinas in America

by Jennifer Pokorney

The curriculum unit described here is designed for a ninth or tenth grade American History class and has been taught at St. Luke's School, an urban private school with a ninety percent Euro-American population whose affluent families have high expectations for their children to attend prestigious universities. African-American, Asian American, and Latino/a American students constitute the other ten percent of the student population. Many of these ethnic minority students receive academic scholarships and often have a difficult time acclimating themselves to the school due to economic and social differences. Learning about diversity and ethnic American history is important for all of these students. What they learn about the past helps them to understand present-day America, to appreciate America as a multicultural nation, and to see themselves as part of that diversity. I have chosen to focus on Latino/a American history because this group is the largest and fastest growing ethnic minority in America and the most underrepresented in our curriculum. Teaching Latino/a history and visual literacy with written texts, films, and other popular media by means of a topic of interest to this age level, "Who Can Obtain the American Dream?" opens student discussion to issues of historical representation, including under-representation, misrepresentation through stereotyping, and ethnic minority efforts at self-representation.

This three-week unit on Latino/Latina history is part of a yearlong curriculum that explores the American Dream from a number of perspectives, including Euro Americans, African Americans, Asian Americans, American Indians, and Latinos/as, concluding with a unit on women of all ethnicities. At the beginning of the year, students are asked to consider this series of questions in relation to our theme: What is the American Dream? Who is allowed to pursue the American Dream? Has this journey towards the American Dream been the same for all people, including those from America's ethnic minority populations? Students brainstorm their answers to these questions in journals, a practice they develop throughout the year. At the end of each segment of the population we study, students review and revise their journal ideas, noting specific differences between what they thought initially and what they now think, as well as the sources of their old and new ideas. At the beginning of the year, students are also introduced to and are expected to continue to use in class discussions and in written assignments such terms as race, ethnicity, melting pot theory, salad bowl theory, tolerance/intolerance, racism, prejudice, discrimination, stereotype, representation, misrepresentation, and self-representation. Also early in the year students see the documentary *A Place at the Table* (Bobby Houston, 2000) featuring teenagers from a variety of ethnic backgrounds discussing their notions of the American Dream and the history-making struggles of their ancestors to achieve it. This film invites students to consider the idea that the American dream means equal opportunity and equal rights for all Americans and that ethnic minorities have endured many hardships in attempting to make this dream a reality. The film engages students in the topic because they can identify with other teenagers struggling with identity issues and hoping to claim their place at the American table.

This unit on the Latino/Latina quest for the American Dream asks students to achieve four main goals. The first is for students to learn specifics about Latino/a history from various kinds of texts: a textbook, a timeline and a world map, a primary document, cartoons, documentary and narrative films, and the Internet. The second objective asks students to learn basic film techniques and then apply their knowledge in analyzing how visual images can both represent and misrepresent Latino/a history and identity. Third, students draw parallels between Latino/as and other ethnic minority groups — African Americans, Asian Americans, American Indians — who have also experienced the effects of misrepresentation and are increasingly using film to re-present themselves. Finally, students learn about and report on the contributions of Latino/Latinas to help themselves and others attain the American Dream.

To help students become critical readers of all texts, both print and non-print, we begin with the basic teaching tool, the history textbook, and then compare it with both what and how we learn from other kinds of texts. Student reading assignments in our textbook, *The Unfinished Nation*,[1] include historical accounts of the Mexican-American War (1846–1848) and the Spanish-American War (1898), which influence the students' understanding of the basic and related questions we next address: Who are Latino/a Americans? Why and when did they become Americans? Were they in pursuit of the American Dream, or were they forced to become Americans? To answer these questions, students again brainstorm in their journals and identify their sources of information, which most often include movies, their parents, and their textbook. This exercise reinforces an important objective for the year: students coming to an understanding of what their ideas are, where they got them, and what sources influenced them to confirm, reconsider, or change these ideas.

A timeline of Latino history[2] and a large world map help students to work together to identify the many different backgrounds of Latino/a culture both outside of and within America. Using the timeline and world map, we review the geography of the exploration age and the impact of Spanish explorations on central Latin America and the United States. We note on our timeline that the former Spanish colonies of Puerto Rico and Cuba became U.S. possessions following the Spanish-American War, that in 1917 Puerto Rican residents acquired U.S. citizenship and started to immigrate in large numbers, and that a Cuban wave of immigration to the U.S. began in 1959 when Castro took power in Cuba. Our timeline also informs us that in the late 1970s, an economic crisis in Mexico and political turmoil in Nicaragua, Honduras, Guatemala, and El Salvador caused new waves of immigration to the U.S. We identify New York and Miami as large communities of Puerto Rican and Cuban Americans respectively, but I remind them that there are Latino/a communities in every part of America. Working from our textbook, we also note that Mexican Americans were living in parts of this country before it became America and that, as a result of the Treaty of Guadalupe Hidalgo ending the Mexican-American War, they became Americans when the United States forced Mexico to surrender much of its land. Students identify on our map pre–1848 Mexico as the present-day states of California, Nevada, and Utah, and parts of what are now New Mexico, Arizona, Colorado, and Wyoming. Our timeline also informs us that Mexican Americans, including U.S. citizens, were deported during times of U.S. economic downturns and imported during economic upturns when the U.S. wanted cheap labor. This section of the unit includes a list of vocabulary words for students to define and discuss, including Manifest Destiny, Hispanic, Latino/a, Chicano/a, migration, immigration, emigration, migrant worker, refugee, deportation, Mestizo, Creole, and Spanglish.

We read, and identify as such, both primary and secondary sources in Mexican American history. Beyond our secondary-source textbook, we read as our primary source the Treaty of Guadalupe Hidalgo. Students engage in textbook-informed discussions about why this treaty — which agreed to grant U.S. citizenship to all Mexican inhabitants in the ceded region and to protect their rights to property, religion, and liberty — was largely ignored. Although the treaty was ratified in 1848, Congress never passed the specific provisions guaranteeing Mexican American equal rights. Students discuss how the U.S. policy of Manifest Destiny (which assumed that Euro-American culture was superior to that of Mexico) and the resultant stereotyping of Mexicans (as inferior and thus undeserving of equal treatment) were primarily responsible for official and unofficial attempts to keep Mexican Americans from realizing the American Dream.

Moving to other kinds of texts, such as cartoons, demonstrates how a history class is an opportunity for students to investigate how various historical accounts each have a point of view and to draw conclusions on their own. We examine cartoons to explore how Latino/a Americans became a part of the American "salad bowl" model. Using Ilan Stavans' *A Cartoon History: Latino Culture*,[3] I guide a review lesson through specific cartoon overheads on "The Treaty of Guadalupe Hidalgo." The Latino/a history created by this Latino artist is a productive way to reach students and get them actively involved. The cartoons are well illustrated, political, and funny. Students analyze the cartoons using a visual literacy approach, identifying point of view (noting the perspective from which the story is told and analyzing how the images direct viewers to identify with this perspective) and reactive characters (characters who react to other characters in order to direct viewers to respond the same way), and discussing historical accuracy as compared to our textbook and the actual treaty itself. This activity gives students an opportunity to practice their visual literacy skills on media other than film and to expand their ideas about the use of such skills. Divided into groups of three or four, students are given a section of the Latino/a history cartoons. Student groups decide which cartoons are significant for the class to see, read, and interpret, and present them to the class on the overhead projector to describe how this type of media presents specific messages with a point of view and reactive characters through captions and dialogue. All the students address the importance of visual literacy by choosing one image from their cartoon lesson and describing what they learned about Latino/a history and how they learned it.

We then discuss what media consists of and why visual literacy is an important aspect of their critical reading skills. I introduce many types of media to make students aware that not only are books, periodicals, and film considered media worthy of analysis but so are cartoons, advertising, and the Internet. We review the various media they initially identified as the sources of their knowledge about Latino/as and discuss how we need to apply our critical reading skills to all of them. We then review a standard vocabulary of film techniques that they become familiar with and use to analyze the films they watch, including point of view, reactive characters, match cuts, cross cuts, intertitles, voice over, visual metaphors, sound effects (including noises and music) and, for documentaries, on-camera authorities and voice-over narration.

At this point, we review short excerpts from *A Place at the Table*, the documentary that they saw in its entirety at the beginning of the year, in order to practice their visual literacy skills and to compare the experiences of different ethnic groups in light of their new knowledge of Latino/a history. In one segment, an American Indian student, an Asian American student, and a Latina student describe how they have been hurt when called derogatory names derived from stereotypes. My students identify the point of view and the authorities in this documentary as the young people themselves, and identify the historical evidence as archival photos and film footage showing how these young people's ancestors faced the same prejudice and discrimination on a larger scale. The documentary excerpts also serve as an historical review of how and why Latino/as became Americans, what they endured and sacrificed for the benefit of their children, and how ethnic identity depends on knowledge of one's ancestral past. These film excerpts also serve to open for discussion issues of assimilation, racism, and stereotypes.

Our next task is to identify and respond to recurring stereotypical representations of Latino/as. Students brainstorm in their journals and share their ideas so I can write them on the board. They often identify stereotyped traits of Latino/a Americans as ignorant and lazy and stereotyped portrayals as gangsters and drug dealers, most students pointing to movies and television as their main sources of such oversimplified images. I then show the introduction to and a seven-minute excerpt from the film *Americanos: Latino Life in the U.S.* (Susan Todd and Andrew Young, 1999) in which Latinos/as define the terms Latino, Hispanic, and Chicano and remind us of the diversity of Latino/as in American. In the short excerpt, self-identified Puerto Rican, Cuban, and Mexican Americans discuss the Latino/a stereotypes that disturb them the most — ignorant and lazy gang members and drug dealers, loose women, and young mothers always named Maria with three kids — while the film illustrates these pervasive stereotypes with clips from advertising, movies, and television.

We move on to a series of excerpts from popular Hollywood films that helped perpetuate these limited and limiting images of Latino/as in the minds of Americans. Students are asked to identify and react to the stereotypes they recognize. The first excerpts from *West Side Story* (Robert Wise, 1961) include the performance of the song "America," expressing the struggles of Puerto Rican immigrants attempting to assimilate in the midst of white privilege in New York City and trying to attain the American Dream. Students recognize that the movie's depictions focus on Puerto Ricans as gangsters and loose women. Similar representations of gangs and violence among Latinos appear in a number of films. For example, I include a film excerpt from *Scarface* (Brian DePalma, 1983) that shows its Cuban immigrant protagonist as a drug dealer and gangster who participates in extreme violence to get ahead in American society. Students also recognize how film excerpts from *The Three Amigos* (John Landis, 1986) perpetuate the Latino stereotypes of inferiority and stupidity. There are many humorous scenes that invite students to laugh at the Mexican characters that can also serve to initiate serious discussions about how Mexicans are often used as comic-relief characters unable to solve their own problems. Re-watching the excerpts from *The Three Amigos* for point of view, reactive characters, and camera positions, students analyze how the film encourages viewers to identify with the perspective of the white savior protagonists. Students begin to recognize the detrimental effects of repeated stereotypes on viewers' perceptions of Latinos/as and on Latinos/as' perceptions of themselves.

To focus on the current relevance of our "Latino/as and the American Dream," theme, I ask students a recurring and currents event question: Should immigrants from Mexico who are not United States citizens be allowed to freely cross the U.S./Mexican border to work and then return home to visit relatives? This question opens provocative discussions about borders, citizenship, and economically controlled migration and immigration policies. The question also provides a good segue to a film by Latino filmmaker Gregory Nava that depicts illegal immigration from the point of view of Guatemalan immigrants.

We watch extended scenes from *El Norte* (Gregory Nava, 1983), an independent feature film about a brother and sister who leave their homeland of Guatemala to escape political persecution and to realize the American Dream they have heard about and seen advertised in American magazines. A viewing sheet students complete while watching the film asks them to focus on the filmmaker's use of crosscutting (editing that cuts back and forth between independently shot scenes to give viewers the impression that two or more events are happening simultaneously) that invites them to identify with the young protagonists. Students note, for example, how one crosscutting sequence cuts from the brother and sister struggling to cross the U.S./Mexican border in a sewer tunnel to a border patrol helicopter outside the tunnel, ready to capture and return them to Mexico, and then back to the struggling protagonists being attacked by sewer rats. Students also recognize how other crosscutting scenes represent these young protagonists as family oriented, hardworking, honest, and resourceful, traits that successfully challenge the stereotypical representations with which we are familiar. The entire film, or just extended excerpts of crosscutting scenes, can help students to understand the reasons people cross the Mexican/U.S. border, the suffering they endure to do so, and the discrimination they face when they arrive. The film includes several scenes that depict American economic dependence on low-paid Latino/a workers, scenes that prompt students to think about not just how far the American Dream is from some people's grasp but also who benefits by keeping it out of their reach.

To initiate discussion about Latino/a efforts to have equal opportunity in education, I show excerpts from the docudrama *The Lemon Grove Incident* (Paul Espinosa, 1985), the documentary *Fear and Learning at Hoover Elementary School: Prop 187* (Laura Angelica Simone, 1998), and the short narrative film *Victor* (Dianne Haak Edson, 1989). The first two films document actual cases of discrimination against Latinos/as in their quest for an equal education in American school systems, and the fictional story in *Victor* dramatizes the trauma of a young man who is caught between two worlds: his Spanish-speaking home and his English-speaking school. Together, the three films initiate further discussion about current events issues, including the pros and cons of a bilingual classroom, and continue to challenge stereotypes. Both before and after they see portions of these films, students brainstorm answers to the following questions: Is it discriminatory to segregate students based on English-language deficiencies? Should English be the only language of instruction in America? In a multi-language world, what is the value of being bilingual? Students view scenes about the history of a 1930s court decision that ended segregated schools for Latino/a youth in *The Lemon Grove Incident* and about more recent discrimination in American schools in *Fear and Learning*. Like *El Norte*, these films challenge pervasive stereotypes with realistic portrayals of Latino/as as a diverse group of hardworking and intelligent individuals and engage students because they are about students like themselves who are also in school to better themselves through education as part of their quest for the American Dream.

For students to practice their visual literacy skills while comparing representations of attempts by African Americans and Latinos/as to gain

equal rights, we view and compare selections from two related documentaries: *A Time for Justice: America's Civil Rights Movement* (Charles
Guggenheim, 1992) and the four-part series *Chicano! History of the Mexican American Civil Rights Movement* (Hector Galon, 1996). These documentaries trace the struggles of civil rights workers to end segregation, to
receive a living wage, to have livable working and living conditions, to
have better schools for their children, and to get full citizenship by having a voice in government. In these documentaries, African Americans
and Latinos/as each chronicle their own struggles and successes and address
the continuing conditions of inequality that students have been discussing
as current events.

With viewing sheets to complete while watching selections from these
films, students identify and record their reactions to film techniques. Students note, for example, that both films have voice-over (off-screen) narrators to explain and interpret what viewers see. Students also note that
these narrators are identified in the credits as being members of each ethnic group represented, so that the historical perspectives presented are
from within each ethnic community. Asked to pay attention to historical
evidence, students note that both films include archival photos and film
footage to illustrate the past and document the people and the struggles
involved in attaining civil rights through non-violent civil disobedience.
Students find that *Chicano!* also includes live testimony of the people
involved in the movement as well as those who were opposed to it in order
to encapsulate various opinions (of both farm works and growers, for
example) and includes a variety of issues (regarding wages and protection
from pesticides, for example). The films chronicle how two large-scale and
multifaceted movements worked to secure the American Dream denied to
African Americans and Latinos/as for so long. Comparing civil rights
movements demonstrates the comparable struggles of ethnic minorities to
gain the rights that are supposed to be guaranteed to all Americans and
shows the means by which historical representations document those
struggles for those of us who follow.

Final projects for the Latino/a unit are threefold. Students complete
and turn in their journals of what they learned about the history of Lati-
nos/as pursuing the American Dream and how they learned it. Each student also writes an essay and gives a presentation to the class on the topic
of Latinos/as and the American Dream. For the essay and presentation,
each student chooses a person, an event, or an issue that we have studied
to research further on the Internet. Because students know about the essay
and the presentation before they begin the unit, they have chosen their
individual topics of interest over the course of the previous weeks and are

ready to do further research. Because they also know that each presentation requires a related media image as an illustration of how Latinos/as have been represented or have represented themselves, they are ready to choose from the images we have seen or to choose a comparable image on their own.

The values of teaching American history through the lens of multicultural and visual literacy are many. Most important is that students learn the origins of and new respect for the diversity that comprises America, and they learn to read critically the images that inform their ideas on a daily basis, both within and outside of school. Also important is the fact that the students' excitement level is easily sustained when examining an interesting variety of sources, and their retention level is greatly enhanced when asked to remember what they learned and where and how they learned it.

11

Teaching Social Studies: The U.S. (Unfinished Sojourn) on Freedom Road

by Mel Didier, Jr.

This two-week unit is designed for a sophomore-level American gov-ernment/civics class but could serve equally well in an American or African-American history class. Subscribing to the ideas that we are the sum of where we have been and that America is still struggling along free-dom's road for true equality and justice, the unit traces the background and history of the Civil Rights Movement and explores how and why the work of the movement is not yet over. In this unit of study, we examine the racist prejudices and stereotypes that made the Civil Rights Movement necessary, and we explore current media images of African Americans to see how far our society has or has not come in terms of progress toward equality. It is important for students to understand that the prejudice behind racist stereotypes inflicts serious damage, that the need to chal-lenge these prejudices and stereotypes continues today, and that students can play an active role in this process.

Screening a combination of whole films and film excerpts allows stu-dents to see for themselves the pernicious images of the past, their recent incarnations, and new images that challenge the old with recognizably realistic portrayals with which students can identify. Students come to learn how early films such as *The Birth of a Nation* (D.W. Griffith, 1915) popularized myths and prejudices about African Americans. Additional films that students view in whole or in part in order to examine how film representations can perpetuate or dispel such myths include *A Place at the Table* (2000), *A Time for Justice: America's Civil Rights Movement* (1992), *Separate But Equal* (1991), *Black and White in America* (1985), *A Class*

Divided (1985), *Midnight Ramble* (1994), *Black Caricature* (1995), *Ethnic Notions* (1987), *Nightjohn* (1996), and *Amistad* (1997).

This unit has been successfully taught at Northside High School, an inner city high school for "at risk" students in Lafayette, Louisiana. Our student population is 75% African American, 23% Euro American, and 2% combined Asian American and Latino/a. While approximately 40% of our students enroll in college, a much lower percent actually complete high school. Because my students have been raised on media images, this unit, invigorated by the use of excerpts and short films, stimulates their interest while engaging them in lively discussions about specific issues and images. Within the larger context of civil liberties in America, we focus on African-American images in film and how to deconstruct them. My goals are to have students complete this unit with a basic understanding of the harmful effects of prejudice, including internalized and institutionalized prejudice, and the skills necessary to read both documentary and feature films actively and critically.

I begin the unit with a lesson in epistemology by having students examine how they know what they know about the history of ethnic diversity and prejudice in America. Some of this lesson uses a strategy known as webbing: I write a word on the board, and students think of as many definitions and descriptions of that word as they can. I write their responses on the board around the word, so the whole ends up looking like a spider web. I start with the word "prejudice." I then encircle it with the following words: "meaning," "methods," "sources," and "victims." Student responses around the word "meaning" usually include such definitions as lack of knowledge, learned dislike, bias, and unreasonable hatred. Around the word "methods" are such responses as name-calling, exclusion, and isolation. Student responses around "sources" of prejudice include friends and relatives as well as movies and television. And finally, under the word "victims," my students include African Americans, Asian Americans, Native Americans, Latinos/as, women, and homosexuals. I reduce long definitions to short phrases for the board and underline the ones we will focus on during this lesson. Students copy the entire web into their notebooks for reference and — although for this lesson we do not focus on stereotypes of and prejudices against Asian Americans, Native Americans, Latino/as, women, or homosexuals — I do not discourage comparisons between ways African Americans and other groups have been discriminated against. Other webbed words, examined and defined in the same way throughout the lesson, include "stereotypes," "ethnicity," "justice," and "equality," as well as any other words that need extensive defining as we encounter them.

Following our webbing exercise to examine the word "prejudice," we explore the nature of prejudice. Several films provide us with specific examples and spark further discussions about how visual media can contribute to what we know about prejudice. Students view portions of two documentaries made specifically for the high school classroom. We first watch the introduction (approximately five minutes long) of *A Place at the Table* (Bobby Houston, Teaching Tolerance, 2000), which is narrated by teens talking about the prejudice they and their families have experienced. For example, a young African American talks about how her grandfather reacted to the Jim Crow segregation that existed in Mississippi, and an Asian American describes how his grandparents survived a Japanese American internment camp during World War II. These narrations are powerful because they come from young people just like those in my classroom. The film's introduction ends with all the different students confirming that what any group wants is "a place at the table," a metaphor that inevitably comes up again when we discuss the word "equality." The second documentary is *A Time for Justice: America's Civil Rights Movement* (Charles Guggenheim, Teaching Tolerance, 1992). The excerpt I use describes how a young African American from Chicago, Emmett Till, was beaten to death when visiting his uncle in Mississippi because he said something flirtatious to a white woman in a store. The young man could be one of my students, and the story of his death adds to my students' understanding of the horror of bigotry and the humanity of its victims. As the film makes clear, these acts of prejudice — both the individual prejudice that caused the brutal murder of this young man and the institutionalized prejudice that resulted in the acquittal by an all-white, all-male jury of the two men who killed him — helped precipitate the Civil Rights Movement.

Two additional film excerpts illustrate for students the everyday harm and persistence of prejudices when they are internalized by a victimized group. The first excerpt is from the made-for-television feature film *Separate but Equal* (George Stevens, 1991), which depicts the road taken by Thurgood Marshall as he prepares the way for the landmark Supreme Court case Brown v. the Board of Education proving that segregation is wrong. The scene I show is when Marshall asks his friend Kenneth Clark to go to South Carolina to interview African-American children in a segregated school. Using black and white dolls, Dr. Clark asks the children to choose the "pretty doll." Most pick the white doll. When he asks them to choose the "ugly doll," they invariably pick the doll that looks most like them. My students quickly recognize how the children have internalized a white standard of beauty that excludes African Americans. A second excerpt, this one from the documentary *Black and White in America* (ABC, 1985), demonstrates how the harmful effects of color prejudice have persisted years after Clark's experiment. I show the segment depicting the results of a University of Michigan study that asks African-American children to choose between drawings of children that are identical except for skin color. All but two children choose the pictures of white children as the "prettiest" girls and the "smartest" boys. I ask my students to consider how color prejudice is internalized and why it is so persistent.

To show how easily prejudice can be learned and integrated into a social structure, I show excerpts from *A Class Divided* (*Frontline*, PBS, 1985), a documentary about Jane Elliott's experiment with her class of third graders in Riceville, Iowa. In 1968, spurred by the assassination of Martin Luther King, Jr., and wondering how to explain it to her students, Elliot created an exercise, which she repeated many times in subsequent years, to teach her students about prejudice. She divided her class into groups of blue-eyed and brown-eyed students and told them, on alternate days, that first one and then the other was the superior group. Effective excerpts show Elliott explaining her theory and the mornings of the first and second days, where she easily convinces the two groups of children on succeeding days that they are either superior or inferior. The second excerpt is from the afternoon of the second day when she summarizes the exercise, explains how poorly both groups of children performed their lessons on the day they were the inferior group, and allows the children to reunite. My students discuss how easy it is for teachers and students to pass on unexamined prejudices based on arbitrary physical features such as skin, or, in this case, eye color. They also learn how prejudiced behavior adversely affects victims and how prejudice can be both taught and untaught.

With an overview from the documentaries of how readily young people can accept prejudiced attitudes and how prejudicial acts affect victims in ways that may not be immediately obvious, we move closer to the Civil Rights Movement. But first students need to learn something about the experience of African Americans before the Civil Rights Movement in order to understand how that experience was shaped by institutionalized prejudice. I begin this portion of the unit by giving students a chronological outline and briefly discussing each event so that students can take notes and ask questions. The outline begins with the first slaves brought to Jamestown in 1619 and follows with the Amistad case before the Supreme Court in 1841. Then we examine the Dred Scott v. Sanford decision (Supreme Court, 1857), the 13th Amendment (1865), Juneteenth (which marks the occasion in 1865 when slaves in Texas did not find out about the end of slavery, legally abolished on January 1st, until June 19th), the

14th Amendment (1867), the 15th Amendment (1870), the Plessey v. Ferguson decision in which the Supreme Court abandoned African American rights won during Reconstruction (1897), and the Niagra Movement (1905) leading to the formation of the NAACP. We conclude with Brown v. the Board of Education of Topeka, Kansas (1954). These key events in American history show students exactly how arduous the struggle for equity and freedom has been for African Americans.

After learning about the African-American experience up to the time of the Civil Rights Movement, we watch the documentary *A Time for Justice: America's Civil Rights Movement* in its entirety. The video offers a visual summary of the Civil Rights Movement from 1954 to 1965. Students take notes on the persons, places, and events chronicled, and we discuss at length what they learned and how they learned it. The latter includes a comparison of the differences between taking notes on an outline of historical events and seeing a visual summary of a series of related events. Students usually conclude that the documentary is an easier way to learn history, with voice-over narration to interpret what we are seeing and with sound effects added to the onscreen images to give us an audio as well as visual experience of important events. But further probing, encouraging students to recall what they learned from the video and to question whether they felt any important events were missing or not completely explained, leads to their recognition of how difficult it is to get the whole picture of any significant event in American history from any one source. Our discussions center on how this documentary attempts to give viewers the experience of directly observing the events by eliminating on-screen experts and providing both photographs and film footage, and how it appeals to young people like themselves by focusing on young activists and victims. This documentary covers the period up to the Voting Rights March in Mississippi — which culminated in the Voting Rights Act that guaranteed people of color, and particularly African Americans in the South, the right to vote — and concludes this segment with the words, " it is done, it is done." The video, however, ends with a strong reminder that civil rights work is not done. I ask my students the question that leads to the next portion of my lesson: "What isn't done?" We then open discussion to ideas about what prejudices have not changed and what barriers still persist on America's freedom road.

For this part of the lesson, we study recurring media stereotypes as one source of how we learn to be prejudiced. I remind the students what they had earlier determined were among our most powerful sources of information: television and movies. We discuss how, since feature films in theatres show seemingly realistic images seen by multitudes of people in various locales at the same time, and since television replays both old and recent films and repeats its own shows over the years, recurring media stereotypes of African Americans are readily available for viewing and reviewing. Continuing our ongoing discussion of how documentaries show reality from a specific and limited point of view, we now add feature films to our study of the ways we can learn and unlearn prejudice. We discuss how feature films are as influential as documentaries because they draw viewers into the story and create a seeming reality that is often difficult to dismiss as simply fiction.

Midnight Ramble: The Story of the Black Film Industry (PBS, *The American Experience*, 1994), and *Black Caricature: The Black Image in Movies, Literature and Music* (Black Entertainment Network, 1995) are excellent sources to learn how the film industry helped solidify stereotypes in the minds of Americans. I show only the introduction of both documentaries (about five minutes each). In *Midnight Ramble,* we learn that early feature films made by Euro Americans caricatured African Americans to such a degree that they could not recognize themselves. Students also learn that African Americans began to create their own films in order to have recognizable images and stories of themselves, but that these films—called "race movies" because they were shown to black audiences after hours—were not shown in many parts of the country. *Midnight Ramble* highlights the African-American independent filmmaker Oscar Micheaux, whose "race movies" attempted to give black viewers an alternative to Hollywood and to portray serious issues within the African-American community. The introduction of the second documentary, *Black Caricature,* contains a number of experts sharing ideas about the damaging effects of racist stereotypes, focusing on how stereotypes cause internalized oppression and self-hatred. My students are reminded of the African-American children who passed over images of themselves in choosing dolls and drawings of Euro-American children to fit the categories of pretty and intelligent.

To learn what the recurring stereotypes of African Americans are and where they originated, we watch several segments from the documentary *Ethnic Notions* (Marlon Riggs, 1987). Students learn that long before movies, radio, or television, print media and live entertainment created and reinforced African-American caricatures. Though they were not as powerful as the moving images that followed, they established the stereotypes that movies would later exploit. Through repetition, these images became both readily available and seemingly believable ways to portray any and all African Americans in film. My goal here is to have students learn to identify the stereotypes prevalent in early films and to able to recognize recurrences in today's films. *Ethnic Notions* identifies and describes a number of popular stereotypes: the Mammy, the Uncle Tom, the Sambo, the Coon, and the Brute. The Mammy's only interest is in serving the white family for whom she works. The Uncle Tom is the male equivalent of the Mammy. The Sambo is a dim-witted and irresponsible male who is always smiling and is often musical. The Coon is an African -American male who tries to imitate the Euro-American male but fails dismally. The Brute is violent and often in pursuit of white women. As usual, students take notes as they watch to record what they learned and how they learned it, here from experts, images, artifacts, and voice-over explanations.

Discussion following this introduction to stereotypes focuses on how recent films often repeat the same images. I show several film excerpts to provide students with the opportunity to recognize what they have just learned to identify. For example, from a short excerpt in *Gone with the Wind* (Victor Fleming, 1936), students easily identify as a stereotype the-slave-turned-servant after the Civil War who holds the white family together. Here the character of the Mammy has no name other than Mammy and no life of her own. They also recognize how a scene from *The Patriot* (Roland Emmerich, 2000) repeats the Mammy stereotype, as the hero and his children are enthusiastically, and unrealistically, welcomed by his former slave who is supposedly in hiding. Scenes from *The Green Mile* (Frank Darabont, 1999) recall for students the Uncle Tom stereotype, as a black death row prisoner is pleased to save the lives of a white woman and a white man at the expense of his own. I also ask students to provide their own recent examples of these stereotypes, and they can now do so, armed with the knowledge that they are seeing repeated stereotypes rather than accurate representations.

The final portion of this lesson teaches students how to read films in terms of film techniques used by directors to create a sense of reality and to guide viewer reactions. After providing students with a list of film techniques (listed in the Glossary of this book), I take students back to the beginnings of film by showing them excerpts from *The Birth of a Nation* (D. W. Griffith, 1915) so that they learn to recognize these techniques and can read them in individual films. *The Birth of a Nation* not only provides examples of most of the film techniques still used today, but also allows students to see how the original stereotypes of African Americans came into film. We also examine excerpts from more recent films to show students how the same techniques can be used in multiple ways.

As students learn to identify important techniques, they also need to develop an awareness of how they are used to create a specific point of view, in this case about African Americans. One of the methods we dissect is the match cut. This is an editing cut where two shots are matched by objects similar in shape. The first example from Griffith's *The Birth of a Nation* matches an empty room with the same room now filled with African Americans. Griffith's scene uses a photograph of a southern legislative room with no one in it to establish the authenticity of his scene. His next shot shows the same room filled with black actors (most of them whites in black face), drinking, eating, and acting inappropriately, representing Griffith's interpretation of the incompetence of the South Carolina legislature controlled by African Americans during Reconstruction. The first part of the match cut creates a sense of reality for viewers and suggests that Griffith's scenes are historically real, even though they are far from historically accurate. The second example of a match cut is from the movie *Nigthjohn* (Charles Burnett, 1996), a film about African Americans' attempts to overcome the horrors of slavery. The first part of the match cut shows the agony on the face of a young slave as his master is about to whip him for leaving the plantation without a pass. The second part shows the same agonized look on the young man's face as other slaves treat his wounds. Through this match cut, viewers are transferred in time without noticing it, so their sense of reality is maintained, while also being led to understand the horrific treatment of slaves without having to see an actual whipping. The two examples allow students to see how the same film technique can be used to different ends and that they need to be attentive to the particular use of each technique in order to be active, rather than passive, viewers.

Other techniques we see examples of include the voice over (an omniscient, all-knowing voice of authority), intertitles (words on the screen that give us the sense that the story must be true), reactive characters (who react to other characters and invite viewers to have the same reaction), camera angles (from below to make a figure seem powerful or from above to make a character seem helplessness), crosscutting (to create the illusion of simultaneous action in two or more places at the same time), and sweetened sounds (exaggerated or intensified sounds to add to the emotional impact of a scene). Once familiar with these film techniques, my students become eager learners in order to be in control of what they see, using their new awareness of what a film encourages them to think.

As a closing activity, I ask my students, "Why should we worry about deconstructing our mediated past in our efforts to construct a more tolerant future?" To give them specifics to discuss, I show an excerpt from *Amistad* (Steven Spielberg, 1997), a feature film version of an actual historical event that we studied earlier. The excerpt shows the closing arguments used by John Quincy Adams before the Supreme Court when he states, "Who we are is who we were." I ask students to discuss the significance of that remark in light of the fact that two of the Founding Fathers mentioned in his speech were slave owners. With my students' help, I make the point that, despite our best efforts to generate an entirely new tomorrow, their past and the past of our society has created the present we now live in, and that present will have an effect on the future.

By studying the prejudices of our past and the history of the Civil Rights struggle, and by practicing methods to identify stereotypes and to read film techniques used to create a point of view, this lesson provides students with a means to avoid learning or accepting prejudice and to have a real appreciation of the work still needed for the creation of a free and equal America. Students are given a final assignment to become civil rights activists. Their assignment is to write a letter to the editor of our school newspaper, or to our local newspaper, stating their opinion about a current events issue recently reported in the news that has to do with civil rights for an ethnic minority group. The issue could be, for example, racial profiling or affirmative action. I read several newspapers carefully while teaching this unit and clip articles to be ready to offer students help in choosing an issue should any need it. Another possibility is for students to write a film review for our student newspaper of a recent or current film, carefully reading its film techniques to highlight the way the film represents ethnic minorities stereotypically or realistically. Students are expected to use the vocabulary of terms we have been using throughout the unit, and to reflect what they have learned in terms of multicultural and visual literacy. We work on drafts in class, sharing and refining ideas, until students are ready to take their own active role on freedom road and continue the work for civil rights by sharing their ideas publicly.

12

Teaching American Literature: Representations of Japanese American Internment

by Nancy Shay

The unit described here is taught in a senior-level Advanced Placement Literature and Composition class at Richard Montgomery High School in suburban Rockville, Maryland. It requires about four weeks of class time. The title of this unit — "Questions of Loyalty" — refers to questions 27 and 28 of the U.S. government's loyalty questionnaire that all interned people of Japanese descent on America's west coast were forced to answer early in 1943. Question 27 read, "Are you willing to serve in the armed forces of the United States on combat duty wherever ordered?" And question 28 asked, "Will you swear unqualified allegiance to the United States of America ... and forswear any allegiance or obedience to the Japanese Emperor...?" The questions required "yes" or "no" answers, but the doubts and suspicions raised about Japanese Americans and the questions they themselves posed regarding their loyalty to community and country following the bombing of Pearl Harbor did not lend themselves to such simple responses.[1] To study the literature of the internment is to study the complexity associated with being of Japanese descent in America, a complexity that continues to resonate today. This unit includes literature and film to educate students about representations in both media and to engender a multi-perspective understanding of the internment of Japanese Americans during World War II — its origins, implementation, and especially its effects.

Because the central texts for this unit are John Okada's (1957) novel *No-No Boy,*[2] Rea Tajiri's (1991) experimental documentary *History and Memory: For Akiko and Takashige,* and a number of film excerpts on the

253

topic, we follow their emphasis on the residual effects of internment. Okada wanted to explore perspectives on internment other than this own, and we also follow his lead here by comparing his novel with internment accounts in documentary films. Although Okada himself served in the U.S. Army in World War II, his protagonist in *No-No Boy*, twenty-five-year-old Ichiro Yamada, does not. The novel opens as Ichiro returns to his postwar community in Seattle after having spent two years in an internment camp and then two years in prison for answering "no-no" to loyalty oath questions 27 and 28. Faced with the choice between loyalty to his Japanese heritage and loyalty to America, the country of his birth and citizenship, Ichiro has chosen the path of greatest resistance. Okada's use of an omniscient narrator allows him to reveal Ichiro's public and private conflicts in considering the wisdom of choices other than his own. In order to teach students to read various types of texts—both print and non-print—and to explore perspectives about internment that compare and conflict with Okada's novel, we screen excerpts from a number of film documentaries that raise the same issues as those in *No-No Boy* but from different points of view. We conclude the unit by watching in its entirety Rea Tajiri's *History and Memory* to help students understand the importance of visual representations and of adding the private histories of Japanese Americans to create more accurate public memories of their internment.

The first step in the lesson occurs well before the unit commences in class. Students are assigned *No-No Boy* about a month before our in-class discussion. They are also given a timeline of events important to Japanese American history in general and the internment in particular and a list of terms, such as *Issei* (the first generation of Japanese to emigrate to the United States), *Nisei* (the Japanese American generation born in the United States), and *Sansei* (third-generation Japanese Americans) useful to understand the readings. Such materials can be found on the Internet.[3] I encourage students to explore sites on the World Wide Web on the subject of Japanese American Internment because they include maps, photographs, film clips, and primary documents from this period. Students are also given James A. Mackey and William E. Huntzicker's article, "Racism and Relocation: Telling the Japanese American Experience."[4] The article demonstrates how one family's internment experience is both unique and representative and models for students the importance of placing representations of historical events within their historical context. I require students to refer to the timeline, terms, and article as they read Okada's *No-No Boy*.

My students find their study of *No-No Boy* useful for their AP exam. In recent years, *No-No Boy* and other multicultural works that are relatively new to the canon have been included in the AP exam. Periodically, the third essay question of the AP exam asks students to write about the setting, both geographical and historical, in a work of literature. *No-No Boy* offers students an opportunity to read a book of literary merit that is enriched by their understanding of its historical context. Should the third essay question on the AP English exam instead ask students to address traditional themes—such as parent-child relationships, moral decisions, the importance of celebrations or homecomings, or the significance of secondary characters—students can easily draw from Okada's novel to demonstrate their understanding of such ideas.

By the completion of the unit, students will be able to meet a number of additional objectives: 1) understand essential aspects of the history of Japanese American Internment, which helps to determine the point of view expressed in various literary and film representations; 2) identify and compare recurring themes in various accounts of the internment; 3) identify and interpret narrative techniques in literature; and 4) identify and interpret cinematic techniques in both documentary and feature films. Ultimately, the objective that most matters in an AP Literature course is the third one, identifying and interpreting narrative techniques in literature. This is the skill students will be expected to demonstrate for the three-hour exam. I would, however, be remiss if I did not incorporate visual literacy skills into the curriculum as well, especially in light of recent state curricular mandates and the National Council of Teachers of English standards regarding media. One of the important benchmarks of a strong high school education is for students to develop keen critical thinking and writing skills. Teaching students to read films offers them rich opportunities to do so. Not insignificantly, my county's on-level twelfth-grade curriculum includes an entire unit on film. To privilege the written text over the visual for Advanced Placement students by not including film texts would be doing my students a disservice. As teachers are well aware, many students are likely to stop reading classic literature as soon as they can; very few, however, will ever stop watching movies. By teaching this unit, I want to provide my students with the opportunity to develop a deeper understanding of the internment while also reinforcing the notion that reading literature and reading film require the same kinds of analytical and interpretative skills and insights.

I begin the in-class portion of this unit with two bridge activities. The first is a reading quiz on *No-No Boy* to help students determine their comprehension of plot, characterization, setting, narrative point of view, and the relation of the events chronicled to the historical context provided on their timeline. Bridge activities use students' prior knowledge to help them make a connection to what they are currently studying. The comprehension quiz allows students to determine what they know as a base line for what they do not yet know about the novel in particular and the internment in general. The second bridge activity introduces students more directly to critical reading of both written and visual texts. We read the trial scene passages from Harper Lee's 1960 novel *To Kill a Mockingbird*[5] and David Guterson's 1995 novel *Snow Falling on Cedars*[6] and view the same scenes from the two feature film adaptations, Robert Mulligan's (1962) *To Kill a Mockingbird* and Scott Hicks' (1999) *Snow Falling on Cedars*. After determining that the trial scenes address issues of justice, racism, prejudice, and loyalty, students discuss how the literary techniques compare with the cinematic techniques as a means to direct reader and viewer reactions. Main characters whose point of view is privileged by our understanding of their backgrounds, private thoughts, and motivations — via interior monologues and direct speech/dialogue in the novels and voice over, camera angles, and the reactions of secondary characters in the films — catch the attention of my students immediately. This bridge activity gives me the opportunity to ascertain how much the students know, especially about film, and to introduce or review important novel and film techniques accordingly. The juxtaposition of these novel and film texts not only inevitably results in lively discussions about where prejudice comes from, how it is reinforced, what effects it has on its victims, what both individuals and societies can do to recognize and work towards ending it, but also creates an interest in Okada's *No-No Boy* and in how verbal and visual texts provide us with different ways of knowing.

The unit consists of journal assignments and student-led discussions and concludes with an in-class essay. In their written work, students are asked to place *No-No Boy* in its historical context, to compare how its treatment of one major theme relates to the treatment of the same theme in a selection from a documentary that we view in class, and to compare how the novel and the documentary excerpts use the narrative techniques of their mediums to convey their points of view on that theme. I organize our discussions around thematic comparisons and points of view because we discuss *No-No Boy* as one representation of Japanese American Internment among many. In the interests of space, my discussions here will focus on film techniques, rather than the techniques of the novel that literature teachers are already familiar with.

Because my method of instruction is student-centered in its approach, my students are responsible for leading class discussion. Students are assigned one of the following themes and asked to explore it in their journals as treated in Okada's novel and in a documentary excerpt shown at the beginning of each class discussion. The themes are loyalty and patriotism; generational differences and tensions; ruptures (economic, social, psychological) affecting the individual, the family, and/or the community; marginalization of individuals and groups; individual and group identity; and celebrations and homecomings. We devote about two class periods to a discussion of each theme. Students assigned to discuss that day's theme connect specific passages from *No-No Boy* to the themes presented in the documentary selection.

Before we begin our comparable themes discussions, we view the eleven-minute Office of War Information documentary newsreel entitled *Japanese Relocation* narrated by relocation director Milton Eisenhower. Because it is only eleven minutes long, we view it in its entirety. The newsreel's one-sided assurances invite students to think critically about point of view in documentary films—rather than passively accepting what they see as an objective record of events—and their influence on our ideas about history. Eisenhower appears on screen behind a desk and in uniform as the U.S. Government authority on Japanese American Internment. His declaration that Japanese Americans "cheerfully" responded to Executive Order 9066 and his claim that the government was providing "plenty of healthful food for all" contrast with the account in *No-No Boy* and, as students are quick to note as they see them, with the views and images presented in the other documentaries. The government's motive of justifying to the American public its internment of 120,000 men, women, and children behind barbed wire determines its point of view that the action was the right decision. Eisenhower claims that the Japanese Americans interned are of the same opinion and have been willingly transported to the camps as their patriotic contribution to the war effort. Comparisons between Okada's novel and the government film highlight for students how important it is to read and see Japanese American perspectives to get the complete story. The official version of history provided by the government clearly does not reflect the internment experience of most Japanese Americans.

Following our viewing and analysis of the government film, we begin student-led discussions to examine what *No-No Boy* and the documentary excerpts reveal about the assigned themes. Beginning with the loyalty and patriotism theme, we see an excerpt from the documentary *Honor Bound: A Personal Story* (Joan Saffe, 1995). This film explores the option some Japanese Americans during World War II chose rather than endure internment: serving in the military as their expression of patriotism and loyalty to the United States. Students note that the film does not focus on the psychological effects such a decision had, whereas these effects are a prominent topic in *No-No Boy*, as the protagonist, Ichiro Yamada, must bear the criticism that he has betrayed other *nisei* and their chance for success in America because he has refused to prove his loyalty in battle. The veterans of the 442nd combat unit who had been gathered for the documentary only admit that, although their service was exemplary (this unit is the most decorated in U.S. military history and suffered one of the highest casualty rates in the war), they sometimes felt "expendable." When reflecting on the wartime experience that still haunts many of these Japanese American Army veterans, one man observes, "It was worth it." The film excerpt offers students a point of contrast between the decision Ichiro makes to be a "no-no" and the effects that different choices had on individuals and their families. Students who have prepared the topic of loyalty and patriotism note that families of the veterans in the film voice no criticism of their choice. And students invariably refer to contrary passages in the novel when Ichiro's mother claims, "If I had a son and he had gone in the American army to fight Japanese, I would have killed myself with shame" (23) and to Ichiro's recollection in Chapter 1 of how and why he made the decision to become a "no-no" (31–35). Comparing the documentary excerpt with passages chosen by students from the novel helps them realize that loyalty and patriotism among Japanese Americans had multiple meanings and motivations especially among the *Issei* and *Nisei* and that to dissent from the often popular *Nisei* position of joining the war to prove one's loyalty was not a position many dared to take.

The theme of generational differences and tensions experienced by *Issei* parents and their *Nisei* children is of personal interest to students of this age who often experience similar tensions. Excerpts from *Rabbit in the Moon* (Emiko Omori, 1999) that directly relate to issues raised by *No-No Boy* work particularly well because they depict the generational frictions that existed in some Japanese American families before the war that were exacerbated by internment. In *Rabbit in the Moon*, the filmmaker's older sister and a camp survivor, Chizuko Omori, observes that when the government issued Order 9066, her American upbringing had made her feel American, not Japanese, as her parents felt. She also recounts in the film that when internees were forced to sign the loyalty oath, her parents resolved to repatriate to Japan (as Ichiro's mother intends to do in *No-No Boy*). She states that "Our parents decided they no longer wanted to stay in the United States" since they saw no future for their family in this country after being treated so poorly.

In viewing this film — as well as the others they watch — students are asked to develop their visual literacy skills, not just to write down the facts from the film that parallel our text, but to pay attention to how the filmmaker tells her internment story. Omori uses such conventions as experts looking straight into the camera in a medium shot (from the waist up and close enough to see facial expressions and gestures) so that we can identify with them literally on our own level as they speak. As Chizuko Omori tells us of her rebellion against her parents, we first see her filmed in a medium shot. Then, we see her image in a family photo—a smiling thirteen-year-old all–American girl with curly hair and glasses—as she confesses in a voice over that her parents' decision to return to Japan "was devastating for me personally." The juxtaposition of the happy girl in the photograph and the voice over recounting her suffering prompted by the U.S. government policy invites us to empathize with her conflicted situation and its effect. In connecting this excerpt from the documentary, students often select a passage from Chapter 2 of Okada's novel focusing on Ichiro's younger brother Taro's ideological clashes with both his parents and Ichiro, which culminates in his joining the army. Another incident showing generational differences and tensions occurs in Chapter 6, where Okada shows the difficulties the *Issei* faced when trying to understand their Americanized children, many of whom had become "unrecognizable shadow[s] among other shadows" to their parents (125–26). *Rabbit in the Moon* also illustrates this aspect well in a segment describing how families disintegrated in the camps, as children no longer ate with their parents and often did not even live with their own families.

Economic, social, and psychological ruptures affecting the individual, the family, and the community serve as the focus of our next discussion. The opening scene from the experimental documentary *Who's Going to Pay for These Donuts Anyway?* (Janice Tanaka, 1993), which includes a brief history of the internment, records the filmmaker's personal recollections of her father's emotional distancing and eventual physical distancing from his family during and after internment. The excerpt reminds students of many of the key themes we have been discussing in regard to the novel: the relationship between children and their parents as well as the emotional ruptures experienced by many members of the Japanese American community. Okada's descriptions of Ichiro's parents at the beginning of Chapter 8 and his mother's eventual suicide by the chapter's end make these difficulties apparent. Students note the parallels: both the filmmaker's father in the film and the protagonist's mother in the novel slip into insanity and death, and both texts suggest that discriminatory treatment, including internment, were responsible.

Tanaka's experimental film offers a distinct kind of documentary for students to consider in their efforts to understand the internment. Tanaka uses many techniques most students haven't seen in a documentary before — slow motion, a tilted hand-held camera resulting in canted angles in the frames, intertitles running horizontally at the bottom of the screen simultaneously with voice overs and visuals, and fictional reenactments of events being described by archival radio broadcasts. Students can examine how experimental documentaries such as this are created not only to inform but to draw our attention to their form as a subjective construction by the filmmaker rather than pretend to be an objective recording of history. Tanaka suggests that all discourse is mediated while also providing varying kinds of evidence to support her point of view. Students come to recognize that documentary filmmakers can employ a variety of film techniques to communicate that theirs is a personal view of the past.

A documentary that addresses our fourth theme, the emotional ruptures caused by internment as well as the marginalization of individuals and groups, is *Children of the Camps* (Stephen Holsapple, 1999). An appropriate excerpt for this part of the lesson features camp survivors discussing the specific ways their childhood camp experiences continue to affect them in adulthood. It includes the poignant moment when one survivor claims: "[As a child,] I knew I was responsible for World War II." Students connect the excerpt to *No-No Boy* in its emphasis on how many Japanese Americans felt deeply — and mistakenly — culpable for the treatment they received during the war. Throughout *No-No Boy*, but especially in Chapters 1 and 7, Ichiro confronts his marginalized position in both Japanese and mainstream American society.

For our discussion of the conflict between asserting one's individuality versus conforming to group identity, we watch a segment from *A Personal Matter: Gordon Hirabayashi versus the United States* (John de Graaf, 1992). The film suggests the range of choices— all of which were difficult and none truly desirable — that Japanese Americans were forced to make during World War II. The excerpt includes Gordon Hirabayashi's description of what he endured once he stated his unwillingness to abide by the government's unconstitutional curfew for Japanese Americans only. Students note just how American Gordon Hirabayashi is as he describes his experiences, stressing all the more the injustice of denying American citizens their constitutional rights. We hear from supporters of Hirabayashi, but also from one of his relatives who confesses that the family felt ashamed and embarrassed by his decision. Students point to parallels in *No-No Boy*. For instance, Ichiro faces both rejection and acceptance from varying members of his community in a confusing mix of reactions that range from being spit upon in Chapter 1 to receiving encouragement and acceptance from his war veteran friend Kenji in Chapter 7.

For the theme of celebrations and homecomings, the documentary *Family Gathering* (Lise Yasui, 1988) serves as another good comparison to *No-No Boy*. The filmmaker's grandfather, so shamed by the government's suspicion of him and by his community's doubts about his loyalty to the United States, commits suicide a few years after being released from prison. Like many contemporary Asian American documentaries, Yasui's film is very personal. It is autobiographical and historical, recording her search for the truth of her family's history. Students learn from the film that from the moment of his immigration, Lise Yasui's grandfather had labored hard to establish himself in his community — moving from domestic servant to store clerk to property owner and president of the local apple growers association. But when his reputation was ruined by the war, he never felt at ease or welcome in his community again, as Yasui learns from her father only when she is an adult. The film excerpt where Yasui discovers this fact about her grandfather introduces the idea that homecomings following internment were often anticlimactic at best and terribly painful at worst. Students point out how Lise Yasui's grandfather and Ichiro's suicidal mother clearly had different American experiences. Yasui's grandfather and his family were assimilated and well respected by their community before the war whereas Ichiro's mother, who had resisted becoming American, lives in a primarily Japanese neighborhood, longs to go back to Japan, and commits suicide when she can no longer sustain the illusion that Japan would win the war. Although their motivations for suicide differ, each suggests the same struggle to maintain dignity and principles in a world that seemed to deny them of both. Neither was ever able to consider America a secure home after enduring the indignities of internment.

The film tests students' visual literacy skills in that it emphasizes that the truth about the past is not readily available. Like many documentaries, Yasui provides us with testimony, in this case from her father, aunts and uncles, and old friends of her grandparents. Unlike most documentaries, she adds her own voice and experience at the beginning of the film — to show her attempt to understand the Japanese part of her bicultural heritage. It may also be helpful to show a few minutes from the beginning of the film, where both she and we realize that she doesn't have the truth and that it is going to take probing on her part to find it. The form of the film requires critical reading and thinking as Yasui challenges herself and her viewers to discover how her grandfather's life and death can be understood through the prism of internment. In considering the effects of internment as Okada explores them, students often refer to passages which focus on

Ichiro's emotionally barren homecoming in Chapter 1 and contrast it with the festive dinner his friend Kenji's family has prepared prior to Kenji's ultimately fatal hospitalization to repair the leg that was shattered in the war (126–132). Both the documentary and novel suggest that even supposedly happy events continued to be tainted by memories and reminders of internment.

Rea Tajiri's *History and Memory: For Akiko and Takashige* (1991) serves as an appropriate and interesting conclusion to bring together all the ideas the students have been discussing in relation to *No-No Boy* and the film excerpts we have viewed. This documentary is the final and primary visual text for our unit for a number of reasons. First, it is an experimental documentary that students could have trouble understanding without an understanding of Japanese American Internment and the experience with experimental form provided earlier with Tanaka's *Who's Going to Pay for These Donuts Anyway?* Additionally, it includes excerpts from the 1942 Office of War Information film that students have viewed earlier as well as excerpts from such Hollywood feature films as *Bad Day at Black Rock* (John Sturges, 1954) and *Come See the Paradise* (Alan Parker, 1990) to make a compelling statement about America's long cinematic history of representing ideas about Japanese American Internment without the input of Japanese Americans, a fact that many students find helpful in attempting to understand the cultural climate that made internment possible. Specifics in Tajiri's film invite students to review what they have learned and add to their knowledge. Newly alert to point of view in both written and visual texts, students discuss the voice over by the filmmaker's nephew during the scenes from *Come See the Paradise*. He criticizes Hollywood's recurring convention of telling an ethnic group's story from a white leading man's perspective because it suggests that Euro Americans would not be interested in protagonists who didn't look like them and it marginalizes the ethnic group whose story is supposedly being told. Here students come to understand how they learn what they learn from the film. Students note how the voice over combined with compelling visual evidence creates a point of view for viewers. They discuss how when Euro Americans become the lead characters in films about ethnic minorities, the perspective belongs to the Euro Americans and the stories often become their stories. Tajiri explores for herself her family's actual internment experience to distinguish it from government and Hollywood movie history. Her film combines various film techniques — film excerpts, voice overs, intertitles, reenactments, contemporary footage of her visit to the Arizona site of the camp where her mother was interned — to provoke new ways of thinking about how we know what we think we know. *History and Memory,* through its juxtaposition of public and private points of view, documents one chapter of American history through a personal lens. Consequently, her private experience becomes a borrowed memory for students, a compelling memory, and like *No-No Boy*, not easily forgotten.

While the unit described here was designed for a literature course, both Okada's novel and the documentary films could work equally well in a number of contexts. A twentieth-century American history course or a social studies course focusing on Japanese American Internment, the U.S. Constitution, or civil rights would certainly find ample material appropriate for their studies. Including fictional literature and documentary films engages my students in a period in our nation's history that many of them otherwise know little about and presents, in the specific experiences of Japanese Americans, themes and ideas important to all Americans.

13

Teaching Film Studies: Images of Ethnicity and Justice in America

by Billie Smith

"Major Themes in American Cinema" is a course offered at McKinley Senior High School in Baton Rouge, Louisiana. The first semester of the course focuses on film depictions of American institutions and government; the second semester covers film depictions of personal and social issues such as growing up, love, and family life. McKinley is an inner city school with a diverse student body. The student population of 850 includes the system's only programs for gifted and visually impaired students, one of two parish-wide programs for talented students, and a core program for traditional students. Approximately sixty percent of the students are African American and forty percent are Euro American. Asian Americans, Latino/as, and American Indians represent less than one percent of the student body. This film course, open to juniors and seniors only, meets every day for a 53-minute class period. During the first semester, we examine cinematic depictions of three elements of the American judicial system: crime, the court system, and incarceration. Although ethnicity is part of every unit, it is the focus of the lesson described here, which takes about two and a half weeks and explores the role ethnicity plays in deciding a defendant's fate. The lesson consists of documentary, newsreel, and feature films, corresponding readings, journal assignments, a test, and a final project. Our focus on Clarence Brown's *Intruder in the Dust* (1949) and Joseph Sargent's *A Lesson Before Dying* (1999) is designed to have students recognize and analyze stereotyping, point of view, intended audience, and cinematic techniques that guide viewer response. We examine the role that ethnicity—with a focus on being African American—plays in film representations as a means to explore issues of ethnicity and justice in America.

We begin this lesson by watching extended selections from *Ethnic Notions* (Marlon Riggs, 1987), a documentary about African-American stereotypes in popular culture, including popular films since the beginning of filmmaking in America, and a reading that illuminates the film history and significance of those stereotypes. With a viewing guide directing their attention, students note the characteristics associated with recurring stereotypes of African Americans in films— the Mammy, Uncle Tom, Sambo, Pickaninny, Black Brute, and Coon — illustrated in *Ethnic Notions*. The Brute stereotype caricatures African-American men as animalistic and oversexed, prone to violence, and destructive of Euro-American civilization; it catches students' attention as a caricature they see repeated in current films. The Coon stereotype, which is also at the heart of the injustice depicted in the feature films we examine, caricatures African-American men as trying to emulate white speech, dress, and behavior but failing ludicrously. These two figures, according to *Ethnic Notions*, were introduced after the Civil War in an effort to depict African American men as naturally inferior and thus unfit for citizenship. Students also read about the history of these stereotypes in American cinema. Excerpts from Donald Bogle's book on African-American stereotypes categorize the stereotypes illuminated in *Ethnic Notions* and discuss how these stereotypes are repeated in some recent films and challenged as false to reality in others.[1] The documentary and readings make students aware of the long history of continued and contested stereotyping of African Americans in American cinema.

Students then watch a brief film montage of examples of brutality and injustice directed at African Americans and read current statistics about incarceration. The montage includes newsreel reports of Civil Rights events such as marches and sit-ins at lunch counters from the documentary *Eyes on the Prize* (Henry Hampton, 1986), film coverage of the Rodney King beating from the opening of the feature film *Malcolm X* (Spike Lee, 1992), and recent television news coverage about racial profiling that I have taped from local and national news programs. The images move from recent American history to the present to dispel the notion that ethnic injustice is a thing of the past. We view and discuss the montage images in conjunction with the stereotypes identified in *Ethnic Notions*, especially the images of the Black Brute and the Coon, to analyze how stereotypes can contribute to unequal and unjust treatment of African Americans. Students then read and discuss recent statistics[2] detailing the inordinately large number of African Americans who are presently incarcerated. A journal writing assignment asks students to reflect on how the stereotypes identified in *Ethnic Notions* relate to issues of judicial inequity reflected in both the montage excerpts and the statistics. This assignment requires students to think seriously about the harm that stereotypes can cause. The journal also provides a record of each student's evolution in thinking as we continue to probe issues of ethnicity and justice.

The class then watches *Intruder in the Dust* (Clarence Brown, 1949) in its entirety. Produced after World War II, it is one of the first cinematic attempts to seriously address the problem of racial injustice in America. Based on William Faulkner's 1948 novel of the same title, *Intruder in the Dust* tells the story of Lucas Beauchamp, a proud African-American man arrested for the murder of a member of the Gowrie family, a tough, poor Euro-American family. Lucas is brought to jail, but everyone believes he will not live to see a trial. As he enters the jail, Lucas turns and commands Chick Malleson — a sixteen-year-old white boy — to bring his uncle, a local lawyer, to the jail. In a flashback, the audience learns that Chick owes Lucas a debt since Lucas once helped Chick when he fell into a frozen lake. Although Chick had crassly tried to pay Lucas for his help and hospitality because he did not wish to owe a black man anything, he now feels his obligation to repay Lucas keenly. Lucas and the Lawyer Stevens cannot seem to trust each other because of a profound distrust rooted in the past. Chick thus gets his opportunity to help Lucas. While the town grows restless for Lucas's blood, Chick, Aleck (Chick's young African-American friend), and Mrs. Haversham (an elderly Euro-American woman) dig up the Gowrie grave to find proof that Lucas' gun was not the murder weapon and thereby prove Lucas's innocence. This task is left to the young men and the older woman because women and children, the film implies, are not as vested in the oppressive system of racial discrimination as adult Euro-American males.

Although the film is dated, it provides students the chance to examine the significance of intended audience and use of stereotypes in a film. For instance, when Chick's uncle piously says, "Lucas wasn't in trouble. We were in trouble," his statement clearly delineates who the intended audience is: white America. *Intruder*, however, remains interesting in its early, but not completely successful, attempts to undercut ethnic stereotypes. On one hand, the audience is asked to identify with Lucas, not with the Euro-American characters. Lucas clearly defies the African-American stereotypes of the Brute and the Coon, and trouble befalls Lucas because he has maintained his dignity in a Jim Crow world. He is proud, arrogant, well dressed, and refuses to cower before other men, which flies in the face of the Brute and Coon stereotypes by which the town defines him. On the other hand, the courageous Aleck occasionally slips into the slow, dull responses and grotesque, pop-eyed stares of the Sambo and Pickaninny illustrated in *Ethnic Notions* and defined by Donald Bogle.

Students receive a video guide to be completed over the days it takes to watch *Intruder,* part of which asks them to read Gordon Allport's "Formation of In-Groups"[3] and respond to Lucas's character in light of this article. Allport states that "what is familiar tends to become a value" (292) and theorizes that, to some extent, group membership and group identification can determine an individual's attitudes and behavior. Students discuss Allport's idea of how, for example, for the individual who is Euro American, being Euro American is valued as good. Allport also argues that individuals recognize "reference groups," which are any groups an individual admires, respects, and would like to be included as a member. Allport states that for ethnic minority individuals who are victims of racial discrimination, the Euro-American majority can come to represent their reference group. It is important for students to apply these ideas to Lucas's character because Lucas clearly sees Euro Americans as his reference group. This notion of reference groups is also helpful for students to understand the way the Euro Americans in town unite across socioeconomic lines against their perceived enemy: the uppity African-American male.

Screening *Intruder* requires two 53-minute class periods. After the class has watched the entire film, it is important to review pertinent scenes—easily gathered on a tape of excerpts—as the class reviews their viewing guides. The focus is twofold: to teach and review cinematic concepts while analyzing and discussing issues of representation. The viewing guide for *Intruder* includes such questions as intended audience, point of view, and depictions of stereotypes. Students discuss who the film was intended for (Euro Americans), point of view (the story is told from Chick's perspective), and with whom viewers are invited to identify (Lucas Beauchamp). We discuss how and why the film lapses into some stereotypes (Alec as Sambo) and defies others (Lucas is not an Uncle Tom, a Brute, or a Coon). Thematic issues raised in the film include other stereotypes (such as Euro-American Southern Womanhood), male dignity and honor, group identification, class structure, and the nature and causes of social change. Each of these concepts can be tied to at least one specific scene in the film. A scene that subverts the ideal of southern womanhood is Mrs. Haversham's standoff with the mob. She is in many ways the ideal, gentile southern woman, but any discussion of the film must address the scene where she holds the mob at bay while she knits. Key scenes that raise the issue of male dignity include Chick's visit to Lucas's home, Lucas's trip to the store, and the scene where the sheriff and lawyer talk to Lucas about his behavior. The latter, which follows their realization that Lucas is innocent, is the ideal scene for discussing male honor, the formation of ingroups, and the system of class structure in America. The mob scenes are instructive for class structure and group identification. The breakfast and the final scene illustrate the nature and causes of social change.

Film techniques on the viewing guide include *mise-en-scène*, flashbacks, intercuts, reactive characters, and extreme close ups. These cinematic techniques illustrate how issues of injustice and justice are depicted in the film. The *mise-en-scène* (the background, objects, and people in the scene and the way they interact) in the opening sequence establishes the when and where of the story. *Intruder* opens with a police car, siren wailing, entering a small southern town. Clothes and setting make it clear that this is the mid-twentieth century. There is the agitated, angry movement of a mob of Euro-American men, speaking with distinctly southern accents. As the handcuffed African American, Lucas Beauchamp, steps forth from the police car, viewers are invited to identify with him and understand his plight. In an intercut flashback, viewers learn of Chick's relationship with Lucas. Reactive characters include the mob at the beginning and at the end of the movie (first conveying anger and a thirst for blood, later representing shame and deflated anger), the men at the point when Mrs. Haversham tells them they should be ashamed, and Aleck when Chick and they dig up the grave and discover it is empty. The scene with Lucas and Chick in the jail is a good one for discussing how close-ups and camera angles direct viewers' attention and emotions.

The next part of the unit examines *A Lesson Before Dying* (Joseph Sargent, 1999), based on Ernest J. Gaines' 1997 novel of the same title. The film opens with an establishing shot of Louisiana sugar cane fields and a Huey P. Long billboard, which ironically promises that "Every Man's a King." A young African-American man, Jefferson — his name is another touch of irony — accepts a ride from two acquaintances. The audience is invited to sense that this is an unwise decision. Shortly thereafter, Jefferson's cohorts become embroiled in a dispute with a Euro-American storeowner over a bottle of whiskey. When the confrontation turns violent, all but Jefferson are dead. Jefferson, though only an innocent bystander, is quickly apprehended, tried, convicted, and sentenced to death by the all-white male jury of "his peers." It is at his trial that the impetus for the story occurs. Jefferson's Euro-American lawyer, in an attempt to "defend" him, refers to Jefferson as an "animal," specifically a "hog," and states that he is incapable of planning and executing a murder. The central plot conflict is precipitated by Jefferson's godmother who decides Jefferson will not go to his death defined by the lawyer's demeaning characterization of him. The local African-American schoolteacher, Grant Wiggins, is pressured by his aunt to go to the jail and teach Jefferson a "lesson before dying." Although resentful and sullen, Grant fulfills the expectations of his aunt and community only to find that Jefferson has as much to teach the teacher and the community as he has to learn. The film provides an excellent foil to *Intruder in the Dust* because *Lesson* has an African-American point of view, an African-American savior, and a more realistic ending. However, both films are also alike: both undercut stereotypes and focus upon the theme of what it means to be a man, specifically, an African-American man in need of justice.

A viewing guide again directs student attention and discussions and leads to a journal assignment. The viewing guide for *A Lesson Before Dying* asks students to look for stereotypes of the Mammy and the Uncle Tom (both caricatures of African Americans as happily subservient) in the film, as well as the Brute, Coon, and Sambo and to determine whether the caricatures they find are being upheld or subverted. The majority of students find that the film offers a mixed message: that depictions of the women are stereotypical and troubling, but that the men defy and undercut these stereotypes. The viewing guide also asks students to respond to the film from a number of perspectives, beginning with statistics related to judicial inequities in America, specifically those comparing the percentage of ethnic minorities in prison with the percentage of ethnic minorities in the general population that we read about earlier. A number of photographs illustrating these inequities are readily available. One which I ask students to discuss in conjunction with the film has a photo of Martin Luther King, Jr. on the left side of the page and a photo of Charles Manson on the right, accompanied by the caption: "The man on the left is 75 times more likely to be stopped by the police while driving than the man on the right,"[4] which provokes a good deal of discussion. Another perspective offered for discussion is in Claude McKay's poem "If We Must Die,"[5] written in response to the white-provoked race riots of the "bloody summer" of 1919. A follow-up journal assignment asks students to respond to the following: What does McKay mean when he says "die like men?" What do you think it means to die like a man? How do McKay's and your own response correspond with and illuminate the characterization and treatment of Jefferson in *A Lesson Before Dying*?

To help students recognize and read film techniques, the viewing guide also asks them to consider the film's use of *mise-en-scène*, visual metaphor, reactive characters, and dissolves to guide viewer response. After viewing the film, we review the guides in conjunction with appropriate excerpts from the film to examine the film techniques used and how they affect thematic issues related to ethnic minorities and justice. For *mise-en-scène* and visual metaphor (an object that is part of the realistic setting but also possesses a larger significance), students comment on the signi-ficance of the time and place of the story as well as the irony of the words printed on the Huey P. Long billboard. Jefferson's godmother, Miss Emma, is a particularly good figure to watch as someone who directs our responses. Her reactions in the courtroom as the lawyer calls her godson a "hog" is a poignant scene, as is the scene when she demands that Mr. Henry ask his brother, the sheriff, to allow the schoolteacher to visit Jefferson in prison. The conflict that takes place between the minister and Grant Wiggins over the radio Wiggins has given Jefferson provides students another opportunity to watch the godmother's reactions and to make judgments about how the film invites viewers to respond to the actions and dialogue. The dissolve from the store to the courthouse is compelling because it metaphorically represents the swiftness of "justice" for poor African-Americans like Jefferson. Throughout the film, two other visual metaphors recur: the positioning of educational objects intermingled with religious objects and the continual references to the globe. The film high-lights religion and education as the two sources of help available to the African-American community. It also develops the tension that can and does arise between them as they vie for control in the community. Throughout the film, references are made to running, to leaving Louisiana and the South for a better place. The presence of the globe constantly high-lights the ambiguity that Grant feels about staying in the South. Themat-ically, students focus on the division of time in the film: the Christmas season and the Easter season. These events are tied to Jefferson's role as savior, as are the scenes when the children bring Jefferson gifts to honor him, when Grant brings him an Easter egg, and when Grant's fiancée gives the speech about "the one."

The lesson concludes with a test with a twofold purpose: first, to assess the student's grasp of ethnic stereotypes and their impact on the conscious and unconscious actions of Americans regarding issues of justice; and second, to ascertain the student's understanding of point of view and intended audience and how they shape what viewers take away from a film. An essay question directing students to compare and contrast point of view, intended audience, and overall effectiveness in depicting issues regarding justice for African Americans as presented in these films is essential to any summative evaluation of this lesson.

Students also complete a project where they apply what they have learned from *Intruder in the Dust* and *A Lesson Before Dying* to another film of their own choice. Projects allow for a variety of interests and a variety of assessments. Suggested projects include examining how justice and injustice are depicted for other ethnic groups—as a way to broaden the impact of the unit. Interlibrary loan and local universities provide excellent help in securing a variety of useable films. Students are also encouraged to evaluate new and popular films for their projects. Projects can take a variety of forms: papers describing or oral presentations accompanied by film excerpts highlighting how film techniques are used to support the film's thesis; papers with specific scene descriptions or presentations with film excerpts to demonstrate how stereotypes are upheld or undercut in a particular film; graphic organizers to illustrate the complex and often ambiguous forces which impede our justice system; and student films (documentary or imaginative) on issues related to ethnicity and justice.

The unit described here works very well in my film course, but it could be adapted easily to a number of other contexts. Since both of these films are based on novels by major American writers, both the literary and film texts could be taught in an American literature course. And since the thematic focus I have chosen is America's legal system — and in this section the often unequal justice meted out to African Americans— my approach to these films would be appropriate for a social studies, history, or government class. Both of these films go a long way in helping students understand what films say to us by understanding how they say it.

Appendix: Selected Video and DVD Distributors and Websites

Video Distributors

Arab Film Distribution, 2417 10th Ave. E. Seattle, WA, 98102 (206) 322-0882, info@arabfilm.com

Bullfrog Films, P.O. Box 149, Oley, PA 19547, (800) 543-3764, video@bullfrog films.com

CAAAV, 2473 Valentine Ave., Bronx, NY 10458, (718) 220-7391 x15, etang@caaav.org

California Newsreel, 500 Third Street Suite 505, San Francisco, CA 94107, (415) 284-7801, contact@newsreel.org

Catticus Corporation, 2600 10th St., Berkeley, CA 94710, (510) 548-0854, skgarden@aol.com

Center for New American Media, CNAM Film Library, 22-D Hollywood Ave., Hohokus, NJ 07423, (800) 343-5540, tmcndy@aol.com

Corvision Media, Inc., 3014 Commercial Ave., Northbrook, IL 60062, (800) 537-3130, corvision@aol.com

Deep Dish TV, 339 Lafayette St., Second Floor, New York, NY 10012, (212) 473-8933, deepdish@igc.org

Direct Cinema Ltd., P.O. Box 10003, Santa Monica, CA 90410, (800) 525-0000, directcinema@attmail.com

Edge Video, P.O. Box 430, Fanwood, NJ 07023, (908) 769-3250, ceetv@aol.com

Electronic Arts Intermix, 535 West 22nd St., 5th floor, New York, NY 10011, (212) 337-0680, info@eai.com

Facets Video, 1517 W. Fullerton Ave. Chicago, ILL 60614 (800) 331-6197, www.facets.org and sales@facets.org

Filmmakers Library, 124 E. 40th St., Suite 901, New York, NY 10016, (212) 808-4980, info@filmakers.com

Films for the Humanities and Sciences, P.O. Box 2053, Princeton, NJ 08543-2053, (800) 257-5126, custserve@films.com

First Run/Icarus, 32 Court St., 21st Floor, Brooklyn, NY 11201, mail@frif.com

Frameline, 346 9th St., San Francisco, CA 94103, (415) 703-8650, distribution@frameline.org

Great Plains National, P.O. Box 80669, Lincoln NE 68501, (800) 228-4630, gpn@unl.edu

KJM3, 788 Riverside Drive, New York, NY 10032, (212 334-4402, KJM3274@aol.com

Movies Unlimited, 3015 Darnell Rd., Philadelphia, PA 19154 (800) 466-8437, www.moviesunlimited.com, movies@moviesunlimited.com

Na Maka o ka 'Aina, P.O. Box 29, Na'alehu, HI 96772-0029, (808) 929-9659, namaka@interpac.net

National Asian American Telecommunications Association, 346 9th St., 2nd Floor, San Francisco, CA 94103 (415) 552-9550, distribution@naatanet.org

National Film Board of Canada, 22-D Hollywood Ave., Hohokus, NJ 07423 (800) 542-2164, j.sirabella@nfb.ca

National Latino Communications, Educational Media, Los Angeles, CA 90039, (323) 663-8294, emedia@nlcc

New Day Films, 22-D Hollywood Ave., Hohokus, NJ 07423 (888) 367-9154, orders@newday.com

PBS Video, 1320 Braddock Place, Alexandria, VA 22314 (703) 739-5388, kostafinski@pbs.org

Phil Lucas Productions, P.O. Box 1274, Issaquah, WA 98027 (206) 979-9819, Iphil1@qwest.net

Portia Cobb, 2932 N. Weil Street, Milwaukee, WI 55212 (414) 964-1991

Pyramid Media, P.O. Box 1048, Santa Monica, CA 90406 (800) 421-2304, info@pyramidmedia.com

Red Carnelian Films, 1380 Dean, Brooklyn, NY 11216, (718) 735-4247

SAI Communications, 22-D Hollywood Ave., Hohokus, NJ 07423 (800) 343-5540, MyAmerica1@aol.com

Teaching Tolerance, Southern Poverty Law Center, 400 Washington Ave., Montgomery, AL 36104, www.teachingtolerance.org for Teaching Tolerance Videos only.

Teatro Campesino, P.O. Box 1240, San Jan Bautista, CA 95045 (831) 623-2444, teatro@hollinet.com

The Cinema Guild, 130 Madison Ave., Second Floor, New York, NY 10016, (212) 685-6242, orders@cinemaguild.com

The Working Group, 1611 Telegraph Ave., #1550, Oakland, CA 94612 (510) 268-9675, info@theworkinggroup.org

Third World Newsreel, 545 8th Ave., 10th Floor, New York, NY 10018 (212) 947-9277, twn@twn.org

Transit Media, 22-D Hollywood Ave., Hohokus, NJ 07423 (800) 343-5540, tmcndy@aol.com

Upstream Productions, 3926 NE 105th St., Seattle, WA 98125 (206) 526-7122, uproduct@aol.com

Urban Life Productions, 22-D Hollywood Ave., Hohokus, NJ 07423 (800) 343-5540, TMCNDY@aol.com

Video Databank, 112 South Michigan Ave., Chicago, IL 60603 (312) 345-3550, info@vdb.org

Video Finders (800) 343-4727, www.videofinders.com

Women Make Movies, 462 Broadway, Room 500, New York, NY 10013 (212) 925-0606, info@wmm.com

Websites for Independently Produced Media About Ethnicity

http://www.viewingrace.org
http://www.naatanet.org
http://www/JAInternment.org
http://www.lib.berkeley.edu/MRC/
http://www.pbs.org.pov

Notes

Preface

1. See Daniel Bernardi, ed., *The Birth of Whiteness: Race and the Emergence of United States Cinema* (New Brunswick: Rutgers UP, 1996) and Daniel Bernardi, ed. *Classic Hollywood, Classic Whiteness* (Minneapolis: The U of Minnesota P, 2001).
2. See Richard T. Schaefer, *Race and Ethnicity in the United States*, 2nd ed. (Upper Saddle River: Prentice-Hall, 2001) 9–13; Mark Nathan Cohen, "Culture, Not Race, Explains Human Diversity," *Chronicle of Higher Education* 17 April 1998.
3. See Noel Ignatiev, *How the Irish Became White* (New York: Routledge, 1995), and Jennifer Guglielmo and Salvatore Salerno, eds., *Are Italians White? How Race Is Made in America* (New York: Routledge, 2003).
4. See Michael Omi and Howard Winant, *Racial Formation in the United States: From the 1960s to the 1980s* (New York: Routledge, 1986); F. J. David, *Who Is Black: One Nation's Definition* (University Park: Pennsylvania State UP, 1991); and James S. Olson, *The Ethnic Dimension in American History*, 3rd ed. (St. James: Brandywine P, 1999).
5. See also Peggy McIntosh, "White Privilege: Unpacking the Invisible Knapsack." http://www.utoronto.ca/acc/events/peggy1.htm.

Introduction

1. Over thirty years ago, Donis A. Dondis described this shift in *A Primer in Visual Literacy*: "In print, language is the primary element, while visual factors, such as the physi-

cal setting or design format and illustration, are secondary or supportive. In the modern media, just the reverse is true. The visual dominates; the verbal augments. Print is not dead yet, nor will it ever be, but nevertheless, our language-dominated culture has moved perceptibly toward the iconic." (Cambridge: MIT Press, 1973) 6–7. More recently, In *The Rise of the Image, The Fall of the Word*, Mitchell Stephens predicts that "we are going to continue staring at those magical moving images and obtaining more and more of our entertainment, information, art and ideas from them." (New York: Oxford UP, 1998) 8.
2. We compare, of course, both shocking events and everyday occurrences to movie images. Our frequent use of movies as a frame of reference points to Susan Sontag's conclusion in *On Photography*, where she says our image-dominated culture is producing a "chronic voyeuristic relation to the world" (New York: Farrar, Straus and Giroux, 1977) 11. See also Sontag's discussion of people who insist that "their experience of a violent event," such as "a plane crash, a shoot-out, a terrorist bombing — seemed like a movie ... in order to explain how real it was," including her idea that "our inclination is to attribute to real things the qualities of an image" 161, 165.
3. See Diane Negra's *Off-White Hollywood: American Culture and Ethnic Female Stardom* (New York: Routledge, 2001) for an analysis of celebrity culture and ethnicity.
4. In *Visual Intelligence: Perception, Image, and Manipulation in Visual Communication* (Albany: State U of New York P, 1997), Ann Marie Seward Barry notes that "visual communication dominates every area of our lives" and advises that "As sleeping becomes the only activity that occupies children more than watch-

ing a video screen, we must become more sensitive to how images shape the fabric of our lives" (3).

5. David Grubin, creator of several film documentary biographies for PBS's *The American Experience*, joins others in his claim that "more Americans seem to prefer the image to the word" and says that "more and more of us are learning our history from [documentaries on] television." Grubin notes that *The American Experience* series "garners six million viewers each week, not counting the millions more who see the series in reruns, on home videos, or at schools and colleges all over the country." "From Story to Screen: Biography on Television," *Humanities* May/June 1997: 12–13.

6. In journals such as *Cultural Studies* and the *Journal of Visual Culture*, visual scholars are exploring such questions as the following: Can the literary notion of reading be applied to images? Is there a visual language? Do words and images constitute equally valid forms of reasoning? Is the shift from the word to the image a shift to be regretted and opposed or embraced? While this book does not directly engage these issues, we do endorse the idea of reading visual texts, offer a basic visual vocabulary for film, propose that reading visual images engages students in critical thinking, and embrace the future with the proviso that in our visually dominant society we need to become, and to educate our students to become, visually literate.

7. Steven Mintz and Randy Roberts, eds., preface, *Hollywood's America: United States History Through Its Films* (St. James, NY: Brandywine, 1993) ix–x.

8. In *Identity, Community, and Pluralism in American Life*, William Fischer writes, "Increasingly, our population profile looks very different than it did in the mid–twentieth century. Simply in racial terms alone, we are changing rapidly and will continue to do so well into the next century. By the year 2020, it is estimated that of a total U.S. population of 265 million, approximately one in three citizens will be a person of color, with Hispanics surpassing African Americans as the largest racial group except for Caucasians of European descent. Even in the late 1990s, looking at our demographics from an urban point of view, in the school systems of the country's twenty-five largest cities students of color are for the first time in the majority. Of the 25 million people who will enter the work force in the last decade of the twentieth century, 85 percent will be women, people of color, and immigrants. The implications are enormous for any person participating in the society of the United States in whatever capacity. At a minimum, in order to make one's way economically and socially, one will be increasingly pressed to possess a functional literacy of that complex diversity." Introduction, *Identity, Community, and Pluralism in American Life*, ed. William C. Fischer, et al. (New York: Oxford UP, 1997) xiii. The 2000 U.S. Census provides further evidence, revealing a U.S. population more diverse than at any time in its history; see http://www.census.org.

9. See Ana Maria Villegas and Tamara Lucas, "Preparing Culturally Responsive Teachers: Rethinking the Curriculum," *Journal of Teacher Education* 53 (2002): 20–32.

10. Tracing changing census categories and numbers reveals a country transforming its identify. The following information is from a report on the history of the U.S. Census in the *San Jose Mercury News* 13 March 2001: 1A+. In 1790, the first U.S. Census categorized Americans only as white, free blacks, and slaves. More than 9 out of 10 blacks were slaves. The 1860 census marked the first time its categories were expanded beyond blacks and whites, as an "Other" category was added and American Indians and Chinese Americans were tallied separately. The 1980 Census added "Asian and Pacific Islander," "American Indian, Eskimo, and Aleut," and "Hispanic" as categories. (The racial categories do not include Hispanic origin, which the Census Bureau considers an ethnic distinction, separate from race. The term "Latino/a" rose in the late 1980s and 90s in opposition to the U.S. government's term "Hispanic," which refers to Spanish language and culture, as a claim to identity. The Census Bureau may eliminate the Hispanic category in the next census, based on challenges to its accuracy and appropriateness.) The 2000 census had six major categories, including Black, Asian and Pacific Islander, American Indian and Alaska Native, Hispanic, White (Non-Hispanic whites), and "Other" (which includes those who identified themselves as having multiracial backgrounds).

11. National Video Resources offers a "Viewing Race After 9.11" collection, which includes videos of Arab-American communities in the United States, to "promote knowledge, understanding, and tolerance." See http://www.viewingrace.org for a list of available titles.

12. Spike Lee and Josh Getlin, "Distant Re-

lations," *St. Paul Pioneer Press* 14 May 1990: C10.

13. Toni Morrison. *The Bluest Eye* (New York: Simon and Schuster, 1970) 19, 57–58, 97–98.

14. Nellie Wong, "When I was Growing Up," *Women: Images and Realities* (Mountain View, Calif.: Mayfield, 1999) 118–19.

15. Henry Louis Gates, Jr., *Colored People: A Memoir* (New York: Knopf, 1994) 24.

16. See Catherine Clinton's assessment of *Gone with the Wind* in *Past Imperfect: History According to the Movies* , ed. Mark C. Carnes (New York: Henry Holt, 1995) 132–35.

17. See Nora Villagran's "Unknown Soldiers," *San Jose Mercury News* 23 Aug. 2003: 1E+.

18. An Independent Television Service online interview with David Riker is available at http://www.itvs.org.thecity./filminterview.html.

19. "The Revised National History Standards," *The History Teacher* 30.3 (1997): 302–45.

20. National Council for the Social Studies, *Expectations of Excellence: Curriculum Standards for Social Studies* (Washington, D.C.: National Council for the Social Studies, 1994).

21. National Council of Teachers of English, *NCTE Guidelines for the Preparation of Teachers of English Language Arts* (Urbana: NCTE, 1996).

22. See http://arsedge.kennedy-center.org/professionslresources/standards/natstandards/index.html.

23. Robert Kubey and Frank W. Baker, "Has Media Education Found a Curricular Foothold?" *Education Week* 27 Oct. 1999, 25 May 2000 http://www.med.sc.edu:81/medialit.statelit.htm.

24. For teachers who are interested in television programming, a documentary on the history of television programming and African American representation is Marlon Riggs' (1992) *Color Adjustment*. The organization Children Now publishes *Colors: Prime Time Diversity Report* annually; see www.childrennow.org. Also, the video series called *Scanning Television*, created by Katherine Tyner, John Pungente, and Neil Anderson, consists of 51 short 6-minute videos described as classroom friendly. The series includes issues of diversity and anti-racism and is available from www.facetofacemedia.com.

Chapter 1

1. The dramatic cross cutting/parallel action of the film had been used by narrative cinema since Edwin S. Porter's *The Great Train Robbery* (1903), a hugely successfully film. Griffith himself had used the technique countless times in his smaller, two-reel films, such as *The Lonely Villa* (1909) and The *Lonedale Operator* (1911). Neither the length of the film nor its epic scope were necessarily innovative, having been used extensively by Italian filmmakers in the early part of the decade in such films as *Quo Vadis* (1912), *The Last Days of Pompeii* (1912), and *Cabiria* (1914).

2. See Pearl Bowser and Louise Spence's *Writing Himself into History: Oscar Micheaux, His Silent Films, and His Audiences* (New Brunswick: Rutgers UP, 2000); J. Ronald Green's *Straight Lick: The Cinema of Oscar Micheaux* (Bloomington: Indiana UP, 2000); and Manthia Diawara's *Black American Cinema* (New York: Routledge, 1993).

3. There are, of course, a number of notable exceptions: Melvin Van Peebles' *Sweet Sweetback's Baaadasss Song* (1971), Charles Burnett's *The Killer of Sheep* (1977), and Haile Gerimas' *Bush Mama* (1979). These films, and the struggles their makers went through to complete them, demonstrate that black independent cinema never died but was relegated to the margins.

4. This is not to say that all white people have an equally privileged place within society; the operations of class and sexism ensure that a significant percentage of white people (if not a majority) will also face social obstacles and will suffer from an unequal distribution of social wealth. The privilege of being white, however, translates into what is made to seem a raceless existence within a racialized society of inequity.

5. Ed Guerrero, *Framing Blackness* (Philadelphia: Temple UP, 1993) 114.

6. Sharon Willis, *High Contrast: Race and Gender in Contemporary Hollywood Film* (Durham: Duke UP, 1997) 159.

7. Toni Cade Bambara, "Reading the Signs, Empowering the Eye: *Daughters of the Dust* and the Black Independent Cinema Movement," *Black Cinema*, ed. Manthia Diawara (New York: Routledge Press, 1993) 119.

8. For a more extensive analysis of *Daughters of the Dust* and its resistance to the finalization of meaning see my "*Daughters of the*

Dust and the Figurative as a Mode of Resistance," *Reel Racism: Confronting Hollywood's Construction of Afro-American Culture* (Boulder: Westview P, 2000) 173–89.

Chapter 2

1. Minor portions of this article appeared previously in "America's Asia: Hollywood's Construction, Deconstruction, and Reconstruction of the 'Orient,'" *Out of the Shadows: Asians in American Cinema*, ed. Roger Garcia (Milan, Italy: Edizioni Olivares, produced in conjunction with the 54th Locarno International Film Festival, 2001) 37–57.

2. While "experimental" and "avant-garde" are usually used interchangeably when referring to films that do not fit easily into the categories of narrative fiction or documentary, operate well outside the commercial film industry, and attempt to contribute to aesthetic debates within the fine arts, a distinction can be made between "experimental" films that interrogate film form and technique and "avant-garde" films that are more in conversation with schools, movements, and genres in the fine arts in general. Certainly, many films fit both criteria, and avant-garde artists very often make "experimental" films.

3. Said 3.

4. http://www.angrylittlegirls.com.

5. Many of the issues mentioned in this section may also be appropriate for inclusion in film studies classes.

6. See http://www.esc2.net/TIELevel2/projects/joyluck/ and http://www.vocabulary.com/VUctjoyluck.html.

7. See Sandra Liu, "Negotiating the Meaning of Access: Wayne Wang's Contingent Film Practice," *Countervisions: Asian American Film Criticism*, ed. Darrell Y. Hamamoto and Sandra Liu (Philadelphia: Temple UP, 2000) 90–111.

Chapter 3

1. I use the term "Indian" when referring to fictional characters and American Indian (or a specific tribal designation) when referring to actual people.

2. David Wark Griffith, "Pictures vs. One

Night Stands," *The Independent* 11 Dec. 1916, qtd. in Richard Koszarski, ed., *Hollywood Directors: 1914–1940* (New York: Oxford UP, 1976) 37.

3. Christian Metz, *Film Language: A Semiotics of the Cinema* (Chicago: U of Chicago P, 1974) 9.

4. Ana M. Lopez, "Are All Latins from Manhattan?" *Mediating Two Worlds*, ed. John King, et al. (London: BFI, 1993) 68.

5. "Realism" is in some ways an unfair expectation of a film or filmmaker. He or she is creating a film, not a reality. However, I believe the use of a real people's identity requires a more responsible attention to real lives.

6. Alice P. Sterner, "A Guide to the Discussion of the Technicolor Screen Version of *Northwest Passage*," *Photoplay Studies* 6.9 (New York: Educational and Recreational Guides, 1940).

7. Donald Culross Peattie, "Braves on the Warpath," *Reader's Digest* July 1943: 79, qtd. in Mary Ann Weston, *American Indians in the News: Images of Indians in the Twentieth Century Press* (Westport, Conn.: Greenwood P, 1996) 87.

8. It was also difficult for American Indian soldiers of World War II, Korea, and Vietnam, many of whom came from urban areas, who found themselves assigned to point duty because their officers believed in the Hollywood Indian.

9. Marius Barbeau, "The Disappearance of the Red Man's Culture," *Scientific American* Jan. 1933: 22–24, qtd. in Mary Ann Weston, *American Indians in the News: Images of Indians in the Twentieth Century Press* (Westport, Conn.: Greenwood P, 1996) 65.

10. Historians hotly debate the causes of the Cold War, and fear of nuclear war is an accurate but partial explanation.

11. Pauline Kael, "Americana: 'Tell Them Willie Boy Was Here,'" *The Pretend Indians: Images of Native Americans in the Movies*, ed. Gretchen Bataille and Charles L. P. Silet (Ames: Iowa UP, 1980) 164.

12. Jace Weaver, "Ethnic Cleansing, Homestyle," *Wicazo Sa Review* 10. 91 (1994): 27.

13. See Louis Menand, "Nanook and Me," *The New Yorker* 9 Aug. 2004. http://www.new yorker.com.

14. For a more in-depth discussion of these films, see "Keeping the Carcass in Motion," *Filming World Literature: The Dialogics of Adaptation*, ed. Robert Stam, forthcoming from Blackwell Publishing.

Chapter 4

1. "Chicano/a" is used to specifically refer to U.S. citizens of Mexican descent, a term popularized in the mid-sixties as Mexican Americans began to celebrate and recognize their distinct cultural identity as valuable in their struggle for equal rights in the U.S. "Latino/a" is an umbrella term used to refer to U.S. citizens of Latin American descent, including the Caribbean. It encompasses Chicanos/as.

2. *Greaser* originally referred to people of Mexican descent who came to the United States illegally during the early twentieth century, later becoming synonymous with the Latino Youth Culture that developed in the Southwest during the 1940s and 1950s. The Spitfire and loose women are stereotypical representations of Chicanas and Latinas as irrational, morally suspect, and sexually promiscuous women. Silent films such *Loves of Carmen* (Raoul Walsh, 1927) established this type early on. *Bandido* translates literally to *bandit* but is used in this context to refer to the stereotypical representation of lawless Mexicans and Mexican Americans who populate so many Westerns and other films from the U.S., e.g. the *bandidos* in *Treasure of the Sierra Madre* (John Huston, 1948). As the Chicano and Latino populations began to shift from rural to urban locales, the image of the gangster (also known as *pachuco, cholo,* and *vato*) became more prominent.

3. "The Hispanic Population." *Census 2000 Brief,* U.S. Census Bureau, May 2001 http://www.census.gov.

4. Experimental films generally attempt to explore and expand the formal and thematic structure of visual media. Independent films are generally produced outside of the studio and major production company infrastructure, though distribution rarely occurs without such funding.

5. Particularly effective is *No Movies, 1975– 1978.* In these series of still images the artist uses ironic subject matter and juxtapositions to explore the varying trends in Latino media production, from overly macho aesthetics to revolutionary hubris.

6. Rosa Linda Fregoso, "Hanging Out with the Homegirls? Allison Ander's '*Mi Vida Loca.*'" *Cineaste* 21.3 (1995): 36–37.

7. The Treaty of Guadalupe Hidalgo provided for the forced sale of what now constitutes all of California, Arizona, New Mexico, Nevada, Utah, most of Colorado, and parts of Wyoming, Oregon and Oklahoma. The price was 15 million dollars.

8. "U.S. and Mexico Agree on Immigrant Plan." *BBC NEWS* 10 Aug. 2001. http://news.bbc.co.uk./1/hi/world/americas/1483656.stm.

9. The website www.atomfilms.com remains a leader in this domain.

Chapter 5

1. The Copyright Act of 1976 allows schools and colleges to use small portions of copyrighted material for instruction without securing copyright holders' permission. The legislation applies only to accredited, nonprofit educational institutions.

Chapter 6

1. Paul B. Weinstein, "Movies as the Gateway to History: The History and Film Project," *The History Teacher* 35:1 (2001) http://www.historycooperative.org/journals/ht/35.1/weinstein.html.

2. Editorial, *Cineaste* 29.2 (2004): 1. The "Film and History" supplement includes Robert A. Rosenstone's "Inventing Historical Truth on the Silver Screen," Robert Brent Toplin's "Cinematic History: An Anatomy of the Genre," Charles Tashiro's "Passing for the Past: Production Design and the Historical Film," Mark C. Carnes's "Shooting (Down) the Past: Historians vs. Hollywood," Richard LaMotte's "Designing Costumes for the Historical Film," and "Film and History: Questions to Filmmakers and Historians" 29–70.

3. "The American Historical Association ... in 2000 published a poll that asked a representative cross-section of the American population to rank their history-related activities during the previous year. More than eighty percent cited watching a historical movie or TV program, while only slightly more than fifty percent indicated reading a history book or visiting a museum or historical site." Quoted in the editorial, *Cineaste* 29.2 (2004): 1.

4. See Leon F. Litwack, "The Birth of a Nation," *Past Imperfect: History According to the Movies,* ed. Mark C. Carnes (New York: Henry Holt, 1995) 136–41.

5. The print of *The Birth of a Nation* that includes Griffith's conversation with Walter Huston about his childhood and the need for the Klan in the 1860s is available on video from Critics Choice Video Masterpiece Collection (1993) and on DVD as the *Griffith Masterworks DVD Box Set* from Kino (2002).

6. Qtd in Jenni Calder, *There Must Be a Lone Ranger: The American West in Film and in Reality* (New York: McGraw-Hill, 1977) 213.

7. Quoted in Gary Crowdus and Richard Porton, "The Importance of a Singular, Guiding Vision: An Interview with Arthur Penn," *Cineaste* 20.2 (1994): 11, 12.

8. "A Conversation between Eric Foner and John Sayles," *Past Imperfect: History According to the Movies,* ed. Mark C. Carnes (New York: Henry Holt and Company, 1995) 19, 20.

9. Dee Brown, *Bury My Heart at Wounded Knee* (New York: Holt, Rinehart and Winston, 1971); Steven Mintz, ed., *Native American Voices: A History and Anthology* (St. James, NY: Brandywine Press, 1995).

10. According to Angela Aleiss's article "Iron Eyes Cody: Wannabe Indian," Cody passed as an Indian because he "fit the white ideal of the Noble Savage." Cody looked, Aleiss quotes UCLA Cherokee anthropologist Russell Thorton as saying, "like what white Americans thought Indians should look like." *Cineaste* 25.1 (1999): 31.

11. To reinforce the film's parallels between the Revolutionary and Depression eras (economic hardships and war overcome by perseverance and loyalty to country), according to film historian John O'Connor, the studio asked local theatres to sponsor essay contests in which housewives would answer the question, "Is the modern economic frontier as hard to combat as the primitive one of 1777?" John E. O'Connor, "A Reaffirmation of American Ideals: *Drums Along the Mohawk,*" *American History/American Film: Interpreting the Hollywood Image,* eds. John E. O'Connor and Martin A. Jackson (New York: Frederick Unger, 1979) 113.

12. President Harry S Truman integrated American's armed forces by Executive Order in 1948.

13. See Sumiko Higashi, "Walker and Mississippi Burning: Postmodernism versus Illusionist Narrative," *The Historical Film: History and Memory in Media,* ed. Marcia Landy (New Brunswick, NJ: Rutgers UP) 227–28, and William H. Chafe, "Mississippi Burning," *Past Imperfect: History According to the Movies,* ed.

Mark C. Carnes (New York: Henry Holt, 1995) 274–77.

14. Mark C. Carnes, Introduction, *Past Imperfect: History According to the Movies* (New York: Henry Holt, 1995) 9.

15. For example, in "The Historical Film: Looking at the Past in a Postliterate Age," Robert Rosenstone notes as "an invention of something that could well have happened" the film's fictional depiction of the "quartermaster of the division to which the Fifty-fourth belongs" refusing to "give boots to the black troops" in *The Historical Film: History and Memory in Media,* ed. Marcia Landy (New Brunswick, NJ: Rutgers UP, 2000) 63–64. And in his essay about *Glory,* James M. McPherson notes that the Fifty-Fourth was not, as the movie would have it, made up of former slaves, but of free African Americans from the north. McPherson justifies this and other fictions in *Glory* as part of its successful effort to tell not just the story of the Fifty-Fourth but the story of blacks in the Civil War. "*Glory,*" *Past Imperfect: History According to the Movies,* ed. Mark C. Carnes (New York: Henry Holt, 1995) 130.

16. See Alex Haley and Malcolm X, *The Autobiography of Malcolm X* (New York: Ballantine, 1965); David Gallen, *Malcolm X as They Knew Him* (New York: Carroll and Graf, 1992); Joe Wood, *Malcolm X: In Our Own Image* (New York: Anchor, 1992); Bruce Perry, *Malcolm: The Life of a Man Who Changed Black America* (Barrytown, NY: Station Hill, 1991). Students can also read filmmaker Spike Lee's (1992) *By Any Means Necessary: The Trials and Tribulations of Making of Malcolm X, Including the Screenplay* as well as historical critiques of Lee's film, such as Clayborne Carson's historical analysis and comparisons between Malcolm X and Martin Luther King, Jr., in *Past Imperfect: History According to the Movies.*

17. Spielberg's Dream Works (via Lifetime Learning Systems) sent a controversial study guide titled "Amistad: A Living Legacy" to teachers to promote use of the film in the classroom. Clifton J. Johnson, founder of the Amistad Center at Tulane University, says of Spielberg's film, "Since the early '50s I've been interested in the Amistad. I've written many articles about it, and I founded this center. But Steven Spielberg did more to promote it in a year than I did in a lifetime.... Now that he's informed the public, I'll spend the rest of my life correcting the errors." *Chronicle of Higher Education* 9 Jan. 1998: A12. For discussions about teaching Spielberg's *Amistad* and

other teaching resources, see "*Amistad*: Controversy About the Film and Its Use" Special Section *The History Teacher* 31:3 (1998): 369–402 and "Resources for Teaching about the Amistad Incident" in the *OAH Newsletter* Feb. 1998: 11.

18. John Grierson coined the word "documentary" in his review of Robert Flaherty's (1926) film *Moana* in the *New York Sun*. He later defined the term documentary as the "creative treatment of actuality." For a short history of the documentary form, see Ira Konigsberg's *Complete Film Dictionary* (New York: Penguin, 1989) 88–89. For a book-length investigation of Grierson's phrase, the "creative treatment of actuality," see Brian Winston's *Claiming the Real: The Documentary Film Revisited* (London: BFI, 1995).

19. In "The Life and Times of Rosie the Riveter: The Experience and Legacy of Wartime Women Wage Earners," Alice Kessler-Harris positions Field's film within the historical debates about women's place during the time depicted and within Field's contemporary feminist ideology. *World War II: Film and History*, eds. John Whiteclay Chambers II and David Culbert (New York: Oxford UP, 1996) 107–22.

20. The Southwest Indian Foundation in Gallup, New Mexico, offers additional resources: the video *Navajo Code Talkers* and two books, *Warriors: Navajo Code Talkers* and *The Navajo Code Talkers*. The Independent Television Service promotes the documentary *True Whispers: The Story of the Navajo Code Talkers* as providing the historical context of the code talkers, including the forced relocation of the Navajo Nation in 1863 and some of the code talkers' boarding school ordeals, as well depictions of their service and valor in World War II.

21. See Karen L. Miksch and David Ghere's "Teaching Japanese-American Incarceration," an essay describing research, writing, and discussion topics about Japanese American Internment that include parallels from recent debates about the balance between security and civil liberties in the war on terror. *The History Teacher* 37.2 (2004): 210–25.

22. Roger Daniels, Sandra C. Taylor, and Harry H.L. Kitano, *Japanese Americans: From Relocation to Redress* (Seattle: U of Washington P, 1994).

23. John W. Blassingame, *The Slave Community: Plantation Life in the Antebellum South* (New York: Oxford UP, 1979); Charles Blockson, *The Underground Railroad* (New York: Berkeley, 1994).

24. Eric Hoover, "Myth Understood," *Chronicle of Higher Education* 16 April 2004: A16+.

25. Toni Morrison, *Beloved* (New York: Plume, 1987); Gary Paulsen, *Nightjohn* (New York: Bantam, 1993).

26. Regarding filmmakers who proclaim their films to be historically "accurate" or "truthful," Mark C. Carnes writes: "Viewers should neither accept such claims nor dismiss them out of hand, but regard them as an invitation for further exploration." Introduction, *Past Imperfect: History According to the Movies* (New York: Henry Holt, 1995) 9–10.

Chapter 7

1. Susan Orlean, *Saturday Night* (New York: Random House, 1990).

2. As reported by Greg Braxton in the *Los Angeles Times* 19 May 2004.

3. Donald Bogle, *Toms, Coons, Mulattoes, Mammies, and Bucks: An Interpretive History of Blacks in American Films*, 4th ed. (New York: Continuum, 2003).

4. Such stereotypes affect the lives of real women. Tricia Rose's (2003) collection of interviews with African-American women, *Longing to Tell: Black Women Talk About Sexuality and Intimacy*, concludes that "Until about thirty to forty years ago, it was a commonly held belief in legal courts that black women were too sexually loose to be raped. This made charges for raping a black woman virtually impossible to prosecute successfully. As late as 1971, a judge admonished the jurors not to apply ordinary presumptions of chastity to black women." (New York: Farrar, Straus and Giroux, 2003). Afterword.

5. Patricia Turner, *Ceramic Uncles and Celluloid Mammies* (New York: Bantam Doubleday Dell, 1994) xvi, 280–81.

6. See John Wu's "Making and Unmaking the 'Model Minority,'" a college student research-based essay written in 1994 that examines assumptions about his ethnic identity and family values. Rpt. in *Creating America: Reading and Writing Arguments*, eds. Joyce Moser and Ann Watters, 2nd ed (Upper Saddle River: Prentice Hall, 1999) 287–91. For an ethnic scholar's discussion of the Model Minority, see Ronald Takaki, *A Different Mirror: A History of Multicultural America* (Boston: Little, Brown, 1993). Takaki claims that Asian

Americans have become the Model Minority "not only for blacks and Chicanos, but also for whites on welfare and even middle class whites experiencing economic difficulties" (8, 414–17).

7. See the NAATA Forum on "The Return of Charlie Chan" at http://www.naatanet.org /forumarchive/charliechan.html.

8. For discussions of how Asian Americans are often seen as foreigners and how this relates to the importance of ethnic studies, see the Introduction to Ronald Takaki's *From Different Shores: Perspectives on Race and Ethnicity in America*, 2nd ed. (New York: Oxford UP, 1994) 3–9, and the introduction to Takaki's *A Different Mirror: A History of Multicultural America* (Boston: Little, Brown, 1993) 1–17.

9. Loni Ding, "Strategies of an Asian American Filmmaker," *Moving the Image: Independent Asian Pacific American Media Arts*, ed. Russell Leong (Los Angeles: UCLA Asian American Studies Center, Visual Communications, Southern California Asian American Studies, 1991) 46–48.

10. Teachers may find it helpful to have students apply Fredric Jameson's theory that "movies are a physical experience, and are remembered as such, stored up in bodily synapses that evade the thinking mind." Fredric Jameson, *Signatures of the Visible* (New York: Routledge, 1992) 1. His idea is that repeated images and repeated experiences with those images in movies, especially where there are no alternatives, implant themselves in our collective memories.

11. Martin Barker and Roger Smith's book, *The Lasting of the Mohicans: History of an American Myth* (Jackson: UP of Mississippi, 1995), counts over ten film versions, some now lost, and also lists numerous plays, radio shows, television shows, and comic book versions.

12. See Paula Gunn Allen, "Who Is Your Mother: Red Roots of White Feminism." *The Sacred Hoop: Recovering the Feminine in American Indian Traditions* (Boston: Beacon, 1986) 209–21.

13. Particularly relevant is Hilger's first chapter, "From Savage to Nobleman: Traditional Images of Native Americans," *From Savage to Nobleman: Images of Native Americans in Film* (Landham: Scarecrow, 1995) 1–16. John E. O' Connor's "The White Man's Indian," *Film and History* 23.1–4 (1993): 17–26 also gives an overview of Indian stereotypes.

14. Charles Ramirez Berg, *Latino Images in Film: Stereotypes, Subversion, Resistance* (Austin:

U of Texas P, 2002); David J. Weber, *Myth and the History of the Hispanic Southwest* (Albuquerque: U of New Mexico P, 1988) 153–67. Chapter 9, "'Scarce More than Apes': Historical Roots of Anglo-American Stereotypes of Mexicans in the Border Region," in Weber's book deals directly with the origins of Latino stereotypes.

15. See Carlos A. Cortes, "Chicanas in Film: History of an Image." *Chicano Cinema: Research, Reviews, and Resources*, ed. Gary D. Keller (Binghamton: Bilingual Review/Press, 1985) 94–108; Clara E. Rodriguez, *Latino Looks: Images of Latinas and Latinos in the U.S. Media* (Boulder: Westview P, 1997).

16. See, for instance, Allen Woll, "Bandits and Lovers: Hispanic Images in American Film." *The Kaleidoscopic Lens: How Hollywood Views Ethnic Groups*, ed. Randall M. Miller (Englewood, N.J.: Jerome S. Ozer, 1980) 54–72.

17. The Special Classroom Section called "50 Years Later: Brown v. Board of Education," in *Teaching Tolerance*, Spring 2004 and at http://www.teachingtolerance.org offer photos, a Brown v. Board timeline of school integration in the United States, an analysis of how the Brown decision affected children of all ethnicities, a timeline of Supreme Court decisions on Civil Rights, essays entitled "Where are we Now?" and "A New Milestone Decade," and a section on classroom activities for students in grades 7–12. An article by Sara Hebel, "Segregation's Legacy Still Troubles Campuses" in the *Chronicle of Higher Education* 14 May 2004 reports on the history of the Brown ruling, offers a timeline with photos, and provides an update on the current status of the struggle to end segregation in colleges and universities.

18. See Jay Rosenstein's website for the documentary which includes news reports about the mascot issue at http://www.inwhosehonor.com/; the Native Circle's website on "How 'Indian Mascots' Oppress" at http://www.nativecircle.com/mascots.htm; and the Wisconsin Indian Education Association's website on Indian mascots and logos at http://pages.prodigy.net/munson/.

19. The Justice Department announcement was carried in newspapers, news magazines, and on television news programs across the nation; see, for example "U.S. Reopening '55 Racial Slaying Case" in the *San Jose Mercury News* 11May 2004: 3A+. Film historian and critic Thomas Doherty reviews the documentaries and the history behind them in "The

Ghosts of Emmett Till" in the *Chronicle of Higher Education* 17Jan. 2003: B12+.

Chapter 8

1. A number of watchdog groups decry violence and gratuitous sex in the movies and on television. Other groups are equally concerned about the lack of ethnic diversity. The organization Children Now http://www.children now.org has been tracking and reporting on ethnic representations on television since its 2001-02 *Fall Colors: Prime Time Diversity Report* in subsequent annual newsletters entitled "Media Now." Other groups advocating for ethnic diversity in media representations include the National Association for the Advancement of Colored People (NAACP); the Non-Traditional Casting Project (NTCP); NOSOTROS, founded to improve portrayals of Latinos/as in the entertainment industry; the National Hispanic Media Coalition (NHMC), Media Action Network for Asian Americans (MANAA), National Asian American Telecommunications Association (NAATA); and First Americans in the Arts. The Screen Actor's Guild (SAG) works with many of these groups and has a number of subcommittees: the African American Subcommittee, the Asian/Pacific Subcommittee, the Native American Subcommittee, and the Latino/Hispanic Subcommittee). For example, according to SAG's website http://www.sag.org, "SAG's Native-American Subcommittee is actively seeking solutions to the under-representation problem, and to help reverse misinformed racial stereotypes of this group in film and television."

2. In 2002, the *Farewell to Manzanar* Education Initiative (a partnership consisting of the State of California, the California Teachers Association, Universal Studios, the California Civil Liberties Public Education Project of the California State Library, and members of California's Japanese American community) devised a *Farewell to Manzanar* kit (consisting of the memoir *Farewell to Manzanar*, a teaching guide for the book, a video of the made-for-television film *Farewell to Manzanar,* and a study guide to accompany educational excerpts included on the video). The lessons for the video are aligned to the California History-Social Science standards and the English-Language Arts standards for grades

11 and 12. The purpose of the kit is to provide California teachers with resources to teach students about the Japanese American experience during World War II and to respond to a parallel backlash against Americans of Middle Eastern descent in the aftermath of September 11.

3. Reported in *Literature Connections Sourcebook: Farewell to Manzanar and Related Readings* (Evanston: McDougal Littell, 1998) 6. Houston says of her memoir that "The voice is mine, the viewpoint is mine. The technique and the craft is James's" (9). This text is provided in the *Farewell to Manzanar* Education Initiative kit cited above.

4. According to the *Literature Connection Source Book* cited above, "From February to June of 1942, the U.S. military relocated approximately 10,000 German and Italian aliens (non–U.S. citizens) from their homes on the California coast to inland 'safe zones.'" Although this is a comparatively short relocation period, it also "separated families, interrupted educations, and forced people to find new jobs and homes" (33).

5. In Chapter 11, Ko Wakatsuki warns his son Woody that to answer "No No" on the loyalty questionnaire could bring deportation. The *Literature Connection Source Book* cited above reports that "Of the 74,000 male internees who filled out loyalty questionnaires, 65,000 — including Mr. Wakatsuki and Woody — answered 'yes yes,' swearing unqualified allegiance to the U.S. and agreeing to be drafted into combat. The 9,000 who refused to answer, who answered 'no no,' or who qualified their answers were classified as 'disloyal,' and most were moved to Tule Lake. There an active community of resistance developed and protested the entire government program of relocation and imprisonment" (27).

6. A "Chronology of Japanese American History" reports that in 1913 the California Alien Land Act forbid ownership of land by aliens "ineligible to citizenship" which was quickly followed by similar statutes in most far-western states. In 1920 the Second California Alien Land Act adopted by initiative forbid leasing of land to aliens "ineligible to citizenship," and in 1922, in Ozawa v. U.S., the Supreme Court confirmed that Japanese and other Asians were ineligible for naturalization by reason of race. *Japanese Americans: From Relocation to Redress*, eds. Roger Daniels, Sandra Taylor, and Harry Kitano (Seattle: U of Washington P, 1991).

7. To his credit, Costner wanted his Indian characters to speak in their native language but, since there are not enough proficient speakers of Comanche left alive to translate the dialogue, he changed the characters from Comanche to Sioux.

8. Edward D. Castillo's review of *Dances with Wolves* shortly after the film was released refers to the Indian outcry against the film's depiction of the Pawnee, notes that it was the Pawnee who "were subjected to the purposeful introduction of smallpox by traders along the Santa Fe trail in 1831" and cites two reference sources for accurate Pawnee history in *Film Quarterly* 44 (1991): 14–13. The sources are William Miles, "Enamored with Civilization: Isaac McCoy's Plan for Indian Reform," *Kansas Historian* 38 (1972): 168–86, and Thomas Dunlay, *Wolves for the Blue Soldiers, Indian Scouts and Auxiliaries with the United States Army, 1869–90* (Lincoln: U of Nebraska P, 1987).

9. Michael Dorris' review of *Dances with Wolves* shortly after the film was released notes how it was filmed on the Pine Ridge Reservation in South Dakota (still one of the most economically impoverished areas of the United States today) and generates sympathy for the Sioux, but Dorris worries that this movie sympathy would not translate into support for "restoration of Lakota sacred lands (the Black Hills) or water rights, for tribal sovereignty, for providing the money desperately needed by reservation health clinics" partly because it leaves movies "the only good Indians ... are lodged safely in the past." Michael Dorris, "Indians in Aspic," *New York Times* 24 Feb. 1991: Sect.4, 7.

10. A good example for students of an Asian American serving as the comic relief butt of humor in a story about Euro Americans is Mickey Rooney's performance as an Asian-American buffoon in Blake Edwards' (1961) *Breakfast at Tiffany's,* and a good example of a Euro American serving as guide into and instant expert on Asian American experiences is the labor leader in Alan Parker's (1990) *Come See the Paradise.*

11. Clyde V. Haupt's *Huckleberry Finn on Film: Film and Television Adaptations of Mark Twain's Novel, 1920–1993* (Jefferson: McFarland, 1994) describes all of the films up to 1993, which does not include the latest Disney version. John C. Tibbetts and James M. Walsh's *The Encyclopedia of Novels into Film* (New York: Facts on File, 1998) lists and briefly describes a number of Huck Finn films.

The book also describes a number of other novels and film adaptations about and by ethnic minorities.

12. On July 8, 2004, the National Endowment for the Arts released the results of a survey conducted by the Census Bureau in 2002 at the NEA's request, which reads in part: "Literary reading is in dramatic decline with fewer than half of American adults now reading literature, according to a National Endowment for the Arts (NEA) survey released today. *Reading at Risk: A Survey of Literary Reading in America* reports drops in all groups studied, with the steepest rate of decline — 28 percent — occurring in youngest age group.... The rate of decline for the youngest adults, those aged 18 to 24, was 55 percent greater than that of the total population." The "Executive Summary" section of the report states that "Literature now competes with an enormous array of electronic media. While no single activity is responsible for the decline of reading, the cumulative presence and availability of these alternatives have increasingly drawn Americans away from reading" (http://arts.endow.gov/news/news04/ReadingAtRisk.html). Narrative films account for a great deal of the draw away from literary reading. Rather than hopelessly bemoan the change, teachers and students need to become visually literate. They can then join the conversation with a knowledge base that allows them to compare the relative merits of written and visual literature.

13. A more recent film, Sergio Arau's (2004) *A Day Without a Mexican*, provides a humorous version of what would happen to California's economy if its huge Latino/a population disappeared for a day.

Chapter 9

1. See "Contexts, Reviews, and Commentaries," Robert Lang, ed. *The Birth of a Nation: Griffith, Director* (New Brunswick, NJ: Rutgers UP, 1994) 159–293.

2. American film history on film includes records of independent filmmakers who protested Griffith's representations and countered with images of their own. PBS's (1994) *Midnight Ramble: The Story of the Black Film Industry*, part of *The American Experience* series, recounts the story of the "race film" industry that operated outside of Hollywood and pro-

duced close to 500 movies for African-American audiences between 1910 and World War II. This documentary highlights films that were produced to counteract *The Birth of a Nation* with more diverse images and actual issues (poverty, discrimination, alcoholism) and chronicles the career of one of the most prolific and controversial of those filmmakers: Oscar Micheaux. The (1998) documentary *That's Black Entertainment* contrasts films by the black film industry in the 1920s, 30s, and 40s with stereotyped portrayals in Hollywood films. Another documentary, *A Century of Black Cinema*, celebrates African-American cinema with footage from films by Oscar Micheaux to Spike Lee, and *The African American Cinema* series compiled by the Library of Congress offers feature films by Micheaux: his (1919) *Within Our Gates*, which confronts racism with the story of a black schoolteacher and responds to Griffith's film with scenes of lynching and attempted white-on-black rape, as well as his (1926) *The Scar of Shame*, a melodrama that depicts poverty, ambition, and prejudice within the black community. Looking to television for movies made for them, high school students can find *You Must Remember This*, a (1993) *Wonderworks* afterschool special based on a story by Karen Evans and Pat Dale, about an African-American girl who discovers the history and importance of independent black filmmaking. See also Thomas Cripps, *Slow Fade to Black: The Negro in American Film, 1900–1942* (New York: Oxford UP, 1992).

3. Students can discuss the two positions in regard to what scientists know today, that humans are genetically more alike than different, that genetic differences among people in the same ethnic (formerly racial) group are often larger than genetic differences between people from different ethnic groups, and that racial markers (such as skin color) are superficial differences that do not point to differences in intelligence, sexuality, or any other basic human quality. The three-part film *Race: The History of an Illusion* is helpful for students to understand that race and racial differences are fictions, but are still believed, and that institutionalized racism (including within the film industry in the repetition of film stereotypes and other demeaning caricatures) is still the cause of discrimination. Cultural differences among ethnic groups are, however, very important to a person's sense of self, an issue that *Guess Who's Coming to Dinner* does not directly address.

4. Additional African-American interethnic romance films include Elia Kazan's (1949) *Pinky*, in which a woman who successfully passes for white and finds the love of a Euro-American man returns to her Southern home and her African-American heritage; Larry Peerce's (1964) independent film *One Potato Two*, which takes viewers inside a marriage between an African-American man and a Euro-American woman as they battle racist discrimination; Douglas Sirk's (1967) *Imitation of Life*, which includes a subplot romance between a woman who attempts to pass for white and a Euro-American man who irrationally rejects her when he discovers she is bi-racial; Mira Nair's (1991) *Mississippi Masala*, where an African-American man and an Indian American woman defy her relatives to form a successful relationship; Anthony Drazan's (1992) *Zebrahead*, where in high school an African-American female student and a Euro-American male student attempt to form a relationship; Marc Forster's (2001) *Monster's Ball*, where an African-American woman and the Euro-American man who was in charge of executing her imprisoned husband form a love relationship; Todd Haynes' (2001) *Far from Heaven*, where racist attitudes in their community keep an African-American man and a Euro-American woman apart in 1940s America; and Robert Benton's (2003) *The Human Stain*, in which a young African-American man conceals his identity, passing for the rest of his life, after he is rejected by his Nordic Minnesota girlfriend when she meets his darker skinned mother.

5. Other Asian American interethnic romance films include Cecil B. DeMille's (1915) *The Cheat*, with a diabolical Asian American who tries to take advantage of a Euro-American woman; Griffith's (1919) *Broken Blossoms*, where a Chinese American man is not allowed to love (platonically) a Euro-American girl; Joshua Logan's (1957) *Sayonara*, where U.S. soldiers fall in love with Japanese women; Richard Quine's (1960) *The World of Suzy Wong*, where an American artist falls in love with a Hong Kong prostitute; John Korty's (1976) *Farewell to Manzanar*, with a (subplot) secret romance between a Japanese American man interned at Manzanar and a Euro-American nurse's aid; George Cosmatos's (1985) *Rambo: First Blood*, where a Euro-American soldier falls in love with a Cambodian woman until her untimely death; Michael Cimino's (1985) *Year of the Dragon*, where a Euro-American man has a love/hate relationship

with a Chinese American woman; Nancy Kelly's (1990) *A Thousand Pieces of Gold*, a made-for-television movie where a Chinese American woman sent to America as a prostitute finds love with a Euro-American man; Alan Parker's (1990) *Come See the Paradise*, where a Euro-American man and a Japanese American woman, who is interned during World War II, fall in love and marry; Mira Nair's (1991) *Mississippi Masala*, where an Indian American woman and an African-American man defy her relatives to form a successful relationship; Oliver Stone's (1993) *Heaven and Earth*, where a Euro-American soldier brings home and marries a Vietnamese woman until his suicide; Maggie Greenwald's (1993) *The Ballad of Little Jo*, where a Euro-American woman passes as a man and has a secret love relationship with a Chinese American man; Ang Lee's (1993) *The Wedding Banquet*, where a Chinese American man loves a Euro-American man but marries a Chinese American woman to please his parents and also comes to love her; Wayne Wang's (1995) *The Joy Luck Club*, where two Chinese American women marry Euro-American men.

6. Interethnic romance films with American Indians include George Seitz's (1925) *The Vanishing American*, where a Navajo man loves but is rejected by a Euro-American woman; Cecil B. DeMille's (1931)*The Squaw Man*, with an English aristocrat who marries an American Indian woman but sees her as a primitive being even as she realizes how he feels and commits suicide; Delmar Daves' (1950) *Broken Arrow*, where a Euro-American man marries an Apache woman until her untimely death; Elliott Silverstein's (1970) *A Man Called Horse*, where an English aristocrat marries a Sioux woman until her untimely death; Michael Mann's (1993) *Last of the Mohicans*, where a (subplot) budding romance between a Mohican man and a Euro-American woman ends with their deaths; Ralph Nelson's (1970) *Soldier Blue*, where a Euro-American woman is briefly married to a Cheyenne man; Arthur Penn's (1970) *Little Big Man*, with a Euro-American man married to a Cheyenne woman until her untimely death; Jonathan Wack's (1989) *Powwow Highway*, with a budding (subplot) romance between a Cheyenne man and a Euro-American woman; and Eric Goldberg and Mike Gabriel's (1995) *Pocahontas*, a Disney animation where an Algonquian chief's daughter rejects an Indian suitor and falls in love with a Englishman.

7. Interethnic romance films featuring Latinos/as include Stanley Kramer's (1952) *High Noon*, where an Mexican-American woman has affairs with all of the main Euro-American characters, including the sheriff, the villain, and the deputy sheriff; Mervyn LaRay's (1953) *Latin Lover*, where a Euro-American female goes to Brazil with her fiancée but falls in love with a Brazilian; Robert Wise's (1961) *West Side Story*, a musical where the budding romance between a Puerto Rican female immigrant and a Euro-American male is doomed by ethnic gang rivalry; Brian DePalma's (1983) *Scarface*, where a Cuban immigrant becomes rich selling drugs and marries a Euro-American woman; Luis Valdez's (1987) *La Bamba*, where the young Mexican-American rock star Ritchie Valens loves his Euro-American high school girlfriend until his untimely death; Arnie Glimcher's (1992) *The Mambo Kings*, where a Cuban-American marries a Euro-American but cannot forget his first love; John Sayles (1995) *Lone Star*, where the Euro-American protagonist and his Mexican-American high school sweetheart who were forced to separate meet later in life and decide to marry; and Patricia Cardoso's (2002) *Real Women Have Curves*, where a Mexican-American high school student has a brief romance with a Euro-American male student.

8. Additional interethnic buddy films include Richard Donner's (1987) *Lethal Weapon*, (1989) *Lethal Weapon 2*, (1992) Lethal Weapon 3, and (1998) *Lethal Weapon 4*, where Mel Gibson and Danny Glover are police and Glover's character often serves as the butt of jokes and humiliations for comic relief; Philip Kaufman's (1993) *Rising Sun* with Sean Connery and Wesley Snipes; Quentin Tarantino's (1994) *Pulp Fiction* with John Travolta and Samuel L. Jackson; Frank Darabont's (1994) *The Shawshank Redemption* with Tim Robbins and Morgan Freeman; David Fincher's (1995) *Seven* with Morgan Freeman and Brad Pitt; Barry Sonnenfield's (1997) *Men in Black* with Tommy Lee Jones and Will Smith; and Antoine Fuqua's (2001) *Training Day* with Denzel Washington as a corrupt policeman and Ethan Hawk as a good rookie cop who opposes him. In Michael Mann's (2004) *Collateral*, Tom Cruise plays a contract killer who commandeers Jamie Foxx as his driver.

9. David A. Cook recognizes Griffith as having done "more than any single individual to establish the narrative language of cinema and turn an aesthetically inconsequential medium of entertainment into a fully articulated art form." *A History of Narrative Film* (New York: Norton, 1996) 59.

10. Griffith, "Pace in the Movies," *Liberty*, 13 Nov. 1926, qtd. in Larry May, *Screening out the Past: The Birth of Mass Culture and the Motion Picture Industry* (Chicago: Chicago UP, 1980) 77.

11. Qtd. in Cook, *A History of Narrative Film* (New York: Norton, 1996) 83.

12. Lee's latest (2004) feature *She Hate Me*, not a film for young viewers, is as personal as any of Lee's independent films, and, like a number of his other films, benefits from Lee's explanations of what he was trying to accomplish. In one nude scene, the male protagonist is eyed by a number of women. Lee's explanation — that this is "an allusion to slavery, and people aren't getting it. He's being inspected, prodded and poked at, just the way a slave might have on the auction block" — illustrates his continued interest in referencing African-American history as meaningful for contemporary stories, and in telling what he calls "incendiary" stories to incite his viewers to rethink their ideas about African Americans in contemporary America. See Mary F. Pols' "Seven 'Misconceptions' About Lee," *Contra Costa Times* 15 Aug. 2004: 5E+.

13. D.W. Griffith, "Five Dollar Movies Prophesied." Qtd. in Robert Lang, ed., *The Birth of a Nation: D.W. Griffith, Director* (New Brunswick: Rutgers UP, 1994) 4.

Chapter 10

1. Alan Brinkley, *The Unfinished Nation: A Concise History of the American People* (Boston: McGraw Hill, 2003).

2. Denis Lynn Daly Heyck, *Barrios and Borderlands: Cultures of Latinos and Latinas in the United States* (New York: Routledge, 1994) xiii–xviii.

3. Ilan Stavans and Lalo Alcaraz, *A Cartoon History: Latino Culture* (New York: Basic Books, 2000).

Chapter 12

1. For an extensive discussion of the loyalty question and other matters of the war in the Pacific, see John Dower, *War Without Mercy* (New York: Pantheon, 1987).

2. John Okada, *No-No Boy* (Seattle: U of Washington P, 1957).

3. The Japanese American Internet Curriculum http://www.bss.sfsu.edu/internment/documents.html site, as well as the site for the Internment documentary entitled Children of the Camps http://www.children-of-the-camps.org/history/timeline.html, provide timelines and term definitions.

4. James A. Mackey and William E. Huntzicker, "Racism and Relocation: Telling the Japanese American Experience," *Social Education* (1991). Rpt. *American History*, vol. 2, 12th ed. (Guilford, Conn.: Dushkin, 1993) 141–43.

5. Harper Lee, *To Kill a Mockingbird* (New York: Warner, 1960).

6. David Guterson, *Snow Falling on Cedars* (New York: Vintage, 1995).

Chapter 13

1. Donald Bogle, *Toms, Coons, Mulattoes, Mammies, and Bucks: An Interpretive History of Blacks in American Film*, 4th ed. (New York: Continuum, 2001).

2. Such statistics are available from the U.S. Department of Justice website, which provides statistics on criminal offenders: http://www.ojp.usdoj.gov/bjs/crimoff.htm.

3. Gordon Allport, "The Formation of In-Groups." *Rereading America: Cultural Contexts for Critical Thinking and Writing*. Ed. Gary Columbo, et al." 2nd ed. (New York: St. Martin's, 1992) 292–305.

4. The image of King and Manson is available at http://archive.aclu.org/graphics/man_on_left.gif.

5. Claude McKay's poem "If We Must Die" is available at http://www.English.uiuc.edu/maps/poets / m_r/mc.

Glossary:
The Language of Film

Students who have a film vocabulary can define, analyze, interpret, discuss, and write about what they see on the screen with intelligence and authority and can recognize how film techniques are designed to guide viewer response rather than being passively guided themselves.

SET DIRECTION **determines what viewers see**

Mise-en-scène— refers to all the elements in a scene: the locale, the physical setting and props, and the arrangement and movement of the properties and actors within that environment.

Visual metaphor— something natural to a scene (in the *mise-en-scène*) also serves a metaphorical or thematic purpose. (In John Singleton's 1991 *Boys 'N the Hood,* the opening scene street signs— STOP, ONE WAY, WRONG WAY— serve as visual metaphors to indicate that the children are headed — to view the body of a young African American murdered by another young African American — in the wrong direction.)

CINEMATOGRAPHY **determines how viewers see**

Viewers see from the perspective offered by the camera. Cinematography is a general term for all manipulations by the camera in the shooting phase (and also later in the editing and development phase).

Frame— the smallest compositional unit of film, the individual photographic image.

Shot— a single run of the camera before a cut. A single shot is joined with others in the editing phase to create scenes.

Scene— an episode united by time, location, and dramatic action.

Master scene— a shot that includes all of the action in a particular sequence, with the camera fairly distant. A master scene allows viewers to see the big picture and to choose what to focus on, creating the illusion that viewers are participants in the scene. During the editing phase, medium shots, close ups, parallel action shots, reaction shots, intercuts, intertitles, and digitalized computer images are inserted to direct viewer participation and response.

CAMERA ANGLES **create perspective**

Wide-angle shot— the camera shot captures a broad field of vision. Viewers have an overview of surroundings, a privileged perspective not shared by all the characters.

Overhead shot— the camera is high, tilted down toward the object. Objects are seen from above, putting the viewer in a commanding position.

Eye-level shot— the camera is placed at

the eye level of a person sitting or standing, so that viewers see surroundings from the perspective of that person.

Low-angle shot—the camera is low, tilted up. Objects and people are seen from below, which gives them the commanding position.

Tilt-angle/canted-angle shot—the camera is tilted off its horizontal and vertical axis. (In Spike Lee's 1989 *Do the Right Thing*, young African-American men are viewed at a titled angle as they enter Sal's pizza parlor to give viewers a visual sense that they are at odds with Sal's promotion of Italian-American images and ethnicity in their neighborhood.)

Camera distance from an object shows vistas or creates intimacy

Long shot—the camera appears to be far from objects and people of interest. (In John Ford's *Stagecoach*, and hundreds of other Westerns, the attacking Indians are seen primarily in long shots, physically and emotionally distanced from viewers as encroaching threats rather than human beings.)

Medium shot—the field of vision is between the long and the close shot.

Close up—the camera appears to be very near to the object.

Extreme close up—the camera appears so close that a face (or faces) fill the entire screen. (In Spike Lee's 1998 documentary *Four Little Girls*, faces of the relatives of the four young girls killed by a church bombing during the Civil Rights movement fill the screen, encouraging viewers to identify with them to understand the deaths as a personal, as well as a national, tragedy.)

Camera movement involves viewers

Stationary camera shot—the camera remains stationary. The camera was stationary in early filmmaking, which was done in a theatrical mode. (In D.W. Griffith's 1915 *The Birth of a Nation*, viewers watch the characters move in and out of interior scenes, seeing them as actors on a stage.)

Tracking shot—the camera (hand held or on a dolly or a vehicle) and its entire support move ahead of, behind, or beside characters who are also moving. (In D.W. Griffith's 1915 *The Birth of a Nation*, tracking shots show the Ku Klux Klan on horseback as they gallop to the rescue of besieged whites. The camera moves with the Klan actors to create the sense that viewers are participating in the rescue.)

Boom shot—the camera moves through the air by crane, giving viewers an overview.

Pan shot—the movement of the camera is from left to right, or vice versa, along a horizontal plane, pivoting (unlike the tracking shot) from a stationary point. (In Jonathan Wacks' 1989 *Powwow Highway* and in Michael Apted's 1992 *Thunderheart*, pan shots bring viewers into the sacred circle of American Indian unity with the land, each other, and the past.)

Camera focus directs attention

Soft focus—an object or parts of a shot are slightly out of focus, to draw viewer attention to the people and things that are in focus.

Deep focus—objects are in focus at both near and far distances, making everything equally important. (In Julie Dash's 1991 *Daughters of the Dust*, wide-angle, deep-focus shots of the members of an extended family of former slaves and the land they have cultivated show the close relation of the family to the place and to the African-American customs they have developed, as an alternative to the Hollywood convention of focusing on one or two heroic figures.)

Point of view shots

Subjective shot—the camera views a scene from one character's point of view.

(In D.W. Griffith's 1915 *The Birth of a Nation*, the motivation and inspiration for the creation of the Ku Klux Klan are shown from the point of view of a white southerner, Ben Cameron, who feels blacks are responsible for the death of his younger sister and for the harassment and disenfranchisement of whites. And in Charles Burnett's 1996 *Nightjohn*, viewers understand the economic motivations for slavery from the perspective of a young slave girl who recounts the monetary worth of each slave from what she read in the slaveholder's account book.)

Objective shot—the character looks directly into the camera, speaks to, and directly involves the viewer, breaking our willing suspension of disbelief and confounding the movie's reality with our own. (In Spike Lee's 1989 *Do the Right Thing*, members of different ethnic groups look directly into the camera and shout ethnic slurs, demonstrating how similarly foolish ethnic slurs are, no matter who shouts them, and allowing viewers to be on the receiving end.)

Omniscient shot—the camera and audience are privileged to see what the characters in the scene cannot.

Establishing shot—an omniscient shot, usually a long shot, that identifies the location where an action takes place. (In Michael Apted's 1992 *Thunderheart*, shots of the U.S. Capitol, the Washington Monument, and the Lincoln Memorial establish the setting as Washington, D.C., to inform viewers that government policy for American Indian reservations is still created and recreated far from and without direct knowledge of reservations and the people who live on them.)

EDITED IMAGES guide viewer response

The iris—highlights a character by showing him or her in a circle of light (In D.W. Griffith's 1915 *The Birth of a Nation*, the heroine and hero are highlighted in irises to become the focus of viewers' attention. Spike Lee's 1991 *Jungle Fever* al-ludes to Griffith's film with an iris shot of his African–American hero.)

Superimposed images—separate images are combined into one. (In Herbert Biberman's 1953 *Salt of the Earth*, images of the husband and wife protagonists are superimposed to suggest that their struggles as striking Mexican-American miners are similar and they must act together to be successful.)

Split screen—the frame is divided into separate, rather than superimposed, images. (In Gregory Nava's 1997 *Selena*, split-screen images of Selena as she is performing on stage suggest aspects of her life and personality that make her attractive to audiences.)

Reaction shot/reactive characters—a shot, usually a cut away, in which an actor or actors react to action that has just occurred, in order to evoke the same response in viewers. (In Robert Townsend's 1987 *Hollywood Shuffle*, a black actor's family reacts negatively to his efforts to play a stereotypical African-American role and reacts positively when he refuses it, inviting the same viewer reaction.)

Intertitles—words on the screen to be read by the viewing audience. Intertitles in silent films identify the setting, give important dialogue, and explain the action. Intertitles in sound films identify the setting or offer commentary, usually to communicate real-world facts relevant to the story or to explain what happened to the characters following the story seen by viewers. (In Mario van Peebles' 1993 *Posse*, intertitles at the end of the film first cite little-known statistics about black cowboys and black settlements in America and then cite related statistics about African Americans in late twentieth century America.)

Subtitles—words superimposed over action, usually at the bottom of the frame, used to translate foreign language dialogue or identify a scene in translated language. (In Kevin Costner's 1990 *Dances with Wolves*, subtitles translate the spoken Lakota into English.)

EDITING manipulates viewers' sense of time and reality

Slow motion—action shown at a rate slower than normal. Slow motion can indicate graceful movement, nostalgia, thoughtfulness, or a lyrical, dreamy, or romantic moment.

Accelerated motion— action shown at a rate faster than normal, often used for comic effect.

Freeze frame— the frame is the smallest compositional unit of film, the individual photographic image. A freeze frame is a frame printed repeatedly so that, although the projector is still operating, one frame is seen without movement for a designated length of time. A freeze frame can change into a moving picture and vice versa. (In Mike Gabriel and Eric Goldberg's 1995 *Pocahontas*, an opening freeze-frame picturing an English town takes on life as elements of the picture began to move, to suggest that what follows is recorded history coming to life before viewers' eyes— in animation. The end of the film returns viewers to the still picture.)

Wipe—a new scene gradually pushes the old one across and off the screen to suggest that time has passed.

Fade out/dissolve—the old scene fades out while the new scene fades in. Rapid dissolves can indicate a rapid passing of time, slow dissolves a slow passing of time.

Continuity editing/invisible editing— unobtrusive editing creates the impression that events move forward seemlessly in terms of space and time continuity, hiding the fact that film scenes are built of shots that are normally filmed out of sequence, and creating a sense of real time passing before our eyes.

Collapsed time—editing that shows time passing at a normal rate in a compressed period of viewing. (In John Singleton's 1991 *Boys 'N the Hood*, four editing cuts in a two-minute scene show that it takes a boy all day and into the evening to rake the leaves in his yard—

to make the point that his African-American father takes pride in his neighborhood and expects his son to be responsible — giving viewers the sense that they have witnessed the son's day-long efforts.)

Match cut—an editing cut where two shots are matched by similarity in the shape and form of two objects or by similarity in the action of one or more characters. (In Edward James Olmos' 1992 *American Me*, a scene of Mexican-American boys playing handball in reform school becomes a scene of the same boys grown into men playing handball in prison, to show how childhood affects adulthood and to suggest an uninterrupted transition from reform school to prison.)

Discontinuity editing/conflict montage— a dynamic juxtaposition of shots to emphasize conflict, often an abrupt juxtaposition of shots from different times and places. (Christine Choy and Renee Tajima's 1988 documentary *Who Killed Vincent Chin?* opens with a series of disjointed shots, to give the impression of a puzzle that needs to be pieced together in order to solve the mystery and ascertain the multiple causes of the murder of Vincent Chin during the course of the film. And Robert Young's 1983 *The Ballad of Gregorio Cortez*, opens with discontinuous shots of men on horseback chasing Gregorio Cortez, Cortez fleeing, a wagon of dead bodies, men arresting a Mexican, and Texas Rangers in pursuit on a train, all seen as aspects of Cortez's story to be pieced together during the film narrative.)

Crosscutting/parallel action—two or more independently shot scenes are edited together to give the illusion that the several actions are happening simultaneously. (At the end of D.W. Griffith's 1915 *The Birth of a Nation*, different groups of Ku Klux Klan members appear to save groups of besieged whites simultaneously. In Peter Wang's 1986 *A Great Wall*, crosscutting scenes show how Chinese and Chinese Americans have much in common but are not culturally identical and how each harbors cultural stereotypes of the other.)

Insert shots/intercuts—something outside the time and or locale is inserted into a scene as a flashback, a flash forward, a vision, or for metaphoric or thematic purposes. (In Jonathan Wacks' 1989 *Powwow Highway*, a twentieth-century Cheyenne is imagined in an intercut as a nineteenth-century Cheyenne warrior to show links between the past and present.)

SOUND creates a sense of reality

Sound track—all the sounds heard in a film

Multiple sound tracks—more than one recording source for the sound. For easier control in sound mixing, music, noises, and voices are recorded on separate tracks, which are then mixed onto one track (or several tracks for stereophonic sound).

Sound editing—the process of adding, arranging, and mixing sounds—music, noises, and voices—to enhance the image and create or reinforce meaning.

Synchronized sound—music, noises, and voices that match the lip movement and action seen on the screen at the time it is heard.

Asynchronous sound—sound derived from a source not in the image on the screen at the time it is heard.

VOICES create a sense of reality

Dialogue—seemingly spontaneous speech between two or more characters, synchronic with lip movement.

Voice over—an off-screen (asynchronous) voice of authority that provides narration or commentary. (In Marlon Riggs' 1986 documentary *Ethnic Notions*, the voice of Esther Rolle explains the visuals, but she is never seen by viewers. In Kevin Costner's 1990 *Dances with Wolves*, the protagonist, Lieutenant Dunbar, tells portions of his own story via voice over.)

MUSIC sets a mood, comments on action, elicits emotions, conveys ideas

Foreground music (synchronized sound) is heard by both viewers and characters and comes from an on-screen source — such as a radio, jukebox, live band, or singer — within the world of the film. (In Randal Kleiser's 1978 *Grease*, verses of songs that are sung alternately by the young man and young woman protagonists from different ethnic groups reveal how differently they interpret the same events.)

Background music (asynchronous sound) is heard on the soundtrack by viewers but is not heard by the characters. It does not come from any on-screen source in the world of the film. (In Robert Young's 1983 *The Ballad of Gregorio Cortez*, the *corrido* "The Ballad of Gregorio Cortez" is heard by viewers as the film opens, to convey the idea that the story is about the Mexican-American borderballad hero.)

Background establishing music—a specific type of music or a specific song is repeated during the course of the film as background music so viewers associate it with a group of people or with a specific character. (In John Ford's 1939 *Drums Along the Mohawk*, stereotypical Indian background music identifies those who attack the white settlers as savage Indians. In Kevin Costner's 1990 *Dances with Wolves*, heart-swelling, orchestral music is heard in the background whenever the Sioux are shown living in harmony with the vast plains, to emphasize an ideal connection between the Sioux and the land and to help convey the idea that the Sioux are superior caretakers of the land.)

NOISES create an experiential reality and evoke emotions

Realistic sound—sounds that normally accompany the kind of action seen on the screen: a door slamming, footsteps, a telephone ringing, an airplane in take off (In Charles Guggenheim's 1992 documentary *A Time for Justice: America's*

Civil Rights Movement, the sounds of sirens, people screaming, and crackly fire accompany a still photograph of a burning Civil Rights Freedom Fighter bus to give viewers the sense that they are experiencing the event.)

Enhanced and sweetened sounds—combined sounds (layering recorded sounds over other recorded sounds) to create never-before-heard sounds that will have an emotional effect on viewers. Gunshots, munitions blasts, explosions, storms (volcanoes and twisters), and monsters typically get enhanced and sweetened sounds. (In John Singleton's 1991 *Boyz 'N the Hood,* gunshots are enhanced to make them seem louder and more powerful than they are in reality to momentarily enhance the expected thrill of seeing a violent act.)

Sound bridge—a segment of the soundtrack (music, a noise, or a voice) that continues from one shot into another to connect the two. (In Frank Christopher's 1985 docudrama *The Lemon Grove Incident,* the same period-piece background music that is heard as background music while old documentary photographs are seen becomes foreground music as viewers see a man playing the piece on a piano, to connect actual documents from the period with a dramatic reenactment of the conflicts that arose when a California school district attempted to segregate Mexican-American from Anglo-American school children.)

Discontinuity editing—the sound and image do not match, causing viewers to note conflicting perspectives and to question what they hear and feel uncomfortable with what they see. (In Valerie Soe's 1987 experimental film *New Year,* a recorded voice from World War II media propaganda says that Americans tried to "save the Japs" while a photograph of the atomic bomb mushroom cloud shows the opposite. And in Marlon Riggs' 1987 documentary *Ethnic Notions,* a recorded voice from the past tells of happy darkies while a photograph of a badly whipped and scared slave shows that the opposite

was true. Also in *Ethnic Notions,* Ethel Waters is seen as a docile mammy from an old Hollywood film and heard singing "Darkies Never Dream" even as Martin Luther King, Jr., is heard giving his 1963 "I Have a Dream" speech.)

FILM TYPES:

The documentary is a nonfiction film about real people and real events (no actors and no invented plot) that is shot in real locations. The primary function of a documentary is to inform. Common features include voice-over narration, a variety of experts and authorities giving their informed opinions, interviews with people (or their descendents) involved in the events, and artifacts (photographs, paintings, maps, films) and music from the period. Documentaries are mediated, not objective views; filmmakers choose whose story to tell and how to tell it.

The persuasive documentary (P.O.V. = point of view) attempts to persuade the viewer to accept a given thesis. Film footage is assembled so as to make a point and narration is common. (In Jay Rosenstein's 1996 documentary *In Whose Honor?* film footage of an Indian mascot dancing at halftime for the University of Illinois and film footage of American Indian Charlene Teters protesting the use of Indian mascots, logos, and nicknames for sports teams is combined with expert testimony, interviews, and voice-over narration, to persuade viewers that Indian mascots and nicknames are degrading to Indians and should be replaced.)

The propaganda documentary is used for persuasive purposes (often political) and therefore tends to manipulate and distort actuality and to appeal to emotion rather than to rational thought. (In Frank Capra's World War II propaganda film series *Why We Fight,* Adolph Hitler and the Japanese are made to seem inhumanly diabolical.)

The docudrama is a documentary that includes dramatized reenactments of events.(In Frank Christopher's 1985 docudrama *The Lemon Grove Incident,* old photographs, documents, and interviews are combined with dramatic reenactments of situations showing the positions taken by Anglos and Mexican Americans when an all–Anglo school board decided to put the children in segregated schools.)

The feature film is a fictional narrative, sometimes based on actual events, usually longer than eighty minutes and made for showing in commercial theatres. Narrative films have a beginning, middle, and end, not necessarily in that order. The main purpose of a feature film is to provide entertainment, although some feature films encourage viewers to think about serious issues and some aim to represent the essence of an historical event or era.

Shorts are narrative films under eighty minutes, usually made as independent films

Realism—a common feature film technique is continuity (invisible) editing, to give the impression of real life so viewers can identify with the characters on the screen as if they were real people and think of the settings as real places. Realism includes the use of scripts, staging, costuming, and edited camera shots. (In D.W. Griffith's 1915 *The Birth of a Nation,* historical facsimiles—photographs and reenactments of historical events—and realistic Union and Confederate costumes create a sense of actuality. In Spike Lee's 1992 *Malcolm X,* newsreel film footage and real people playing themselves on screen contribute to the impression that viewers can see history unfolding before their eyes.)

Kinds of feature films—feature films are fictionalized stories based on a variety of sources: real-life events, original scripts, short stories, novels, plays, comic books, autobiographical memoirs, and earlier films.

Film adaptations—transformations to the screen of stories, novels, plays, or memoirs. There are both faithful and loose adaptations. (John Korty's 1976 *Farewell to Manzanar* is faithful to Jeanne Wakatsuki-Houston's autobiographical memoir of her childhood experiences in an internment camp during World War II but eliminates Wakatsuki-Houston's account of her experiences when her family left the camp.)

Feature film genres—common genres are the western, the gangster film, the detective film, the combat film, the romantic comedy, the musical, the action-adventure film, the science-fiction film, the horror film, the history film, and the biography.

KINDS OF FILMS:

Hollywood feature films—productions financed by commercial studios to make money.

Independent films—film productions initiated by a person or persons not under contract to a commercial studio who often wants to make a film other than those that Hollywood makes. Some independents may produce films without use of union personnel or commercial facilities; others may subcontract. Independent films include documentaries and feature films; experimental films (which are personal and personalized) are by definition independent. Digital technology is making the independent filmmaking process easier, but filmmakers still need to find distributors.

Selected Filmography

In the list that follows, the designation "D" indicates that the film is a documentary.

Films about and by African Americans

Adventures of Huck Finn (Richard Thorpe, 1939)

Adventures of Huckleberry Finn (Michael Curtiz, 1960)

Adventures of Huckleberry Finn (Peter Hunt, 1985)

The African American Cinema (Library of Congress). Two parts: (1) African American Cinema I: *Within Our Gates* (Oscar Micheaux, 1919); (2) African American Cinema II: *The Scar of Shame* (1926), *Sissle and Blake* (1923)

Africans in America (D, PBS, Orlando Bagwell, Susan Bellows, 1998), Four Parts: (1) The Terrible Transformation; (2) Revolution; (3) Brotherly Love; (4) Judgment Day

Ali (Michael Mann, 2001)

An American Love Story (D, Jennifer Fox, 1998)

Amistad (Steven Spielberg, 1997)

Another 48 Hours (Walter Hill, 1990)

The Autobiography of Miss Jane Pittman (Made for TV, John Korty, 1973)

Bamboozled (Spike Lee, 2000)

Beloved (Jonathan Demme, 1998)

The Betrayal (Oscar Micheaux, 1948)

Beverly Hills Cop (Martin Brest, 1984)

Beverly Hills Cop II (Tony Scott, 1987)

Beverly Hills Cop III (John Landis, 1994)

The Birth of a Nation (D.W. Griffith, 1915)

Black Caricature: The Black Image in Movies, Literature, and Music (D, Black Entertainment Network, 1995)

Black Shadows on a Silver Screen: The Black Film Industry from 1915–1950 (D, 1975)

Black, White, and Brown: Brown versus the Board of Education of Topeka (D, 2004)

Blazing Saddles (Mel Brooks, 1974)

Blue-Eyed (D, Bertram Verhaag, 1996)

Body and Soul (Oscar Micheaux, 1925)

Bowling for Columbine (Michael Moore, 2002)

Boyz 'N the Hood (John Singleton, 1991)

A Class Divided (D, PBS *Frontline* William Peters, 1985)

Classified X (D, Mark Daniels, 1998)

Clockers (Spike Lee, 1995)

Clueless (Amy Heckerling, 1995)

Collateral (Michael Mann, 2004)

Color Adjustment (D, Marlon Riggs, 1992)

The Color Purple (Steven Spielberg, 1985)

Corrina, Corrina (Jessie Nelson, 1994)

Crash (Paul Haggis, 2005)

Crooklyn (Spike Lee, 1994)

Daughters of the Dust (Julie Dash, 1991)

The Defiant Ones (Stanley Kramer, 1958)

Do the Right Thing (Spike Lee, 1989)

Driving Miss Daisy (Bruce Beresford, 1989)

Ethnic Notions (D, Marlon Riggs, 1987)
Eyes on the Prize I: America's Civil Rights Years (D, PBS, Henry Hampton 1986). Six parts: (1) *Awakenings* (1954–56); (2) *Fighting Back* (1957–62); (3) *Ain't Scared of Your Jails* (1960–61); (4) *No Easy Walk* (1962–66); (5) *Mississippi: Is This America?* (1962–64); (6) *Bridge to Freedom* (1965)
Eyes on the Prize II: America at the Racial Crossroads (D, PBS, 1989, Eight Parts)
Family Across the Sea (D, Tim Carrier, ETV, 1990)
Far from Heaven (Todd Haynes, 2001)
The Five Heartbeats (Robert Townsend, 1991)
48 Hours (Walter Hill, 1982)
Four Little Girls (D, Spike Lee, 1995)
Freedom on My Mind (D, *The American Experience*, Connie Field, Marilyn Mulford, 1994)
Freedom Song (Made for TV, TNT, Phil Robinson, 2000)
Get on the Bus (Spike Lee, 1996)
Ghosts of Mississippi (Rob Reiner, 1996)
Glory (Edward Zwick, 1989)
Gone with the Wind (Victor Fleming, 1939)
Great Books: Huckleberry Finn (D, PBS, 1995)
The Green Mile (Frank Darabont, 1999)
Guess Who's Coming to Dinner (Stanley Kramer, 1967)
Hitch (Andy Tennant, 2005)
Hollywood Shuffle (Robert Townsend, 1987)
Home of the Brave (Mark Robson, 1949)
Hoop Dreams (D, Steve James, Frederick Marx, Peter Gilbert, 1994)
The Human Stain (Robert Benson, 2003)
Imitation of Life (John Stahl, 1934)
Imitation of Life (Douglas Sirk, 1959)
Intruder in the Dust (Clarence Brown, 1949)
The Invisible Soldiers: Unheard Voices (D, PBS, William H. Smith, 2000)
Jungle Fever (Spike Lee, 1991)
The Legend of Bagger Vance (Robert Redford, 2000)
A Lesson Before Dying (Joseph Sargent, 1999)

Lethal Weapon (Richard Donner, 1987)
Lethal Weapon 2 (Richard Donner, 1989)
Lethal Weapon 3 (Richard Donner, 1992)
Lethal Weapon 4 (Richard Donner, 1998)
The Life and Times of Rosie the Riveter (D, Connie Field, 1980)
The Littlest Rebel (David Butler, 1935)
The Long Walk Home (Richard Pearce, 1990)
Malcolm X (Spike Lee, 1992)
Malcolm X: Make It Plain (D, PBS, *The American Experience*, Orlando Bagwell, 1993)
The Massachusetts 54th Infantry (D, PBS, Jacqueline Shearer, 1991)
Men in Black (Barry Sonnenfield, 1997)
Menace II Society (Allen and Albert Hughes, 1993)
Midnight Ramble: The Story of the Black Film Industry (D, PBS, *The American Experience*, 1994)
Mississippi Burning (Alan Parker, 1988)
Mississippi Masala (Mira Nair, 1991)
Mo' Better Blues (Spike Lee, 1990)
Monster's Ball (Marc Foster, 2002)
Murder in Mississippi (Made for TV Movie, Roger Young, 1990)
The Murder of Emmett Till (D, Stanley Nelson, 2003)
Nat Turner: A Troublesome Property (D, Charles Burnett, 2002)
The Negro Soldier (D, Frank Capra, 1944)
Nightjohn (Hallmark, Charles Burnett, 1996)
One Potato, Two (Larry Peerce, 1964)
The Patriot (Roland Emmerich, 2000)
Pinky (Elia Kazan, 1949)
Posse (Mario Van Peebles, 1993)
Pulp Fiction (Quetin Tarantino, 1994)
A Question of Color (D, Kathe Sandler, 1995)
Rising Sun (Philip Kaufman, 1993)
The Road to Brown (D, William Elwood, Mykola Kulishm, 1989)
Roots of Resistance: A Story of the Underground Railroad (D, PBS, *The American Experience*, Orlando Bagwell, 1989)
Rush Hour (Brett Ratner, 1988)
Rush Hour II (Brett Ratner, 2001)
The Scar of Shame (Oscar Micheaux, 1926)

School Daze (Spike Lee, 1988)

Scottsboro: An American Tragedy (D, PBS, 2001)

Separate but Equal (Made for TV Movie, George Stevens, 1991)

The Shawshank Redemption (Frank Darabot, 1994)

She Hate Me (Spike Lee, 2004)

Soul Plane (Jessy Terrero, 2004)

Sounder (Martin Ritt, 1972)

That's Black Entertainment (D, William Greaves, 1989)

The Tiger Woods Story (LaVar Burton, 1998)

A Time for Justice: America's Civil Rights Movement (D, Charles Guggenheim, 1992)

To Kill a Mockingbird (Robert Mulligan, 1962)

To Sleep with Anger (Charles Burnett, 1990)

Training Day (Antonia Fuqua, 2001)

The Tuskegee Airman (HBO, 1996)

Unchained Memories: Readings from the Slave Narratives (D, HBO, 2004)

Uncle Tom's Cabin (Harry Pollard, 1927)

The Underground Railroad: Flight to Freedom (D, History Channel)

The Untold Story of the Murder of Emmett Till (D, Keith Beauchamp, 2004)

The Untold West: The Black West (D, TBS, Nina Rosenblum, 1995)

Whitewash (script by Ntozake Shange, 1994)

Within Our Gates (Oscar Micheaux, 1919)

You Must Remember This (PBS, Helaine Head, Wonderworks, 1993)

Zebrahead (Anthony Drazan, 1992)

Films about and by Asian Americans

After Silence: Civil Rights and the Japanese American Experience (D, Lois Shelton)

a.k.a. Don Bonus (D, PBS, Sokly Ny and Spencer Nakasako, 1995)

Alamo Bay (Louis Malle, 1985)

All Orientals Look the Same (D, Valerie Soe, 1986)

American Made (Shanat Raju, 2003)

American Sons (D, Steven Okuzaki, 1997)

Anatomy of a Springroll: Vietnam Roots/American (Paul Kwam, 1997)

Animal Appetites (D, Michael Cho, 1991)

Another America (D, Michael Cho, 1996)

Asian American History Series (D, Loni Ding, 1997). Two parts: (1) Ancestors in the Americas: Coolies, Sailors, Settlers; (2) Ancestors in the Americas: Chinese in the Frontier West, An American Story

Back to Bataan (Edward Dymtryk, 1945)

Bad Day at Black Rock (John Sturges, 1955)

The Ballad of Little Jo (Maggie Greenwald, 1993)

Becoming American: The Chinese Experience (D, PBS, Bill Moyers, 2003, Three Parts)

Benaat Chicago (Daughters of Chicago): Growing Up Arab and Female in Chicago (D, Jennifer Bing-Canar, Mary Zerkel, 1996)

Better Luck Tomorrow (Jason Lin, 2002)

Beyond Barbed Wire (D, Steve Rosen, 1997)

The Bhangra Wrap (Nandini Sikand, 1994)

Blue Collar and Buddha (D, Taggart Siegel, 1988)

Bontoc Eulogy (Marlon Fuentes, 1995)

Breakfast at Tiffany's (Blake Edwards, 1961)

Broken Blossoms (D.W. Griffith, 1919)

Bui Doi: Life Like Dust (D, Ahrin Mishan, 1994)

Chan Is Missing (Wayne Wang, 1982)

Charlie's Angels: Full Throttle (McG, 2003)

Charlotte Sometimes (Eric Byler, 2003)

The Cheat (Cecil B. DeMille, 1915)

Children of the Camps (D, Stephen Holsapple, 1999)

The Color of Honor (D, Loni Ding, 1988)

Come See the Paradise (Alan Parker, 1990)

Conversations: Before the War/After the War (D, Robert Nakamura, 1986)

Crusin' J-Town (Duane Kubo, 1976)

Die Another Day (Lee Tamahori, 2002)

Dim Sum: A Little Bit of Heart (Wayne Wang, 1984)

Double Happiness (Mina Shum, 1994)

Dragon: The Bruce Lee Story (Rob Cohen, 1993)

Eagle Against the Sun (John Akahoshi, 1992)

Eat a Bowl of Tea (*American Playhouse*, Wayne Wang, 1989)

Enter the Dragon (Robert Clouse, 1973)

The Face of Fu Manchu (Don Sharp, 1965)

Family Gathering: A Search for a Japanese-American Past (D, PBS, American Experience, Lisa Yasui, 1988)

Farewell to Manzanar (Made for TV, John Korty, 1976)

Fargo (Joel Cohen, 1996)

Filipino Americans: Discovering Their Past for the Future (D, John Wehman, 1994)

Flower Drum Song (Henry Koster, 1961)

From a Different Shore: The Japanese-American Experience (D, 1996)

The Good Earth (Sidney Franklin, 1937)

A Great Wall (Peter Wang, U.S. & China, 1986)

The Green Berets (John Wayne, 1968)

Harold and Kumar Go to White Castle (Danny Leiner, 2004)

Heaven and Earth (Oliver Stone, 1993)

History and Memory: For Akiko and Takashige (Experimental D, Rea Tajiri, 1991)

Hito Hata: Raise the Banner (Robert Nakamura, 1980)

Honor Bound: A Personal Journey (D, Joan Saffe, 1995)

I'm on a Mission from Buddha (D, Deborah Gee, 1991)

In My Own Skin: The Complexity of Living as an Arab in America (D, Nikki Byrd, Jennifer Jajeh, 2001)

The Iron Road (D, American Experience, Neil Goodwin, 1990)

Japanese Relocation (D, Department of War Information, 1942)

Jazz Is My Native Language: A Portrait of Toshiko Akyoshi (D, Renee Cho, 1983)

The Joy Luck Club (Wayne Wang, 1995)

Juxta (Hiroka Yamazaki, 1989)

Kelly Loves Tony (D, Spencer Nakasako,

Kane Ian "Kelly" Saeteurn, Nai "Tony" Saelio, 1998)

Kill Bill Vol. I (Quentin Tarantino, 2003)

Lest We Forget (D, Jason DaSilva, 2003)

Letter Back Home (D, Nith Lacroix, Sang Thepkaysone, 1994)

Letters to Thien (D, Trac Minh Vu, 1997)

Made in China: A Search for Roots (D, Lisa Hsia, 1986)

Manzanar (D, Robert Nakamura, 1971)

Maya Lin: A Clear Strong Vision (D, PBS/POV, Freida Lee Mock, 1994)

Me, Mom, and Mona (Mina Shum, 1993)

Memories from the Department of Amnesia (Experimental D, Janet Tanaka, 1991)

Mississippi Masala (Mira Nair, 1991)

Monterey's Boat People (D, Spencer Nakasako, Vincent DiGirolamo, 1982)

Mulan (Tony Bandroft, Barry Cook, 1998)

My America ... or honk if you love Buddha (D, Renee Tajima-Pena, 1998)

My American Grandmother (Aysha Ghazoul, 1999)

New Year, Parts I and II (Experimental D, Valerie Soe, 1987)

Nisei Soldier: Standard Bearer for an Exiled People (D, Loni Ding, 1984)

Of Civil Rights and Wrongs: The Fred Korematsu Story (D, Eric Paul, 1999)

A Personal Matter: Gordon Hirabayashi vs the United States (D, John DeGraaf, 1992)

Picture Bride (Kayo Hatta, 1995)

A Place Called Home (Persheng Sadegh-Vaziri, 1998)

Portraits from the Cloth (Alberto Justiniano, Roger Schmitz, 1996)

Rabbit in the Moon (D, POV, Emiko Omori, 1999)

Rambo: First Blood, Part II (George P. Cosmatos, 1985)

Romeo Must Die (Andrzej Bartkowiak, 2000)

Rush Hour (Brett Ratner, 1998)

Rush Hour II (Bret Ratner, 2001)

Sa-I-GU (D, PBS/POV, Dai Sil Kim-Gibson, Christine Choy, 1993)

Sayonara (Joshua Logan, 1957)

Searching for Asian America (D, Donald

Young, Sapana Sakya, Kyung Sun Ya, 2004)

Sewing Woman (D, Arthur Dong, 1982)

Shanghai Express (Josef van Sternberg, 1941)

The Shot Heard 'Round the World (D, Christine Choy and Spiro Lampro, 1997)

Slaying the Dragon (D, Deborah Gee, 1988)

Snow Falling on Cedars (Scott Hicks, 1999)

Some Questions for 28 Kisses (D, Kip Fulbeck, 1994)

Starting Over: Japanese Americans After the War (D, PBS, Dianne Fukami, 1996)

Strawberry Fields (D, Rea Tajiri, 1998)

A Tajik Woman (Mehrnaz Saeed-Vafa, 1994)

Tales from Arab Detroit (Joan Mandell, 1995)

Teahouse of the August Moon (Daniel Mann, 1956)

The Thief of Bagdad (Raoul Walsh, 1924)

Turbans (Erika Surat Andersen, 1999)

Unfinished Business (D, Steven Okazaki, 1986)

Wataridori: Birds of Passage (Robert Nakamura, 1976)

The Wedding Banquet (Ang Lee, 1993)

Who Killed Vincent Chin? (D, Christine Choy, Renee Tajima, 1988)

Who's Going to Pay for These Donuts Anyway? (Experimental D, Janice Tanaka, 1992)

The World of Suzie Wong (Richard Quine, 1960)

Year of the Dragon (Michael Cimino, 1985)

Yellow (Chris Chan Lee, 1998)

Yellow Tale Blues: A Tale of Two American Families (D, Christine Choy, Renee Tajima, 1990)

Yuri Kochiyama: A Passion for Justice (D, Rea Tajiri, Pat Saunders, 1993)

Films about and by American Indians

Allegheny Uprising (William Seiter, 1939)

The Apache Kid (George Sherman, 1941)

The Battle of Elderbrush Gulch (D.W. Griffith, 1913)

Broken Arrow (Delmer Daves, 1950)

Broken Rainbow (Maria Florio, Victoria Mudd, 1985)

The Business of Fancy Dancing (Sherman Alexie, 2002)

Captain John Smith and Pocahontas (Lew Landers, 1953).

Clouded Land (D, Randy Croce, 1989)

The Covered Wagon (James Cruz, 1932)

Dances with Wolves (Kevin Costner, 1990)

Drums Along the Mohawk (John Ford, 1939)

The Far Horizons (Rudolph Matte, 1955)

500 Nations: Attack on Culture (D, Jack Leustig, 1944, Eight Parts)

Grand Avenue (Made for TV, HBO, Daniel Sackheim, 1996)

Images of Indians (D, KCTS-TV, Phil Lucas, Robert Hagopian, 1979). Five parts: (1) *Great Movie Massacre*; (2) *How Hollywood Wins the West*; (3) *War Paint and Wigs*; (4) *Heathen Injuns*; (5) *Movie Reel Indians*

Imagining Indians (D, Victor Masayesua, 1992)

In Search of the Oregon Trail (D, PBS, Joel Geyer 1996)

In the White Man's Image (D, PBS, *American Experience*, Christine Lesiak, Matthew Jones, 1991)

In Whose Honor? (D, PBS/POV, Jay Rosenstein, 1996)

Indian Princess Demystified (D, Lorraine Norrgard, 1988)

Iola's Promise, or How the Little Indian Maid Paid Her Debt of Gratitude (D.W. Griffith, 1912)

The Iron Horse (John Ford, 1924)

Keep Your Heart Strong: The Powwow (D, Deb Wallwork, 1986)

Lakota Woman: Siege at Wounded Knee (Made for TV, TNT, Frank Pierson, 1994)

The Last of the Mohicans (Maurice Tourneur, Clarence Brown, 1920)

The Last of the Mohicans (George Seitz, 1936)

The Last of the Mohicans (Michael Mann, 1992)

The Last of the Redmen (George Sherman, 1947)

Last Stand at Little Big Horn (D, PBS, The American Experience, Paul Steckler, 1992)

Leatherstocking (D.W. Griffith, 1909)

Legend of the Lone Ranger (George Seitz, 1949)

Little Big Horn: The Untold Story (D, The History Channel)

Little Big Man (Arthur Penn, 1970)

A Man Called Horse (Elliot Silverstein, 1970)

Nanook of the North (D, Robert Flaherty, 1922)

Navajo Code Talkers: In Search of History (D, History Channel, 1996)

Northwest Passage (King Vidor, 1940)

The Oregon Trail (Ford Beebe, 1939)

The Outsider (Delbert Mann, 1961)

Paha Sapa: The Struggle for the Black Hills (D, Mel Lawrence, 1993)

Paleface (Norman McLeod, 1948)

Peter Pan (Hamilton Luske, Clyde Geronimi, Wilfred Jackson, 1953)

Pocahontas (Eric Goldberg, Mike Gabriel, 1995)

Powwow Highway (Jonathan Wacks, 1989)

Return of a Man Called Horse (Irwin Kirschner, 1976)

Rocks with Wings (D, Rick Derby, 2002)

The Searchers (John Ford, 1956)

She Wore a Yellow Ribbon (John Ford, 1949)

Skins (Chris Eyre, 2002)

Smoke Signals (Chris Eyre, 1998)

Soldier Blue (Ralph Nelson, 1970)

The Spirit of Crazy Horse (D, PBS, Michel DuBois and Kevin McKieran, Frontline, 1991)

The Squaw Man (Cecil B. DeMille, 1931)

The Squaw's Love (D.W. Griffith, 1911)

Stagecoach (John Ford, 1939)

Standing Tall (Harvey Hall, 1977)

Tell Them Willie Boy Is Here (Abraham Polonsky, 1969)

They Died with Their Boots On (Raoul Walsh, 1941)

Thunderheart (Michael Apted, 1992)

The Unforgiven (John Huston, 1960)

The Vanishing American (George Seitz, 1925)

War Code: Navajo (D, Lena Carr, Amy Wray, 1996)

Where the Spirit Lives (American Playhouse, Bruce Pittman, 1989)

Windtalkers (John Woo, 2002)

Films about and by Latinos/as

¡Alambrista! (Robert Young, 1978)

The Alamo (John Wayne, 1960)

The Alamo (John Lee Hancock, 2004)

American Me (Edward James Olmos, 1992)

Americanos: Latino Life in the U.S. (D, Susan Todd, Andrew Young, 1999)

The Ballad of Gregorio Cortez (Robert Young, 1983)

La Bamba (Luis Valdez, 1987)

Bataan (Tay Garnett, 1943)

Blackboard Jungle (Richard Brook, 1955)

Blacklist: Hollywood on Trial (D, Christopher Koch, 1995)

Border Incident (Anthony Mann, 1949)

Born in East L.A. (Richard "Cheech" Marin, 1987)

Boulevard Nights (Michael Pressman, 1979)

The Bronze Screen: 100 Years of the Latino Image in American Cinema (D, Susan Racho, Nancy de los Santos, Albert Dominquez, 2001)

Chicana (Sylvia Morales, 1979)

Chicano! History of the Mexican American Civil Rights Movement (D, Hector Galon, 1996). Four parts: (1) Quest for a Homeland; (2) The Struggle in the Fields; (3) Taking Back the Schools; (4) Fighting for Political Power

Chicano Park (D, Marilyn Mulford, 1988)

La Ciudad (The City) (David Riker, 1998, Four Stories)

Colors (Dennis Hopper, 1988)

Conversations with Intellectuals about Selena (D, Lourdes Portillo, 1999)

Corpus: A Home Movie for Selena (D, Lourdes Portillo, 1999)

Corridos: Tale of Passion and Revolution (D, Luis Valdez, 1987)
Crossover Dreams (Leon Ichaso, 1985)
Cuba 15 (D, Elizabeth Schub, 1997)
A Day Without a Mexican (Sergio Arau, 2004)
The Gaucho (F. Richard Jones, 1928)
Giant (George Stevens, 1956)
Girlfight (Karyn Kusame, 2000)
Grease (Randal Kleiser, 1978)
The Greaser's Gauntlet (D.W. Griffith, 1908)
Guadalcanal Diary (Lewis Seiler, 1943)
Hangin' with the Homeboys (Joseph Vasques, 1991)
High Noon (Fred Zimmermann, 1952)
Hispanic Americans (D, Radames Soto, 1998, Seven Parts)
I Am Joaquin (Luis Valdez, 1969)
Latin Lover (Mervyn LeRay, 1953)
The Lemon Grove Incident (Docudrama, Frank Christopher, 1985)
Lone Star (John Sayles, 1995)
The Mambo Kings (Arnie Glimcher, 1992)
Martyrs of the Alamo (W. Christy Cabanne, 1915)
The Mask of Zorro (Martin Campbell, 1998)
A Medal for Benny (Irving Pichel, 1945)
The Merrow Report: Lost in Translation: Latinos, Schools and Society (D, 1998)
Mi Vida Loca (My Crazy Life) (Allison Anders, 1993)
The Milagro Beanfield War (Robert Redford, 1988, 58 min)
Los Mineros (D, PBS, *The American Experience*, Hector Galan, 1990)
My Family, Mi Familia (Gregory Nava, 1995)
Napolean Dynamite (Jared Hess, 2004)
El Norte (The North) (Gregory Nava, 1983)
The Perez Family (Mira Nair, 1995)
Raices de Sangre (Jesus Salvador, 1977)
La Raza Nueva (Jesus Salvador Trevino, 1969)
Real Women Have Curves (Patricia Cardoso, 2002)
Salt of the Earth (Herbert Biberman, 1954)
Scarface (Brian DePalma, 1983)

Selena (Gregary Nava, 1997)
Senorita Extraviado — Missing Young Women (Lourdes Portillo, 2002)
Soldados: Chicanos in VietNam (D, Sonya Rhee, 2003)
Stand and Deliver (Ramon Menendez, 1988)
Sweet 15 (PBS Wonderworks, Sharon Weil, Victoria Hochbert, 1990)
Three Amigos (John Landis, 1986)
Touch of Evil (Orson Welles, 1958)
Training Day (Antoine Fuqua, 2001)
Treasure of the Sierra Madre (John Huston, 1948)
Victor (Dianne Haak Edson, 1989)
West Side Story (Robert Wise, 1961)
Zoot Suit (Luis Valdez, 1981)
Zoot Suit Riots (D, American Experience, Joseph Tovares, 2001)

Films about American Ethnicity

Bowling for Columbine (Michael Moore, 2002)
Crash (Paul Haggis, 2005)
Culture Shock (PBS, 1999)
Domino: Interracial People and the Search for Identity (D, 1994)
Hate.Com: Extremists on the Internet (D, HBO, 2000)
Media Literacy: The New Basic? (D, Rutgers University, 1996)
A Place at the Table (D, Southern Poverty Law Center, Hudson and Houston, 2000)
Race: The Power of an Illusion (D, Three Parts: *The Difference Between Us* [Christine Herbes-Sommers], *The Story We Tell* [Tracy Heather Strain], *The House We Live in* [Llewellyn Smith], 2003)
The Shadow of Hate: A History of Intolerance in America (D, Southern Poverty Law Center, Charles Guggenheim, 1995)

Selected Bibliography

Multicultural and Visual Literacy

Abrash, Barbara, and Catherine Egan. *Mediating History: The Map Guide to Independent Video by and About African American, Asian American, Latino, and Native American People.* New York: New York University Press, 1992.

Benshoff, Harry M., and Sean Griffin. *America on Film: Representing Race, Class, Gender and Sexuality at the Movies.* Malden, Mass.: Blackwell, 2004.

Bernardi, Daniel, ed. *The Birth of Whiteness: Race and the Emergence of U.S. Cinema.* New Brunswick, N.J.: Rutgers University Press, 1996.

_____. *Classic Hollywood, Classic Whiteness.* Minneapolis: University of Minnesota Press, 2001.

Carnes, Mark C., ed. *Past Imperfect: History According to the Movies.* New York: Henry Holt, 1995.

Considine, David M., and Gail E. Haley. *Visual Messages: Integrating Imagery into Instruction.* 2nd ed. Englewood, Col.: Teacher Ideas Press, 1999.

Costanzo, William V. *Great Films and How to Teach Them.* Urbana, Ill.: NCTE, 2004.

_____. *Reading the Movies: Twelve Great Films on Video and How to Teach Them.* Urbana, Ill.: NCTE, 1992.

Dyer, Richard. *The Matter of Images: Essays on Representations.* New York: Routledge, 1993, 1995.

_____. *White.* New York: Routledge, 1997.

Friedman, Lester D., ed. *Unspeakable Images: Ethnicity and the American Cinema.* Urbana: University of Illinois Press, 1991.

Girgus, Sam B. *America on Film: Modernism, Documentary, and a Changing America.* New York: Cambridge University Press, 2001.

Goldfarb, Brian. *Visual Pedagogy: Media Culture, in and Beyond the Classroom.* Durham, N.C.: Duke University Press, 2002.

hooks, bell. *Reel to Real: Race, Sex, and Class at the Movies.* London: Routledge, 1996.

Konigsberg, Ira. *The Complete Film Dictionary.* 2nd ed. New York: Penguin, 1997.

Landy, Marcia, ed. *The Historical Film: History and Memory in Media.* New Brunswick, N.J.: Rutgers University Press, 2001.

McFarlane, Brian. *Novel Into Film: An Introduction to the Theory of Adaptation.* New York: Oxford University Press, 1996.

Mintz, Steve, and Randy Roberts. *Hollywood's America: United States History Through Its Films.* St. James, N.Y.: Brandywine, 1993.

Monaco, James. *How to Read a Film: The World of Movies, Media, and Multimedia.* 3rd ed. New York: Oxford University Press, 2000.

Naremore, James, ed. *Film Adaptation.*

305

New Brunswick, N.J.: Rutgers University Press, 2000.

Reynolds, Larry J. *National Imaginaries, American Identities: The Cultural Work of America Iconography.* Princeton, N.J.: Princeton University Press, 2000.

Rosenstone, Robert A. *Visions of the Past: The Challenge of Film to Our Idea of History.* Cambridge, Mass.: Harvard University Press, 1995.

Shohat, Ella, and Robert Stam. *Unthinking Eurocentrism: Multiculturalism and the Media.* London: Routledge, 1994.

Sklar, Robert. *Movie-Made America: A Cultural History of American Movies.* New York: Vintage, 1975, 1994.

Summerfield, Ellen. *Seeing the Big Picture: Exploring American Cultures on Film.* Yarmouth, Me.: Intercultural Press, 2001.

Teasley, Alan B., and Ann Wilder. *Reel Conversations: Reading Films with Young Adults.* Portsmouth, N.H.: Heinemann Boyton/Cook, 1997.

Tyner, Kathleen R. *Literacy in a Digital World: Teaching and Learning in the Age of Information.* Mahwah, N.J.: Erlbaum, 1998.

Cinematic Representations of African Americans

Anderson, Lisa M. *Mammies No More: The Changing Image of Black Women on Stage and Screen.* Lanham, Md.: Rowman and Littlefield, 1997.

Bogle, Donald. *Toms, Coons, Mulattoes, Mammies, and Bucks: An Interpretive History of Blacks in American Films.* 3rd ed. New York: Continuum, 2001.

Bowser, Pearl, and Louise Spence. *Writing Himself into History: Oscar Micheaux, His Silent Films, and His Audiences.* New Brunswick, N.J.: Rutgers University Press, 2000.

Cripps, Thomas. *Black Film as Genre.* Bloomington: Indiana University Press, 1978.

_____. *Slow Fade to Black: The Negro in American Film 1900–1942.* New York: Oxford University Press, 1992.

Dash, Julie. *Daughters of the Dust: The Making of an African American Woman's Film.* New York: The New Press, 1992.

Davis, Natalie Zemon. *Slaves on Screen: Film and Historical Vision.* Cambridge, Mass.: Harvard University Press, 2000.

Diawara, Manthia, ed. *Black American Cinema.* New York: Routledge, 1993.

George, Nelson. *Blackface: Reflections on African Americans in the Movies.* New York: HarperPerennial, 1994.

Gubar, Susan. *Racechanges: White Skin, Black Face in American Culture.* New York: Oxford University Press, 1997.

Guerrero, Ed. *Framing Blackness: The African American Image in Film.* Philadelphia, Pa.: Temple University Press, 1993.

hooks, bell. *Black Looks: Race and Representation.* Boston, Mass.: South End, 1992.

Klotman, Phyllis R., and Janet K. Cutler. *Struggles for Representation: African American Documentary Film and Video.* Bloomington: Indiana University Press, 1999.

Lang, Robert, ed. *The Birth of a Nation.* New Brunswick, N.J.: Rutgers University Press, 1994.

Lee, Spike, and Ralph Wiley. *By Any Means Necessary: The Trials and Tribulations of the Making of Malcolm X, Including the Screenplay.* New York: Hyperion, 1992.

Lupeck, Barbara Tepa. *Literary Adaptations in Black American Cinema: From Micheaux to Morrison.* Rochester, N.Y.: University of Rochester Press, 2002.

Nesteby, James R. *Black Images in American Films, 1896–1954.* Washington, D.C.: University Press of America, 1982.

Peters, William. *A Class Divided: Then and Now.* New Haven, Conn.: Yale University Press, 1987.

Reid, Mark. *Redefining Black Film.* Berkeley: University of California Press, 1993.

Roberts, Diane. *The Myth of Aunt Je-mima.* New York: Routledge, 1994.

Rocchio, Vincent F. *Reel Racism: Confronting Hollywood's Construction of Afro-American Culture.* Boulder, Co.: Westview Press, 2000.

Smith, Valerie, ed. *Representing Blackness: Issues in Film and Video.* New Brunswick, N.J.: Rutgers University Press, 1997.

Turner, Patricia. *Ceramic Uncles and Celluloid Mammies: Black Images and Their Influence on Culture.* New York: Anchor, 1994.

Yearwood, Gladstone Lloyd. *Black Film as a Signifying Practice: Cinema, Narration, and the African American Aesthetic Tradition.* Trenton, N.J.: Africa World Press, 2000.

Cinematic Representations of Asian Americans

Ditman, Linda, and Gene Michaud, eds. *From Hanoi to Hollywood: The Vietnam War in American Film.* New Brunswick, N.J.: Rutgers University Press, 1990.

Feng, Peter X. *Identities in Motion: Asian American Film and Video.* Durham, N.C.: Duke University Press, 2002.

_____. *Screening Asian Americans.* New Brunswick, N.J.: Rutgers University Press, 2002.

Gee, Bill J., ed. *Asian American Media Reference Guide.* 2nd ed. New York: Asian CineVision, 1990.

Gordon, Avery F., and Christopher Newfield. *Mapping Multiculturalism.* Minneapolis: University of Minnesota Press, 1996.

Hamamoto, Darrell Y., and Sandra Liu, eds. *Countervisions: Asian American Film Criticism.* Philadelphia, Pa.: Temple University Press, 2000.

Hsing, Chun (Jun Xing). *Asian America through the Lens: History, Representations, and Identity.* Walnut Creek, Calif.: AltaMira Press, 1998.

Leong, Russell, ed. *Moving the Image: Independent Asian Pacific American Media Arts.* Los Angeles, Calif.: UCLA Asian American Studies Center, 1991.

Marchetti, Gina. *Romance and the Yellow Peril: Race, Sex, and Discursive Strategies in Hollywood Fiction.* Berkeley: University of California Press, 1994.

Cinematic Representations of American Indians

Bird, Elizabeth, ed. *Dressing in Feathers: The Construction of the Indian in Popular Culture.* Boulder, Co.: Westview Press, 1996.

Churchill, Ward. *Fantasies of the Master Race: Literature, Cinema, and the Colonization of American Indians.* Monroe, Me.: Common Courage, 1992.

Deloria, Philip Joseph. *Playing Indian.* New Haven, Conn.: Yale University Press, 1998.

Hilger, Michael. *From Savage to Nobleman: Images of Native Americans in Film.* Lanham, Md.: Scarecrow, 1995

Kilpatrick, Jacquelyn. *Celluloid Indians: Native Americans and Film.* Lincoln: University of Nebraska Press, 1999.

O'Connor, John E. *The Hollywood Indian: Stereotypes of Native Americans in Film.* Trenton: New Jersey State Museum, 1981.

Rollins, Peter C., and John E. O'Connor, eds. *Hollywood's Indian: The Portrayal of the Native American in Film.* Lexington: University of Kentucky Press, 2003.

Singer, Beverly R. *Wiping the War Paint Off the Lens: Native American Film and Video.* Minneapolis: University of Minnesota Press, 2001.

Smith, Andrew B. *Shooting Cowboys and Indians: Silent Western Films, American Culture, and the Birth of Hollywood.* Boulder: University of Colorado Press, 2003.

Stedman, Raymond William. *Shadows of the Indian: Stereotypes in American*

Culture. Norman: University of Oklahoma Press, 1982.

Cinematic Representations of Latino/as

Berg, Charles Ramirez. *Latino Images in Film.* Austin: University of Texas Press, 2002.

Berumen, Frank J.G. *Brown Celluloid: Latino/a Film Icons and Images in the Hollywood Film Industry.* New York: Vantage, 2003.

Biberman, Herbert J. *Salt of the Earth: The Story of a Film.* Boston, Mass.: Beacon, 1965.

Fregoso, Rosa Linda. *The Bronze Screen: Chicana and Chicano Film Culture.* Minneapolis: University of Minnesota Press, 1993.

Hadley-Garcia, George. *Hispanic Hollywood: The Latins in Motion Pictures.* Secaucus, N.J.: Carol, 1991.

Keller, Gary D., ed. *A Biographical Handbook of Hispanics and United States Film.* Tempe, Ariz.: Bilingual Press, 1997.

_____, ed. *Chicano Cinema: Research, Reviews, and Resources.* Binghamton, N.Y.: Bilingual Press, 1985.

_____. *Hispanics and United States Film: An Overview and Handbook.* Tempe, Ariz.: Bilingual Press, 1994.

Noriega, Chon, ed. *Chicanos and Film: Representation and Resistance.* Minneapolis: University of Minnesota Press, 1992.

Noriega, Chon, and Ana M. Lopez, eds. *The Ethnic Eye: Latino Media Arts.* Minneapolis: University of Minnesota Press, 1996.

Pettit, Arthur G. *Images of the Mexican American in Fiction and Film.* College Station: Texas A & M University Press, 1980.

Reyes, Luis. *Hispanics in Hollywood: An Encyclopedia of 100 Years of Film and Television.* Hollywood, Calif.: Lone Eagle Publications, 2000.

Richard, Alfred Charles. *Contemporary Hollywood's Negative Hispanic Image, 1956–1993.* Westport, Conn.: Greenwood, 1994.

_____. *The Hispanic Image on the Silver Screen: An Interpretive Filmography from Silents into Sound, 1889–1935.* New York: Greenwood, 1992.

Rodriguez, Clara E., ed. *Latin Looks: Images of Latinas and Latinos in the U.S. Media.* Boulder, Colo.: Westview Press, 1997.

Torrans, Thomas. *The Magic Curtain: The Mexican-American Border in Fiction, Film, and Song.* Fort Worth: Texas Christian University Press, 2002.

Wilson, Michael, and Deborah Silverton Rosenfelt. *Salt of the Earth: Screenplay and Commentary.* New York: Feminist Press, 1978.

Index